S. A. Lloyd proposes a radically new interpretation of Hobbes's *Leviathan* that shows transcendent interests – interests that override the fear of death – to be crucial to both Hobbes's analysis of social disorder and his proposed remedy to it.

Most previous commentators in the analytic philosophical tradition have argued that Hobbes thought that credible threats of physical force could be sufficient to deter people from political insurrection. Professor Lloyd convincingly shows that because Hobbes took the transcendence of religious and moral interests seriously, he never believed that mere physical force could ensure social order. Lloyd's interpretation demonstrates the ineliminability of that half of *Leviathan* devoted to religion, and attributes to Hobbes a much more plausible conception of human nature than the narrow psychological egoism traditionally attributed to Hobbes. Recognizing the religious and moral interests that could drive human beings even to the point of self-sacrifice, Hobbes undertakes to redescribe those transcendent interests that fuel civil strife in order to show his readers that their interests, once properly understood, give them overwhelming reasons to adhere to a principle of political obligation that could, if generally followed, ensure perpetual domestic stability.

In the concluding chapter the author argues that Hobbes succeeded in providing a powerful original method for resolving conflict rooted in transcendent interests, a method that may be usefully applied to problems in contemporary political philosophy.

Ideals as interests in
Hobbes's *Leviathan*

Ideals as interests in Hobbes's *Leviathan*

The power of mind over matter

S. A. LLOYD

UNIVERSITY OF SOUTHERN CALIFORNIA

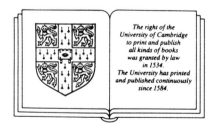

The right of the
University of Cambridge
to print and publish
all kinds of books
was granted by law
in 1534.
The University has printed
and published continuously
since 1584.

CAMBRIDGE UNIVERSITY PRESS

CAMBRIDGE

NEW YORK   PORT CHESTER   MELBOURNE   SYDNEY

Published by the Press Syndicate of the University of Cambridge
The Pitt Building, Trumpington Street, Cambridge CB2 1RP
40 West 20th Street, New York, NY 10011–4211 USA
10 Stamford Road, Oakleigh, Victoria 3166, Australia

First published 1992

Printed in Canada

Library of Congress Cataloging-in-Publication Data
Lloyd, S. A., 1958–
Ideals as interests in Hobbes's Leviathan : the power of mind over
matter / S. A. Lloyd
p.   cm.
Includes bibliographical references and index.
ISBN 0–521–39243–8
1. Hobbes, Thomas, 1588–1679. Leviathan.   2. Hobbes, Thomas,
1588–1679 – Contributions in political science.   3. Hobbes, Thomas,
1588–1679 – Contributions in political stability.   4. Hobbes, Thomas,
1588–1679 – Contributions in social conflict.   I. Title.
JC153.H659L56   1992
320.1 – dc20   91-19370
                                                                         CIP

A catalog record for this book is available from the British Library.

ISBN 0-521-39243-8 hardback

To Greg Kavka
My teacher and friend

Contents

Acknowledgments

In the years since I began this work on Hobbes I have benefited from the generous advice and aid of numerous friends and colleagues. Ken Anderson encouraged me to sit down and begin the project, and served as philosophical sounding board throughout. In the initial stages of the project I profited from many discussions with Liz Anderson, Michele Moody-Adams, Nick Pappas, Thomas Pogge, Marya Schechtman, and Paul Weithman. An early draft was vastly improved by the illuminating, extensive comments I received from Robert Brenner and Larry Solum, and by the acute criticism I received from Alan Donagan and Jim Woodward when I discussed the project with them.

Josh Cohen's careful criticism of the first more or less complete draft caused me to revise my view on many central points, saving me from some serious errors, and his encouragement sustained me. My concerns about the historical plausibility of my view were relieved, and the view was further refined, as a result of the feedback I received from Richard Ashcraft, Amos Funkenstein, and Lawrence Stone. David Johnston's generous comments helped me clarify my argument at many points.

The final version was much improved by efforts to respond to four very formidable sets of criticisms. Greg Kavka's flawless Hobbes scholarship and philosophical rigor kept me honest while I tried to counter his replies to my arguments against his most sophisticated version of the standard philosophical interpretation. Perry Anderson presented me with a number of criticisms that were simply unanswerable from within the view I then held. Answering them required me to revise the entire structure of my view and to rework completely my interpretation of Part 1 of *Leviathan*. The anonymous reader at Cambridge University Press helped me address the most important remaining historical questions about my thesis, by both alerting me to them and often suggesting means for dealing with them. Finally, Paul Weithman zeroed in on virtually every point of philosophical interest in the manuscript, urging me to expand, qualify, or otherwise rework my remarks on many of these.

My greatest debt is to my thesis advisers John Rawls and T. M. Scanlon, under whose supervision I developed the central ideas of this work. Scanlon went through several versions with a fine-tooth comb, chasing down incomplete or invalid arguments, and enabling me to improve on my general argumentative strategy at many points. It was Rawls who oversaw the shape of the project, who vigilantly herded me away from the philosophically uninteresting, and who required me to keep at the hard problems until they cracked.

Finally, I owe a great debt to the philosophy department at the University of Southern California. I would like to thank my dean, Marshall Cohen, my chairman, John Dreher, and my colleagues Hartry Field, Barbara Herman, Janet Levin, Frank Lewis, Chet Lieb, Brian Loar, Ed McCann, Kevin Robb, and Dallas Willard for granting me the leave time and flexible teaching schedule that helped me to complete the book, and for the intellectual support and encouragement they provided.

A note on references

Leviathan (herein abbreviated *L*) page references are to the
original Head edition page numbers as these are indicated
in square brackets in C. B. Macpherson's Pelican edition of
Leviathan (1968), from which I quote. *Behemoth* (*B*) references
are to the edition by Sir William Molesworth, Source Works
Series No. 38 (New York: Burt Franklin Research, 1962).
Hobbes's Thucydides references are to the edition by Richard
Schlatter (New Brunswick, N.J.: Rutgers University Press,
1975). *Elements of Law* (*EL*) references are to the Ferdinand
Tönnies (2nd) edition (London: Frank Case, 1969). References to others of Hobbes's works are to *The English Works
of Thomas Hobbes*, Molesworth edition in nine volumes (*EW*
1, 2, etc.) (London: John Bohn, 1839). In my quotations of
Hobbes I have modernized capitalization, and in a very few
cases when Hobbes's punctuation has obscured his meaning,
I have modernized punctuation.

Introduction

What good is it to promise allegiance and then by and by to
cry out, as some ministers did in the pulpit, To your tents, O
Israel!?

> — Hobbes (*B* 181)

Human beings will fight for their beliefs. People go to war
over their moral ideals and religious principles, and are capable not only of risking death in the service of their values
but even of embracing death when they believe it will further
their cause. The Christian martyrs, Buddhist monks in Viet-
nam, and some Shiite Muslims in Lebanon today are among
countless examples of the human capacity for pursuing religious or moral convictions even at the expense of one's own
life. People are capable of forming, and acting on, *transcendent*
interests. Of pursuing principles over preservation. Of ex-
erting mind over matter.

We all know this. Hobbes knew it too, and it worried him
deeply. It worried him because he believed that transcendent
interests very often cause civil wars.

It is difficult to call to mind any modern war that did not
contain as one element moral or religious transcendent interests. Correctly or incorrectly, combatants usually view
themselves as engaged in a struggle for some value of overriding importance, such as liberty, equality, human dignity,
or true religion. Their struggle appears to them in the form
of a struggle for right. As the French Revolution, the Amer-
ican Civil War, and the Russian Revolution suggest, civil

1

wars are no exception to this rule. Many people on both sides believe themselves to be fighting for moral or religious interests of overriding importance. Hobbes viewed the English Civil War in this way, as a conflict appearing in the form of – indeed, actually generated by – competing transcendent interests. And he believed that any permanent solution to that war – any prospect for a perpetual domestic peace – would have necessarily to address the disruption generated by such conflicts of transcendent interests.

Part of the thesis of this book is that Hobbes's masterwork, *Leviathan*, is intended to address precisely this problem of the domestic social disorder generated by transcendent interests. The sorts of transcendent interests that particularly worried Hobbes were religious interests. This is why he devotes more than half of *Leviathan* to a discussion of religion, which is crucial to his task of providing a permanent remedy to the internal social disorder caused by transcendent religious interests. I shall try to show that Hobbes's conception of the *problem* of social disorder cannot be understood without close attention to Parts 3 and 4 of *Leviathan*. Thus, the first sense in which Hobbes's political theory is a theory of mind over matter is that it analyzes disorder as the result of the primacy of religious interests over material interests, including the interest in self-preservation.

The second part of this book's thesis is that Hobbes develops an effective, stable *solution* to the problem of disorder generated by transcendent interests. His theory works to solve the problem he was addressing. His solution has much less to do with coercive force than is generally supposed. His solution is to reproduce perpetually a proper, stability-reinforcing conception of people's transcendent religious interests by a process of education that continually generates consensus. It is education, and not might, that makes for social order in Hobbes's system. This is the second way in which Hobbes's theory is a theory of mind over matter.

The final part of the thesis of the present book is that Hobbes succeeds in providing a powerful original *method* for addressing social conflict rooted in transcendent interests, a method that is instructive for political philosophy generally. His method is to begin from the interests people actually claim as their own (rather than from some physical-scientific account of human beings as matter in motion, or from some idealized notion of what interests people ought, given their physical natures, to have), and through a process of rationalizing their beliefs and redescribing their interests, to provide people with *reasons* linked to the interests they actually affirm, including their transcendent interests, for acting in a way that can ensure the perpetual maintenance of peaceful social order. Hobbes's method provides the third sense in which his theory is a theory of mind over matter.

Of course, there is a fourth sense of that notion in which Hobbes's theory is not a theory of mind over matter. Hobbes believed that all that is (with the possible exception of God, whose nature we cannot know) is material. Or, more precisely, he believed that the contents of the world could in principle be comprehensively described making reference only to bodies and their motions. But because there is, in Hobbes's view, a bidirectional causal relation between mental phenomena and the physical bodies that ground them, and because scientific understanding is not sufficiently developed to allow us to say all we must in the language of physics, any adequate social theory will properly take such things as beliefs, interests, and passionate attachments seriously, as moving parts and explanatory components of primary importance to the theory. Thus, Hobbes's ontological commitments do not preclude a theory that favors mind over matter in the three senses I've described.

This book focuses primarily on the political theory Hobbes presents in *Leviathan*, although the interpretation I offer of that theory is supplemented by considerations from others of Hobbes's writings, most importantly from *Behemoth* and the *Elements of Law*. Although I make use of Hobbes's history of the English Civil Wars, and, from time to time, adduce historical considerations in support of my interpretation of his political theory, I do not intend this interpretation as a work of intellectual history or history of philosophy.[1] My

aim, as will become clear, is to speak to a particular philosophical school of Hobbes interpretation, and to provide a
philosophically defensible alternative interpretation in the
style of the Western analytic philosophical tradition.

I should forewarn the reader that this book does not present its argument in a linear fashion. It elaborates a preliminary sketch, adding, chapter by chapter, successively thicker
layers of detail. None of the chapters stands on its own. It
is not until the end of the book that a full account of any of
the discrete components of Hobbes's political theory will
have been completed. But it is my hope that by the end, the
reader will be satisfied that she or he has received a full
account of all of the components of Hobbes's political theory.

The first chapter begins by offering considerations that may
cast some doubt on the adequacy of the standard philosophical interpretation of Hobbes's political theory, and
thereby justify yet another contribution within philosophy
to the mountainous literature on *Leviathan*. It ends with a
thumbnail sketch of the alternative interpretation I propose
to develop in the remainder of the book.

The next four chapters collectively elaborate the interpretation outlined in Chapter 1. By the end of Chapter 5, three-
quarters of the theory presented in *Leviathan* will have been
introduced, including all of Hobbes's compositive reconstruction of a stable society, and half of his resolutive analysis
of disorder.

Chapter 6 attempts to provide preliminary confirmation of
the theory developed in the first five chapters, using
Hobbes's own history of the period of disorder to which his
political theorizing is most intimately tied. Chapter 7 inte-
grates the remainder of *Leviathan*, the final phase of Hobbes's
resolutive analysis of disorder, into the theory already presented. This order of exposition may surprise those who have
worked on *Leviathan*. It is not until Chapter 7 that I discuss
Part 1 of *Leviathan*, including its Chapter 13 on the state of
nature. I have ordered my discussion in this way because I
think that our philosophical tradition of Hobbes scholarship
makes it difficult for us to understand the actual function of

Part 1 without having first understood what is going on in the remainder of the book. Not that there is anything wrong with Hobbes's order of exposition; it's just that our particular philosophical interests prevent us from grasping Hobbes's argument when it is presented in the order he presents it. All of this should become clear in Chapter 7.

Chapter 8 offers some bird's-eye observations about Hobbes's treatment of transcendent religious interests, and presents Hobbes's arguments on the topic of other sorts of potentially transcendent interests such as liberty and justice. Chapter 9 completes our discussion of transcendent interests by examining the status of those interests, on Hobbes's understanding of them. It goes on to examine Hobbes's claim to have established both the necessity and desirability of political absolutism, and argues that Hobbes succeeded – from within his own assumptions, of course – both in validly deriving, and in actually justifying, absolutism. The chapter, and the book, end by suggesting several ways in which Hobbes's work provides us with invaluable insight into the practice of political philosophy, and the constraints on fruitful work in this field.

Chapter 1

The standard philosophical interpretation

> It must be extreme hard to find out the opinions and meanings
> of those men that are gone from us long ago, and have left
> us no other signification thereof but their books.
> — Hobbes (*EW* 4:75)

Listen in on most any undergraduate philosophy course in which *Leviathan* is discussed and you will hear a familiar story. Hobbes the individualist. Hobbes the theorist of power, advocate of the view that sheer might makes order. Hobbes the pessimist, defender of the view that the only alternative to anarchy is absolute subjection, that an overriding fear of death drives men to embrace an apparent but necessary tyranny. Hobbes the moral skeptic, subjectivist, or relativist. Hobbes the atheist. There is a received wisdom about Hobbes's political theory that has been passed from generation to generation – admittedly not without refinements or emendations, and occasional challenges – that pervades and conditions almost all serious philosophical work on Hobbes.

Among the interpretations of Hobbes's political philosophy that begin from this general picture of Hobbes is a family of views that composes what I shall loosely term the "standard philosophical interpretation." Variants of the standard philosophical interpretation appear in the seminal works on Hobbes by David Gauthier and J.W.N. Watkins, as well as in the writings of Macpherson, Nagel, Plamenatz, and Skinner, and, more recently, of Kavka and Hampton.[1] Indeed,

6

most works on Hobbes contain elements of the standard philosophical interpretation, although some few writers, most notably Taylor, Warrender, and Hood, have advanced interpretations deeply at odds with the standard philosophical view; and others, such as Barry, Oakeshott, and, more recently, Johnston, have developed interpretations that would require rejection of substantial portions of the standard philosophical view.[2]

THE STANDARD PHILOSOPHICAL INTERPRETATION

Interpretations of this standard bent differ considerably, and there is some room for disagreement as to which interpretations should be counted as belonging to this group. But the rough grouping I have in mind is of interpretations holding some significant subset of the following views: that Hobbes intended to derive a necessary form of political organization from fundamentally egoistic human nature, that Hobbes was a moral subjectivist or relativist, that the essentials of Hobbes's theory can be captured without reference to religious interests, that political obligation is solely prudentially based, that might makes order, and correspondingly that fear of death and the desire for self-preservation are the strongest motivating forces.

One feature shared by almost all of the interpretations I would characterize as philosophically standard is the view that the sole reason Hobbes offers for why men ought to submit themselves to an absolute political authority – the reason to which all other considerations are ultimately reducible – is narrowly prudential. It is that it is in men's individual rational self-interest to live under a political authority that has the power to secure their preservation, and that resistance to such an authority invites a civil war resembling the state of nature in its effects. Hobbes attempts to demonstrate this result, say the standard interpreters, by means of a thought experiment (a resolution of society into its component parts – namely, individual persons – and a

7

new recomposition of the whole) designed to show that given fundamental human nature, people living in a condition in which there was no sovereign power (the state of nature) would find themselves in such an insecure and miserable condition (a state of war) that they would find it rational to subject themselves to an absolute civil sovereign. The fact that people in a state of nature would find it rational to contract into a state of subjection to an absolute political authority is supposed to show that it is rational for people already living under such an authority to do all they can to maintain that authority, including, most importantly, obeying it.

Several features of this account deserve special attention. First, the idea of a social contract made within a state of nature is a purely expository device intended not to describe a historical event, but to represent what it is prudent for people to do. An interpreter might hold either that obedience to one's political authority is required because it is what we would *agree* to from an appropriate point of view (because, from that point of view, it is rational to do so), or alternatively, that obedience is required simply because it is prudent, where the notions of agreement and agreement from a specified and standardized point of view have no independent force. The difference between these two ideas becomes evident when we consider whether or not Hobbes's argument prohibits subjects from disobeying the laws of their political authority even when they could rationally expect to profit by disobeying: If the reason for obeying is simply that obedience is in one's rational self-interest, then one would have, it seems, no reason to obey in cases where obedience isn't in fact in one's rational self-interest; if the fact that one would agree to be obedient from a specified point of view has some independent force, one might have reason to obey even in such cases. Because most standard interpreters fill the gap of profitable disobedience by referring to Hobbes's argument that one can never reasonably expect to profit by disobedience, it seems that they do not think the notion of agreement has any independent force. The idea of agreement

8

or consent is used solely to vivify the conclusions of individual rational self-interest.

Second, the state of nature depicted by means of this mental exercise is not to be thought of as some actual pre-political state of primitive man. The state of nature is the state of affairs that would actually obtain if the existing political order were suddenly to be dissolved, given current, actual, and *fundamental human nature*. This point is crucial: The standard philosophical interpreters contend that Hobbes is attempting to derive the need for an absolutist form of political organization from a description of human nature as it actually, and fundamentally, is.[3]

Third, since the argument from the state of nature is supposed to demonstrate the rationality of submitting oneself to an *autocratic* political authority, Hobbes attempts to show both that the state of nature is worse than the condition of subjects under an absolutist government, and that these are the only two alternatives. The former is supposed to be accomplished by Hobbes's argument that the state of nature is a state of war, by which is meant a condition in which people have a known disposition to violence, and there is no reasonable assurance that one will not become the victim of such violence. The latter requires an independent argument to the effect that a state of nature will ensue whenever there are disputes in the absence of a complete decision mechanism to resolve them, and that a complete decision mechanism requires – indeed, consists in – a single, undivided, unlimited, active authority, that is, a sovereign authority.

Hobbes's argument that the state of nature is a state of war is often characterized by the standard philosophical interpreters as the description of a prisoner's dilemma: The pursuit by each of the most rational individual course of action results in the perpetuation of a state of affairs in which each individual fares worse than he would if everyone were to pursue a less rational course. The state of nature is a state of war because scarcity of resources relative to demand leads to competition; competition, to fear of invasion (compounded by fear of invasion, not by the needy but by prideful people

9

in pursuit of glory); fear of invasion, to preemptive aggression; and fear of preemptive aggression, to further preemptive aggression. Given this state of affairs, it is rational for people to make preemptive attacks on their fellows. Nor is this condition subject to remedy by observance of those of Hobbes's laws of nature that dictate the keeping of contracts, mercy, equity, complaisance, submission to arbitration, and so on, because in the absence of assurances that others will comply with the laws of nature, one's own compliance may just make one easy prey. Moreover, each individual will reason, in the state of nature, that he stands to fare better by refusing to comply with the laws of nature, *no matter what others do* (if they comply, he has the benefit of free riding, and if they don't, he avoids being victimized); and because individual compliance is known to be individually irrational, no one has reason to think that others will comply.

If the problem is that given fundamental or actual human nature, people will find it irrational to behave sociably and cooperatively, then a reasonable remedy would be to find a way to change the conditions that make cooperation individually irrational. According to the standard philosophical interpretation, this is achieved, in Hobbes's theory, by the erection of an absolute sovereign with the power and authority to resolve disputes, make laws, distribute property, and enforce the laws of nature. By attaching punishments to the perpetration of antisocial acts, such a sovereign power provides people with strong incentives for cooperative behavior, bringing individual rationality into line with collective rationality, and short-term rationality into line with long-term rationality. The threat of punishment serves to deter antisocial acts, thereby simultaneously diminishing one's fear of being victimized by others, and discouraging one from committing antisocial acts oneself; combined, these factors make compliance with the sovereign's laws and decisions (which, it is supposed, contribute to peace and security) individually rational.

One may belong to the standard philosophical school without holding the view that the disorder of the state of nature is the result of a prisoner's dilemma, although the most recent and sophisticated standard interpretations do include this view. Some standard interpreters hold that uncooperative behavior is always irrational, but that men are inclined to lose sight of this fact and to sacrifice their long-term rational self-interest for the satisfaction of more immediate desires. Macpherson writes that Hobbes sees that, because individuals are not fit for social living unless subject to a power mighty enough to overawe them, "a coercive state built from a multitude of isolated wills is necessary. Fear of death and desire for more commodious living drive the individuals to it; their ability to calculate the consequences of continuous atomic competition makes them capable of it; but only a coercive state can prevent them backsliding from it."[4] Even though obedience to a political authority is rational, it must be reinforced by the imposition of sanctions for disobedience, "For men would still be appetitive creatures, and would be apt to take back some of their old right whenever they saw an immediate advantage in doing so."[5] On this interpretation, the role of a sovereign power is not so much to *make* sociable behavior rational as it is to remedy a defect in men's calculations of their rational self-interest (the defect being a temptation to give priority to short-term over long-term interests).

According to the standard interpretation, then, the long-term, though motivationally weaker, reason why one ought to obey the commands of whatever sovereign power one lives under (whether instituted or imposed) is that unless a sufficient number of people obey it for its power to be effective in securing social order, civil society will deteriorate into a state of war, and because such a turn of events would pose a threat to one's preservation and commodious living, it is rational for one to do what one can to maintain civil society. The immediate, and most motivationally efficacious, reason why a subject ought to obey the sovereign power is that it will *punish* him if he doesn't. Central to this interpretation is the idea that fear of personal harm is sufficient to motivate obedience – it is the fear of social collapse (which poses a threat to individual self-preservation) and the fear of punishment by the state that motivate political obedience. We might capture this feature of the standard philosophical interpretation in the slogan "Might plus fright makes order."[6]

The standard philosophical interpreters' account of the reason Hobbes offers for political obedience is strengthened by the prima facie plausible claim that Hobbes held an egoistic theory of human motivation.[7] If it is true that the only motive of voluntary human behavior is the desire for one's own good (narrowly construed, as excluding altruistic and moral concerns), then it follows that self-interest must be the motivating ground of political – indeed, of all – "obligation." Moral considerations could not possibly have played any functional role in Hobbes's political theory because either (1) the demands of morality and prudence are counterposed, in which case there cannot be any genuine moral obligation in Hobbes's system, since "ought" implies "can," but egoists cannot act against their perceived self-interest, nor from any motive except self-interest;[8] or (2) the demands of morality and prudence serendipitously coincide, in which case although it would be *possible* for men to act in *accordance* with the requirements of morality, they could not be moved to act by moral considerations (they could not be acting for moral reasons). Even if political obedience were morally required, this observation could play no role in Hobbes's argument, because it couldn't, of itself, induce anyone to obey one's political authority. One could assert, with Warrender, a distinction between why one *ought* to obey, and why one *can* obey, but the moral requirement will be a lame ox, incapable of doing any motivational work in the theory.[9]

In turn, the claim that Hobbes was a psychological egoist has been thought[10] to be bolstered by what the standard interpreters identify as Hobbes's mechanistic materialism. They point out that in Part 1 of *Leviathan*, Hobbes seems to begin with a scientific conception of man as matter in motion. Hobbes's account, in its bare essentials, is that all of a man's actions (except for those caused by a very few innate appetites, e.g., the appetite for food) are ultimately the result of the impingement on him of external forces. One is struck by a stimulus that causes one to move either toward or away from that stimulus, depending upon whether the stimulus enhances or decreases one's vital motion (one's life-force, literally, it seems, the circulation of one's blood). A man will always try to move toward a stimulus that increases his vital motion, the increase of which is experienced as pleasure, and away from a stimulus that decreases it, thereby causing pain. Because a man will always try to increase his vital motion, the end of deliberation will always be the action that seems to him to be best for himself.[11] In this way Hobbes's mechanistic materialism is supposed to support his psychological egoism: Given the former, it becomes a truism that the only motive of voluntary human behavior is the desire for one's own good. In Gauthier's words, "From this account of vital and voluntary motion, it follows that each man seeks, and seeks, only, to preserve and to strengthen himself. A concern for continued well-being is both the necessary and sufficient ground of human action. Hence man is necessarily selfish."[12]

Standard philosophical interpretations often include the further claims that Hobbes's moral theory (he is taken to have one, even though moral considerations can have no independent motivational force in the theory) is subjectivist or relativist, and that Hobbes himself was an atheist (or, at least, that theism is inessential to, detrimental to, or positively prohibited by Hobbes's political theory).[13] Although neither claim either entails or is entailed by materialism or egoism, they complement these other features of the standard interpretation. If men always and necessarily seek to obtain the objects of their desire, then it is not surprising they should call "good" all and only those things they desire. If what a man will call good, evil, and so on, depends on whether it produces in him an appetitive or an aversive reaction, and if his reaction will vary depending on the constitution of his body and his previous experience (the components of the passions), then it will be reasonable to suppose that 'good' and 'evil' have no universal and objective application.[14] If

there is no God, and if there are no objective moral requirements, then one would not expect there to be any source of
political obligation other than narrow self-interest.

Let us review the most characteristic features of the standard philosophical interpretation. These are that Hobbes is
attempting to derive a necessary form of political organization from fundamentally egoistic, even preservation-
centered, human nature; that Hobbes was a materialist,
moral subjectivist or relativist, and atheist; that political obligation is prudentially based; that might makes order and,
correspondingly, that fear of death and the desire for self-
preservation are the strongest motivating passions; and that
the state of nature represents a prisoner's dilemma.

A paradigm case of the standard philosophical interpretation would attempt to make a strict derivation of the need
for political subjection from mechanistic materialism via psychological egoism. It would afford what Hobbes calls the laws
of nature the status of mere maxims of prudence, even when
those laws were considered (by some "superstitious" persons) as the commands of God, since even one's "obligation"
to obey God would have to be merely prudentially grounded.
It would hold that the problem of social order is that given
fundamentally egoistic human nature, in the absence of any
coercively empowered authority, human beings will be
moved to act in ways that undermine the preservation of
themselves and others. Hobbes's solution to this problem is
to make it irrational for people to act antisocially by having
them subject themselves to an absolute political authority,
which can make rules for the regulation of conduct and which
has the power to coerce compliance with the rules.

Each of the standard interpreters identified earlier endorses some of the steps of the argument I've sketched, although not every standard interpreter endorses all of these
steps. For example, Watkins denies that Hobbes's psychological egoism can be strictly derived from his mechanistic
materialism, and Gauthier denies the link between egoism
and political obligation because, in his view, human beings
as Hobbes describes them aren't sufficiently tractable to sub-

mit themselves to an absolute sovereign. Nevertheless, these discontinuities in the argument that the standard interpreters attribute to Hobbes reflect not a denial that Hobbes held these views, but a faulty inference, or unwarranted conclusion, on Hobbes's part.

PRELIMINARY ASSESSMENT OF THE STANDARD PHILOSOPHICAL INTERPRETATION

The standard philosophical interpretation appears to fit well with Hobbes's legal positivism, his compatibilist theory of free will, his argument for obedience to any de facto power, and the scientific tone of the first part of *Leviathan*. It rationalizes Hobbes's emphasis on the utility of punishments in maintaining social order, and it seems the natural outgrowth of an egoistic, antisocial conception of human nature. In general, the standard interpretation captures one's sense upon reading the book that Hobbes is trying methodically, rigorously, and rationally to overcome what he sees as men's natural inaptitude to social living.

Before we proceed to evaluate this interpretation, it may be useful to make a provisional list of general criteria by which interpretations of great philosophical works are to be assessed. The best interpretation will be the one among those available that meets these criteria to the fullest extent. The criteria may be separated into two general headings, under each of which fall three distinct requirements. Ronald Dworkin terms these general headings – or dimensions, as he calls them – "fit" and "evaluation." Under the heading of "fit" we may distinguish three requirements. A good interpretation should have (1) *precise fit*, reflecting the author's particular claims, assertions, and arguments (it should fit with the specific things she or he says). It should be (2) *complete*, capable of accommodating most if not all of the author's text; and (3) *structurally explanatory*, capable of making sense of the way the author has organized his or her material, that is, it should account for the structure of the text. Under the heading of "evaluation" we may demand that an interpretation make the theory it yields (4) *coherent*, that is, the theory should be reasonably logically consistent, without major gaps or self-contradictory components (put another way, the author's argument must not be rendered blatantly invalid, or, at minimum, it must be shown why the argument should be invalid, and why an interpretation that makes it so is to be preferred over any available one that doesn't); (5) *plausible*, that is, the interpretation should not produce a theory that it would be wildly implausible to suppose the author could have formulated given his or her period, education, experience, milieu, and so forth (i.e., the attribution to him or her of the theory should not be "historically absurd"), and within this constraint, the theory should not rely on obviously false or seriously doubtful assumptions (it must not be blatantly unsound); and (6) the author's theory should have theoretical power, that is, it should be capable, at least in principle, of carrying out the task the author has set him- or herself.

Given the standard philosophical interpretation's wide acceptance, one might expect it to be able to account for most if not all of Hobbes's particular remarks. In fact, the standard interpretation does not fit the text precisely, as we shall presently see. Warrender and Taylor brought attention to a number of passages that would seem to be at variance with it,[15] and I present many more such passages a bit later.

When faced with textual evidence that challenges it, those committed to the standard philosophical interpretation are inclined either to throw out the recalcitrant passages, assuming that Hobbes was simply confused, or had some ulterior motive for including them, or to admit the recalcitrant passages, footnoting that Hobbes was inconsistent here, rather than to question their interpretation. For example, Plamenatz seems to favor conceding Hobbes's inconsistency ("Are philosophers so seldom inconsistent that we are entitled to conclude that they do not mean what they say, when to conclude otherwise would be to accuse them of inconsistency?"), and to prefer confusion to deceit as the explanation of such inconsistencies as there may be in Hobbes's theory on the standard interpretation of it ("Mr. Warrender mentions the critics who believe that Hobbes was guilty either of confusion or pretence when he brought God into his political philosophy. He does not agree with them. Yet, surely, if it was not pretence, it was confusion. . . . We may suspect [Hobbes] of atheism, but we cannot prove it against him. We can, however, prove against him the charge of confusion.")[16] The standard interpreters are not inclined to count incompatible textual passages as evidence against the adequacy of their interpretation.

Their disinclination to do so would be less noteworthy if such incompatible passages were few and far between, and the standard interpretation were capable of accommodating most of Hobbes's text and of explaining the structure of the work as a whole. But, surprisingly, the standard interpretation virtually ignores half of the book. The fact that almost exactly half of *Leviathan* is devoted to a highly detailed discussion of religious doctrine, practice, and history – which fact, it seems, cannot adequately be understood on the standard interpretation – has failed to diminish allegiance to that interpretation, again owing to a settled willingness to excuse Hobbes even such extensive lapses, chalking them up to mere confusion, ornamentation, or insincere concessions to tradition.

On the standard philosophical interpretation, the second half of *Leviathan* becomes quite mysterious. Why should Hobbes have been so concerned with the details of Christianity? Few standard interpreters even address this question. But some have suggested that the half of the book concerned with religion is intended to, as it were, cover Hobbes's atheistic tracks, both to protect Hobbes from persecution and to make his irreligious theory more palatable by its seeming concern for religion. This explanation is quite implausible, particularly once one sees that the religious view Hobbes develops in the second half of *Leviathan* is extremely unorthodox and inflammatory. (Indeed, many of his contemporaries focused their scathing attacks solely on Hobbes's religious views.) Moreover, Hobbes was well aware of the unorthodoxy of his religious views, and makes no secret of it: "I confess they are very hardly to bee reconciled with all the doctrines now unanimously received" (347) and "this doctrine will appear to most men a novelty" (241). Had Hobbes been doing what these interpreters suggest, he would surely have adopted a less radical and contentious religious position.[17]

What other explanation of this half of the book is available to the standard interpreter? Given that interpretation's assumptions of mechanistic materialism and (consequently) of egoism, the perception of a religious or moral *duty* cannot in itself motivate anyone to do anything, least of all, to jeopardize one's preservation. Even a concern for salvation seems problematic if one is going to take mechanistic materialism seriously, since that assumption is usually taken to imply the primacy of men's concern for *temporal* self-preservation, by showing that all of a man's actions are going to be directed toward the preservation of his *body*. If this were true, religious concerns could not motivate disobedience in the face of threatened corporal, especially capital, punishment, so there would seem to be no theoretical reason to discuss them at all, let alone at such length and in such detail.

Nevertheless, if the standard interpreter is to be able to account for the religious half of *Leviathan* in a way that (consistent with his assumptions about human motivation) makes that half a working part of Hobbes's theory, he would have, it seems, to appeal to special prudence – to one's interest in securing one's own salvation. But two considerations cast doubt on the claim that the religious half of the book's sole function is to reconcile the requirements of salvation with obedience to one's sovereign.

First, the claim that the half of *Leviathan* devoted to religion is included only to address people's self-interested concern in their own salvation seems to rely on an impoverished conception of what is involved in having religious concerns. People with religious concerns very often care about doing God's will for its own sake, about bringing about certain states of the world, and about securing the salvation of others. Their religious interests are not reducible to an interest in securing their own salvation. Of course, the standard interpreter might acknowledge this to be true while nonetheless insisting that *Hobbes* thought they were reducible in this way. But it is difficult to see how Hobbes could have thought this: A majority of the people to whom he was addressing his theory were Protestant (indeed Calvinist) predestinarians who did *not* believe it was *possible* for them to affect their own salvation, yet who were devoted to doing God's will in this world, many of them attempting to bring about a "biblically directed commonwealth." Hobbes's readers would not have been open to persuasion by a reductionist argument, and it is quite unlikely that Hobbes could have failed to realize this.

Second, if it were true that Hobbes had devoted half of his book to the issue of salvation, that would suggest he regarded people's interest in their own salvation as *extremely important* – important in a way it could not be unless that interest were often and widely given *priority* over men's interest in securing their temporal preservation and well-being, and could thus motivate disobedience to the state even in the face of threatened capital punishment. If the interest in salvation didn't *override* fear of bodily harm, then it would not undermine the effectiveness of the sovereign's threatened punishments and the threats to preservation posed by a state of nature, and so would not need to be dealt with for Hobbes's argument to work. If it *does* need to be dealt with, then it must be that religious interests can jeopardize order, which they could do only if they could override concerns to avoid bodily death. But if the concern to secure one's own salvation were *overriding*, then the role of the argument from the state of nature – of the argument the standard interpreter takes to be the centerpiece of Hobbes's theory – becomes not just radically incomplete, but clearly of secondary importance. If Hobbes thought that people have an overriding concern for their own salvation, then fear of death couldn't possibly provide the fundamental foundation for political obedience, as the standard philosophical interpretation insists it does.[18] The significance of the first half of the book would be radically diminished. And this will be true even if there are many people who have themselves no religious interests and who would be deterred by threat of death, because so long as there are enough others who *do* have overriding religious concerns that they can disrupt social order, it is not clear that even atheists have any reason to obey a state that cannot maintain social order. If the state can neither protect me nor credibly threaten to punish me, as it may not be able to do if religious resisters impede its functioning, then I have no reason from narrow prudence to obey it, even though I myself have no religious interests. On the one hand, if religious interests do not pose any serious threat to social order, then Hobbes's extended treatment of religion in the second half of *Leviathan* becomes an inexplicable mystery. On the other hand, if any significant portion of the population has overriding religious interests, then (on the standard interpretation's account of the first half of *Leviathan*) the importance of the first half of the book would be substantially reduced. But the standard interpretation can hardly afford such devaluation, since it concentrates *exclusively* on that portion of the book, and proposes a solution to disorder (namely changing the payoffs by threatening punishment) that would be completely undermined by acknowledging religious interests to override narrow self-interest. If the standard philosophical interpretation makes the second half of *Leviathan* a working part of the theory as a whole, its very foundation collapses. So, it concludes, the second half must be an irrelevant addendum.[19]

But Hobbes himself regarded his scriptural exegesis as crucial to his project: "That which perhaps may most offend, are certain texts of Holy Scripture, alledged by me to other purpose than ordinarily they use to be by others. But I have done it with due submission, *and also (in order to my subject) necessarily;* for they are the outworks of the enemy, from whence they impugne the civill power."[20]

The use of Scripture is *necessary* to Hobbes's task, yet it seems that the standard interpretation cannot provide an adequate account of Hobbes's massive and careful scriptural exegesis and his painstaking analysis of Christian religion. Either the religious half of the book is rendered superfluous, or it presents considerations that undermine the standard interpretation's account of disorder and its solution. Nevertheless, few standard interpreters say anything at all about that half of the book. If Hobbes's extremely extended discussion of religion sits badly with the standard interpretation, so much the worse for that discussion: the standard interpreter will not question the accuracy of his interpretation, but rather say with Stephen that Hobbes's system "would clearly be more consistent and intelligible if he simply omitted the theology altogether."[21]

The standard philosophical interpretation is defective in point of fit. It is imprecise (in the sense stipulated earlier), and it is particularly weak in the completeness and structural reflectiveness aspects of fit explained earlier. Yet that interpretation is very widely accepted among philosophers, and one might suppose that this is so because it is thought to render Hobbes's theory particularly coherent and plausible. It would appear, then, that any inroad into the territory of the standard interpretation must employ interpretive criteria other than fit, bringing to bear, for example, arguments that on the standard understanding of his theory Hobbes's assumptions are implausible, his arguments invalid, and his remedy for social chaos inconsistent with his conception of human nature. If Hobbes's theory, on the standard interpretation of it, is subject to serious and obvious objections, then, given its problems of fit, the accuracy of that interpretation ought, perhaps, to be called into doubt.

Astonishingly, so committed are philosophers to the traditional interpretation, that this implication of the principle of charity in interpretation has been roundly rejected by virtually everyone; the standard interpreters themselves have not failed to criticize Hobbes on the grounds that his theory depends on an implausible conception of human nature (psychological egoist), that his argument that the state of nature is a war of all against all is unsound, that his argument against divided sovereignty is unsound, that his mischaracterization of human nature leads him to argue that absolutism is necessary when it in fact isn't, and that given his conception of human nature, absolutism is impossible to establish.[22] In short, none of the standard interpreters we've discussed think the argument they attribute to Hobbes actually works.

Of course, it is always possible that even a thinker of Hobbes's stature will make logical or factual errors, and the standard philosophical interpreters are often careful to excuse the errors they take him to have made, saying, for example, that there is something valuable in Hobbes's "interconnected system of ideas, all of them fallible, most of them controversial, and some of them outrageous," namely, that it is "just because Hobbes tried, unsuccessfully, to demonstrate his political conclusions, he succeeded in elaborating a richly criticizable philosophy – which is what we should ask from a political philosopher."[23] Similarly, Gauthier maintains that "the content [of Hobbes's theory] is, as we have shown in the case of the moral theory, and will show in the political theory, inadequate. But the conceptual structure may provide us with insights into the construction of a more adequate theory . . . Hobbes has something of value for us . . . even if what is of the most value is not what he intended."[24] It doesn't matter that Hobbes's argument fails miserably, because, in Gauthier's words, "The outstanding merit of Hobbes's political theory is not to be found in its content."[25]

It would seem that what is of interest in Hobbes's theory to the standard interpreters is not the somewhat incoherent and implausible argument that they take Hobbes actually to have made, but rather some suitably restructured and corrected theory that one's reading of Hobbes might inspire one to create. Perhaps it is the standard interpretation's suggestion that Hobbes's work contains the raw material for a really interesting political theory, that has made that interpretation so attractive to philosophers that they have been willing not only to discount incompatible textual and structural evidence, but also to waive conditions of plausibility and internal consistency.

Whatever the reason, the standard interpreters are quite unmoved by the fact that their interpretation fails adequately to satisfy reasonable conditions on interpretation, namely, precision, completeness, structural explanatoriness, coherence, and plausibility. Perhaps they think that their interpretation's failure to satisfy the criteria under "fit" is because of the incoherence and implausibility of Hobbes's own argument, and is, in any event, no worse than that of any alternative interpretation.

THE THEORETICAL POWER CRITERION

Suppose that, temporarily and for the sake of argument, we grant all of this to the standard philosophical interpretation. There remains an important consideration: It is one thing to discount textual and structural features that would count against one's interpretation, or to accept inconsistencies, logical errors, and false empirical assumptions into the theory, for the sake of constructing or preserving a theory capable, at least in principle, of carrying out the task the author set himself; it is quite another thing to do this in the service of a hopeless theory. Whether or not we will find it reasonable to accept an interpretation that commits Hobbes's theory to inconsistencies, excesses, and errors will depend on both the theoretical power of the theory despite its faults, and the relative potential of the theory on any available alternative interpretations of it.

The simplest way to evaluate the strength of the standard philosophical interpretation of Hobbes's theory is to see how the theory fares in solving the fundamental problem that all philosophers take Hobbes to have been addressing: the problem of establishing and maintaining order. Everyone agrees that Hobbes saw himself as constructing a theory that could provide an answer to the question of how peaceful social order is to be established and maintained; thus, the power of his theory will be proportionate to its success in providing a solution to this problem. Once we see how successful Hobbes's theory is on the standard interpretation of it, we will have some idea of the extent to which that interpretation meets the theoretical power criterion for interpretation, mentioned earlier. The question of how it compares on this point to other available interpretations will have to await further investigation.

To evaluate what is alleged to be Hobbes's solution to the problem of order, we have to know the precise character of the problem of order as Hobbes saw it. What are the sources of social disorder, according to Hobbes? Because the standard interpretation sees Hobbes as seeking to derive from fundamental human nature the social arrangements necessary for enduring social order, and because it takes the state of nature to lay bare the characteristics of fundamental human nature, it seems we must analyze the state of nature: Why is it that when left to their own devices, men will engage in war?

We may immediately distinguish between two possible sources of disorder, namely, rational and extrarational: Does a state of war result from the rational activities of actors in pursuit of their rational self-interest, or is it the effect of action motivated by the passions or other such perturbations of reason? It might be that the state of nature has certain characteristics (e.g., extreme scarcity relative to demand) such that perfectly rational individual action leads to a miserable state of general warfare and insecurity; alternatively, it might be that normally rational actors would find the state of nature only a somewhat inconvenient, but not miserable, state were it not for the disruptive effects of certain perturbations of reason such as feelings of pride, vengeance, envy, and so forth. This distinction is not, of course, perfectly tidy; fear, for example, is a passion, but well-grounded fear is not to be accounted irrational. Likewise, the knowledge that others will be moved by passion to act irrationally may give a dispassionate person rational reason to be fearful. Nevertheless, this rough distinction is clear enough for our purposes: Is the primary source of disorder the rational activities of egoists engaged in competition for scarce resources, or is it the irrational behavior of persons under the influence of passionate interferences with reason? Or is disorder the result of some combination of the two?

The most compelling of the standard philosophical interpretations describe the belligerent behavior of individuals in the state of nature as the result of a cooperation problem, placing their interpretations firmly in the rational side of our dichotomy. Under conditions of scarcity relative to demand, rough equality of power, and the absence of any coercively empowered arbiter of disputes, the perfectly rational activities of entirely self-interested individuals will lead to a war of all against all.

Gauthier writes, "The natural condition of mankind is inherently unstable.... The actions which men naturally and reasonably perform in order to secure their ends prove self-defeating. We cannot suppose that men in Hobbes's state of nature are irrational. They do not engage in the war of all against all merely in order to satisfy immediate passion, or even to secure short-term interests."[26] It is clear that in Gauthier's view, the feature of the state of nature that sets in motion a downward spiral into the state of war is scarcity relative to desire, and the war that ensues is the effect of individually rational responses to such a situation:

> Men become enemies because they desire the same commodities as needful to their preservation. If the state of nature were a state of plenty, then men might refrain from hostility. But given that a man, in order to survive, may need some object which is also needed by his fellows, then competition necessarily follows. And as Hobbes shows, diffidence follows competition. Men acting on their own, however reasonable they may be, are doomed to the war of all against all.[27]

Likewise Kavka (who in other respects departs from the standard interpretation) sees the state of nature as the description of a cooperation problem in the form of a prisoner's dilemma with respect to promise-keeping and attack behavior. According to Hobbes, on Kavka's reading of him, individuals in a state of nature will find it rational to break their promises and preemptively to attack one another, and it is actions like these that create and perpetuate a war of all against all.

If these interpreters are right to think that Hobbes views social disorder as the result of individually rational behavior under certain unfavorable conditions, then the solution one would expect Hobbes to offer to the problem of order would be to alter those unfavorable conditions that make antisocial behavior rational.[28] This is, in fact, the solution these standard interpreters attribute to Hobbes: Hobbes's solution is to set up a coercively empowered sovereign that can, by threat of punishment, compel individuals to behave in a manner that does not threaten the security of their fellows.[29] Nagel, for example, writes that the laws of nature, which are rational precepts dictating to men the means to secure that peace which is a prerequisite of the self-preservation of each, "do not enjoin men to renounce the basic motivation to seek their own immediate benefit. They urge the establishment of conditions such that the results of men's acting from this same motivation will differ from the universal condition of war."[30] According to Gauthier, Hobbes's attempted solution to the problem of order is "to devise arrangements which will enable men to terminate this war. The well grounded state is that condition of human affairs which enables men to overcome obstacles to their security which make their natural condition one of permanent war."[31] What is alleged to be Hobbes's solution to the problem of order, on this conception of the problem as one of cooperation only, is most lucidly stated by Kavka: "Hobbes proposes a plausible solution to the problem of diverging individual and collective rationality: the creation of a power to impose sanctions that would alter the parties' payoffs so as to synchronize individual and collective rationality."[32] If the problem is that circumstances make rational individual patterns of behavior that cause social disorder, then the solution to disorder is to change those circumstances. The solution is to set up a coercive authority powerful enough to make antisocial behavior individually irrational.

If this is the problem of order as Hobbes conceives it, then the kind of solution the standard interpreters attribute to him might be capable, at least in principle, of *originally* establishing order out of anarchy.[33] If so, that would accomplish part of Hobbes's task. But the major portion of Hobbes's task – the project of showing how order can be maintained perpetually – remains as yet unaddressed. In order to achieve its end of giving directions for a perpetual peace, Hobbes's theory must speak to the causes of social *collapse,* providing both an analysis of, and a remedy to, *recurrent* disorder.

Now *if* we accept the standard interpreters' account of disorder and its solution, what explanation shall we give of *recurrent* disorder? Once a coercively empowered authority has been established – once the "payoff matrix" has been altered to bring individual rationality into line with collective rationality – disorder *ought* to have been permanently eradicated. States should not collapse. But clearly, Hobbes thought that states of order frequently collapse, that setting up a state was no guarantee whatsoever of permanent stability. Indeed, Hobbes says as much when he identifies the task he is undertaking as that of discovering how states may be made permanently stable – internally indestructible: "So, long time after men have begun to constitute commonwealths, imperfect, and apt to relapse into disorder, there may, principles of reason be found out, by industrious meditation, to make their constitution (excepting by externall violence) everlasting. And such are those which I have in this discourse set forth" (176).

The question of how order collapses is absolutely central because whatever account of disorder one wishes to attribute to Hobbes must provide a plausible explanation of the particular period of disorder in response to which Hobbes declared he was writing. There can be no doubt there had been a government in England that made laws and effectively punished violations of those laws before the onset of that conflict which Hobbes says occasioned his writing of *Leviathan*; it would be simply false to assert that there had never in England been a political authority with sufficient power to establish social order. Indeed, Hobbes acknowledges that there had been periods of stability in the commonwealths of the world in his remark that "in those nations whose commonwealths have been long-lived, and not been destroyed, but by forraign warre, the subjects never did dispute of the sovereign power" (107).

How then, on the standard interpretation's account of the problem of order, does a state of *order* collapse into a state of civil war? And can that collapse be explained (on the assumptions of the standard interpretation) in a way that would allow the solution they attribute to Hobbes to work? In order to evaluate the standard interpretation we must see what account it can give of the collapse of order; whether the English case, or any other case of disorder, could reasonably be thought to fit with that account; and whether, on that account of disorder, order could in fact be (re)established by setting up a coercive authority to "change the payoffs."

The first possible explanation of the collapse of order is destabilizing external forces (attack or invasion by an enemy nation, plague, or natural disaster). But it would be wildly implausible to suppose that all or even most disorder is the result of such events. Certainly Hobbes does not attribute the particular disorder with which he was concerned to this sort of factor.[34] If this were the only, or the primary, source of disorder, disorder would be a relatively minor problem, hardly worth spending some six hundred pages on, particularly since this sort of problem could not be solved by erecting a national civil sovereign to make laws and impose punishments (on other nations? on natural disasters?). If the intervention of external forces is the explanation for most social collapse, there is *nothing* to be done about it – the preservation of society is beyond the control of its members, subject to the uncontrollable forces of nature or foreigners. No one, including the standard interpreter, thinks that this is the lesson *Leviathan* teaches.

A second explanation of recurrent disorder is that the sovereign voluntarily surrenders all or essential parts of his sovereignty. Though it is not impossible that such a thing could happen, it seems very unlikely that this should be the proper account of most recurrent disorder. Certainly this was not the problem in Hobbes's period – Charles I was not known for his eagerness voluntarily to distribute parts of the sovereign power. Moreover, the standard interpretation's assumption of egoism makes it doubtful that Hobbesian sovereigns would be moved to give away pieces of their sovereignty. Again, of course, if this were the problem, it could hardly be solved by adopting the standard philosophical interpretation's solution of erecting a national civil sovereign to impose punishments (on himself?).

The clear implausibility of "destabilizing external forces" and "voluntary resignation of sovereignty" as the explanation of most recurrent social disorder allows us to see that a third prima facie reasonable explanation of recurrent disorder is a nonstarter. A standard interpreter might claim that social order collapses because the sovereign does not have enough power. This position is not open to the standard interpreter. "Enough power," on the standard philosophical interpretation, can only mean enough power to change the payoff matrix. If there is order, the sovereign ipso facto has enough power. For order to collapse, he would have somehow to cease to have enough power. How could this happen? As we've seen, he won't voluntarily give his power away. Subjects will be deterred from usurping it by effective threats of punishment – this is entailed by the hypothesis that the payoff matrix has been changed. He could cease to have enough power if some external force intervened that made it more rational for subjects to attempt to fend for themselves (risking punishment as well as the ills of a state of nature) than to obey the sovereign. But in this case it is the external force that is accounting for disorder, and we are again left with that unsatisfactory explanation. Note also that no amount of power will be enough to change the payoff matrix in such a case. No amount of power will be enough as long as people reason that their prospects for survival are worse if they attempt to comply with the law than if they don't. If their reasoning this way is the source of collapse, then order could not be reestablished by simply erecting a sovereign (since in the face of such reasoning he could not effectively change the payoffs), and the standard interpretation's "solution" would be no solution at all.

Similar reasoning allows us to see the failure of a fourth possible account of recurrent social disorder. A standard interpreter might wish to claim that order collapses because sovereignty is divided. Certainly Hobbes expresses concerns about divided sovereignty.[35] But how is the *standard interpreter* to make out a case against divided sovereignty? On the one hand, if disorder *always* obtains whenever sovereignty is divided – then an account of how a state of order can collapse will have to include some explanation of how sovereignty *becomes* divided. But the standard interpreter cannot provide the required explanation: once the payoff matrix has been changed, subjects will find it *irrational* to attempt to usurp sovereignty; and given the standard interpretation's psychological egoism assumption, it is exceedingly unlikely that an egoistic sovereign will voluntarily give away his power. That is, if divided sovereignty is enough to cause disorder, then a state of order will have to have undivided sovereignty. But if it is a state of order, where the payoffs have been changed, and subjects find it irrational to attempt to seize power, and sovereigns won't give it away, how can the sovereignty become divided, as it would have to if the explanation of the subsequent collapse is to be attributed to divided sovereignty?

On the other hand, a standard interpreter might try to avoid the problem of explaining how sovereignty can become divided by suggesting that sovereignty was always divided, and that the division at some point "just becomes" problematic. Sometimes divided states are stable, and sometimes they aren't. So a divided sovereign power might well succeed in changing the payoffs, thus maintaining order, for a while, and then somehow cease to be able to change the payoffs.

Something happens that makes a divided government incapable any longer of changing the payoffs (though the same event would not have that result were the government undivided). But notice that this "something" would then be the variable that accounts for social collapse. The government's dividedness per se would not be the explanation of disorder. The actual explanation would be that something else, in the face of divided sovereignty, causes disorder. What could the *ultimate* explanans be? It will not be any familiar element of the standard interpretation's account of disorder – it will not be simply that cooperation is suddenly irrational, or that preemptive aggression is once again rational. Recall that, in its rationality variant, the standard interpretation analyzes disorder solely as the result of competition for scarce resources and the diffidence it produces. But to explain collapse as the result of a resurgence of these factors would be inadequate without the addition of some further variable, foreign to the standard interpreter's analysis, such as plague, famine, or invasion, to account for the resurgence. The *ultimate explanans* will be ad hoc from the perspective of the standard interpretation.

The same argument will hold for limited sovereignty. If that is to be the account of disorder, then either the standard interpreter will have to explain how an unlimited, order-securing government becomes limited (which he cannot do from within his assumptions), or he will be left with a strange and unfamiliar variable to explain why a previously stable limited government suddenly collapses. The important point here is not only that the standard interpreter has not succeeded in explaining recurrent disorder, but is also that although *Hobbes* does worry greatly about divided and limited sovereignty, the standard interpreter's account of the cause of disorder cannot explain why this should be so.

If disorder is, as Hobbes thought it was, a genuine problem, its causes will be deeper, and wider, than these explanations allow. In claiming that his aim in *Leviathan* was "to set before men's eyes the mutual relation between protection and obedience" (395–6), Hobbes suggests that the problem

of order lies not with sovereigns, natural disasters, or foreigners, but with *subjects* (including, of course, those subjects
who also carry out governmental functions, e.g., in Hobbes's
day, members of Parliament, justices of the peace, and
judges); and this is also why he wrote that in domestically
stable commonwealths "the subjects never did dispute of the
sovereign power" (107). If the problem of disorder lies with
subjects, Hobbes's theory of disorder would seem to be a
theory of *rebellion*. What motivates subjects to rebel? Is it
reason, or is it the passions? We will consider each possibility
in turn, evaluating the standard philosophical interpretation's solution on either of these construals of the problem
as one, not of the impingement of external forces or of defects
inherent in the apparatus of the state, but as one of rebellious
subjects.

Let us consider the first possible explanation of the dissolution of order by rebellion available to a standard interpreter (of either the cooperation or the long-term rationality
variety). Perhaps order collapses because subjects fail to see
that disobedience or rebellion are not in their rational self-
interest. This would be a reasonable explanation if one had
to grasp some very complicated argument in order to see
that disobedience was not in one's interest. (If, for example,
one had to understand Hobbes's argument about the state
of nature.) But recall that this is supposed to be an explanation of how a state in which the payoffs *have been changed*,
reconciling individual and collective rationality, and short-
term and long-term rationality (through effective legislation,
and law enforcement *by threat of punishment*) collapses. The
standard interpreter's suggestion here is that subjects are
failing to see that disobedience is not in their interest *in the
face of the sovereign's threatened punishments.*

Now, if this were the cause of disorder, how could the
threat of punishment restore order? The threat of punishment will only motivate self-interested persons who *correctly
identify* their self-interest; it cannot be expected to have any
effect on self-interested people who are so irrational as to fail
to see the imprudence of disobedience even in the face of

32

credibly threatened punishments. That is, if recurrent disorder is caused by widespread irrationality, how can the solution be to "make" disorderly conduct irrational? It is *already* irrational, once the payoffs have been changed. Do people respond to the threat of punishment or don't they? (That is, can they be relied upon correctly to perceive and to act upon their rational self-interest, or not?) If they do, then there will be no recurrent disorder; if there is recurrent disorder, then clearly they don't respond to threat of punishment, and no mere reiteration of the threat is going to reestablish order.

Perhaps the standard interpreter is suggesting that order collapses because subjects fail to see that disobedience is not in their self-interest, and that order can be restored by increasing the obviousness, certainty, and magnitude of threats. That is, order collapses because, for example, people fail to see that incarceration is not in their self-interest, but that order can be restored by threatening to hang disobedient subjects. (This would allow for degrees of irrationality.) But how can this be an explanation of how order collapses? If there was order at t_1, then the threatened punishments must have been obvious, certain, and great enough that people perceived the irrationality of disobedience. Why, then, does order collapse at t_2, in the face of these very same threats? If they are insufficient at t_2, then they should also have been insufficient at t_1.[36] We do not yet have any explanation of how a state of order collapses. If collapse were due to a failure of rationality, pure and simple, there would be no reason to expect coercive sanctions (which are effective only on rational agents) either to restore or initially to establish order.

On neither the cooperation-problem nor the long-term irrationality variant of the standard interpretation, is order really a problem – it's easier to get than Hobbes supposes, and once it is established there's no reason why it should collapse. If the so-called Hobbesian solution is capable of working (which requires both that antisocial behavior can be made irrational *and* that most people can be counted on to act rationally), then a collapse of order, once order has been established, should not be possible. But such collapses are

possible and do in fact occur (as do reestablishments of order), and if these collapses were the result of irrationality,
then the "Hobbesian solution" wouldn't be capable of re-
storing order. If this is Hobbes's analysis of and proposed
solution to the problem of order, his theory is very weak
indeed.

Let us then examine the second possible source of disorder
distinguished above, namely, perturbation of reason, to see
whether the standard philososophical interpretation's solution fares any better on that account of disorder. (Some standard interpreters do recognize "glory seeking" as one source
of disorder.) Perhaps sociable behavior is individually rational, but people are caused to act irrationally by forces that
undermine or override their reason. On this analysis of disorder, we could certainly account for the phenomenon of
recurrent disorder. But could "Hobbes's solution" ever succeed in establishing order, if this were the problem?

For the passions to cause disorder, they would have to be
able to *override* reason, that is, rational self-interest, because
both general social order and avoidance of punishment are
in one's rational self-interest. They would also have to be
capable of overriding one particular sort of passion – fear of
death – if they are to be able to motivate disobedience in the
face of threatened corporal, especially capital, punishment.
But if this is the case, the standard interpretation's solution
won't work to establish order, because threats of punishment, which rely for their effectiveness on a calculation of
possible costs to self-interest, or fear of personal harm, especially of death, won't motivate sociable behavior. If disorder is caused by forces that *override* reason, or that *override*
fear, then an appeal to reason, or to fear, cannot solve the
problem. And if the passions are not forces of this sort, then
they cannot be the cause of recurrent disorder. If fear of
death, or the desire to avoid punishment or to preserve oneself, are sufficient to prevent antisocial behavior, then recurrent disorder ought not to be any problem. And if it is a
problem, it is either because people are chronically and systematically irrational, or because their other passions are ca-

pable of overriding their fear. Either way, the standard solution will not be effective on this account of disorder.[37]

If disorder is caused by passionate interferences with rational self-interest, the problem is real, but insoluble on the standard philosophical interpretation's reading of Hobbes; changing the payoffs won't work, precisely because the passions are capable of overriding rational self-interest.[38] If, on the other hand, there is no extrarational source of disorder (no passions involved except rational fear) and the problem is one of cooperation or long-run irrationality only, then either there is no significant problem of maintaining order once established (which is false), or that characteristic of human beings which makes disorder common and recurrent (either an inability correctly to calculate their rational self-interest, or susceptibility to overriding passions) also deprives "Hobbes's solution" of any possibility of success. In short, given the solution the standard interpretation attributes to Hobbes, and the available analyses of Hobbes's problem, the problem of order is either negligible or insoluble, and his solution is either unnecessary or useless.

This dilemma for the standard philosophical interpretation might seem to suggest either that Hobbes's solution to the problem of order is *not* simply to change the payoffs (that he does not think that might makes order), or that Hobbes does not view human beings as motivated only by considerations of narrow self-interest, or even that the source of social disorder is not to be found in the state of nature. Although I shall later offer arguments in support of all three of these conclusions, all I am suggesting at this point is that Hobbes's theory, on the standard philosophical interpretation of it, is too weak to warrant dismissing contrary textual and structural evidence, or admitting inconsistencies and errors into the theory, for the sake of preserving it. If the standard interpreters had built Hobbes a powerful theory, one that could address, and was capable at least in principle of solving, a genuine problem, then we might find it reasonable to accept such omissions and admissions. But because they have not, let us reexamine various of Hobbes's

remarks with an eye to seeing both how the standard interpretation stands up against them, and whether there emerges
a more compelling picture of the problem with which Hobbes
was concerned.

TOWARD A DIFFERENT ACCOUNT OF DISORDER

Hobbes makes assertions that would seem to suggest there
are forces other than considerations of rational self-interest
capable of affecting behavior, contrary to the materialism–
egoism assumption of the standard philosophical interpretation. Hobbes asserts that "the passions of men are *commonly*
more potent than their reason" (241, emphasis added), and
that "the understanding is by the flame of the passions never
enlightened, but dazzled" (242). These remarks suggest both
that the passions can override reason and that passion does
not aid ratiocination, but is rather counterposed to it. If there
are forces such as these that can oppose and override the
process or result of calculation of rational self-interest, then
disorder might be a function of more than just a lack of
cooperation or a nearsightedness in calculation.

Nevertheless, perhaps despite occasional interferences by
passions, human beings are at least crude calculators of their
self-interest. They may be prone to minor lapses of rationality, but when it comes to their self-preservation, self-
interest with its correlative passion, fear of personal harm,
will override all other motivating forces.

On the contrary, according to Hobbes, fear is often *not* the
strongest motivating passion. He writes, for example, that
one cannot be obligated to kill one's parent because "a son
will rather die than live infamous and hated of all the world"
(*EW* 2:83), that "*most* men choose rather to hazard their life,
than not to be revenged" (76, emphasis added), that "indignation carrieth men, not onely against the actors and authors
of injustice, but against all power that is likely to protect
them" (183), and that "most men would rather lose their
lives . . . than suffer slander" (*EW* 2:38). We can see from his

lengthy discussion of dueling that Hobbes recognized that pride could override fear of death; and seeing that legal prohibitions against dueling (with their concomitant punishments) had failed to eradicate that practice, he recommended a strategy of persuading people to think that dueling was ignoble (thereby fighting pride with pride, and not with fear). Fear of death, and the desire for self-preservation, seem *not* to be the strongest motivating forces after all.

The standard interpreter may reply that these are cases where a man simply does not realize the consequences of his actions (and that if he did, fear would override the self-destructive passion). Not only does this reply fail to salvage the interpretation – because if people are prone to ignorance of the consequences of their actions, making disruptive actions irrational will hardly prevent them from performing them – but Hobbes gives the lie to this "blinding passion" account of irrationality in his reply to Bishop Bramhall: "He [Bramhall] thinks, belike, that if a conqueror can kill me if he please, I am presently obliged without more ado to obey all his laws. *May I not rather die if I think fit?*" (*EW* 5:180, emphasis added).

The answer to this rhetorical question is obviously "Yes."[39] To "think something fit" is not to be driven by raging passion to do it. If the cause of disorder is (or contains an element of) these reason-resistant passions, the standard solution will not be effective.

What does Hobbes say about the cause of disorder? He undoubtedly thinks that disruptive actions are irrational, but he never says that irrationality is the cause of disorder. What he does say is this:

> *The most frequent praetext of sedition and civil war,* in Christian commonwealths hath a long time proceeded from a difficulty, *not yet sufficiently resolved,* of obeying at once both God, and Man, then when their commandments are one contrary to the other. It is manifest enough that when a man receiveth two contrary commands, and knows that one of them is God's, he ought to obey that, and not the other, though it be the

command even of his lawfull Soveraign (whether a monarch,
or a soveraign assembly) or the command of his father. (321,
emphasis added)

The most frequent reason for a collapse of order is the perceived conflict between duty to God and duty to man. This
assertion appears at once to sit badly with the standard interpretation. The standard interpreter need not, on the basis of
this passage, forgo his attribution of egoism; he can maintain
that one's interest in obeying God reduces to a self-regarding
interest in salvation, although we have already discussed
several reasons for thinking that Hobbes did not attempt to
make any such reduction. The standard interpreter's problem
is more basic: If people are taking up arms, risking their
preservation, because they believe their duty to God to be
at stake, how can the threat of punishment preserve social
order? This problem is only made worse once salvation is
brought into the picture. When faced with a choice between
eternal damnation and temporal punishment, the rational
egoist will surely choose the latter.[40] The sovereign cannot
hope to maintain order by his might under such conditions,
and it is difficult to see how any theorist could think that
disorder could be remedied by pointing out that rebellion
threatens self-preservation. (Furthermore, if the sovereign
cannot maintain social order, then even egoistic, preserva-
tion-driven atheists may have no reason to obey him. The
disruptive influence of religious factions may undermine
everyone's reason for civil obedience.)

In fact, Hobbes acknowledges quite explicitly that "changing the payoffs" is *not* sufficient to preserve social order:

> And the grounds of these rights [of sovereignty] have the
> rather need to be diligently, and truly taught, *because they
> cannot be maintained by any civil law, or terrour of legal punishment.*
> For a civill law that shall forbid rebellion (and such is all re-
> sistance to the essentiall rights of soveraignty) is not (as a civill
> law) any obligation, but by vertue onely of the law of nature
> that forbiddeth the violation of faith; which naturall obligation
> if men know not, they cannot know the right of any law the
> soveraign maketh. And for the punishment, they take it but

for an act of hostility; *which when they think they have strength enough, they will endeavour by acts of hostility, to avoyd.* (175–6, emphasis added)

Equally to the point, Hobbes writes, "If men know not their duty, what is there that can force them to obey the laws? An army, you will say. *But what shall force the army?"* (B 75, emphasis added). Not only are threats to self-preservation inadequate reliably to motivate people to obey, but the sovereign's very ability to wield coercive force depends on the uncoerced obedience of his subjects.[41] Generally stated, "The power of the mighty hath no foundation but in the opinion and belief of the people" (B 22). Opinion, not might, makes order.

Opinion and the related concepts of doctrine, belief, and judgment seem to be the key to Hobbes's political theory. These are very often cited as the cause of disorder:

If it be lawfull then for subjects to resist the king, when he commands anything that is against the Scripture, that is, contrary to the command of God, and to be judge of the meaning of Scripture, it is impossible that the life of any King, or the peace of any Christian kingdom, can long be secure. *It is this doctrine* that divides a kingdom within itself, whatsoever the men be, loyal or rebels, that write or preach it publicly. (B 63–4, emphasis added)

If there had not first been an *opinion* received of the greatest part of England that these powers [essential rights] were divided among the King and the Lords and the House of Commons, the people had never been divided, and fallen into this civil warre. (93, emphasis added)

This is why Hobbes writes that "the actions of men procede from their opinions, and in the well governing of opinions, consists the well governing of men's actions, in order to their peace and concord. . . . It belongeth therefore to him that hath the soveraign power, to be judge, or constitute all judges of opinions and doctrines, *as a thing necessary to peace*, thereby to prevent discord and civill warre" (91, emphasis added).

Opinion again appears in Hobbes's discussion of the cause of disorder as rooted in the translation of Scripture into vulgar languages for perusal and interpretation by individuals, "For what could that produce, but *diversity of opinion, and consequently,* as man's nature is, disputation, breach of charity, disobedience, and *at last rebellion?"* (*B* 66, emphasis added).

Indeed, even if men could be deterred from open hostility by the threat of punishment, their condition would be tenuous and would not count as peace of the sort Hobbes has in mind:

> It is true, that in a commonwealth, where by the negligence, or unskilfullnesse of governours and teachers, false doctrines are by time generally received, the contrary truths may be generally offensive: Yet the most sudden, and rough busling in of a new truth that can be, does never breake the peace, but only sometimes awake the warre. For those men that are so remissely governed, that they dare take up armes to defend, or introduce an opinion, are still in warre; *and their condition not peace but only a cessation of armes for fear of one another;* and they live as it were, in the procincts of battaile continually. (91, emphasis added)

Forbearing to take up arms for fear only, is not peace but at best a fragile cease-fire (something, perhaps, like a cold war). But this is the most that the standard interpretation could hope to achieve. The standard interpretation's solution relies on fear of the threats to preservation caused by disorder, and more immediately on fear of punishment, to maintain social order; even if, *pace* Hobbes, social order could be maintained this way, the condition of men would not be one of that peace which Hobbes is after.

Now the sorts of opinions that disrupt peace, and in the governing of which consists the government of men's actions in order to their peace and concord, would appear to be opinions about, not self-preservation or self-interest narrowly construed, but about such things as men's duty to God, the justice and injustice of actions and policies, and the distribution of legitimate authority. Moreover, these opinions and doctrines seem to be capable of motivating actions inimical to the maintenance of social order generally, and to self-preservation and other forms of self-interest particularly.

It seems reasonable to suppose that these opinions are resistant to self-interest because they are associated with the passions: We might say that the cause of social disorder is *opinion, passionately held*. And if this is the cause of disorder, disorder becomes a substantive, genuine, problem. Because the passions are resistant to modification by calculations of rational self-interest, we should expect passionately held opinions to be not effectively *modifiable* by threat of force. On this point Hobbes confirms our expectation: "A state can constrain obedience, but convince no error, nor alter the mind of them that believe they have the better reason. Suppression of doctrines does but unite and exasperate, that is, increase both the malice and power of them that have already believed them" (*B* 80).

Moreover, because the passions are reason-resistant, we should expect the failure of any strategy that relies on *suppressing* passionately held opinions. Sheer force might slow the dissolution of order, but it cannot, in the end, prevent it. Passionately held beliefs, in particular those concerning one's duty to God, when they require actions opposed to the policies of the state, or to the aims of competing religious factions, are bound to destroy the peace, and no exercise of coercive power – no amount of alteration in the payoff matrix – will help:

> [T]he emperours, and other Christian soveraigns, under whose government these errours and the like encroachments of ecclesiastics upon their office, at first crept in to the disturbance of their possessions, and of the tranquillity of their subjects ... may neverthelesse bee esteemed accessaries to their own, and the public dammage: for without their authority there could at first no seditious doctrine have been publically preached. I say they might have hindred the same in the beginning: *But when the people were once possessed by those spirituall men, there was no humane remedy to be applied, that any man could invent.* And for the remedies that God should provide ... wee are to attend his good pleasure, that suffereth

many times the prosperity of his enemies, together with their ambition, to grow to such a height, as the violence thereof openeth the eyes . . . *whereas the impatience of those that strive to resist such encroachment before their subjects eyes were opened did but encrease the power they resisted.* (384, emphasis added)

The opinions men have of their religious duties can be held with such devotion and passion that they cannot be squelched, even by the *united* forces of Christian sovereigns,

till preaching be better looked to, whereby the interpretation of a verse in the Hebrew, Greek, or Latin Bible, *is oftentimes the cause of a civil war* and the deposing and assassinating of God's anointed. . . . It is not the right of the sovereign, though granted to him by every man's express consent, that can enable him to do his office; *it is the obedience of the subject, that must do that. For what good is it to promise allegiance and then by and by to cry out, as some ministers did in the pulpit, To your tents, O Israel!?* (B 181, emphasis added)

The degree of influence of "spirituall men," preachers and theologian-philosophers, is, in Hobbes's view, absolutely staggering. He relates Diodorus's history of the Ethiopians, according to which, not only subjects, but Ethiopian kings, would commit suicide when their priests so directed them, obeying the priests, "not as mastered by force and arms, but as having their reason mastered by superstition" (B 119). Hobbes tells this story intending "not by these quotations to commend either the divinity or the philosophy of those heathen people, but to show only what the reputation of those sciences can effect among the people" (B 120). If one's religious beliefs can motivate one actually voluntarily to kill oneself, they can certainly motivate one to *risk* death or lesser punishment in their service. One's interest in doing what one believes to be religiously required can override one's interest in self-preservation. It is precisely this *transcendence* of religious interests that makes them incorrigible by means of coercion. And it is the affirmation within a society of competing transcendent interests, or the affirmation by any significant portion of society of an inherently disruptive transcendent interest, that is inimical to the preservation of social order. This is why the sovereign *must* control religious doctrine; because "if he give away the government of doctrines, men *will be frighted into rebellion* with the feare of spirits" (93, emphasis added).

If, then, the problem Hobbes is concerned with is the disruption caused by competing passionately held beliefs, beliefs in particular about one's duty to God, then his solution to the problem of social order will have to deal with these beliefs. This would make sense of the structural feature of *Leviathan,* mentioned earlier, that roughly half of that book involves a detailed discussion of various religious beliefs. Now those struggles over beliefs which bring about a collapse of social order will have to involve at least one party that is affirming a *false* belief, because in Hobbes's view, the truth can never be repugnant to peace (91). Hobbes has already said that suppressing these beliefs will not maintain social order. The remaining alternative is to correct them. Experience is an inadequate teacher. Even the experience of social collapse will not sufficiently correct men's false opinions, for they will continue to acknowledge the lesson experience has taught them only "till all their miseries are forgotten, and no longer, except the vulgar be better taught than they have hitherto been" (93). Nor can these beliefs be corrected by coercing those who hold them. Hobbes is quite explicit about this in his attack on the practice of inquisition.[42]

How do *we* ordinarily correct false beliefs? Presumably, what is called for is a process of reeducation, preferably one that begins from the true beliefs a man holds, and uses these to show the falsity of his disruptive beliefs. We won't correct his errors by simply and flatly contradicting his beliefs, but there is this more profitable way to educate. And if we can get him to hold true beliefs as passionately as he held his false and disruptive beliefs, we will have passion working for, rather than against, the maintenance of peace. We will then find ourselves in a condition that is not just a modus vivendi, or a fragile cease-fire, but a stable, self-perpetuating peace, "for ambition can do little without hands, and few hands it would have, if the common people were as diligently instructed in the true principles of their duty, as they are terrified and amazed by preachers, with fruitless and dangerous doctrines" (B 90).

The sources of disorder are passionately held opinions concerning their transcendent interests, particularly in matters of religion; and what is required to combat these disruptive opinions is active and systematic reeducation:

> Common people know nothing of right or wrong by their own meditation; they must therefore be taught the grounds of their duty, and the reasons why calamities ever follow disobedience to their lawful sovereigns. But to the contrary, our rebels were publicly taught rebellion in the pulpits; and that there was no sin, but the doing of what the preachers forbade, or the omission of what they advised. (*B* 181)

It appears then, that Hobbes's solution to the disruption created by men's pursuit of competing transcendent interests is to reeducate men so that they all hold the (same) correct views. But a seemingly fatal flaw in this plan is immediately apparent. Perhaps uniform preaching and education could bring about uniform judgment. But how are we to get uniform preaching and education? After all, these not only condition judgment, but also *reflect* it. And, as we've seen, differences in judgment cannot be overcome by force. Competing transcendent interests would have to be largely reconciled *before* a system of uniform preaching and education could be established.

One of Hobbes's central tasks, then, is to find a way to reconcile competing transcendent interests. This, I will argue, is precisely the task he undertakes in the second half of *Leviathan:* The function of the second half of the book is to reconcile competing religious interests through an elaborate process of redescription. Hobbes aims to redescribe competing substantive descriptions of men's transcendent interest in fulfilling their duties to God in such a way that each former faction can affirm the redescription as accurately capturing its interest, while all will be affirming the very same

44

description. Hobbes's careful scriptural exegesis and his detailed discussion of Christian doctrine, practice, and history are employed in this project of reconciling transcendent interests, and they become, on our suggested interpretation, an indispensable part of Hobbes's solution to the problem of social order. Once transcendent interests have been reconciled, consensus in judgment is then to be maintained and reproduced by means of an aggressive system of education.

In sum, we can see that on the supposition that Hobbes viewed certain disruptive, or competing, passionately held beliefs – beliefs upon which people are willing to act even at the expense of their self-preservation – to be the cause of disorder, Hobbes was concerned with a genuine problem, genuine in two senses: First, this analysis makes disorder a substantive problem, rather than one of cooperation only, and thus a problem likely to recur again and again. Second, this analysis of disorder rings true; if men had *no* transcendent interests, if there were nothing for which they would risk their preservation, how could they be motivated to resist the state? And when people do resist the state, they very often do so in the name of religion, liberty, or a similarly devotion-inspiring interest. Hobbes's analysis of disorder, on this hypothesis, becomes much more sensible. Moreover, his solution – to correct through a process of redescription and reeducation the beliefs that when passionately held underlie socially disruptive activities – is capable, at least in principle, of solving the problem of order as he has posed it. If *this* is the problem, then it is a serious problem that could, theoretically, be solved by the means Hobbes suggests. And it is not ludicrous to suppose that this formulation of the problem of order is approximately right, at least vis-à-vis the English case with which Hobbes was concerned. In both of these senses, Hobbes's political theory becomes a *powerful* theory, on this interpretation of it.

Further consideration of our interpretation reveals two additional prima facie benefits. First, this interpretation makes sense of the fact that attacks on the universities, and arguments in favor of better education, abound in Hobbes's writ-

ings. On the standard interpretation, according to which social order is achieved merely through changing the payoffs
(by making antisocial behavior irrational), it is not at all clear
why education should have such a central role in Hobbes's
theory as it seems to have; given their attribution to Hobbes
of an egoistic theory of motivation, and given what they take
to be Hobbes's solution to the problem of order (namely,
creating an authority to change the payoffs), education would
have to be education about what activities threaten self-preservation and other forms of self-interest. It would have to
teach, for example, that armed rebellion threatens self-preservation, that civil war threatens preservation, that illegal
acts bring with them the threat of punishment (which is not
in one's self-interest), and so on. But, in fact, this does not
seem to be the sort of education Hobbes has primarily in
mind – he speaks very often of teaching men about their
duty, about moral and political virtue, and, of course, about
true religion.

Second, on our hypothesis we can see why Hobbes should
have been deeply concerned with the problem of pride – so
concerned, in fact, that he named his major political treatise
for "the King over all the children of pride" (*L* 167). The
passionately held beliefs that disrupt social order are beliefs
about what God wants, what is just, what is righteous, what
is sinful, and so on. These passionately held beliefs appear
in the form of a transcendent interest in acting righteously,
justly, and so on. A person willing to take up arms (risking
his own preservation and threatening social order generally)
to defend or to impose these beliefs, must feel very certain
that he knows what God's will is. He must think, in fact,
that he knows better than anyone whose ideas oppose his
own, even if that person is his civil sovereign, or the head
of the state church, what God's will is, what is just, righteous,
sinful, and so forth. This, Hobbes will argue, is *hubris*.
Hobbes's recurrent attack on pride is an attack on the sort
of pride exhibited in private judgment generally, and in religious judgment particularly – the pridefulness involved in
taking one's own private opinion of right and wrong, good

and bad, just and unjust, or one's own interpretation of Scripture, as right reason, and then acting on it in defiance of constituted authority, and attempting to impose it over and against the judgments of others. Social disorder arises from diversity of opinion in conjunction with each person's insistence that his judgment is authoritative; and this insistence bespeaks tremendous hubris. Pride becomes a central concept in Hobbes's analysis of social disorder.

In contrast, the standard philosophical interpretation seems hard-pressed to explain Hobbes's obsession with pride: If its analysis of and alleged solution to the problem of order is correct, pridefulness can have no important role to play, since whatever disruptive actions men might be tempted by this passion to perform would be prevented by their overriding fear of death and desire for self-preservation; they would have to be – otherwise, the alleged solution wouldn't be capable of maintaining social order.

In light of the failure of the standard philosophical interpretation satisfactorily to meet reasonable criteria for good interpretations, it should not seem unreasonable for us to attempt to construct an alternative interpretation that pursues the line of reasoning we've been sketching. It may be that the standard interpretation is the best we can do for Hobbes (and if it is, we may have to rest satisfied with it, despite its problems of fit, coherence, plausibility, and power); but this we will not know until we see, in detail, what alternative there is.

Chapter 2

Hobbes's compositive reconstruction, phase one: identification of the principle of political obligation

> It is not the bare words, but the scope of the writer that giveth the true light by which any writing is to bee interpreted; and they that insist upon single texts, without considering the main designe, can derive no thing from them cleerly.
>
> – Hobbes (*L* 333)

Although interpreters of Hobbes's political philosophy have all agreed that Hobbes took as his primary task providing an answer to the question of how domestic social order can be established and maintained perpetually,[1] there remains among Hobbes interpreters serious disagreement over what might be called the *strategy* that Hobbes is thought to employ in executing this fundamental task. The specific characterizations of Hobbes's strategy put forward by the various interpreters – their views of *how* Hobbes was proceeding – differ in ways that have a profound effect on the resulting positions attributed to Hobbes – their views of *what* Hobbes actually argued. Nonstandard interpreters such as Warrender and Taylor have held that Hobbes sought to provide a basis for social order by demonstrating that people have a *moral obligation* to obey their sovereign, and have thus attributed to him views and arguments that differ dramatically from those alleged by standard philosophical interpreters, who see Hobbes as attempting to provide a basis for social order by demonstrating that people, who desire their self-preservation above all else, would be *irrational* ever to disobey their sovereign. Indeed, such differing characterizations of

48

Hobbes's strategy for solving the problem of order – of the "main designe" of his theory – result not only in the attribution to Hobbes of incompatible positions and arguments, but also in differing assessments of the success of Hobbes's political theory.

It is not surprising that interpretations and evaluations of Hobbes's political theory will differ depending on the interpreter's belief as to which strategy Hobbes is employing in his attempt to solve the problem of order. But perhaps it is surprising that there could be such a wide range of disagreement about what it is that Hobbes is trying to do. Hobbes's text is sufficiently rich that the members of each school of interpretation can muster reasonable textual evidence for their claims as to the strategy Hobbes is employing. Some pieces of the text will bear the standard interpretation, with its claim that Hobbes is trying to derive the conclusion that men ought (prudentially) to obey the state from fundamentally preservation-centered human nature, whereas other portions of the text can be used to support those nontraditional interpretations that see Hobbes as trying to derive a moral obligation to obey the state from either a moral duty to obey the laws of nature, or a moral duty to obey the commands of God. Nevertheless, to the extent that each type of interpretation claims Hobbes to be deriving the requirement of political obedience *solely*, or *primarily*, from considerations of rational prudence, or solely, or primarily from a prior moral or religious obligation, they will be mutually incompatible. Because the major philosophical interpretations are usually taken to be incompatible in this way (philosophers have a lively sense that Hobbes has an elegantly simple master plan), yet none can be strictly ruled out on the basis of Hobbes's text, virtually all of the philosophical interpreters agree in thinking that Hobbes's political theory is itself inconsistent.

I suggested in Chapter 1 that many Hobbes interpreters of the standard philosophical school have attributed to Hobbes a political theory that fits poorly with Hobbes's text, is internally inconsistent, reliant on a highly implausible conception of human nature, full of mistakes and insincere arguments, and ultimately fails, even in its own terms, to provide a solution that successfully addresses the problem it poses. These problems, as I see it, are most immediately the result of the standard interpreters' having misidentified Hobbes's *solution* to the problem of order. But this very misidentification, and the problematic theory it yields, themselves rest, in my view, on an erroneous specification of the strategy Hobbes was using in his attempt to solve the problem of order. In this and the following two chapters I argue, on the basis of a close textual analysis of Parts 2 and 3 of *Leviathan*, that Hobbes's strategy was *not* to derive the necessity of an absolutist form of government from the individual's overriding desire for self-preservation. I shall argue instead that Hobbes was attempting to provide virtually all of his readers with a *sufficient reason*, given *all* of the interests they actually took themselves to have, for affirming and acting on a *principle of political obligation* that, if generally and widely adhered to, could ensure the perpetual maintenance of effective social order. Let me first elaborate a bit on the components of this hypothesis.

When I speak of a principle of political obligation, I am referring to a statement of the conditions under which subjects or citizens are to obey the commands of the government of the commonwealth of which they are members. Examples of this sort are such principles as "One is to obey the government no matter what" and "One is to obey the government only if all of its commands are just" or "One is to obey the government only in those of its commands that are just." Hobbes's aim is first to identify a principle of political obligation that actually could, if widely followed, ensure the perpetual maintenance of domestic peace, and then to provide each of his readers with what that person can regard as a sufficient reason to affirm and to adhere to that principle. The principle Hobbes seeks to defend as being one that, if widely followed, could ensure perpetual domestic order, and then to give people a sufficient reason to uphold is (in its first formulation): "One is to obey the effective government of the commonwealth of which one is a member in all of its commands not repugnant to one's duty to God."[2]

A "sufficient reason," as I will use that term, is a reason that is not overridden by contrary reasons. Thus, for example, the fact that I have a narrowly prudential reason for cheating my neighbor (I will gain by doing so) will not be a sufficient reason to cheat him if I have an overriding moral reason, or an overriding religious reason, for refraining from cheating him. I will speak of having a reason as recognizing that some action contributes to the satisfaction of one or more of what one *perceives* as one's interests. Because Hobbes holds that people act on their perceived interests, his theory is designed to take seriously the interests that people say they have, providing people with reasons linked to the interests they actually claim as their own, rather than starting from some ideal notion of what interests people "really do" have, or ought to recognize. Hobbes is aiming to identify a principle of political obligation that could, if followed, ensure the perpetual maintenance of effective social order (that is, ensure a commonwealth that could never be destroyed but by foreign war), and that nearly everyone, given what each acknowledges to be his interests, can have sufficient reason to affirm and uphold. This is so even though, as we shall see, Hobbes also argues that through education people can be made even further disposed to act on this principle by fostering in them certain interests, and that they should be so educated.[3]

Now 'interests' here is meant broadly, and may include interests in non-self-referring objects and states of affairs (for example, interests in the happiness of others) and uniformity-requiring interests (such as that everyone fulfill the requirements of true religion, or that everyone act morally). Hobbes recognizes that people are capable of having at least four basic sorts of interests: narrowly prudential interests in their physical survival and in "commodious living," moral interests in fulfilling their natural duties and moral obligations, religious interests in fulfilling their duties to God, and "special prudential" interests in achieving salvation. The latter three sorts of interests may be "transcendent," that is, they may be interests that an individual affords priority over any of his narrowly prudential interests, including his interest in securing his physical survival. One who has an interest in acting morally or in fulfilling his duties to God may be willing to sacrifice his preservation for the realization of these interests, and if so, they are for him transcendent interests. (Interests in the welfare of a loved one, or in enjoying salvation, might also be transcendent in this way.)

What will count as a sufficient reason for a person will thus depend on what he takes his interests to be, and what their relative weight is. A sufficient reason may be composed of a number of independent considerations – for example, prudential considerations, moral considerations, and religious considerations. Although connecting adherence to Hobbes's principle of political obligation with the realization of any single one of these four interests *may* give one a sufficent reason to adhere to the principle (if, say, one has no other interests, or if those other interests do not provide reasons for contrary action), Hobbes is aiming at a *concurrence* of reasons – narrowly prudential, moral, religious, and specially prudential – for affirming his principle.[4] The provision of a merely narrowly prudential reason will not serve Hobbes's purpose, since moral and religious interests may be transcendent; nonetheless, a narrowly prudential reason is generally necessary if people are to be *reliably* motivated to act on the principle, because it would be unwarranted to suppose that people will *always* be willing to sacrifice their preservation or quality of life for their other interests. As we'll see, Hobbes expects these four types of reason to work together, so to speak, in such a way that the number of people who will *not* have a sufficient reason for adhering to his principle of political obligation will, at any given time, be so small that their activities can be expected to have a negligible effect on the maintenance of social order.

Hobbes's strategy, then, is to identify a principle of political obligation that could, if widely followed, ensure the perpetual maintenance of domestic order, and then to show his readers that given all of the interests they take themselves to have, they have on the whole a sufficient reason for adhering to this principle. The argument, as I shall try to show, although very complex (which complexity accounts for the disagreement among interpreters as to Hobbes's strategy, and the initial appearance of inconsistency in Hobbes's argument), is brilliantly conceived, and actually works to solve the problem of order as Hobbes understood that problem.

In Parts 2 and 3 of *Leviathan*, Hobbes offers a multi-partite argument to implement the strategy I have been outlining. He begins in Part 2 by identifying what he calls infallible rules of reason for constructing a perpetually stable commonwealth, or a commonwealth that, barring external forces, will not collapse. These are rules that, if universally followed, would ensure against civil war. He begins from the *concept* of a commonwealth – its function and basic form – and from some empirical observations about the sources of disorder within commonwealths, and traces through the requirements that must be met if such an entity is to be perpetually stable. By this means Hobbes arrives at a set of rules for constructing an indestructible commonwealth. These rules are compiled into a single principle of political obligation, which forms, on the basis of the argument so far, the best candidate for a principle that could, if followed, ensure perpetual stability. Part of this step in the argument involves translating the contraries of these various particular rules of reason into *grounds for disobedience* to an existing government, compiling these contraries into alternative principles of political obligation, and then discrediting the alternative principles one by one, thereby answering objections to Hobbes's own principle of political obligation. The resulting principle of political obligation, although importantly underspecified until the completion of the task undertaken in Part 3, provides the basic principle that Hobbes will show his readers to have sufficient reason to support. The basic principle Hobbes defends is, as I have said, that one is to obey the government of the commonwealth of which one is a member in all of its commands not repugnant to one's duty to God;

and the principle is importantly underspecified because we cannot tell at this point in the argument how much disobedience the exemption concerning duty to God allows, and whether it is enough to undermine the ability of the principle to ensure perpetual domestic peace.

The first two legs of the latter portion of Hobbes's argument showing people to have reasons to adhere to his principle – the linkage between Hobbes's principle of political obligation and the satisfaction of both narrowly prudential and secular moral interests – are also carried out in Part 2 of *Leviathan.* Hobbes sketches two arguments designed to show that adherence to his principle is required for the satisfaction of narrowly prudential and secular moral interests, when these are properly understood. This chapter presents both of these (very distinct) portions of Hobbes's project – the argument identifying a (still underspecified) principle; and the preliminary and partial arguments linking that principle with narrowly prudential and secular moral interests.

The next phase of the compositive portion of Hobbes's argument (carried out in Part 3, and discussed in my next chapter) involves the dual project of fully specifying Hobbes's principle of political obligation, and linking that principle to the satisfaction of his readers' interests in fulfilling their religious duties and in their special prudential interest in achieving salvation. The further specification of Hobbes's principle is indispensable to his task of establishing that the principle really could, if followed, ensure a perpetually stable domestic order, and of showing people to have sufficient reason to adhere to it. This is so for two reasons. The principle must be fully specified, first, because the principle is left at the end of Part 2 in a preliminary formulation that includes an exemption from political obedience the full impact of which on stability cannot be known until the exact character of the class of actions exempted is spelled out. The specification of the principle carried out in Part 3 is thus to be understood not as a wholly separable, subordinate, or even dispensable argument but rather as a continuation of the task, begun in Part 2, of identifying a principle of political obligation that could, if widely followed, ensure perpetual social order. Second, Hobbes cannot complete his argument that people have a narrowly prudential reason to adhere to the principle until he can show that adherence to the principle really would ensure the maintenance of social order, because the rationality of adhering to the principle depends in part on whether doing so would contribute to something people value, such as the maintenance of order. And, because the secular moral interests argument is parasitic on the narrowly prudential interests argument (as we shall see) it too can be completed only once the principle is fully specified.

The arguments offered in Part 3 providing reasons for adhering to Hobbes's principle from religious interests are also indispensable components in Hobbes's project of identifying a principle of political obligation which everyone can have *sufficient* reason to affirm and uphold, again for two reasons. First, because a narrowly prudential reason to do something may not be a sufficient reason when one has a moral or religious reason not to do it, particularly since moral and religious interests may be transcendent, overriding mere prudential interests in cases where they conflict, Hobbes must show that there can be no such conflict if he is to succeed in providing everyone with a sufficient reason for adhering to his principle of political obligation. Second, even if I am a wholly self-interested atheist, if others in my society do have transcendent religious interests, their action on these may upset social order. If this is possible, then I will have to be assured that the principle with its exemption sufficiently restrains their disruptive activities that order can be maintained if I am to be able to see myself as having even a narrowly prudential reason for adhering to it. This is so because if the principle could not, when followed, ensure social order, then I, as a wholly self-interested atheist, could have no reason from narrow prudence to adhere to it.

We should note, too, that the position Hobbes advances is stronger than the mere claim that adherence to his principle of political obligation is *compatible* with the realization of an interest in acting morally (in Part 2), in fulfilling one's duties to God, or in fulfilling one of the necessary conditions for achieving salvation (in Part 3). His argument is that anyone who has those interests will have *further* reasons – moral, religious, and specially prudential – for adhering to his principle. This is because, as Hobbes argues, acting against his principle involves the violation of a moral duty, and acting according to it is a part of one's duty to God, and a necessary, although not sufficient, condition of salvation. Thus, people who desire their survival and material flourishing have not only a prudential reason for affirming and upholding his principle but – to the extent that they have interests in acting morally and in fulfilling their duties to God – also moral and religious reasons for doing so. This *concurrence* of reasons for affirming and adhering to Hobbes's principle makes it likely that any given person will perceive himself as having sufficient reason to do so, and virtually certain that at any given time, enough people will be sufficiently motivated to adhere to his principle that effective social order can be maintained perpetually.

Although the full specification of Hobbes's principle and the provision of reasons from religious duty and special prudence are an integral phase of Hobbes's overall project (rather than a separate project), they require the use of extrarational sources of knowledge, and so Hobbes considers them separately under the heading of Part 3. Nothing is to be inferred about the limits of the compositive portion of Hobbes's project from the division of the argument into Parts 2 and 3; this division merely reflects the differing sources of knowledge to be employed in mounting the argument. Parts 2 and 3 of *Leviathan* form a single complex argument, the compositive portion of Hobbes's overall theory.

Hobbes's project requires that he deal with transcendent interests, not only so that these sorts of interests do not *undermine* people's obedience to their political authority, but also because in cases where that authority comes under attack, it may be necessary for the maintenance of effective social order for people actively to defend their political authority, and this may entail risking their preservation. This consideration further motivates Hobbes's arguments for his principle from transcendent interests, particularly his argument from special prudence (presented at the end of Part 3), designed to show that people ought to regard themselves as having a transcendent interest in acting according to Hobbes's principle *even if they are entirely self-interested.* The final portion of Hobbes's compositive argument (which I present and discuss in Chapter 4) is an analysis of the mechanism by which the characterizations of transcendent interests on which his argument depends can be socially affirmed and reproduced perpetually – of how these interests can be instilled in people – and of how a disposition to act on them is to be cultivated.

If Hobbes's principle of political obligation is, as he argues, both one that when generally followed is capable of ensuring the perpetual maintenance of effective social order, and one that most people can almost always have sufficient reason to follow (and even to defend at risk to themselves), he will have succeeded in providing a solution to the problem of order. Moreover, Hobbes's solution will work even when the problem of disorder is generated by transcendent interests, the most difficult of interests to deal with because coercive threats cannot be effective in the face of these interests, which trump concerns of narrow self-interest (including the interest in self-preservation). This feature of Hobbes's solution, that it can remedy even disorder generated by transcendent interests, is absolutely crucial to the success of Hobbes's political project because, as we shall see in considering Hobbes's resolutive analysis of disorder (in Chapters 5, 6, 7, and 8), Hobbes thought that not only the disorder of his own day but many, if not most, instances of disorder throughout history had been the result of transcendent interests.

Let us now see what the compositive component of Hobbes's political theory looks like when his task is conceived in the way I've described it.

IDENTIFICATION OF A PRINCIPLE OF
POLITICAL OBLIGATION

The concept of a commonwealth

What Hobbes has in mind when he speaks of developing a science of politics is the discovery of a set of certain rules of reason for the construction of an internally indestructible commonwealth – rules such that, *if followed*, would ensure perpetual internal peace and domestic stability. Hobbes writes: "So, long time after men have begun to constitute common-wealths, imperfect, and apt to relapse into disorder, there may, principles of reason be found out, by industrious meditation, to make their constitution (excepting by externall violence) everlasting. And such are those which I have in this discourse set forth" (176).

These rules can all in one way or another be spun out from the concept of a commonwealth because Hobbes defines that concept to include the functions of a commonwealth and the means necessary to carry out its functions. Once these rules of reason are identified, they can be condensed into a single prescriptive principle addressed to subjects, a principle of political obligation that, if followed, will ensure perpetual domestic stability. There are good reasons for so consolidating them, as we shall see when we come to discuss Hobbes's principle. But first, let's see how Hobbes identifies the rules of reason that compose his science of politics. As I enumerate the rules I merely sketch Hobbes's argument for each of them; I fill out these sketches in the discussion of Hobbes's principle and the arguments he advances to support it.

At the end of the first chapter of Part 2, Hobbes characterizes ("defines," as he puts it) a commonwealth as "One person, of whose acts a great multitude, by mutuall covenants one with another, have made themselves every one the author, to the end he may use the strength and means of them all, as he shall think expedient, for their peace and common defense"(88). This definition's seven distinct elements will yield, in conjunction with the considerations that account for their inclusion in the definition, the various rules of reason for constructing an indestructible commonwealth that are then to be transformed into Hobbes's single principle of political obligation. That is, the considerations that justify the rules of reason will be the very same considerations that justify the inclusion of each phrase within the specification of what is to count as a commonwealth, from which phrases the various rules are spun out as elaborations or implications.

We should note that it is not just that these rules of reason follow from some *arbitrary* definition of a commonwealth. Hobbes builds his concept of a commonwealth from certain ordinary empirical observations about the acknowledged features and functions of commonwealths, and, crucially, from his resolutive analysis (presented in Parts 1 and 4) of the *sources of disorder* within commonwealths.[5] Because Hobbes frames his concept of a commonwealth with an eye to taking into account the sources of recurrent disorder within commonwealths, the rules of reason for the maintenance of commonwealths derived from the concept speak directly to what Hobbes took to be the sources of social collapse. Hobbes's rules of reason for the construction of an indestructible commonwealth are thus rules for constructing a commonwealth so structured that it can systematically cope with the causes of relapse into disorder. The form of association we recognize as a state, or a commonwealth, has, Hobbes claims, certain features that make sense given its purpose, and that are necessary for the optimal execution of its function. The rules of reason gathered out of these features, or elements of the concept of a commonwealth, will be rules that cannot be violated without doing damage to a commonwealth – without impeding its proper functioning. Thus, if we wish to build an internally indestructible commonwealth, one that will *certainly* withstand shifts in domestic circumstances and attitudes, all of these rules must be followed. It is not Hobbes's view that no commonwealth can, for any length of time, be orderly and stable unless all of the rules of reason are followed. His point is, rather, that in order to construct a permanently, reliably stable, certainly indestructible commonwealth, one cannot violate any of the rules. States may be more or less stable, and last for lesser or greater lengths of time, depending on their construction, the circumstances they confront, and the beliefs, values, and interests of their members. Hobbes is concerned only to identify the rules of reason for constructing a commonwealth, which, if followed, would ensure perpetual domestic peace.

To see Hobbes's argument for his rules of reason we must examine the various elements of his characterization of a commonwealth. These elements are:

1. One person
2. authorized through mutual covenants
3. by a great multitude
4. to use their strength
5. and their means
6. as *he* shall think expedient
7. for their peace and common defense.

Let us consider these components of Hobbes's characterization of a commonwealth in the order he presents them in the first chapter of Part 2. The reason why people live in commonwealths – their purpose in allowing constraints on their liberty and ability to dominate others – is to increase their prospects of security and a comfortable life (clause 7). "The finall cause, end, or designe of men (who naturally love liberty, and dominion over others,) in the introduction of that restraint upon themselves, (in which wee see them live in common-wealths,) is the foresight of their own preservation, and of a more contented life thereby" (85). If one of people's purposes in submitting to a commonwealth is to receive protection, then one of the functions of a commonwealth may reasonably be taken to be the provision of such protection. People's purpose in submitting to government, the function of a commonwealth, entails several rules of reason for the construction of a stable commonwealth: When people's refusal to obey the state's commands frustrates this end, then they do not have the right to refuse to obey (112); when the preservation of the commonwealth requires the help of all who are able to bear arms, then all of those are obligated to do so (112, 390);[6] because the state is charged with this end, it ought to be allowed the means necessary to carry it out (90), including the right to conduct war, and the right to raise monies to conduct war; as well as the right to make laws, to adjudicate disputes, and to punish violations of the law, and the right to seek good council for advice on matters of internal and external security and prosperity (91–2), and the right to determine titles of honor (92). Moreover, subjects may not interfere with the sovereign's attempts to punish or to harm others (112).[7]

In order for a commonwealth to provide security for its members against the attacks of enemies, it must be fairly large (clause 3), of such a size that no foreign power can be confident of subduing it in a war. Hobbes writes:

> Nor is it the joyning together of a small number of men that gives them this security; because in small numbers, small additions on the one side or the other, make the advantage of strength so great, as is sufficient to carry the victory; and therefore gives encouragement to an invasion. The multitude sufficient to confide in for our security is ... then sufficient, when the odds of the enemy is not of so visible and conspicuous moment, to determine the event of warre, as to move him to attempt it. (86)

A group that is manifestly too small to defend its members when they are working in concert relieves its members of any obligation to refrain from defending themselves by whatever means they can, including fleeing, or submitting to the enemy.[8]

In order to be effective in securing the preservation of its members against the attack of outsiders or harms from one another, a group must be directed by a single person, that is, by a single unified judgment (clause 1). This is because conflicting private opinions about the best means for defense may paralyze the group or cause it to act chaotically, rendering it incapable of fulfilling its end. Hobbes writes:

> And be there never so great a multitude; yet if their actions be directed according to their particular judgments, and par-

ticular appetites, they can expect thereby no defense, nor protection, neither against a common enemy, nor against the
injuries of one another. For being distracted in opinions concerning the best use and application of their strength, they
do not help, but hinder one another; and reduce their strength
by mutuall opposition to nothing: whereby they are easily,
not onely subdued by a very few that agree together; but also
when there is no common enemy, they make warre upon each
other, for their particular interests. (86)

The necessity of direction by a single person, either a single
natural person (a monarch) or a single artificial person (an
assembly), has profound implications for Hobbes's political
theory: It is this claim that supports Hobbes's rule that there
cannot be more than one sovereign of a people over any
given realm of action. A people cannot, for example, be directed both by a king and by a parliament in such matters
as what laws they are to obey, what taxes they are to pay,
and the like, because if the judgments of the two conflict,
the ability of either party to carry out these functions necessary to security is compromised (93, 95, 121).[9]
   Nor can a people be directed by distinct temporal and
spiritual sovereigns in the matter of how they shall act, because if the dictates of the two conflict, a paralysis of action
may be expected to occur (171–2).[10] Nor, as Hobbes will argue, can the rights of sovereignty be divided, because the
ability to ensure security depends on possession of all of the
essential rights of sovereignty (92–3), and so if the various
possessors of partial sets of sovereign rights disagree in their
judgments of what is to be done, a paralysis of effective
government can be expected to ensue. The stricture that a
commonwealth be a single person entails that sovereignty
must be singular and unified, "for powers divided mutually
destroy each other" (170).
   The reason why a multitude must be directed by a single
person if it is to be able to carry out the end for which people
subject themselves to commonwealths is that security requires direction by a *single judgment* (clause 6). Men cannot
achieve security against their enemies and against one an-

other (that is, live peacefully and profitably – sociably – together) unless they are directed by a single judgment, doing what a single person shall think expedient for their peace and common defense. This is because men *differ* in their private judgments as to what is to be done, as well as in their private appetites. Differing education, experience, and constitution account for these differences of judgment and appetite (35); and the differences are very real, and devastating to the achievement of the end for which men unite themselves. Differing private judgment leads to disorder, for the following reasons:

> First, that men are continually in competition for honour and dignity . . . and consequently amongst men there ariseth on that ground, envy and hatred, and finally warre. . . . Secondly, [that the common good differeth from the private, and that] man, whose joy consisteth in comparing himselfe with other men, can relish nothing but what is eminent [86]. . . . Thirdly . . . amongst men, there are very many that thinke themselves wiser, and abler to govern the publique better than the rest; and these strive to reforme and innovate, one this way, another that way; and thereby bring it into distraction and civill warre [87]. . . . Fourthly . . . men can represent to others that which is good in the likenesse of evill; and evill, in the likenesse of good; and augment, or diminish the apparent greatnesse of good and evill; discontenting men, and troubling their peace at their pleasure [87]. . . . Fiftly . . . man is most troublesome when he is most at ease: for then it is that he loves to shew his wisdome, and controule the actions of them that governe the common-wealth. [86–7][11]

Because men are prideful, thinking themselves eminent in wisdom and in the capacity to direct common affairs, striving to be acknowledged as better than others, in competition for honor, and are capable of discontenting their fellows by false representations of good and evil, all of which they will do even when they are comfortable and secure, their judgments will be largely self-promoting and therefore will necessarily differ; thus, direction of the group according to the private

63

judgments of each can be expected to be chaotic and self-defeating.

This claim also has massive implications for Hobbes's rules of reason for the construction of an indestructible commonwealth. It entails the central Hobbesian view that sovereignty cannot be limited because any limitation encourages the use of private judgment, differing judgment, to decide whether the limits have been overstepped. What it means to limit what the one person directing the commonwealth may do, or the means he may use, in securing the end of commonwealth, is to make his judgment subject to limits imposed by the judgments of others. If he is entitled to act for the common peace but not to be sole judge of what that peace requires, then others must be judge. But the variability of private judgment makes it likely that people will disagree about what is to be done, and when they disagree they will be reduced again to chaos and immobility (86, 172).[12] Thus, a commonwealth must be directed by a single person *according to a single judgment,* and that person must be able to use the members' strength and means *as he shall think expedient* (clause 6) for their peace and common defense. He is therefore to be judge of all matters pertaining to domestic peace and common defense, including judge of *what is relevant* to such peace and defense. Hobbes writes,

> And because the end of this institution is the peace and defense of them all; and whosoever has the right to the end, has the right to the means; it belongeth of right, to whatsoever man, or assembly that hath the sovereignty, *to be judge* both of the meanes of peace and defence; and also of the hindrances, and disturbances of the same; and to do whatsoever *he shall think* necessary to be done, both before hand, for the preserving of peace and security, by prevention of discord at home and hostility from abroad; and, when peace and security are lost, for the recovery of the same. (90–1, emphasis added)

The sovereign is to be sole judge of who is a threat, of what doctrines are a threat, of what wars are necessary, of what funding for such wars is required, of what laws are necessary, of what punishments are necessary, and of everything else.

It is through this transition – from a commission to do what is necessary to peace and defense to a sole right to decide what is involved in this commission – that the transformation of a limited sovereign into an unlimited sovereign is effected. If the sovereign were subject to the judgment of other individuals or other bodies about, for instance, what laws he could make, what taxes he could impose, what wars he could wage, what punishments he could stipulate or injuries he could commit, then either the judgment to which he was subject would in reality be sovereign (98–9) (because sole determinant of what is to be done for the peace and common defense), or else the commonwealth is simultaneously subject to multiple judgments, which, when they conflict, as they can be expected to do, may immobilize the commonwealth or reduce it to disputing factions whose difference cannot be resolved but by war, contrary to the end for which people subject themselves to commonwealths.

Peace and defense require, then, the direction of a large group by the single judgment of a single person. To be directed by such a person is to follow his judgment about what they are to do, including deploying their strength (clause 4) and their means (clause 5) as he shall direct them to. Their resources are to be under the direction of their leader – conferred upon him – to use as he thinks fit. Hobbes writes: "The only way to erect such a common power as may be able to defend them from the invasion of forraigners, and the injuries of one another, and thereby to secure them in such sort, as that by their owne industrie, and by the fruits of the earth, they may nourish themselves and live contentedly; is to conferre all their power and strength [clauses 4 and 5] upon one man, or upon one assembly of men, that may reduce all their wills ... unto one will" (87). That subjects confer the use of all their means and strength on their sovereign implies the further rules of reason for the construction of indestructible commonwealths that subjects' property rights do not exclude the sovereign's use of their property (128, 169–70), and so that the sovereign may lay whatever claim to their goods (in the form of taxes, say) he thinks necessary (128, 169–70); that he may require them to serve as councilors, judges, magistrates, or soldiers if he deems their service necessary to peace and defense (112).

The final clause in Hobbes's definition of a commonwealth is that the single person whose single judgment is to direct the use of a multitude's strength and means for their peace and common defense is to be regarded as being *authorized through the mutual covenants* (clause 2) of the members of the multitude, *as if* they had authorized him by mutual covenants with one another. The only way for people to form a commonwealth is, Hobbes writes, for them

> to appoint one man, or assembly of men, to beare their person; and every one to owne, and acknowledge himselfe to be author of whatsoever he that so beareth their person shall act, or cause to be acted, in those things which concerne the common peace and safetie; and therein to submit their wills, every one to his will, and their judgments, to his judgment. This is more than consent, or concord; it is a reall unitie of them all, in one and the same person, made by covenant of every man with every man, in such manner *as if* every man should say to every other man, "I authorise and give up my right of governing my selfe, to this man, or to this assembly of men, on this condition, that thou give up thy right to him, and authorise all his actions in like manner." (87, emphasis added)

The requirement that people regard themselves as having authorized their sovereign is an elaboration of the notion of accepting direction by a single judgment. It is given by the idea, inherent in the idea of a commonwealth, that a multitude of people "reduce all their wills . . . unto one will" (87).[13] The only way to *reduce,* or to unify, many wills into a single will is for the many to appoint a single person to represent them. "A person, is he whose words or actions *are considered* . . . as representing the words or actions of an other man" (80, emphasis added). We authorize a person – we make him our representative – when we *regard* his actions as if they were our own, when we regard ourselves as authors of his actions, thereby submitting our wills and judgments to his will and judgment; just as if we had actually promised all of our fellows that we would take his will and judgment for our own if they do so as well.

This stipulation of a commonwealth as an entity in which members must regard themselves as having owned and authorized all of the sovereign's actions, and must further regard themselves as owing it to one another to accept the directions of their sovereign, again implies a number of rules for the construction of indestructible commonwealths. These include that sovereigns cannot treat subjects unjustly (90, 109), and so may not be resisted on pretense that they have done so; and that subjects act unjustly toward one another when they disobey the sovereign (89).

This last consideration – that subjects must *regard themselves* as having authorized all of the actions of the government if a commonwealth is to function reliably, and to be capable of ensuring perpetual stability – is the consideration that motivates Hobbes's transformation of the various rules of reason into a unified principle of political obligation addressed to subjects. The fact is that most subjects don't directly determine the formal construction of their commonwealth (by and large they inherit a commonwealth that is usually, by Hobbes's lights, only imperfectly constructed); all that they can normally do is control how they *behave* toward their governors. But their behavior will depend chiefly on their attitude toward their government: If they view it as acting by their authority, view it as their representative, as if they had agreed with one another to own all of its actions – if they view it as, in a word, legitimate – then they will be the more inclined to refrain from challenging its right to act as it does. This attitude is *crucial* in Hobbes's view, for "in those nations, whose commonwealths have been long lived, and not been destroyed but by forraign warre, the subjects never did dispute of the soveraign power" (107).

The greatest determinant of domestic stability is subjects' own view about the extent of their sovereign's legitimate authority, and so, correlatively, their view about the limits of their obligation to obey the sovereign. If subjects see the sovereign's authority as unlimited, then they will not view themselves as having any legitimate grounds for refusing to obey it; if they understand the sovereign's power to be limited in certain ways, then they may well view themselves as exempted from obedience in cases where they judge the sovereign to have overstepped the limits of its authority. So their own view of the limits of sovereign authority will affect their view of the conditions under which they are required to obey that sovereign. And their view about their duty to obey is everything, for "take away in any kind of state, the obedience (and consequently the concord of the people,) and they shall not only not flourish, but in short time be dissolved" (177). The civil power depends on the opinion men have of their duty to the sovereign (296), and "it is not the right of the sovereign, though granted to him by every man's express consent, that can enable him to do his office; it is the obedience of the subject that must do that" (B 181). Indeed, his writing of *Leviathan*, as Hobbes sums it up, was "without other designe, than to set before mens eyes *the mutuall relation between protection and obedience; of which the condition of humane nature, and the laws divine, (both naturall and positive) require an inviolable observation*" (395–6, emphasis added). What is crucial, then, is that subjects be brought to affirm the proper view of their duty of obedience, which is most easily done by formulating a simple principle of political obligation – a simple statement of the conditions under which subjects are to obey their sovereigns – addressed to subjects.

Hobbes's principle

The principle of political obligation for which Hobbes argues, on the very same grounds as he argues for his various rules of reason (because the principle consolidates and embodies these rules) is presented on the first page of the final chapter of Part 2. It is this: "That subjects owe to soveraigns simple obedience in all things wherein their obedience *is not repug-*

nant to the laws of God" (186, emphasis added). For the purpose of analyzing it, we might reformulate this principle to
be more explicit, as follows: One is to obey the extant effective
political authority of the commonwealth of which one is a
member in all of its commands, except those that would
require one to violate one's duties to God.

This is the principle Hobbes wishes to defend, and we
can show how the considerations he advanced in support
of his various rules of reason also support this principle by
translating the contraries of those rules into *grounds for
disobedience* to an existing political authority. By showing
that taking the contraries of those rules as legitimate
grounds for disobedience could, in some not very unusual
circumstances, undermine the stability of a commonwealth,
we can see clearly what Hobbes's argument for his favored
principle is, and show that Hobbes's project of identifying
the rules for constructing an indestructible commonwealth
– a perpetual domestic peace – can be captured in this
simple principle of political obligation. This principle will
then (in Part 3) be fully specified, and linked to the satisfaction of people's primary interests (some of which interests are presented in Part 2 and others in Part 3),
completing Hobbes's task of providing enough people at
any given time with a sufficient reason for adhering to a
principle of political obligation capable if followed, of ensuring the perpetual maintenance of effective social order,
that social order can be maintained perpetually.

Let's begin by listing the various contenders for a principle
of political obligation that Hobbes's argument requires us to
consider. These are:

A. Hobbes's principle: One is to obey the extant effective political
   authority of the commonwealth of which one is a member in
   all of its commands except those that would require one to
   violate one's duty to God.
B. One is to obey the extant effective political authority unless it
   fails to enforce and observe the laws of nature, or fails to respect
   the norms of the common law, or fails to respect people's traditional rights and privileges, or exceeds its commission.

69

C. One is to obey the extant effective political authority in all of
   its commands except those that conflict with the resolutions or
   decisions of other legitimate authorities (e.g., representative
   assemblies or courts, duly authorized private franchises, or
   churches).

Notice first that Hobbes's principle contains one condition
on obedience, and one exemption from obedience, to an
existing political authority. The condition is that the existing
political authority of the commonwealth of which one is a
member be effective – meaning that only a state that is able
to protect its members has any claim on the obedience of
members. The exemption is that members are not required
to obey the state in those of its commands that would require
them to violate their duties to God. Both this condition and
this exemption are implied by the *concept* of a commonwealth.
Specifically, both are dictated by a particular feature of a
commonwealth according to Hobbes's definition, namely,
that a commonwealth is an association for the protection,
preservation, and security of its members.

"The end of obedience is protection" (114). The end for
which people accept subjection to a commonwealth is "the
foresight of their own preservation, and of a more contented
life thereby" (85), and provision of this good is a part of
the concept of a commonwealth. Hobbes suggests that "protecting us" is "the very essence of government" (112). Provision of protection is an essential feature of the idea of a
commonwealth, such that "if a monarch or sovraign assembly, grant a liberty to all, or any of his subjects; which
grant standing, he is disabled to provide for their safety,
the grant is voyd; unlesse he directly renounce or transferre
the sovraignty to another" (113). It is because provision
of protection for its members is an essential property of a
commonwealth that "the obligation of subjects to the soveraign is understood to last as long, and no longer, than
the power lasteth, by which he is able to protect them"
(114), and why "when ... there is no farther protection of
subjects in their loyalty; then is the commonwealth dissolved" (175).

70

Because it is part of the notion of a commonwealth that it provide protection for its members, an association providing protection for none of its members cannot be a commonwealth, and those individuals that a commonwealth cannot or does not protect are not to be counted as members. Thus, say, if in a war with a foreign power the state cannot protect any of its members, that state is dissolved and ceases to be a commonwealth; if it cannot protect a particular group of individual subjects – say, a company of soldiers that are outnumbered, or subjects that have become prisoners of war – those subjects are released from any obligation of obedience to it, for "no man is obliged (when the protection of the law faileth,) not to protect himself, by the best means he can" (156). And one who has either not received the protection of the commonwealth, or has expressly rejected the protection that it offers, is no member of that commonwealth.

This notion of membership in a commonwealth seems at first glance a peculiar one because membership comes and goes according to whether or not one is accepting protection. If today I am accepting the protection of a commonwealth, I am a member of that commonwealth and am obliged to obedience. If tomorrow some threat to my preservation arises against which the commonwealth cannot protect me (if I am in the power of a bandit or become a prisoner of war), then tomorrow my membership is suspended, until such time as I either accept protection elsewhere (in which case my prior membership is terminated altogether), or again receive protection from the commonwealth. If the commonwealth permanently ceases to be able to protect me, then I am no longer a member of it. Of course, if a commonwealth never protected me (in the way that any foreign nation never protected me), then I was never a member of it. More peculiar still, Hobbes's notion of membership in a commonwealth implies that if the commonwealth itself is threatening my preservation (if, say, it is attempting to kill me, or capture me for the purpose of inflicting some punishment or harm on me), then I cease to be a member of the commonwealth until such time as I am assured of its continued protection (say, by being

71

offered a pardon). Membership thus depends on openly receiving protection: Acceptance of protection is enough to
make me a member (assuming I have no prior incompatible
obligation); and lack of protection is enough to extinguish
my membership.[14]

Hobbes writes that although a man has never expressly
covenanted to obey the governors of a commonwealth, "yet
if he live under their protection openly, hee is understood
to submit himselfe to the government" (391). This passage
suggests that Hobbes takes acceptance of protection to be
sufficient to make one obligated to obey the commonwealth's commands, and hence sufficient to make one a
member of a commonwealth, provided that one does not
already hold membership elsewhere. Acceptance of protection is one form of tacit consent, a kind of sign by
inference, which can be, as Hobbes writes, "sometimes the
consequence of silence; sometimes the consequence of actions; sometimes the consequence of forbearing an action"
(667). This interpretation is supported by Hobbes's assertion
that one "ought to obey him by whom it is preserved;
because preservation of life being the end, for which one
man becomes subject to another, every man is supposed
[i.e., assumed] to promise obedience to him in whose power
it is to save, or destroy him" (103). The sovereign of a
commonwealth can protect (or destroy) the persons who
live within his territory, and if he protects them (unless
they *explicitly* refuse his protection), they are assumed to
(tacitly) promise obedience to him, and thus to be members
of the commonwealth. This assumption allows Hobbes to
conclude that "the sovereign of each country hath dominion
over all that reside therein" (103), which could not be the
case unless every resident had promised (which they do
tacitly by accepting his protection) to obey him.[15] Acceptance of protection is enough for a previously stateless
person to count as a member of a commonwealth, being
bound not to weaken it by disobedience, for "it is a dictate
of naturall reason, and consequently an evident law of
nature, that no man ought to weaken that power, the pro-

tection whereof he hath . . . wittingly received against others" (142). And the failure of a commonwealth to protect some person is enough to extinguish, temporarily, if not permanently, that person's membership in the commonwealth.

Now the condition on obedience contained in Hobbes's principle of political obligation is that the political authority of the commonwealth of which one is a member be effective, that is, able to protect one. This condition on obedience thus requires (1) that there be a commonwealth, (2) that one be a member of it, and (3) that it be able to protect one. All three aspects of the condition are, as I've said, dictated by Hobbes's idea of a commonwealth. A commonwealth is an association of a certain sort that protects its members; thus, only an association that protects its members can be a commonwealth, and if we want to know who is to be counted as a member of a particular commonwealth, the definition tells us to look to see who is protected by the association. Thus, the effectiveness condition on obedience is most properly viewed as just that, a condition – and not as an *exemption* from obedience to a commonwealth of which one is a member. The condition is not ad hoc but is derived from Hobbes's concept of a commonwealth – if an association can't protect you, then either it is not a commonwealth or you are not a member of it, but in neither case are you obligated to obey its political authority. This means that any principle of political obligation to a commonwealth will have to be understood as implicitly including this condition on obedience, and so principles (B) and (C) above should be taken, like Hobbes's principle, to include this condition. Note also that because the "effectiveness" condition is derivable from the concept of a commonwealth, the stipulation that the commonwealth be effective is technically redundant, and so may be omitted from the formulation of these principles of political obligation.[16]

In addition to the effectiveness condition on obedience, Hobbes's principle includes an exemption from obedience to a generally effective state in one particular set of its commands. What is really interesting about this exemption – the exemption from obedience to commands that would require one to violate one's duties to God – is that it, too, is mandated by the concept of a commonwealth, and for the very reason the effectiveness condition on obedience is required. For a commonwealth to be a commonwealth it must protect its members. In circumstances where it can and does protect one, one is obliged to obey its commands; but in circumstances where it cannot protect one, one is not obliged to obey it. Many commonwealths may be generally effective, but one thing no commonwealth can do, is protect people from God's wrath, because no sovereign is as powerful as God. If, therefore, it demands that one do something that will elicit God's wrath, people are not obliged to accede to its demand. One way of putting this point is that people are bound to obey the commonwealth only *insofar as* it can protect them. If there is a realm in which it cannot, even in principle, protect "subjects in their loyalty," that is, in their obedience, then subjects have no obligation of obedience whatsoever *in that realm*. It is because commonwealths cannot protect their subjects from God's punishment that subjects are not required to obey commands that would require them to violate their duties to God. Because the end of a commonwealth is protection, and this is an essential feature of a commonwealth, the concept itself implies this exemption from obedience.

Hobbes holds that because God is the first cause, and sets the entire causal chain of worldly events in motion, and because he can, and does from time to time, intervene in the course of human events, the enjoyment of both preservation (temporal and eternal) and a contented or commodious life ultimately depends on God's will. Subjects, who may well believe in a god who can affect their fate now and in the hereafter, may reasonably view the fulfillment of God's requirements as a part of their rational self-interest. To disobey God, who is believed to be much more knowledgeable and powerful than any man, or any commonwealth, might well lead to one's ruin. (The Bible contains many examples of such cases.) "It is manifest enough," Hobbes writes, "that when a man receiveth two contrary commands, and knows that one of them is God's, he ought to obey that, and not the other, though it be the command even of his lawfull soveraign" (321). This is true even for people who are moved not by considerations of religious duty per se, but only by consideration of narrow self-interest, since "if the command be such as cannot be obeyed without being damned to eternall death, then it were madnesse to obey it" (321). (Of course, people may possess further, non-self-interested reasons for wanting to fulfill their duties to God; all the more reason to reject any principle that would require them to obey their political authority in violation of those duties.) It would be the height of irrationality for believers to accept a principle of political obligation that required them to jeopardize their present and eternal life-prospects, and they would almost certainly refuse to adhere to such a principle.

The problem with obeying commands that would require one to violate one's duties to God under consideration here is that doing so threatens one's preservation (both earthly and eternal). But the end for which people become subject to a commonwealth – an essential component of the concept of a commonwealth – is that it protect its members. Because obedience to those of their political authority's commands that require violating their duties to God may bring divine punishments from which the political authority cannot protect subjects, there is a very real sense in which such commands are a threat to their preservation, and a form of attack on them. Subjects are thus exempted from obedience to such commands, in much the same way they are relieved of any obligation to obey a sovereign's command that they kill themselves, or not resist those who attempt to kill them. The difference is that in the latter sorts of cases, subjects cease to be members of the commonwealth, and resume all of their natural liberty, until such time as they again receive protection; whereas in the former case, there is a whole class of commands that may be disobeyed without extinguishing subjects' membership in the commonwealth. They remain members, and thus bound to obey all of the sovereign's commands that are not repugnant to their duty to God, despite the fact that they are exempted from obedience to this one special set of commands that compose a realm in which the commonwealth cannot, even in principle, protect subjects in their loyalty.

Hobbes cannot, in consistency, avoid admitting this exemption from obedience into his principle of political obligation, for it is an implication of that feature of his definition of a commonwealth that specifies the end of all such associations. Nevertheless, admitting this exemption poses a very real danger for the successful execution of Hobbes's project, and I want to flag it here so that we can appreciate the importance of Hobbes's later attempts to deal with it. Hobbes's project is to identify a principle of political obligation that could, if followed, ensure the perpetual maintenance of domestic order – that is, that could yield an internally indestructible commonwealth – and then to provide people with what they can regard as a sufficient reason for adhering to that principle. Part of the project is thus to identify a principle that if faithfully followed by (most) everyone, will, in fact, reliably prevent social collapse. But this "duty to God" exemption in Hobbes's principle makes it *very* doubtful, particularly given Hobbes's analysis of the English Civil War (as we shall see), that Hobbes's principle, *as it stands*, could ensure perpetual domestic peace. This is because the "duty to God" exemption is underspecified in a way that introduces the possibility of massive disobedience, and is ambiguous in a way that allows for massive dissension among the members of a commonwealth over whether or not an existing sovereign is to be obeyed. From obedience to *which* commands precisely does this qualifying claim exempt subjects? If the exemption permits anyone who feels that his ability to fulfill his duty to God is jeopardized by some command to exempt himself from obedience to that command, then given the fact that there may be (and often is) a wide range of disagreement about what duty to God involves, it is possible that significant numbers of people might excuse themselves from obedience to certain of the sovereign's commands, while others insist on obedience, causing disruption, and perhaps, in an extreme case, paralysis, civil war, and the complete dissolution of effective sovereignty. This is the problem with making *any* exceptions to a policy of obedience to the extant effective political authority. People may disagree about what the exception allows. In the present case, if it is left to (variable) private judgment to decide what duty to God involves, even universally faithful adherence to Hobbes's principle may not prevent the dissolution of domestic order, and this would utterly defeat Hobbes's purpose. Hobbes must specify what one's duties to God are, and so specify them that the exemption does not produce sufficient disobedience to disrupt social order; and his specification of duty to God must be acceptable to his readers if they are to see themselves as having any religious reason to adhere to his principle, or even to refrain from rejecting it on grounds of their religious convictions.

This is precisely what Hobbes attempts to do in Part 3 of *Leviathan*, and Part 3 is thus an indispensable portion of his project, carrying out the necessary specification of his principle. At the present point in the argument, it is unclear whether the principle Hobbes has identified is adequate to his task of ensuring perpetual domestic order; and whether the "duty to God" exemption will or will not threaten social order depends on what it actually specifies as people's duty to God, the extent to which obedience to a political authority's commands can conflict with religious duty, on that specification of it, and whether people can be brought to affirm that specification of religious duty. An answer to the question of how much of a threat to stability this exemption involves must await the further specification of Hobbes's principle, when one's duties to God will be spelled out. Thus, although the exemption from obedience Hobbes includes in his principle of political obligation is unavoidable, because entailed by the concept of a commonwealth, it is nonetheless extremely problematic. This problem is one that will be shared by any principle of political obligation to a commonwealth, and so the next two principles to be considered are both to be regarded as implicitly containing the "duty to God" exemption from obedience as well.[17]

The principle of limited sovereignty

Let us look at the next candidate for an appropriate principle of political obligation Hobbes discusses. Among the rules of reason Hobbes derived from his concept of a commonwealth were the rules that sovereignty cannot be forfeited (89), that it is unlawful for subjects to punish or kill their sovereigns (90), even if tyrants (179), that sovereigns are not subject to the laws (169), that subjects are not to judge of good and evil (91, 168–9), and that the subjects' property rights do not exclude the sovereign's use of that property (169–70). What all of these rules have in common is the denial of some sort of *limit* on sovereign authority (such as law, or the property rights of others), or on the conditions under which subjects are to obey their political authority (such as that obedience to tyrants, or obedience to commands one believes wrong is not required). We may suppose that Hobbes explicitly discussed each of these implications of the idea of a commonwealth because people had often affirmed that sovereigns were subject to limits such as these. (In Chapter 6, I present evidence that this is in fact why Hobbes discusses them.)

If we take the contraries of these rules and condense them into a single principle of political obligation, we wind up with a principle something like (B): One is to obey one's extant effective political authority unless it fails to enforce and observe the laws of nature, or fails to respect the norms of the common law, or fails to respect people's traditional rights and privileges (including property rights). This principle expresses the frequently advanced view that only *limited* sovereignty can be legitimate, that is, that the rights of legitimate governments are constrained by certain moral considerations – that people have rights, that governments have duties, and that any government that fails to honor these rights and duties is not to be obeyed.

Hobbes argues that if one is aiming to identify a principle of political obligation that can reliably ensure perpetual social order, principle (B) must be rejected. Whenever limits are put on the conditions under which people are to obey the extant effective political authority, there arises the problem of deciding when those limits have been overstepped. To allege that there are limits to what a legitimate government may do is to regard the government as if it had covenanted not to do certain things; but then we are confronted by the difficulty of garnering consensus on the question of whether the covenant has been violated. Hobbes writes of subjects that

> if any one, or more of them, pretend a breach of the covenant made by the soveraigne at his institution; and others, or one other of his subjects, or himselfe alone, pretend there was no such breach, there is in this case, no judge to decide the controversie: it therefore returns to the sword again . . . contrary to the designe they had in the institution. It is therefore in vain to grant sovereignty by way of precedent covenant. (89)

If each subject is to decide for himself whether or not, and how far, the government is to be obeyed, then, given the variability of private judgment and people's tendency toward discontent and partiality, there is every reason to expect recurring widespread disagreement as to whether the extant effective political authority is to be obeyed. If people were to adhere to principle (B), which takes a large field of decision out of the hands of their *only* public representative, it would have to be a matter of *private judgment* whether or not the political authority was violating the laws of nature, failing to respect custom, or failing to respect the traditional rights and privileges of the people; and there is good reason, according to Hobbes's analysis, to expect that people will differ in their judgments. It is likely that many people will excuse themselves from obedience if (B) is adopted (particularly given their partiality and other passions); it is possible that *so* many people will cease to obey the political authority, it will no longer have effective power. And subjects may see fit to take up arms to defend or to resist the political authority. So even if everyone faithfully followed principle (B), the perpetual maintenance of domestic order could not be ensured. Although Hobbes does not offer an argument from the likelihood of various outcomes, we can see that the probability of disruption, civil war, or a complete dissolution of effective social order if subjects adhere to principle (B) is much higher than if they adhere to Hobbes's principle. The additional danger of dissolution principle (B) introduces can be avoided by simply adopting Hobbes's principle.

Unlike the exemption from obedience contained in Hobbes's principle, the further exemption contained in principle (B) cannot be justified by reference to any feature of the idea of a commonwealth; and, indeed, that further exemption is disallowed by the end of commonwealths, and what Hobbes argues to be the means necessary to achieve that end. The sorts of "inconveniences" (as Hobbes puts it) that might have to be tolerated under (B) do not generally threaten preservation; and in the extraordinary event that they become preservation-threatening, subjects are exempted from obedience in any case by the effectiveness condition on political obligation.[18]

The problem of imposing any limit on the authority of one's government is one of who is to decide when that limit has been overstepped. If there is to be any alternative to the inconveniences of unlimited sovereignty on the one hand, and the perils of each subject deciding for himself whether or not obedience is to be rendered on the other hand, people would have to submit to the judgment of some other legitimate public body or bodies that have the authority to evaluate and condemn the actions and policies of the primary political authority. We are thus naturally led to consider principle (C), that one is to obey the extant effective political authority in all of its commands except those that conflict with the resolutions or decisions of other legitimate authorities.

The principle of divided sovereignty

Principle (C) can again be understood as the compilation of the contraries of a number of Hobbes's rules of reason, the denial of such rules as that there cannot be more than one sovereign over a people (170); that ultimate authority over the various functions of government may not be assigned to different groups (172); and that temporal and spiritual sovereignty may not be divided (171–2). What these rules have in common is the denial that sovereignty can be divided, shared, or multiplied.

Principle (C), which incorporates their contraries, is thus a principle of *divided* or of *multiple* sovereignty. Hobbes is conceiving it as a principle allowing either (1) multiple sovereigns with coextensive or overlapping authority (where various distinct bodies have authority over the same sphere such that each may issue legitimate judgments or commands that contradict those of the others), or (2) a division of powers, exemplified by independent legislative, doctrinal, interpretive, executive, and judicial secular and religious authorities, with powers in theory exercisable by each only within some limited social territory (as, for example, church courts, civil courts, and the courts of private franchises, all of which have authority to adjudicate disputes, but only within some circumscribed social domain). Under (2) would seem to fall both the case of a *radical* division of authority in which the various bodies that hold partial authority are completely unconnected, and their interaction is not determinately and systematically ordered or regulated by any set of rules, and the case of what we would call the separation of powers within a government, where the interaction of various branches is governed by a set of rules.[19] The concepts of multiple authority and divided authority are, of course, distinct, but Hobbes sees them as importantly connected – for reasons I explain momentarily – and so treats them together. Principle (C) is included in Hobbes's discussion in order to reflect the actual practice of government in Hobbes's England, and the accompanying ideological commitment of many of his contemporaries to the idea that what a king may legitimately do is limited by the decisions and resolutions of other independent authorities.

Hobbes argues that a situation wherein there exists multiple authority, or duplication of what he calls "the essential rights of sovereignty," is the state of affairs least conducive to the maintenance of effective social order. Indeed, the situation of persons who have no commonwealth – say, of those living during a civil war or without a state entirely – is just the most extreme case of a situation in which there is multiple authority; there is universal duplication of rights over everything, and each individual may evaluate and condemn the actions and claims of any other. In a situation like this, where everyone retains private authority in the face of conflicts, there can be no effective authority; this is why people might be willing to alienate their authority to a public representative in the first place. Hobbes argues that a principle of political obligation that exempts subjects from obedience to those of the extant effective political authority's commands that are in conflict with the resolutions of other legitimate authorities is tantamount to an insistence on a system of multiple authority; and because a situation in which there is multiple authority, with its ensuing chaos and insecurity, is precisely what commonwealths are instituted in order to avoid, for people to obey only when it is required by this principle will likely damage a commonwealth.

Implicit in the first of his arguments is the claim that if there are multiple legitimate authorities whose commands are capable of mutual contradiction, then this is a case in which a number of bodies possess overlapping or coextensive authority. This is a straightforward point of logic; for two authorities to issue contradictory commands, those commands must be about the same thing, and if both of the authorities are legitimate (entitled to issue such commands), then they must have overlapping authority. But when there is a multitude of bodies with overlapping authority, and they put forward mutually conflicting commands, judgments, or policies, it is quite possible there will be a collapse of effective government, in the form either of a paralysis of the government, or of a civil war. The maintenance of effective social order requires, at minimum, the promulgation of laws to regulate conduct, a peaceful means of settling disputes, and the enforcement of laws and decisions. But where there are a number of legitimate authorities issuing contradictory decisions and commands, and subjects are uncertain or in disagreement about which authority is to be obeyed, the various authorities may so undermine one another's activities that these essential requirements of effective social order cannot be satisfied. Take, for example, the hypothetical case in which one legitimate authority proclaims toleration for the public practice of Catholicism, interference with which is a punishable offense, while another legitimate authority accounts such public practice a crime to which subjects who fail to intervene are to be held accessories, subject to punishment. (And we can imagine many other parallel cases concerning, e.g., taxes levied, military service required, land grants and private charters extended, and the like.) This situation presents subjects with a dilemma: Which of these legitimate authorities should be obeyed? There is no reason for people to assume that subjects will always decide this question alike; and in the absence of any *ultimate* authority to settle the question (which is entailed by the hypothesis that these are legitimate authorities with overlapping authority) sufficient chaos may ensue that laws, decisions, and so on cannot function to yield effective, preservation-securing social order. Simply put, where multiple overlapping or coextensive authorities exist, the problem arises of which is to be counted the "primary" authority, and which the "other" legitimate authority; if they are all legitimate authorities, then it is not clear from which of them it is that principle (C) exempts subjects from obedience. (If there were some settled enforceable rule that stipulated that in cases of conflict subjects were always to obey the commands of one and the same particular authority, then, says Hobbes, that authority would actually be sovereign, and there would be no exemption from obedience to any of its commands. By hypothesis, principle [C] rules out this move to resolve the problem.) And whenever disagreement about this occurs, there is the potential for a paralysis of effective government and a breakdown of effective social order. Moreover, should the competing authorities wish to impose their claims over and against those of their competitors, as they will have to do if they are to be effective, there is a real possibility of civil war.

Hobbes's argument here about the problem with multiple coextensive or overlapping authorities is clear enough, but what would be problematic about a situation in which there were different authorities on different matters – where the essential rights of sovereignty were divided among distinct bodies – and subjects were to obey any given authority's commands only when those commands fell within a certain limited field? If this were the case, principle (C) would merely exempt subjects from obedience to the commands of an authority operating out of its jurisdiction, usurping, as it were, authority to which it was not entitled. Why should such a principle undermine the stability of a commonwealth?

Hobbes offers two grounds for thinking that it might. The first, relatively minor, problem with such a principle is that the boundaries among domains of jurisdiction may be sufficiently fuzzy that they allow conflicts for which there is no agreed-upon remedy. We might imagine conflicts between church and civil courts, each of which claims sole authority to try a particular sort of case, or conflicts between king and parliaments, each of which claims sole authority to raise an army or to tax. In such cases, there may be no peaceful way to settle their dispute, and subjects, all of whom are faithfully following principle (C), may be forced to take sides, or to suffer from the partisanship of others who take sides, in a violent resolution of the dispute. Even faithful universal adherence to principle (C) will not be able to ensure the maintenance of effective social order.

But Hobbes's major argument is that there is no guarantee

against the degeneration of a state of divided authority into a state of multiple overlapping or coextensive authority, because any authority whose actions are to have their intended effect (that is, any authority that is to ensure its ability to fulfill its function of securing effective social order) will have to claim possession of *all* of the essential rights of sovereignty. And where multiple bodies claim coextensive authority, there exists the potential for the collapse of effective social order.

Now, Hobbes argues that if these various "independent" authorities were hierarchically organized in such a way that it was agreed that the same authority always prevails in cases of conflict, this would not in fact be a case of divided sovereignty but, rather, a case of a unified sovereignty, certain functions of which have been delegated to other bodies, subject, ultimately, to the approval of the sovereign; and there would be nothing problematic about this. But this is not the kind of case we are considering in considering principle (C). It is important to see that principle (C) is allowing subjects the liberty to resist their *government* (whether it be an absolute monarchy or a democracy with separation of powers) when its commands conflict with those of other legitimate authorities; it proposes to refuse governments sovereign power.

Hobbes's argument that divided authority must ultimately lead to multiple coextensive authorities rests on the claim that the various powers of a government are connected in such a way that a loss of one may entail an inability effectively to exercise the rest. For example, laws without interpretation or application to particular cases will not regulate conduct or resolve disputes, decisions without enforcement will not deter violations of the law, and declarations of war or formulations of social programs without granting of funds will not be implementable. Thus, the possession of any one of these rights, without possession of the others as well, may not enable one to exert any substantial positive influence on the maintenance of social order. Hobbes argues this explicitly, saying,

85

[if the soveraign] transferre the Militia, he retains the judi-
cature in vain, for want of execution of the lawes: Or if he
grant away the power of raising mony, the militia is in vain:
or if he give away the government of doctrines, men will be
frighted into rebellion with the feare of spirits. And so if we
consider any one of the said rights, we shall presently see that
the holding of all the rest will produce no effect in the conservation of peace and justice, the end for which all commonwealths are instituted. (92–3)

This connection between the ability to exercise one right
of sovereignty with the possession of others is why the rights
of legislation, adjudication, interpretation, taxation, punishment, and so on are termed "essential" rights of sovereignty;
any government that is to be effective, whether a monarchy,
aristocracy, or democracy, must possess all of these rights.
Therefore, if these rights are divided among different authorities, and the authorities refuse to cooperate with one
another – to, so to speak, back one another up – it is quite
possible there will be a paralysis of effective government.
"And this division it is," Hobbes writes, "whereof it is said,
'a kingdome divided in it selfe cannot stand': For unlesse
this division precede, division into opposite armies can never
happen. If there had not first been an opinion received of
the greatest part of England that these powers were divided
between the King and the Lords and the House of Commons,
the people had never been divided, and fallen into this civill
warre; first between those that disagreed in politiques, and
after between the dissenters about the liberty of religion"
(93). An ability to achieve one's end in exercising any one of
these essential rights will be dependent on the cooperative
activity of those in possession of other rights. Because this
is so, any body which intends effectively to exercise its right
in the face of noncooperation from other rights possessors,
will be compelled to claim for itself other (and perhaps all)
of the essential rights of sovereignty. This is why unregulated, or *unenforceably* regulated, division of authority may,
when conflicts arise, lead to the formation of multiple overlapping authorities.[20] Whichever event occurs, whether it is

the paralysis of effective government or the emergence of multiple overlapping authorities (which then either undermine one another's authority until none has effective authority, or proceed to fight it out for supremacy), may pose a serious threat to effective, preservation-securing social order.[21]

The increased potential for social collapse that principle (C) introduces makes that principle unsuitable for Hobbes's project. If the aim is to construct an indestructible commonwealth, we must reject principle (C) in favor of Hobbes's principle.

Although it may be true that sometimes, or for some people, a system of limited or divided authority might function quite adequately in maintaining social order, since there might be general consensus on when and how far one's political authority was to be obeyed, as well as perfect cooperation among the possessors of various sovereign rights, the question we are to consider is whether or not we can *count on* the presence of such conditions. Given Hobbes's characterization of human beings as prone to disagree with one another, as subject to partiality, pride, and a multitude of other antisocial passions, who are not always motivated by moral considerations (and who even when they are, may disagree about what morality requires) and who feel equally entitled to press their claims, we may reasonably wonder what are the chances of maintaining effective social order when people with these characteristics are given contrary commands by different authorities, with leave to disobey one or another of those commands (principle [C]) or the right to disobey their government when they personally think it has overstepped its authority (principle [B])? Can we *assume* that they will never receive contradictory commands, or disapprove of their government? Can we *assume* that they will achieve consensus on which authority is to be obeyed, or on whether their government has acted beyond the limits of its authority, even most, let alone all, of the time? And what will happen when there is disagreement? The exemptive clause in Hobbes's principle, which is tantamount to an exemption from obedience to an *in*effective government (and only insofar as it is ineffective), once it is fully specified, will not turn out to undermine the ability of an effective government to maintain social order, whereas (B) and (C), both with clauses that would exempt subjects from obedience to an effective political authority, very well may threaten social order. Hobbes's principle is, of the principles considered, the best candidate for a principle that, if followed, could ensure the perpetual maintenance of peaceful social order. Hobbes thus arrives at the conclusion that if we are aiming to build an indestructible commonwealth, we ought to accept the principle that one is to obey one's extant effective political authority in all of its commands not repugnant to one's duty to God.

PRELIMINARY REASONS FOR ADHERING TO HOBBES'S PRINCIPLE

It is one thing to identify a principle of political obligation that, if followed, could ensure as indestructible a commonwealth as a commonwealth can be. It is quite another thing to provide people with reasons for adhering to that principle. If people's sole or overriding interest were in the construction and maintenance of a perpetually stable commonwealth, then these two tasks would converge. But there is no reason to think this ever is people's overriding interest, and Hobbes certainly does not assume that people have any independent interest in building indestructible commonwealths per se. Rather, as he tries to show, the basic sorts of interests people ordinarily have, such as narrowly prudential, moral, and religious interests, are best satisfied by adhering to a principle of political obligation that would, if widely followed, ensure a perpetual domestic peace. We ought not, then, to conflate Hobbes's argument for the superiority of his principle with his argument offering reasons for adhering to his principle. These are two very distinct, though equally necessary, parts of his political project.

The two sorts of reasons for adhering to his principle that

Hobbes can establish by employing only natural knowledge are offered in Part 2 of *Leviathan*. These are reasons from narrow prudence and from secular morality, the latter including both natural duty and obligation. Neither the argument linking the satisfaction of narrowly prudential interests to adherence to his principle, nor the argument linking the satisfaction of moral interests to his principle could proceed if that principle did not contain the exemption from obedience to commands that would require the violation of one's duties to God. This is because the moral argument is parasitic on (though not derived from) the narrowly prudential argument, and the narrowly prudential argument requires that subjects be shown that it is in their narrow self-interest that the principle be followed, which couldn't be done if adherence to the principle would bring God's wrath down upon them. The inclusion of the "duty to God" exemption in his principle makes it possible for Hobbes to offer these provisional arguments in Part 2, despite the fact that full specification of the principle, and so completion of the argument that this principle is one that, if followed, could ensure an indestructible commonwealth, must await the discussion of Part 3. (The prudential and moral arguments cannot be fully established until the principle is satisfactorily specified, but we here assume that it can be, and so offer these arguments provisionally.) The implication is that people who have Judeo-Christian religious beliefs could not be given *any* reason for adhering to Hobbes's principle, not even a narrowly prudential reason, unless that principle contained the "duty to God" exemption. This is why the argument from revealed religion in Part 3 is improperly conceived as offering a merely supplementary or additional reason for believers to adhere to Hobbes's principle.

Narrow prudence (a)

Hobbes's argument from narrow prudence is not, properly speaking, an argument for always adhering to his principle of political obligation. It is, rather, an argument (a) in favor of having others adhere to the principle, and (b) against oneself violating the principle, under the circumstance that one does so by an act of open rebellion. As we shall see, the first portion of this argument grounds Hobbes's arguments from natural duty and from obligation for his principle, while the second portion provides an indirect argument that one has prudential reason to adhere to that principle in all important cases.

Our narrowly prudential interests can be divided into two sorts: the interest in self-preservation and thus in the security of our persons; and the interest in "commodious living" – in the means to live a contented life, in such a way as "not to be weary of it" (66).[22] The latter requires the possession of personal property and the enjoyment of a certain minimal degree of liberty.

Hobbes argues that both interests are best satisfied by living within a settled, effective commonwealth. This is because an effective commonwealth protects its members from threats to their preservation from one another and from outsiders, and because only within a commonwealth can there be settled, enforceable titles to property, as well as sufficient regulation of individual activity that people can go about their business without having their liberty decreased by the interference of many others. An effective commonwealth increases members' security by deterring attacks on them, and it makes stable possession of property possible by assigning and enforcing titles to property. Hobbes writes that "where there is no commonwealth . . . every thing is his that getteth it, and keepeth it by force; which is neither propriety nor community; but uncertainty . . . therefore the introduction of propriety is an effect of common-wealth" (127–8). A state is needed "to make good that propriety, which by mutuall contract men acquire, in recompense of the universall right they abandon" (72); and "where there is no common-wealth, there is no propriety; all men having right to all things" (72). When men submit to a "civill power" their rights and obligations become enforceable, "and then it is also that propriety begins" (72).

An effective commonwealth also produces a net increase in liberty over a state of license – a state in which each may do as he pleases, "all he lists" – by coordinating and harmonizing (through the promulgation and enforcement of laws) individual activity so that people are not continuously "bumping into" each other. The license of others curtails the liberty of each so that, as Hobbes writes, "if we take liberty for an exemption from lawes, it is no lesse absurd, for men to demand as they doe, that liberty, by which all other men may be masters of their lives" (109).[23]

Because all three components of narrow self-interest are best satisfied by living within a settled, stable, and effective commonwealth, it is in the narrow self-interest of each person that he live within such a commonwealth. But on what does the existence of such a commonwealth depend? It depends on the obedience of a vast number of members of the commonwealth to their political authority. It is thus in the interest of each individual that a number of his fellows sufficient to ensure the maintenance of a stable effective commonwealth so act as to sustain the effective power of their political authority.

What principle of action – of political obligation – ought then an individual to want his fellows to adopt? A principle that, if widely followed, could ensure the maintenance of effective social order if not perpetually, then at least reliably for the whole of one's lifetime, in whatever time period that might be. Hobbes's is the most promising candidate for such a principle. As Hobbes argued, it is the principle best able to ensure the perpetual maintenance (and hence maintenance during our limited natural lifetimes) of effective social order – to secure an indestructible commonwealth – of all principles compatible with the concept of a commonwealth. Thus, individuals have a reason from their narrow self-interest in preservation and commodious living to want others in their commonwealth to adhere to Hobbes's principle of political obligation.

This is Hobbes's argument. But, we may wonder, mightn't the various components of narrow self-interest dictate differing preferences as to which principle of political obligation one's fellow commonwealth members are to follow? For example, mightn't my interest in possessing property, or in enjoying liberty, lead me to prefer that others follow a principle of limited sovereignty (like [B] above) rather than Hobbes's principle, even though that principle best realizes my interest in security?

Hobbes thinks not, for the simple reason that a collapse of order threatens *not only* my preservation, but *also and equally* my possession of property and my liberty. We cannot "trade" decreased security for increased property and liberty, because these three go together, as inseparable effects of an effective commonwealth. If a commonwealth cannot ensure my preservation against attacks by my neighbors, neither can it prevent them from seizing my property or interfering with my liberty (my ability to do or get what I want to do or get). Thus, any principle that decreases security must also decrease one's prospects of ensurable and enforceable property possession, and of liberty. One can expect to be worse off in *each* aspect of narrow self-interest if social order collapses than one would be in the presence of effective social order, no matter what amount of property or liberty one enjoys under that order. Hobbes writes, in two well-known passages:

> But a man may here object that the Condition of Subjects is very miserable; as being obnoxious to the lusts, and other irregular passions of him, or them that have so unlimited a Power in their hands . . . not considering that the estate of Man can never be without some incommodity or other; and that the greatest, that in any forme of Government can possibly happen to the people in generall, is scarce sensible, in respect of the miseries, and horrible calamities, that accompany a Civill Warre; or that dissolute condition of masterlesse men, without subjection to Lawes, and a coercive Power to tye their hands from rapine and revenge. (94)

> And though of so unlimited a Power, men may fancy many evill consequences, yet the consequences of the want of it,

which is perpetuall warre of every man against his neighbor,
are much worse. (107)

The thought, then, that one might do better if one's fellows
adhered to a principle of political obligation that allowed
more exemptions from obedience than Hobbes's principle is
ill-founded, since it makes appeal to the mistaken idea that
social stability might profitably be traded for increases in
property or in liberty. There can be no such trade-offs, according to Hobbes; security, property, and liberty are effects
of a common cause, and are secured in direct, not inverse
proportion to it.[24] The narrowly prudential interests of each
person can be expected to be best secured if others in his
commonwealth adhere to Hobbes's principle of political
obligation.

Natural duty and moral obligation

If this is the case, then each person who has an interest in
securing his own preservation and commodious living has a
reason from narrow prudence to want others to adhere to
Hobbes's principle. And if he wants others to adhere to the
principle, then he has a natural duty to adhere to it himself.
This is because men have a natural duty not to reserve to
themselves any right that they would not be content to have
others reserve as well, in this case a right to violate a principle
they want others to observe. This is Hobbes's tenth law of
nature, against arrogance; and it is an implication of his ninth
law of nature, against pride, "that every man acknowledge
other for his equall by nature" (77). Hobbes writes, "If . . .
men require for themselves that which they would not have
to be granted to others, they do contrary to the precedent
law, that commandeth the acknowledgment of naturall
equalitie, and therefore also against the law of nature" (77).
If we are to reserve to ourselves a right not to adhere to
Hobbes's principle, then we must be willing to allow others
the same right; and if we are not willing to allow them that
right, then we must not claim it ourselves. Thus Hobbes

establishes that those who have an interest in fulfilling their secular moral duties – which is just to obey the laws of nature – have a reason from secular morality for adhering to his principle of political obligation.

Moreover, Hobbes's argument that people have a reason from narrow prudence to want to live within a stable state forms the basis for the further moral argument that people have an obligation to obey an existing political authority insofar as it is effective. If one has a reason to want to live within a stable state, then one has reason to accept the state's protection if it is available to him. If one accepts protection from the political authority of a commonwealth, then, as we saw, one is to be regarded as having tacitly covenanted to obey that authority; and this tacit covenant is limited only by considerations of what a commonwealth is, and of what it is to be a member of a commonwealth. But if one has (tacitly) covenanted to obey the political authority of a commonwealth, then one has an obligation to do so, since an obligation is just what one owes to another by covenant. To have an obligation of obedience to an effective government insofar as it can be effective is tantamount to having an obligation to adhere to Hobbes's principle. This obligation to adhere to the principle is then backed up by the natural duty to keep one's covenants (the third law of nature). Hobbes is thus able to offer two distinct moral arguments for adherence to his principle of political obligation – one from the natural duty to treat others as equals, and one from our obligation to obey an authority from whom we have accepted protection (which obligation is underwritten by the natural duty to keep covenants) – both of which rely on portions of his argument that it is in one's narrow self-interest to live under an effective government, and so that one has reason to want others to adhere to Hobbes's principle of political obligation.[25]

Narrow prudence (b)

Although Hobbes can by this means establish moral reasons for people to adhere to his principle, he has not yet provided any narrowly prudential reason for individuals themselves to adhere to his principle. Hobbes cannot establish that it is *always* in one's narrow rational self-interest to adhere to his principle. What he can show is that it is usually irrational for subjects to act against his principle, particularly when doing so constitutes an act of open rebellion, "for rebellion is but war renewed" (166), and war is rarely in one's narrow self-interest.

This argument is presented largely in Hobbes's famous reply to the "foole." Hobbes argues that it is against one's narrow self-interest to violate his principle by an act of rebellion, for three reasons: first, because one cannot reasonably expect to gain by doing so; second, because even if one does succeed, one teaches others to do the same by one's example; and third, because if one is unsuccessful, one can expect very dire consequences, namely, to die the death of a traitor. Moreover, some of the same considerations apply to lesser violations of Hobbes's principle, to what we would call attempts to free ride: first, assuming reasonably effective law enforcement, one cannot reasonably expect to succeed in gaining by acts of disobedience, and second, the costs of failure are too high to be reasonably risked. The idea is that acts of disobedience – violations of the law – if detected will result either in punishment sufficiently severe to offset any gains one might expect from disobedience, or in the termination of one's membership in, and thus protection by, a commonwealth. One cannot rationally want either of these events to transpire. And one cannot reasonably expect to avoid these consequences in an effective commonwealth, where there is, by implication, effective law enforcement.

Hobbes's argument for the irrationality of violating his principle is stronger for open rebellion than it is for surreptitious acts of disobedience such as tax evasion or isolated acts of theft. And this is no accident. Hobbes, because he was concentrating on the horrors of civil war, was concerned primarily to show the irrationality, iniquity, and sinfulness of rebellion, rather than to address the general problem of crime. His primary argument is that one cannot expect to

95

gain in terms of narrow self-interest by attempting to over-throw one's government; and this argument has a good deal of plausibility. In a system of effective law enforcement, conspirators are often caught before they can initiate a revolution. Revolution usually causes a war, in which one may lose one's life. Hobbes writes that "of them that are the first movers in the disturbance of common-wealth, (which can never happen without a civill warre,) very few are left alive long enough, to see their new designes established" (154). Even if one survives the war, one may lose the war, in which case one can expect the severest of punishments. Even if one wins the war, one's example may provide encouragement to others to attempt the same against oneself. And if a person revolts in the name of religion, he runs a double risk because if he is wrong, as he may be, about what God requires of him, he may be subject to divine punishment as well as the wrath of men. Hobbes writes:

> The foole . . . questioneth, whether injustice, taking away the feare of God . . . may not sometimes stand with that reason which dictateth to every man his own good; and particularly then, when it conduceth to such a benefit, as shall put a man in a condition, to neglect not onely the dispraise, and reviling, but also the power of other men. The kingdome of God is gotten by violence; but what if it could be gotten by unjust violence? were it against reason so to get it, when it is impossible to receive hurt by it? and if it be not against reason, it is not against justice: or else justice is not to be approved for good. From such reasoning as this, successfull wicked-nesse hathe obtained the name of vertue: and some that in all other things have disallowed the violation of faith, yet have allowed it, when it is for the getting of a kingdome. . . . This specious reasoning is nevertheless false. . . .
>
> For the manifestation whereof, we are to consider; First, that when a man doth a thing, which notwithstanding any thing can be forseen, and reckoned on, tendeth to his own destruction, howsoever some accident which he could not expect, arriving may turne it to his benefit; yet such events do not make it reasonably or wisely done. Secondly, that . . . there is no man can hope by his own strength, or wit, to

defend himselfe from destruction, without the help of confederates; where every one expects the same defence by the confederation that any one else does: and therefore he which declares he thinks it reason to deceive those that help him, can in reason expect no other means of safety, than what can be had from his own single power. He therefore that breaketh his covenant, and consequently declareth that he thinks he may with reason do so, cannot be received into any society, that unite themselves for peace and defence, but by the error of them that receive him; nor when he is received, be retayned in it, without seeing the danger of their errour; which errours a man cannot reasonably reckon upon as the means of his security: and therefore if he be left, or cast out of society, he perisheth; and if he live in society, it is by the errours of other men, which he could not forsee, nor reckon upon; and consequently against the reason of his preservation; and so, as all men that contribute not to his destruction, forbear him onely out of ignorance of what is good for themselves.

As for the instance of gaining the secure and perpetuall felicity of heaven by any way; it is frivolous: there being but one way imaginable; and that is not breaking, but keeping of covenant.

And for the other instance of attaining soveraignty by rebellion; it is manifest, that though the event follow, yet because it cannot reasonably be expected, but rather the contrary; and because by gaining it so, others are taught to gain the same in like manner, the attempt thereof is against reason. Justice therefore, that is to say, keeping of covenants, is a rule of reason, by which we are forbidden to do any thing destructive to our life; and consequently a law of nature.

There be some that proceed further, and will not have the law of nature, to be those rules which conduce to the preservation of mans life on earth; but to the attaining of an eternall felicity after death; to which they think the breach of covenant may conduce; and consequently be just and reasonable; (such are they that think it a work of merit to kill, or depose, or rebell against, the soveraigne power constituted over them by their own consent.) But because there is no natural knowledge of mans estate after death; much lesse of the reward that is then to be given to breach of faith . . . breach of faith cannot be called a precept of reason, or nature. (72–4)

By this argument Hobbes offers his readers a narrowly prudential reason for not disobeying their effective political authority – that is, for not violating Hobbes's principle – particularly by an open act of rebellion. Hobbes cannot show that it can *never* be in one's overall narrow rational self-interest to disobey *any* command of one's sovereign. But Hobbes's project does not require that he demonstrate that disobedience is *always* irrational from the standpoint of narrow prudence. It requires only that he provide enough people with a reason that they can regard as sufficient (given their moral and religious interests as well as their narrowly prudential interests) to adhere to his principle of political obligation enough of the time that effective social order can be continuously maintained. The narrowly prudential reasons he offers against rebellion particularly, and disobedience generally, are sufficient, in conjunction with his moral and (upcoming) religious arguments, to serve this purpose.

To summarize, then, the first phase of the compositive portion of Hobbes's argument, presented in Part 2 of *Leviathan*, has two components: the argument that his principle of political obligation, assuming it can be satisfactorily specified, is one that could, if widely followed, ensure the perpetual maintenance of effective social order; and the argument that subjects have (a) a narrowly prudential reason to want others to adhere to that principle, (b) two moral reasons, one from natural duty and one from obligation, for people to themselves adhere to the principle, and (c) a narrowly prudential reason not to violate the principle themselves that will obtain most of the time and in the most important cases. The second, and final, phase of the compositive portion of Hobbes's argument, carried out in Part 3 of *Leviathan*, has an analogous structure: First, Hobbes fully specifies his principle in such a way that it can be shown really to be one that, if widely followed, could ensure the perpetual maintenance of effective social order; and second, Hobbes provides his readers with reasons from both religious duty and special prudence for adhering to his principle. It is to this second phase of Hobbes's compositive project that we now turn.

Chapter 3

Compositive reconstruction, phase two: religion and the redescription of transcendent interests

The most frequent praetext of sedition and civill warre in Christian common-wealths hath a long time proceeded from a difficulty, not yet sufficiently resolved, of obeying at once, both God, and man . . .

– Hobbes (L 321)

To this point, we have reconstructed the portion of Hobbes's compositive argument presented in Part 2 of *Leviathan*. There Hobbes attempts to identify a principle of political obligation that could, if generally followed, ensure the perpetual maintenance of effective social order. That principle is that one is to obey one's extant effective political authority in all of its commands not repugnant to one's duty to God. Hobbes then offers arguments both from narrow prudence and from morality for subjects to adhere to that principle.

But recall that Hobbes is engaged in the project of providing everyone with a *sufficient* reason to adhere to a principle which could, if generally followed, ensure the perpetual maintenance of effective social order. This requires, in part, that he provide people with reasons for adhering to his principle linked to the satisfaction of *all* of their most important interests; and also that he so specify his principle that it can be shown actually to be one that, if generally followed, could ensure perpetual domestic stability. To this point in the argument, Hobbes has not dealt with one crucially important set of interests – religious interests; there has as yet been no argument that people have any religious reason for affirming

99

Hobbes's principle of political obligation. Now, Hobbes is concerned to provide everyone with a *sufficient* reason for adherence to his principle, a reason not overridden by contrary reasons, and the quest for a such reason does not automatically or necessarily require that people have a religious reason. Nor does it necessarily require that they see themselves as having moral reasons for adherence to the principle. It may be that most people can, most of the time, be sufficiently motivated to adhere to Hobbes's principle just by considerations of narrow self-interest.

Still, although it may be true that a narrowly prudential reason can be a sufficient reason if people have no other sorts of interests, it may well not be sufficient if they do have other sorts of interests with which the dictates of narrow prudence conflict. Indeed, it is characteristic of moral and religious considerations that they are regarded as putting limits on how, and how far, narrow self-interest may be pursued, and are thought in this sense to provide stronger reasons than mere prudential considerations. A person's thought that his plan to improve his material well-being is unjust, or sinful, may well motivate him to refrain from implementing it. In fact, people may, and often do, consciously pursue their religious and moral interests at the expense not only of their material well-being, but even of their self-preservation. These are the potentially transcendent interests of which I spoke earlier. Moral and religious interests *need* not be transcendent, but they may be, and often are. The existence of transcendent interests suggests it will likely not be a sufficient reason for affirming Hobbes's principle of political obligation that it is in one's rational self-interest *narrowly* construed, if it is not also in one's interest *broadly* construed, as taking into account one's moral and religious interests, including the special prudential interest in receiving salvation.

We saw that Hobbes's attempt to provide everyone with a sufficient reason for adhering to his principle of political obligation was dictated by his recognition that effective social order depends on *compliance* with the laws made by the political authority – that it depends on the *obedience* of subjects

– and that compliance is most effectively obtained when people can be persuaded that they have what they can see, in their own terms, as a sufficient reason for complying. Effective social order requires the promulgation and enforcement of rules regulating individual conduct, and a mechanism for the peaceful resolution of disputes. For there to be effective social order on a societywide scale by means of political organization, some political authority must be able to carry out these functions.[1] But no political authority can effectively fulfill these functions without the cooperation of those who are subject to it; the ability of a political authority to secure effective social order requires, at minimum, compliance from most of the people, most of the time. This suggests that *general* compliance cannot be reliably coerced by threat of force. General compliance cannot be coerced by a political authority because any political authority's ability to wield force at all depends on a fairly general compliance with its commands and decisions. Hobbes emphasizes this point with a rhetorical question: "If men know not their duty, what is there that can force them to obey the laws? An army, you will say. But what shall force the army?" (*B* 22).[2] Moreover, even if the political authority is obeyed by a sufficiently large number of people that it is capable of exercising coercion, it may not be able to compel obedience from enough of the remaining members of society to secure effective social order.

This is so for the simple reason that in order for obedience to be reliably attainable by means of threat of force, it must be true that fear of death, wounds, or imprisonment (fear of the means of coercion available to a political authority) must be the *strongest* motivating passion. But the existence of transcendent interests shows we *cannot* count on this passion (or, we might say, this interest in avoiding personal harm) to override all other passions and interests. More generally, the fear of personal harm (either "artificially" inflicted, as in the case of punishment by the sovereign power, or "naturally" consequent to the dissolution of any protective power, which disobedience might bring about) may *not* be sufficient to motivate people to obey their extant political authority, because that obedience may frustrate their realization of others of their interests (in, for instance, fulfilling their duties to God and to each other, securing the good of their loved ones, and so on), interests for the satisfaction of which they are willing to risk personal harm. The point about transcendent interests is that they are capable of overriding one's self-interest narrowly construed, so compliance can be *reliably* secured only when people recognize it as in their interest *broadly* construed, as including *all* of their interests. Obviously this cannot be done by appeal only to a subset of their interests, so the threat of harm to their self-interest narrowly construed cannot be relied upon to motivate them to comply. Thus the compatibility of Hobbes's principle with the realization of people's moral and religious interests (which may be transcendent) must be demonstrated.

In the following discussion of Hobbes's identification of and argument from religious duty, we will find that Hobbes not only fully specifies his principle of political obligation and provides two *new* sorts of reason – one from religious duty, and one from the interest in salvation – for adhering to that principle, but he also provides considerations that strengthen his moral interest argument. This is because the laws of morality – the laws of nature – are identical to the laws of God discernible by unaided natural reason, and so Hobbes's argument that obedience to the laws of God entails adherence to his principle automatically demonstrates that moral interests, when properly understood, will require adherence to the principle. Whereas the separate moral interest argument of Part 2 links political obedience to the fulfillment of certain discrete laws of nature, the argument from religion provides a *general* argument that adherence to Hobbes's principle does not impede but, rather, advances, the realization of one's moral interests. Hobbes speaks almost exclusively of religious duties and interests, treating moral duties and interests as if they were a subset of these. It should be made clear that Hobbes does *not* think one must have religious interests in order to have moral interests; in Hobbes's view, knowledge of the moral duties is not dependent on knowledge of (or belief in) the existence of God. An atheist may have moral interests, and he may be a moral person (although, in Hobbes's view, he will be a rationally defective person, and not sufficiently sinless to attain eternal life without faith). Hobbes treats moral and religious interests together because he holds that fulfillment of one's duty to God requires an attempt to follow all of the dictates of morality (plus some other things), so a demonstration that his principle of political obligation is compatible with the realization of one's interest in fulfilling one's duty to God, will automatically show that the principle is compatible with one's interest in fulfilling one's moral duties.[3] Hobbes needn't give a separate general argument that adhering to his principle does not impede the realization of one's moral interests.[4]

Now, at first blush there seems to be *no* possibility that Hobbes's principle could conflict with people's religious interests, because that principle requires obedience to one's extant effective political authority only in those of its commands which are not repugnant to one's duty to God. People's interest in fulfilling their duties to God was taken into account by Hobbes's including a very general exemption in his principle of political obligation. But the matter of whether Hobbes's principle could conflict with people's religious interests will depend upon how we interpret the phrase "one's duty to God" in the clause that exempts one from obedience to commands repugnant to one's duty to God. Are we to understand this phrase as referring to some *objective* fact, in principle possibly quite different from what any individual or group actually (though "mistakenly") *thinks* his duty to God to be? Or are we to understand it as referring to each person's or group's *actual* particular beliefs about one's duty to God? That is, does the principle exempt one from obedience to commands that conflict with what actually, objectively, is one's duty to God (regardless of what one believes), or does it exempt one from obedience to commands that conflict with what one *believes* to be one's duty to God?

The implications of these two readings differ enormously. If Hobbes were to adopt the first reading, then those who *disagree* with whatever he specifies as *the* "objective" content of one's duty to God – those who think Hobbes has misidentified the content of one's duty to God – might well *not* have sufficient reason to affirm Hobbes's principle of political obligation. After all, some people may have a transcendent interest in fulfilling their duties to God, an interest they afford priority over all of their other interests; and if Hobbes's principle would require them to obey their political authority even in those of its commands that conflict with what they believe to be their duty to God, then they will certainly not regard themselves as having sufficient reason to adhere to that principle, and Hobbes's project of trying to provide *everyone* with a sufficient reason to adhere to his principle of political obligation is doomed to failure.

On the other hand, if Hobbes were to adopt the second reading of the "duty to God" clause, then his principle might well exempt *so many* people from political obedience at any given time that the social order would collapse. If each person may disobey his political authority whenever he perceives a conflict between its commands and his own view about what one's duty to God is, it becomes a matter of (infinitely variable) private judgment whether or not the political authority is to be obeyed. Not only is it possible that many people will withhold obedience on religious grounds, but it is not unreasonable to suppose that they will try to organize others to refuse obedience as well in cases where they perceive some important religious issue to be at stake.[5] And where different people or groups have competing conceptions of duty to God, they may attempt to impose their conceptions over and against not only that of the state but those of other factions as well, creating widespread social disorder.[6] But Hobbes's aim in specifying a principle of political obligation that everyone could have sufficient reason to affirm was to ensure, so far as possible, the maintenance of effective social order. If Hobbes's proposed principle is inherently unstable – if even strict, universal adherence to the principle would be insufficient to maintain effective social order – then it cannot possibly serve the purpose for which Hobbes intends it. Because

Hobbes's sole aim in *Leviathan* is to defend this principle, then once again his project is doomed to failure.

There is another way of posing the problem: For a principle to be effective in maintaining effective social order, people must follow it, and it must be true that when people follow it effective social order is maintained. If Hobbes's principle is specified in a way that makes adherence to it incompatible with some people's transcendent interest in fulfilling what they take to be their duties to God, they will not follow it, and so the principle may not be effective in maintaining social order. If the principle is specified in a way that allows adherence to it to be compatible with each of a number of mutually incompatible specifications of the transcendent interest in fulfilling one's duty to God, then even when people follow it, the principle may not be able to maintain effective social order. In this latter case, people would not even have a *narrowly prudential* reason to follow the principle, because even universal adherence to it would not ensure the maintenance of effective social order. Moreover, to the extent that people believe it is imprudent to disobey God, they won't have prudential reason to follow the principle in the former case either. *We won't know whether theists should regard themselves as having even a narrowly prudential reason to adhere to Hobbes's principle until that principle is satisfactorily specified.*[7]

But this specification couldn't be carried out in Part 2, which employed only information available to unaided natural reason, because it requires information from revealed religion. This way of posing the problem again allows us to see how very distinct the two portions of Hobbes's project – the task of identifying a principle of political obligation that could, if followed, ensure domestic order, and the task of providing people with reasons for adhering to such a principle – are. It seems that if we specify the duty to God exemption one way, we cannot effect the necessary link between people's religious interests and adherence to the principle; but if we specify it the other way, the principle turns out to be incapable, even if universally followed, of ensuring domestic peace.

Hobbes would seem, then, to be on the horns of a dilemma: His principle must respect the particular transcendent interests people actually claim as their own if it is to be one they can affirm; but it is precisely the conflict among these particularisms that may well upset social order. He cannot endorse any *one* of these particularisms (or any limited range of them) as truly and uniquely constitutive of one's duty to God, nor can he admit any and every particularism as legitimately exempting its advocates from political obedience. Simply put, the problem is this: If you want to ensure the maintenance of effective social order, you have to respect all people's transcendent interests; but in cases where people's transcendent interests are in conflict, you cannot respect them all and still ensure the maintenance of effective social order.[8]

Hobbes's ingenious solution to this apparent dilemma employs a strategy I am going to call "redescription of transcendent interests." The basic idea is that even though people who have a transcendent interest in fulfilling their duties to God would all affirm the description of their interest as "an interest in fulfilling one's duties to God," they hold differing beliefs that lead them to specify their interest in fulfilling their duties to God in differing and sometimes incompatible or mutually contradictory ways. That is, in the real world, any given religious group will identify the content of one's duty to God with some conjunction of statements about what one must do, believe, and so on, and its trancendent interest in fulfilling its duties to God will amount to (be equivalent to) a transcendent interest in doing, believing, and so on, each of those things. These particular descriptions of one's transcendent interest in fulfilling one's duties to God will be the result of beliefs about what God commands, approves of, and the like, and about what the Scriptures say, about the nature of the world as God has created it, the nature of God, the requirements of salvation, the nature of faith, and so on. So, for example, when two religious factions disagree about whether or not it is pleasing to God that divine worship employ massive pageantry, ceremony, and ornamentation, this difference in beliefs leads one faction to have an interest in abolishing such "vulgar displays, remnants of heathen ceremonies, magical incantations, and like offences to God," whereas it leads in the other faction to an interest in "communicating the awesomeness of the mysteries of Christian religion and an offering to God of the most perfect worship of which we are capable." Because people identify their interest in fulfilling their duties to God with an interest in fulfilling each duty in some determinate conjunction of duties, the differences in particular beliefs on which these differing descriptions depend must be abolished if there is to be a reconciliation of transcendent interests, and consensus on the requirements of one's duty to God.

Now an alteration in the conjunction of particular interests, by adding, deleting, or replacing any or all of the conjuncts, will count as what I am going to call a redescription of one's transcendent interest in fulfilling one's duty to God.[9] My claim is that Hobbes is going to attempt to redescribe his readers' transcendent interests in fulfilling their duty to God in such a way that each former faction can affirm that description as accurately capturing their interest, while all the factions will be affirming the very same description and will be willing to give up allegiance to any other description. Hobbes is aiming to get all of his readers to accept as the proper description of their interest in fulfilling their duties to God, "an interest in professing, practicing, and acting as the appropriate religious authority dictates." I will show that Hobbes tries to carry out this redescription by means of an attack on the causes of those differing beliefs from which spring incompatible descriptions of one's interest in fulfilling one's duties to God.

Now, this strategy would be hopeless were there not already a great deal of agreement about the appropriate sources of religious knowledge. But Hobbes's audience did agree on the appropriate sources of knowledge of one's duty to God; everyone recognized natural reason, personal revelation, and the Holy Scriptures as legitimate – and the only legitimate – sources of religious knowledge. Likewise, it might be impossible to carry out this project of redescription if people thought there was no fact of the matter about what duty to God involves, or that it involved something different for each individual, or that it was impossible to discover what one's duties to God are.[10] But again, the people whom Hobbes is addressing do agree that there is a discoverable fact of the matter about what one's duties to God are, and that these duties are the same for everyone (excepting, of course, differences attached to different functions or offices).

We might wonder how, if people are in substantial agreement about the possibility of, and sources of, religious knowledge, there can be so great a difference in religious belief, and so in people's substantive descriptions of their transcendent interests, among various groups and individuals. Hobbes's answer to this question – and it seems quite a reasonable answer – is that given our available sources of religious knowledge, it will be true that *what* we believe must be a function of *whom* we believe. Hobbes will argue that in holding any religious belief, one cannot be simply "believing God." Unless God has spoken to one directly, one will be believing what men have said or written about what God requires, that is, one will be believing men; and even if one believes that God has spoken to one directly, one is believing in *one's own judgment* that one's dream or vision was immediately caused by God, and not the result of natural causes.

The contention that what one believes about God's requirements is a function of whom one believes is less obviously true for natural reason than it is for revelation, so I will illustrate Hobbes's idea by reference to Scripture. We may agree that the Scriptures, which are the compilation of Judeo-Christian revelations, are an appropriate, and indeed the most important, source of religious knowledge. Nevertheless, the Scriptures do not obviously yield a single, determinate body of doctrine. They require interpretation, and different interpretations will yield different, and possibly incompatible, bodies of doctrine. It may be possible to reject some proposed interpretations on grounds of unintelligibility or of lack of coherence with other of our religious beliefs based on natural reason, but even this is uncertain if one believes there may be religious truths incomprehensible to the human intellect, or that men's sinfulness makes them prone to error, and so their reason untrustworthy. There seem to be very few criteria for choosing among various interpretations of Scripture that do not make reference to either the authority of the interpreter, or the authority of some other body, or officially sanctioned set of doctrines, against which proposed interpretations are to be measured. If the criterion for *deciding* among various interpretations of Scripture is the authority of the interpreter, or the authority of the church leadership, or the authority of an Aquinas – if the criterion for *accepting* a proposed interpretation *as* true is whether or not it is approved by the appropriate authority – then it will be true that what one believes will be a function of whom one believes, and disagreement over what one's duty to God is may stem from a disagreement about who the appropriate interpretive authority is.

Nevertheless, this insight, that divergent descriptions stem from differences in who is believed, also suggests a starting point for Hobbes's project of redescription. His attempt to redescribe various conflicting substantive descriptions of the transcendent interest in fulfilling one's duties to God into a single universally acceptable description proceeds by focusing on the question of what the basis of differing religious beliefs is. After arguing that differences in belief stem from differences in who is believed, Hobbes addresses the question of who *ought* to be believed, that is, the question of whose judgment in religious matters *God* wants us to *take as* authoritative. This is the question of who is the appropriate authority in matters of religion. If agreement on this question can be reached, then those differences in belief which result in conflicting substantive descriptions of the transcendent interest in fulfilling one's duties to God can be resolved, and the problem of specifying a meaning of the "duty to God" exemption in Hobbes's principle of political obligation will be settled in a way that enables that principle to be both acceptable to the people for whom it is supposed to hold (because it will respect their transcendent interest in fulfilling their duties to God) and effective in securing social order (because, as we'll see, it will be specified in such a way that it will not exempt large numbers of people from political obedience). Hobbes's principle would then read: One is to obey one's extant effective political authority in all of its commands not repugnant to one's duty to God as specified by the appropriate (one and only, authorized by God, and universally recognized) religious authority.

At this point we are in a position to take notice of a general feature of Hobbes's strategy for overcoming the problem of competing transcendent interests. We saw that under its most general or formal description as "an interest in fulfilling one's duties to God," there was no perceivable conflict among people's potentially transcendent interests. We also saw that when the content of this interest was spelled out, that is, when it was specified by and identified with some determinate conjunction of particular duties, there was the potential for conflict among people's religious interests. Under a more general description people do not perceive their religious interests as in conflict; under a specific or substantive description, people do perceive themselves as having conflicting interests. So whether people will see their interests as in conflict or not depends on the level of generality or formality of the description of those interests. By transforming the question of what religious beliefs are true into the question of whose judgment we should take to be authoritative, Hobbes has raised the level of dispute to a much more general and formal level. If he can persuade people to accept as the proper description of one's duty to God "the duty to profess and practice as the appropriate religious authority dictates" *rather than* as "the duty to do x and the duty to believe y and the duty to z" (where some other religious faction may substitute not-x, not-y, and not-z), then he will have succeeded in redescribing "one's duties to God" in an extremely general and formal way.

Hobbes's strategy is – theoretically speaking – really quite

sensible. People are attached to highly specific, very particular doctrines and practices, and have an interest (possibly
transcendent) in these *because* they believe them to be part
of their duty to God, in the fulfillment of which they have a
(transcendent) interest. But it is these particularisms that generate conflict, and it is around these specific issues that the
various religious factions struggle. If people could be persuaded that one's true duty to God is properly identified by
a religious authority, and that they should profess, practice,
and act only as he dictates, then all that would be needed
in order to resolve their conflicts with one another would be
the reaching of consensus on who the appropriate religious
authority is. Hobbes would thus reduce the epistemological
problem of knowing what our duties to God are, to (what,
he argues, turns out to be) the less complex epistemological
problem of knowing whose judgments God requires us to
take for truth in matters of religion. Although there had by
no means been a settled consensus on the answer to this
latter question, Hobbes thought he could offer powerful and
persuasive arguments to settle the question, and to generate
consensus among Christian believers. Supposing he could
garner consensus on this question, Hobbes would have eliminated the possibility of those differences in belief that give
rise to differing descriptions among factions of their transcendent interest in fulfilling their duties to God. This done,
Hobbes would then be able to specify his principle of political
obligation in a certain way such that it is rendered both effective and acceptable.

Before examining the argument that instantiates this strategy, I want to answer one objection that might be raised to
my discussion of the strategy of redescription Hobbes employs at this point in his argument. One might claim that
Hobbes could not have been trying to redescribe his readers'
religious interests into a nondisruptive description potentially acceptable to all because the religious arguments and
conclusions he puts forth were so *unorthodox* that virtually
none of his readers accepted them. The suggestion is that
Hobbes couldn't have been *aiming* to develop and support

an acceptable redescription because he *could not possibly have thought* that any of his readers could have accepted his redescription, and this because that redescription was *in fact unacceptable,* as the observation that no one *did* accept it proves. Therefore, Hobbes could not have been employing the strategy I attribute to him.

I shall have more to say about the plausibility of Hobbes's argument and the merits of his strategy when we assess his project in Chapter 9. And we shall not enter into the discussion of the question of how unorthodox Hobbes's views really were.[11] For the moment we might say this: It is certainly true that Hobbes's argument concerning religion provoked outrage and indignation, and was rejected by most of his contemporaries. But this is a fact about the world that will remain true *no matter what* interpretation we give to Hobbes's argument. This fact does not tell us *anything* about what Hobbes was trying to do. It does not follow from the fact that Hobbes's religious views were not accepted, and were in that sense unacceptable, that Hobbes was not trying to persuade people of their truth (rather than, say, trying to get himself into trouble, or trying to make a badly judged joke). Indeed, the length and detail of his argument concerning religion in *Leviathan,* radically expanded and changed from the more orthodox view presented in his earlier works (before the civil war experience had shown him how necessary it was to attempt to reconcile the views of competing religious factions), suggest that Hobbes was making a very serious effort to persuade his readers of the truth of his redescription of religious duty.[12]

So we can set aside the objection that my argument that Hobbes was attempting to redescribe his readers' transcendent religious interests into a uniform widely acceptable description is doubtful because Hobbes's theological arguments were unorthodox, and unorthodox arguments could not have been expected to produce agreement. The orthodox arguments had obviously not produced agreement (as the civil war testifies), so new arguments were needed. Certainly, Hobbes did not think he was articulating an *already shared* and uncontroversial description of religious duty, nor was he seeking to show that the already existing conflicting viewpoints, in their *unaltered* state, were compatible. Either of these *would* have been a losing proposition, and any interpretation asserting that he was attempting to do these would be, to that extent, implausible. What I shall argue, in contrast, is that starting from the conflicting religious positions actually held, Hobbes sought to construct, by means of a new, perhaps unorthodox, argument, a formal description of religious duty that most factions could be brought (by that argument) to see as accurately capturing their true interests. The question, then, is not whether Hobbes's arguments were new but whether they were good arguments. We'll take up this question in Chapter 9. But first we must see how the argument goes.

Let us now examine the actual course of Hobbes's argument in Chapters 31 through 43 of *Leviathan*. Hobbes begins his project of redescription by identifying what he takes to be the only possible sources of religious knowledge, namely, natural reason, personal revelation, and prophecy. It is from these three sources alone that we are to discover what our duties to God are.

NATURAL REASON

In Chapter 31, Hobbes argues that the knowledge of one's duties to God attainable through the exercise of natural reason alone gives people no reason to affirm divergent descriptions of their interest in fulfilling their duties to God. Furthermore, none of those of our duties to God concerning the profession and practice of religion discoverable by means of unaided natural reason conflicts with perfect obedience to one's extant effective political authority. If our duty to God involved nothing more than what can be known by unaided natural reason, all people would affirm the very same description of their interest in fulfilling their duties to God, and the "duty to God" exemption could be so specified that

Hobbes's principle of political obligation would be acceptable to everyone.

The method of discovery from unaided natural reason consists in making arguments based solely on self-evident truths and definitions of words, drawing out the logical implications of each of these. Hobbes supposes that this sort of reasoning yields a unique determinate conclusion in any given instance; because he holds this belief and the further belief that all human beings have the capacity for this sort of reasoning, Hobbes thinks everyone will reach the same conclusion through natural reasoning, and everyone will accept the conclusions of natural reason. So although what one believes on the basis of natural reason does, in some sense, depend on whom one believes (one is believing the judgments of himself and his fellows when arrived at by this method), this fact does not result in differences among people in what is believed. This means that the conclusions of natural reason can be unproblematically used as assumptions for further arguments about who the appropriate authority in matters of religion is, as well as giving us some unproblematic, shared conclusions as to what really is our duty to God.

Hobbes begins by asking what natural reason tells us about our duties to God in the treatment of one another. In his natural kingdom (as opposed to his prophetical kingdom, where he is sovereign over a particular people by pact, and governs by positive laws), God governs those who believe in him by the laws of nature, which tell men their natural duties, violations of which are punished by naturally consequent bad effects. The laws of God discoverable by unaided natural reason are just the laws of nature, considered as commands from a deity who exists, who has given laws and rules of conduct, and who offers rewards and punishments. In his natural kingdom, God governs those who acknowledge his providence by the dictates of "right reason," these laws of God, which concern the natural duties of one man to another. These duties, as we saw earlier, may be "contracted into one easie sum, intelligible even to the meanest

114

capacity, and that is, 'Do not that to another, which thou wouldest not have done to thy selfe'" (79). This is all that natural reason tells us about our duties to God in the treatment of one another, and everyone who has the use of natural reason will agree about this. There is as yet no basis for affirming divergent descriptions of the interest in fulfilling one's duties to God.

Next, Hobbes argues that none of those of our duties to God concerning the profession and practice of religion discoverable by natural reason conflicts with perfect obedience to the commands of one's extant effective political authority. This is so because natural reason informs us that it *doesn't matter* how we profess and practice, that God demands no particular sort of worship such that if the political authority prohibited it, we would be duty-bound to disobey him. There are no grounds in natural reason for preferring some other religious practices to any which the political authority may command us to observe.

The first question to be considered is one of what it is to worship God. Hobbes holds that there are some actions that are natural signs of honor, such as prayers, thanks, obedience to God's laws, public worship, and considerate speech concerning God. Honoring, says Hobbes, consists in inward thought; to honor God is to think as highly of his goodness and power as is possible. Worship is just the external expression of honor, and is naturally expressed by thanks and obedience, which praise God's goodness and magnify his power, and prayers. These are natural forms of worship because they are the natural external expressions of those passions – namely, hope, love, and fear – that arise from the belief that God is infinitely good and powerful. There are also some attributes that are naturally significative of divine honor, that is, qualities that our intention to honor God dictates that we attribute to him, for example, existence, cause of the world, caring for the well-being of men, and being infinite. If we did not attribute these qualities to God, we would be either unable to honor him (if he didn't exist) or unconcerned to do so (if he had no care of the actions of mankind), or we would be dishonoring him by thinking him less than he might possibly be (by thinking him finite, or caused).

These actions and ascriptions of attributes are naturally signs of honor, a part of natural worship. But there are other actions and ascriptions of qualities that are signs of honor only by institution or convention, in themselves indifferent, and these are a part of arbitrary worship.[13] Hobbes speaks here of conventional, as opposed to natural, signs or expressions of honor, but the distinction he has in mind is better captured by the idea that although there are *kinds* of actions that are naturally expressions of honor, that is, prayers, thanks, and so on, the *form* these expressions take – the actual words, gestures, ceremonies, and so on used in prayers, thanks, oblations, and other kinds of worship – are in themselves indifferent, and to be held significative of honor insofar as those who use them intend to convey honor by means of them, or he who is to be honored understands them to convey honor. Hobbes says, "Others [signs of honor] are so by institution or custome of men, and in some times and places are honourable, in others dishonourable, in others indifferent, such as are the *gestures in* salutation, prayer, and thanksgiving, in different times and places differently *used*" (189, emphasis added). This is so, Hobbes explains, because all words, and an infinite number of possible actions and gestures, have their meaning by agreement among speakers, that is, by convention. Whereas it would be impossible to honor one's God by, for example, swearing by other gods, speaking irreverently of him, refusing to obey his commands, or deprecating rather than praising him (and so actions of the type prayer, thanksgiving, obedience, sacrifice, and the like are natural signs of honor), the words or gestures we use in praying, blessing, and so on, are regarded as appropriate depending upon the conventions we've established for their use. So, for example, we might think that spitting, belching, and mooning are irreverent actions and not to be used in religious worship (and the criterion for deciding whether or not we regard the gesture as dishonorable is whether or not we would be ashamed to perform it in front of people whom we respect), but groups of people in other places or at other times may not think that these actions are signs of dishonor; they may afford them a meaning altogether different from that which we afford them, and so think them perfectly acceptable for use in worship.

Now Hobbes argues that if a commonwealth is to be of any religion at all, public worship must be uniform.

> But seeing a commonwealth is but one person, it ought also to exhibite to God but one worship, which then it doth, when it commandeth it to be exhibited by private men, publiquely. And this is public worship, the property whereof, is to be uniforme: For those actions that are done differently, by different men, cannot be said to be a public worship. And therefore, where many sorts of worship be allowed, proceeding from the different religions of private men, it cannot be said there is any public worship, nor that the commonwealth is of any religion at all. (192)

Moreover, since the civil political authority is the representative of the commonwealth, which cannot be said to have a will except as expressed in the laws made by that authority, only the political authority can determine the form of public worship. Because all words have their meaning only by convention, the political authority may ordain for signs of honor to be used in divine worship any utterances he chooses, and there will be no grounds based on natural reason for defending the use of any particular utterances in worship contrary to those he stipulates. Likewise, of that infinite number of actions and gestures that are by nature indifferent, the political authority may ordain the use of any of them as signs of divine honor, and subjects will have no grounds based on natural reason for resisting the use of those actions and gestures in the public worship. Thus men have no reason, discoverable by natural reason alone, not to conduct their public worship in whatever manner the political authority dictates.

Hobbes has argued, then, that our natural reason gives us some knowledge of our duties to God: We can know that we have a duty to endeavor to obey the laws of God (which command justice, mercy, humility, in sum not doing unto others as we wouldn't be done to), and we can know something about "the honour naturally due to our divine soveraign," namely, that we should offer prayers, thanks, sacrifices, public worship, considerate speech, and obedience to God's laws. This is all our natural reason tells us about our duties to God. In particular, it doesn't specify determinate ceremonies, gestures, utterances, or postures as required to fulfill our duties to God. Natural reason can't, for example, tell us which prayer book to use, whether to pray facing the east, standing or kneeling, in Latin or in English, with pomp and circumstance or with Spartan simplicity. What our natural reason suggests is that it *doesn't matter* which of these we use in our worship because whichever words and actions we intend to convey honor, do convey honor. Thus we have *no* natural reason *not* to worship as the political authority commands us to.

Reason tells us further, that a necessary property of public worship is uniformity. Thus, if we want to exhibit public worship (if we want our commonwealth to be of any religion at all), we also *have* reason to worship in public as the political authority commands us to. So it will not be the case that any of the political authority's commands *concerning the profession and practice of religion* can be repugnant to our duty to God.

Moreover, though it might seem that the political authority's commands could be repugnant to our duties to God in the treatment of one another (that is, to the laws of nature), this appearance is misleading. Even if they were repugnant, religion per se wouldn't be a source of disorder because people would not be in disagreement about the requirements of religion, and their only potential grounds for disobeying the political authority would be that his commands required them to violate laws of nature that are as aptly described as moral laws as they are as religious laws. But in fact, Hobbes argues, subjects cannot usually establish that the sovereign *is* violating the laws of nature, because there can be no authority-independent specification of what is to count as a violation of a law of nature. Recall Hobbes's contention in

Chapter 15 of *Leviathan* that "because, though men be never so willing to observe these Lawes [of nature or God] there may neverthelesse arise questions concerning a mans action; First, whether it were done, or not done; Secondly (if done) *whether against the Law, or not against the Law;* the former whereof is called a question of Fact; *the later a question Of Right;* therefore unlesse the parties to the question covenant mutually to stand to the sentence of another, they are as farre from peace as ever" (78, emphasis added). Hobbes seems to be holding that the laws of nature or God do not, as it were, apply themselves; we may agree, for example, that we ought not to act unjustly, while disagreeing about which actions are to be counted as unjust. Hobbes suggests the analogy of adultery: We may know that adultery is sinful, but nonetheless disagree about what copulations are adulterous, because this depends on the notion of a lawful marriage. (Is bigamy a form of adultery? How should we regard the external activities of one who has a "common law marriage"? Or those of a person whose spouse is deceased? And so on.) For the laws of nature or God to have determinate application in particular cases, we must recognize the authority of some arbiter who can specify which actions are to be counted unjust, unequitable, ungrateful, immodest, and so on. This arbiter will turn out to be the sovereign himself.

Thus, if people believed that the whole of one's duty to God were discoverable by unaided natural reason, they would have no grounds for affirming divergent descriptions of that duty, or for resisting their sovereign's specification of it. As it happens, the people whom Hobbes is addressing do *not* believe that one's entire duty to God is discoverable by natural reason alone, so Hobbes's next step is to investigate what more can be known by personal revelation and prophecy.

Now, although natural reason cannot give us the whole truth about our duties to God, Hobbes insists that what it does tell us *is* true, and nothing further that revelation or prophecy might tell us about our duties to God can *contradict* what we have learned by natural reason. We must assume that God does not contradict himself, so we can be assured that any further specification of our duties that an analysis of Scripture might effect will not reveal any duties incompatible with those we can know by reason alone. In evaluating the claims about our duties to God advanced on the basis of revelations or prophecies, we are not to disregard the promptings of our senses, our experience, or our natural reason, "which is the undoubted word of God" (195). We must not forbear to use these, because

> they are the talents which he hath put into our hands to negotiate till the coming again of our blessed Saviour, and therefore not to be folded up in the napkin of an implicate faith, but employed in the purchase of justice, peace, and true religion. For though there be many things in God's word above reason, that is to say, which cannot by natural reason be either demonstrated, or confuted; yet there is nothing contrary to it; but when it seemeth so, the fault is either in our unskilfull interpretation, or erroneous ratiocination. (195)

This is an important argument because it arms Hobbes with several criteria for evaluating competing claims advanced on the basis of personal revelation or Scripture, which criteria are *independent* of any reference to authority. If Hobbes were compelled to attempt to settle the question of who the appropriate religious authority is on the basis of an analysis of Scripture *without* the aid of any independent criteria for choosing among competing interpretations, he would be trapped in a vicious circle: He would have to defend his identification of the appropriate religious authority by an argument from one among many competing interpretations of Scripture; yet his only available means of defending his preferred scriptural interpretation would make use of an appeal to the fact of its endorsement by the appropriate religious authority. By this "nothing true can contradict natural reason" argument, Hobbes has given himself use of tools sufficient to narrow significantly the scope of debate over the major question of who the appropriate religious authority is, and even, he thinks, actually to settle certain particular doctrinal disputes.[14]

PERSONAL REVELATION

With these tools in hand, Hobbes proceeds to examine the other available sources of knowledge of our duties to God, namely, personal revelation and prophecy. Both are forms of supernatural revelation; in the first, God speaks to men immediately, in the second, he speaks to them by mediation of some other man, to whom he has formerly spoken immediately. In order to determine what knowledge claims can be supported by an appeal to supernatural revelation, we need to know something about the nature of revelation.

The methods, Hobbes tells us, by which God reveals his will to individuals are dreams and visions. Both dreams and visions are by their nature private, in other words, inaccessible to others. What separates ordinary dreams and hallucinations from those revealing God's will is, says Hobbes, the manner of their causation. The experience of revelation is not the result of natural causes, as are ordinary dreams and hallucinations, but of the immediate intervention of God.

Now, according to Hobbes, what we believe is always a function of our experience and reason. We cannot simply choose to believe just anything, "for sense, memory, understanding, reason, and opinion are not in our power to change, but alwaies, and necessarily such, as the things we see, hear, and consider suggest unto us; and therefore are not effects of our will, but our will of them" (196).[15] Because it is impossible for us to adopt and sustain beliefs by a sheer act of will, we cannot be under any obligation to believe otherwise than as our senses, experience, and reason dictate. We can incur an obligation not to *express* our disbelief by word or deed, but can be neither obligated nor compelled by force to *believe* anything.[16]

It may be that the quality of the experience of revelation somehow allows its recipient to identify it as an inspiration or revelation as opposed to an ordinary dream or vision, but howsoever this may be, it is clear that no outside observer can be in a position to know whether or not someone else's alleged revelation really is the result of God's supernatural

121

operation.[17] Because neither dreams and visions nor their causes are publicly observable, even if we assume that a person is sincere in reporting his experience, we are in no way compelled to believe that God has supernaturally spoken to him,

> For to say that God hath spoken to him in the Holy Scripture, is not to say God hath spoken to him immediately, but by mediation of the Prophets, or of the Apostles, or of the Church, in such manner as he speaks to all other Christian men. To say he hath spoken to him in a dream, is no more than to say he dreamed that God spake to him; which is not of force to win beleef from any man that knows dreams are for the most part natural. . . . To say he hath seen a vision, or heard a voice, is to say, that he hath dreamed between sleeping and waking. . . . To say he speaks by supernaturall inspiration, is to say he finds an ardent desire to speak, or some strong opinion of himself, for which he can alledge no naturall and sufficient reason. So that although God almighty can speak to a man by dreams, visions, voice, and inspiration; yet he obliges no man to beleeve he hath done so to him that pretends it; who (being a man) may erre, and (which is more) may lie. (196)

Because dreams, visions, and similar possible avenues of revelation are only privately accessible, and their causes are not accessible at all, one may doubt not only the sincerity of another's report of his experience, but also that the experience reported is really an instance of supernatural revelation.

This being the case, we are presented with the question that Hobbes next poses, namely, "How then can he, to whom God hath never revealed his Wil immediately (saving by the way of natural reason) know when he is to obey, or not to obey, his Word, delivered by him, that says he is a prophet?" (196). We need an answer to this question if we are to reach consensus on what those of our duties to God that can be known on the basis of supernatural revelation are. Precisely which duties we take God to have revealed to us supernaturally will depend on whose alleged revelations we believe, or regard ourselves as required to acknowledge. Where different people acknowledge the precepts of different alleged prophets, they may well come to hold incompatible descriptions of their transcendent interest in fulfilling their duties to God. It is important, then, that we identify some means of discriminating between those whose dreams and visions we should acknowledge as genuine revelations, and the rest. To this end, Hobbes cites passages from Deuteronomy, Matthew, and Galatians, all of which Scriptures his readers agree in regarding as canonical, which stipulate two marks by which a true prophet may be known.[18]

The two marks of a true prophet are the performance of miracles, and the teaching of the established religion, each necessary, but only jointly sufficient, to determine whose precepts it is that God would have us acknowledge for his own. Hobbes defines a miracle as "a work of God, (besides his operation by the way of nature, ordained in the Creation,) done for the making manifest to his elect, the mission of an extraordinary minister for their salvation" (235). Hobbes is including accurate predictions of events that could not have been expected to occur on the basis of experience and scientific knowledge as a species of miracle, and holds that in such cases, the thing foretold must come to pass within some fairly short period of time, in order for the prediction to function as evidence for one's being a true prophet.

A couple of features of Hobbes's argument here deserve comment. First, the marks of a true prophet are understood to be those criteria that *God wants us to make use of* in identifying the people he is using to make his will known to us. It is a matter both of Scripture and of logic that one of the criteria he sets forth is that of underwriting previously established doctrine; God does not make mistakes, and he does not contradict himself, so he is not going to direct his prophets to preach against the established religion.[19] Because God wants us to *believe* his prophets (since he wants us to do his will, which we are in a better position to do if we hold correct beliefs as to what it is that God wills), he gives us the further criterion of performance of miracles. What we believe is a function of our experience and reason, so what better way to procure our belief than to provide us with an experience for which our reason can give no natural account? The criterion of performance of miracles thus does double duty: It indicates whom God wants us to believe, and it actually *effects* belief. God has designed our nature in such a way that (other things equal) we believe what we see, so the performance of a miracle really will cause us to believe.[20] In this way, Hobbes is able to synthesize the questions of whose claims we ought to acknowledge, and of whose claims we ought to believe, despite his formal view that beliefs are not subject to "oughts." Second, the question of how to recognize a true prophet is just the question of to whose personal revelations we ought to give credence. So we see that there are really only two distinct sources of religious knowledge, namely, natural reason and revelation, since Scripture is the accumulated personal revelations of the true prophets (or at least of some subset of these). Hobbes concludes that "it is manifest that the teaching of the religion which God hath established, and the shewing of a present miracle, joined together, were the only marks whereby the Scripture would have a true prophet, that is to say, immediate revelation to be acknowledged; neither of them being singly sufficient to oblige any other man to regard what he saith" (198). We needn't believe anyone who preaches against the established religion, and of those who preach for it, we needn't believe anyone unless he performs miracles. Indeed, we *shouldn't* recognize the claims of anyone who fails to satisfy both these conditions.

However, says Hobbes, there have long since ceased to be any miracles. And "miracles ceasing," we are no longer required to acknowledge the doctrine of any pretended prophet "farther than it is conformable to the Holy Scriptures, which since the time of our Saviour, supply the place, and sufficiently recompense the want of all other prophesy" (198). Thus, the only sources we need to employ in discovering our whole duty to God are natural reason and Scripture.

Hobbes wishes to establish this conclusion because he wants to eliminate those doctrinal differences (those differing descriptions of the transcendent interest in fulfilling one's duties to God) that stem from a lack of consensus about which alleged revelations are to be acknowledged. If we acknowledge none of the claims advanced on the basis of personal revelation, we will avoid the possibility of acknowledging – some of us one, some of us another – of the conflicting claims advanced by various alleged prophets.

We might suppose that Hobbes feels entitled to base his argument on the premise that there are no longer any miracles (and so no new prophets to be recognized) because most of his readers agree with him in thinking that Jesus, in his life on earth, completed the task of making our duties to God known to us. But Hobbes is clearly uncomfortable resting his conclusion on this premise, as becomes evident several chapters later. Even if there haven't been any miracles, or new prophets, since the time of Jesus, it doesn't follow that there won't (or couldn't) be any in the future. If God wished to speak to us, he could certainly send us a prophet empowered to work miracles; and if he spoke to us in such a way, we would want to be able to listen to him. So just to dismiss the personal revelations of others as potential sources of religious knowledge would be both foolish and presumptuous. Hobbes needs to find some other way to rule out the possibility of differences in what we believe based on differences in whom, among various alleged prophets, we believe.

He deals with this problem by arguing that even the question of whether or not a miracle has been performed must ultimately resolve into a question of whose judgment we ought to accept in such matters. As we saw, in order for an event to function as a miracle (i.e., to procure among the elect credit to God's prophets) it must be an extraordinary event for which no natural cause is known. But, as Hobbes points out, the same event may strike some as extraordinary, others as ordinary, depending upon how much experience they've had; and whether or not one takes an event to be explicable in terms of natural causes will depend on one's degree of scientific sophistication. So there may be disagreement over whether an event is to be counted as miraculous, even when we assume it has actually occurred. The matter is further complicated by the fact that people can easily deceive others into thinking an event miraculous that is in fact merely the result of natural causes, arranged by a conspiracy of frauds to serve their own ends: "For such is the ignorance, and aptitude to error generally of all men, but especially of them that have not much knowledge of naturall causes, and of the nature, and interests of men [to rule others], as by innumerable and easie tricks to be abused" (236). Hobbes seems to think this latter difficulty is the more common of the two: "For in these times, I do not know one man, that ever saw any such wondrous work, done by the charm, or at the word, or prayer of a man, that a man endued but with a mediocrity of reason, would think supernatural: and the question is no more, whether what wee see done, be a miracle; whether the miracle we hear, or read of, were a real work, and not the act of a tongue, or a pen; but in plain terms, whether the report be true, or a lye" (237). Given these obstacles to making an accurate determination of whether or not someone has performed a miracle, the "performance of miracles" criterion for true prophecy is not very helpful. If we can't know a miracle when we see one, it is as if, for us, miracles had ceased; and miracles ceasing, we can no longer be assured that anyone who now claims to be a prophet is. Even though God has set out for us the marks by which a true prophet is to be judged, in most cases we cannot trust our own judgment as to whether or not these criteria are satisfied, and different people may well reach different conclusions.

The appropriate solution, as Hobbes attempts to prove out of Scripture, is to accept the established religious authority's judgment on the question of whether a miracle has been done:

> And in this also we must have recourse to God's Lieutenant, to whom in all doubtful cases wee have submitted our private judgements. For example; if a man pretend, that after certain words spoken over a piece of bread, that presently God hath

made it not bread, but a God, or a man, or both, and neverthelesse it looketh still as like bread as ever it did; there is no
reason for any man to think it really done, nor consequently
to fear him, till he enquire of God, by his vicar, or lieutenant,
whether it be done or not. If he say not, then followeth that
which Moses saith (Deut. 18.22) "he hath spoken it presump-
tuously, thou shalt not fear him." If he say 'tis done, then he
is not to contradict it. So also if wee see not, but onely hear
tell of a miracle, we are to consult the lawful church, that is
to say the lawful Head thereof, how far we are to give credit
to the relators of it. (237)[21]

This second argument allows Hobbes to concede that there
might be future miracles, signaling future true prophets,
while still accomplishing his goal of removing personal revelation as an important source of doctrinal discord. The problem was that different people might acknowledge the
conflicting claims of different alleged prophets, and this problem is as successfully solved by referring the question of who
is to be regarded as a true prophet to the judgment of an
authority as it is by denying that we ought to regard anyone
as a true prophet. (Of course, this solution won't *really* solve
anything until Hobbes can gain agreement on the question
of who the unique appropriate religious authority is, a question whose answer must await an analysis of Scripture.)

Hobbes thus disposes of that problematic source of religious knowledge, personal revelation, with one interesting,
but ultimately inconsequential, exception. He has shown that
we needn't take seriously the alleged personal revelations of
others – that we are required to do so only when the appropriate religious authority so directs us. But suppose God
reveals his will directly to me? Hobbes holds that if I genuinely believe God has spoken to me, I would be crazy not to
do what I believe God has told me to do. "It is true," says
Hobbes, "that God is the soveraign of all soveraigns, and
therefore, when he speaks to any subject, he ought to be
obeyed, whatsoever any earthly potentate command to the
contrary" (199). In particular, "if the command bee such, as
cannot be obeyed without being damned to eternall death,

then it were madnesse to obey it" (321). This is an exception
to the rule that one should accept the judgment of the religious authority in matters of revelation, but its disruptive
effects can be diminished as greater numbers of people are
brought to see that their dreams and visions most likely have
natural causes; and the disruptive potential of those who do
believe themselves divinely inspired is quite severely limited
by the fact that no one else is required (nor even permitted,
if the religious authority does not approve their claims) to
follow them. The scope of this exception will be further limited, as we shall see, by Hobbes's distinction between what
is and what is not necessary to salvation, and his argument
that God permits disobedience to one's earthly authority only
in those of its commands obedience to which would jeopardize one's salvation (which turns out to be an empty set).
Nevertheless, it is essential that Hobbes allow this exception
because a principle that required a person to ignore God's
commands when God spoke directly to him, thereby undermining his ability to fulfill his duties to God, and jeopardizing the satisfaction of his supremely rational interest in
salvation, would be totally unacceptable to anyone who takes
his religion seriously. So far, then, Hobbes has established
what can be known of our duties to God on the basis of
natural reason, and has dispensed with the problem of conflicting duties advanced on the basis of the alleged revelations
of others. There is to this point no ground for affirming
divergent descriptions of the transcendent interest in fulfilling one's duties to God (excepting only the case of personal
inspiration, the effects of which are negligible). The only
remaining source of religious knowledge is Scripture, which
Hobbes next proceeds to investigate.

SCRIPTURE

Hobbes aims to demonstrate that his principle of political
obligation, when the "duty to God" exemption is fully specified, is one that people have no religious grounds for rejecting, and one that, if followed, would not exempt a

sufficiently large number of people from obedience to the commands of their extant effective political authority that it would be ineffective in maintaining effective social order. His strategy for doing this consists in establishing three conclusions on the basis of Scripture.[22] These three required conclusions are:

1. that one's duty to God is properly identified by the appropriate religious authority, and thus that everyone ought to profess and practice religion as the appropriate religious authority dictates,
2. that a given group of Christians is subject to only one authority in both civil and religious matters, and
3. that the appropriate authority in both secular and religious matters is one's national civil sovereign (political authority).

In proving (1) from Scripture, Hobbes will have completed the transformation of the issue of what one's duty to God is, into the issue of whose specification of our duty to him God himself requires us to acknowledge. The proper description of our interest in fulfilling our duty to God is as an interest in professing, practicing, and acting as the appropriate religious authority dictates. Neither natural reason nor the alleged personal revelations of others give us any ground for resisting this description, and Scripture affirms it. Nevertheless, if people were subject to two distinct authorities, one in religious matters and another in secular matters, then it is not clear that Hobbes's principle of political obligation, even when faithfully followed, could ensure the maintenance of effective social order; subjects might be in disagreement about which authority was to be obeyed in particular cases, (after all, commands may have both secular and religious import), and the ability of either authority to carry out its specified function might require it to claim all of the essential rights of sovereignty, resulting in the formation of multiple overlapping or coextensive authorities. It is thus essential to Hobbes's project of demonstrating the effectiveness of his principle that he establish (2), that there is only one authority to whom a particular given group of persons is subject, and it has authority in secular and religious matters alike. Yet here again, people might agree that their allegiance is to be given to just one authority over all matters, while disagreeing about who that authority is. If people do not all recognize the same authority, then there is a clear possibility of the collapse of effective social order, and Hobbes's principle would be rendered impotent in virtue of disagreement over who the extant effective political (and now also religious) authority is. For this reason, Hobbes must go on to establish (3) that the unique appropriate authority in both secular and religious matters is one's national civil sovereign (for example, the king, or king in Parliament, as opposed to the pope or the bishop of Canterbury). Simply stated, Hobbes will argue on the basis of Scripture that God requires us, first and foremost, to obey our national civil sovereign in all of its commands, including those concerning the profession and practice of religion. Thus, one's duty to God will be formally characterizable as a duty to profess, practice, and act as one's national civil sovereign dictates. Hobbes's principle would then read: One is to obey one's extant effective political authority in all of its commands not repugnant to one's duty to God as it is specified by that same political authority. Obviously, the "duty to God" restriction no longer describes a significant exemption from obedience to one's extant effective political authority, so the principle when followed ought to be effective in maintaining effective social order. And, if one accepts Hobbes's argument for how the condition concerning duty to God is to be specified, one has no religious grounds for rejecting the principle, but, rather, good religious reason for accepting and adhering to it, namely, that it states a primary requirement of fulfilling one's duties to God.

Hobbes is going to take his argument from those books of Scripture which all factions agree in regarding as canonical.[23] He will use conceptual arguments and previously established conclusions both to supplement his preferred scriptural interpretation and to defend that interpretation. As we shall see, he attempts to rest as much of his argument as is possible on an analysis of concepts and on previously established, uncontroversial, or self-evident premises, and to employ interpretations of Scripture only when absolutely indispensable. When he does make an argument from Scripture, he takes care to "ground it on such texts as are both evident in themselves, and consonant to the scope of the whole Scripture" (394).

Conclusion (1)

Now, the first of the conclusions that Hobbes seeks to establish, namely, that one ought to profess and practice religion as the appropriate religious authority dictates, is one that virtually all of Hobbes's readers would want to endorse. Part of the reason there is so much religious strife in this period is that very few people are willing to tolerate differences in religious doctrine and practice; people believe there is a fact of the matter about how religion ought to be characterized and practiced, and they believe it is part of their duty to God to see that it is so practiced in this world. (For example, in the case of Calvinists this comes out as a mandate for a "biblically directed commonwealth," in Catholicism, as an insistence on the performance of all of the traditional sacraments, affirmation of the doctrines of transubstantiation, purgatory, and so on.) Nevertheless, to the extent that people acknowledge the concept of "reforming" religion, they are, at the least implicitly, allowing for the possibility that the fact of the matter about one's duties to God, and the specifications of that duty imposed by (what they had taken to be) the appropriate religious authority, might diverge. Thus, although the desire to see that everyone in the commonwealth professes and practices the true religion drives most everyone to seek uniform practice in line with the dictates of whichever religious authority he recognizes, people are inclined when, so to speak, push comes to shove, to resist the recognized religious authority on grounds of a discrepancy between its dictates and one's true duty to God. It is for this reason, I think, that Hobbes offers an explicit argument for his first conclusion, despite the fact that many of the disputants would seem to affirm it.

Much of the groundwork for this argument has been laid in Hobbes's earlier discussions of natural reason and personal revelation. When one claims there is a discrepancy between one's true duty to God and the dictates of the heretofore recognized religious authority, on what can one be basing one's claim? It cannot be on one's natural knowledge of one's duties to God, for this includes no stipulations of required particular doctrines or practices, and no authority-independent specifications of what is to count as a violation of a law of nature; one cannot claim that the religious authority is objectionably omitting or adding religious doctrines or practices, or that it is violating (or allowing to be violated) the laws of nature. Nor can one's claim be defended on the basis of the personal revelations of others, since God instructs us to acknowledge such revelations only when they conform to the established religion and are accompanied by the performance of a miracle, but the judgment of whether or not these criteria have been satisfied belongs to the religious authority. (My own personal revelation may give me grounds for the claim that the religious authority is mistaken about one's duty to God, but it won't have any effect on other people.) But perhaps one could base this claim on information contained in the Scriptures. If the precepts of the Scriptures have independent authority, then we could use them to assess the dictates of the religious authority.

The question, then, is one of the status of the precepts of the Bible: By whose authority are the Scriptures made law, that is, by whose authority are the dictates contained in them made obligatory for Christians? One might be tempted to say it is God who makes the Scriptures law, but, as Hobbes explains, this answer bespeaks a misunderstanding of the question: As we've seen, those who have not themselves experienced a supernatural revelation can have no way of knowing that some alleged divine positive laws really are God's – they must take someone else's word for what God's positive laws are, so the question is one of whose specifications, if anyone's, we are obligated to take for statements of God's positive laws. Whose commands, if anyone's, concerning God's positive laws have the force of law for us? This is an important question to answer because once we know who it is that makes the divine positive laws contained in the Scriptures obligatory, we will be able to determine whether or not the fact of the matter about our duty to God could diverge from the specifications of that duty imposed by the suspect religious authority. If the Scriptures have *independent* authority, that is, authority that does *not* derive from their having been underwritten by the religious authority, then they might provide a basis for denying Hobbes's first conclusion, that one ought to profess and practice as the appropriate religious authority dictates. If they do not possess independent authority, then there is no basis for rejecting this conclusion.

Hobbes argues that those parts of Scripture that don't differ in content from the laws of God (the laws of nature known to us by our reason) are eternal laws that have intrinsic authority. They do not need to be "made laws" or given authority by anyone.[24] These parts of Scripture *do* have independent authority, but they cannot provide the basis for claims against the religious authority, for the reason given earlier. God's positive laws, on the other hand, cannot be identified by natural reason, so unless God has supernaturally revealed to one that some positive laws are his, one cannot know which positive laws God has given, and so cannot be obligated to obey any alleged divine positive law *except* by an authority whose commands *already have the force of law*. A person obligated to obey whatever positive laws God might make is obligated because he has covenanted, by his baptism, to have God for his sovereign and to obey God's laws; but his obligation to take *these* particular laws *as* God's positive laws depends on his having been commanded to do so by an authority whom he is already obligated to obey. A Christian who has no direct knowledge of God's positive laws cannot be obligated to take X for such a law, except if he is commanded to do so by an authority whose commands already have the force of law.

Now, in a commonwealth there is no private person whom

others are obligated to obey. Men in commonwealths are subjects of the state, but not of one another. Only a *public* authority, a public representative whom they are supposed to have (at least tacitly) covenanted to obey, can issue commands that have the force of law. So unless a subject has had God's will supernaturally and directly revealed to him, he is under no obligation to take for God's positive laws any dictates propounded to him by a private person; he can be obligated to obey those dictates only if they are commanded by a public authority to whom he is subject.

What this means is that the authority – the obligatoriness – of the divine positive precepts contained in the Scriptures is *not* independent of their having been commanded to be observed by a public authority. If the public authority capable of making them law is the "appropriate religious authority" (as it seems it would have to be because one who was not entitled to issue commands concerning religion could hardly be a "religious" authority), then it is clear that the Scriptures will provide no basis for a claim that one's true duty to God is not, in fact, what the religious authority says it is. Thus, neither natural reason, nor the supernatural revelations of others, nor the Scriptures provide any basis for rejecting Hobbes's first conclusion, that one ought to profess and practice religion as the appropriate religious authority dictates.

Nevertheless, this argument is bound to leave one dissatisfied because it does not speak to the thought that the so-called appropriate religious authority (the public authority in matters of religion) is not *really* the appropriate religious authority. But the persistence of this thought does not undermine Hobbes's first conclusion; it does not represent a denial of the claim that one ought to profess and practice religion as the appropriate religious authority dictates, but is, rather, a claim that we have misidentified the appropriate religious authority. Even if Hobbes is correct to say that the precepts contained in the Scriptures can be made obligatory for Christians only if they are commanded by a public authority, there remains room for disagreement over who the public authority in matters of religion is. A public authority is the authorized representative of a people – it must be, in Hobbes's terms, "a person" ("A person is he whose words or actions are considered either as his own, or as representing the words or actions of an other man" [80]), capable of exercising the "personal qualities" of willing, judging, commanding, and so on, and thus of representing a diverse multitude of people by unifying their judgments into a single judgment, their wills into a single will, and so on (82, 206). The question is, Who is our authorized representative in matters of religion? The first step Hobbes will take toward an answer is to argue that *whoever* this authorized representative in matters of religion is, he is *also* the authorized representative in secular matters. This brings us to Hobbes's argument for conclusion (2), that there is only one authority to whom a given group of Christians is subject in matters both secular and religious.[25]

Conclusion (2)

Conclusion (2) will be challenged by those who would claim that the church represents and properly governs the kingdom of God on earth, man's immortal soul, or men's temporal religious life, whereas the national civil sovereign represents and properly governs the kingdom of man, men's earthly bodies, or men's temporal secular life. Even granting that if a multitude of people are to be conceived as a unity at all, they must have a single representative, they might nonetheless be represented in different matters by different public authorities. There might be distinct but coexistent *spheres of existence* or *aspects of men*, governed by distinct authorities. Thus, it might be that a man *qua* man belongs to the temporal sphere and is subject to a civil political authority in all temporal matters, while that same man, *qua* Christian, is also a member of a spiritual realm, and is thus subject to a spiritual authority in all religious matters. In order to combat the claim that there are distinct authorities in different realms or aspects of human life, and so to establish his second conclusion, Hobbes must show that there is only one realm, and so there can be only one representative of a people in all matters.

Hobbes gives three arguments in support of this, his second, conclusion, each of which addresses some variant of the split-sovereignty thesis.

Sovereign of the kingdom of God versus sovereign of the kingdom of man. Those who contend that the kingdom of God is a presently existing spiritual kingdom would seem to have a basis for claiming that there are two independent governments to which men are concurrently subject: the government of the kingdom of God, and the government of an earthly human kingdom. Hobbes attacks this distinction by citing Scripture to show that the kingdom of God is properly understood as a civil government by God, on earth, of those who have consented to have God for their king, and that it does not presently exist. The kingdom of God, writes Hobbes, is not some metaphorical kingdom; it is a kingdom in the literal sense, where God is made king by the consent of those governed, and he governs them in their daily life by positive laws. Hobbes supports this contention with a brief scriptural history of the kingdom of God: It was first instituted when Abraham made a covenant with God that bound him and his posterity (over whom he had paternal dominion) to obedience to God's positive laws for the conduct of civil life, and that was renewed by Moses who, although not descended from Abraham and so without paternal dominion over the Israelites, was given authority to rule them by their own consent; the kingdom of God continued to exist until the Israelites decided they wanted a human king after the manner of the nations, and deposed God in the election of Saul. Hobbes argues that at the time of the termination of the Old Covenant, the high priest's office ceased to be magisterial and became ministerial only, and God's civil government on earth ended. God's civil kingdom on earth will be restored at the Resurrection, when God himself, as Christ, in the "kingdom of glory," will rule over the faithful on earth. It is this restoration of the kingdom of

God, says Hobbes, for which Christians pray in praying "thy kingdom come." *But the kingdom of God does not presently exist.* Thus, no one can now reasonably claim to be administering it, and so there is no possibility that subjects may be bound simultaneously to two different sovereigns, one of the kingdom of God, the other of a purely secular kingdom. Hobbes seems to think that his readers will accept his scriptural account of the kingdom of God and his conclusion, but will shift their ground in order to preserve some distinction between civil and religious authorities.[26] He thus turns to address a second version of the split-sovereignty thesis.

Spiritual sovereign versus temporal sovereign. Even if there can be no present sovereign of the kingdom of God, it might still be the case that there is now an authority in religion, distinct from the civil sovereign, whose job it is to see to the well-being of men's immortal souls, preparing them for the next life. If there were such a division of authority between temporal and spiritual realms, any rational Christian would obey the spiritual authority in cases of conflict. Recognizing this, Hobbes argues that there can be no distinctive spiritual authority for the government of the soul, with an existence separated from the body, because people do *not* by their nature *have* immortal souls, existing separately from their bodies. "The soule in Scripture," writes Hobbes, "signifieth alwaies, either the life, or the living creature and the body and soule jointly, the body alive" (339–40).[27] Mental life attends a living body and brain; when the body dies, mental life ceases. It is true that if Adam had not sinned, he and his posterity, eating from the tree of life, would have lived eternally in their bodies on the earth; but he did sin, and since that original forfeiture of eternal life, God has withheld from men the tree that would have allowed them to overcome their natural mortality. By his nature, Hobbes insists, man is mortal; but Jesus canceled that forfeiture of eternal life for those who believe in him, and at the Second Coming they will be resurrected, body, brain, and mental life, to live in their incorruptible bodies on the earth forever. Correlatively, the damned will be resurrected, judged, and sentenced to a *second* death, after which they will never again exist.[28] Thus, men have eternal life *not by their nature* (i.e., they do not have immortal souls); rather, they are resurrected to live eternally *by God's promise.* Although *after* the resurrection the faithful's bodies will be "spiritual" (i.e., perfect and "thin" or trans-lucent) and eternal, in *this* life they are gross and corruptible, so in this life there are no spiritual and eternal subjects to govern, and there can thus be no government other than *temporal* government in this life. "It is true," writes Hobbes, "that the bodies of the faithful, after the resurrection, shall be not onely spirituall, but eternall: but in this life they are grosse, and corruptible. There is therefore no other govern-ment in this life, neither of state, nor religion, but temporall" (248). There may be two so-called realms, but they are not coexistent. At present we are temporal beings living in the temporal realm, and as such can be subject only to a temporal sovereign.[29]

Temporal religious sovereign versus temporal secular sovereign. Supposing that Hobbes has succeeded in showing that there can be neither a sovereign of the kingdom of God nor a sovereign of the spiritual realm to oppose the civil temporal sovereign (since neither the kingdom of God nor the spiritual realm now exist), he must still address the further objection that there might nevertheless be two coexistent temporal authorities, one in civil matters, the other in matters of re-ligion. His challenge is to show it is not the case that the head of the church (either the pope or the head of the national church, or of any minority church) has sovereignty only in matters of religion, whereas the political authority (the king or a parliament, or a king in Parliament) has sovereignty only in the civil sphere; whoever the temporal sovereign turns out to be, he must have *both* religious and secular authority.

Hobbes begins by reminding his readers that sovereignty

includes coercive authority. No one can be said to have sovereignty in any sphere unless he has the authority to coerce behavior in that sphere, since sovereignty necessarily involves the powers of making and enforcing laws and decisions, and such enforcement requires coercive power. Ecclesiastics would certainly have coercive authority in matters of religion if they were administering a present kingdom, that is, if the kingdom of God currently existed and they were God's vice-regents on earth, but, says Hobbes, we've already seen that no such kingdom presently exists. Likewise, if the mission of ecclesiastics requires them to promulgate, interpret, and especially, enforce laws concerning religion, then they will be entitled to hold coercive power. So the question is whether or not the ecclesiastical function requires coercive power. If ecclesiastics have no coercive authority but are commissioned only to teach and preach, then they cannot themselves be sovereigns and must, moreover, be subject to whoever is the sovereign, since authority over the teaching of all doctrines is an essential right of sovereignty.

It might seem that ecclesiastics have coercive authority because they can excommunicate people, but in fact, holds Hobbes, excommunication is not an exercise of coercive force because it has no effect. It has no effect on the *eternal* prospects of either believers or disbelievers because those who genuinely believe will be saved despite their excommunication, and those who don't wouldn't be saved even if they weren't excommunicate. Hobbes writes that "he that believeth Jesus to be the Christ, is free from all the dangers threatened to persons excommunicate" because "if he beleeve that Jesus is the Christ, he hath the spirit of God [and] can receive no harm by excommunication of men" (278–79).[30]

Nor can it have any significant effect on the weal or woe of men in this life unless it is backed up by civil sanctions.[31] And although it's true that ecclesiastics have the authority to remit or retain sins, they are allowed to do so only by attending to the outward signs of repentance; if one says one is repentant and asks for forgiveness, one's sins must be remitted. Thus, an ecclesiastic has no authority to coerce behavior by threatening to retain one's sins.

We can see, Hobbes argues, that ecclesiastics have no coercive authority because Scripture says that their commission is to convert people to belief, but belief is not subject to coercion. Faith is ultimately a gift of God, worked in men by the natural operations of teaching and persuasion, which cannot be compelled by threat of force. In support of this argument Hobbes cites Paul's statement that "we have no dominion over your faith," and various passages in Scripture that liken the task of Christ's ministers to that of sowing seed or fishing (both forms of persuasion or invitation, so to speak, rather than coercion). Lacking coercive power in matters of religion, mere ecclesiastics can have no sovereignty in matters of religion.

Not only do Christ's ministers *qua* ministers have no authority to punish people for disbelieving or for contradicting or violating the precepts they put forth, Scripture further directs Christians to "obey the king and his governors, for this is God's will" (Peter), and to "put men in mind to be subject to their principalities and powers, and to obey magistrates" (Paul) even though their sovereigns be infidels. Far from having magisterial powers themselves, ecclesiastics and those whom they teach and counsel are required to obey, even in matters of religion, the civil sovereigns whose subjects they are.

Hobbes confirms this argument with a brief biblical history of authority in the Judeo-Christian tradition. Scripture shows, says Hobbes, that whoever occupies Moses' place in a commonwealth has the sovereignty, and because Moses was a civil sovereign and as such made divine positive laws obligatory for his subjects, it is the civil sovereign who occupies his place. Christ did not take away but, rather, confirmed the authority of civil sovereigns. Because there was no kingdom of God for them to administer, the apostles had no authority either to interpret Scripture or to make it law, and there existed no interpretive authority on the Scriptures until civil sovereigns became Christians. If Christ himself had

no magisterial authority (his kingdom being not then existent), then neither did his apostles, and neither can any other
ecclesiastic who is not also a civil sovereign.

To the objection that one must surely disobey the sovereign
if he forbids one to believe in Christ, Hobbes replies that
such a command can have no effect because belief can be
neither instilled nor caused to be lost by means of commands.
Hobbes writes that "such forbidding is of no effect, because
beleef and unbeleef never follow mens commands. Faith is
a gift of God, which man can neither give, nor take away by
promise of rewards, or menaces of torture" (271). Moreover,
one may, indeed ought to, obey the sovereign even if he
commands one actually to deny one's faith, because such an
utterance is merely an external gesture of obedience just like
any other, and if performed, not at one's own initiative, but
because it is commanded, is the act and responsibility of the
sovereign rather than of the subject.[32] That only the sovereign
will be held accountable for inauthentic actions done at his
command is shown by the fact that God allows Naaman, his
subject, to worship before heathen gods; from which, "we
may say, that whatsoever a subject, as Naaman was, is compelled to in obedience to his soveraign, and doth it not in
order to his own mind, but in order to the laws of his country,
that action is not his, but his soveraigns; nor is it he that in
this case denyeth Christ before men, but his governour, and
the law of his countrey" (271).[33]

Finally, Hobbes answers the objection that if his allegations
are true, then the Christian martyrs died needlessly, by conceding that many so-called martyrs did die needlessly, because one is to be accounted a true martyr (having been
obligated to die for one's faith) *only if* one actually witnessed
the Resurrection, was formally commissioned by the appropriate authority to bear witness to the Resurrection, and bore
witness to those who did not already believe in Christ. "To
die for every tenet that serveth the ambition or profit of the
clergy is not required," says Hobbes, "nor is it the death of
the witnesse, but the testimony itself that makes the martyr:
for the word signifieth nothing else, but the man that beareth

witnesse, whether he be put to death for his testimony, or not" (272). Because no one then living could plausibly claim to satisfy all these conditions, the duty to suffer martyrdom was no longer a live concern.

The three foregoing arguments directed against variants of the split-sovereignty thesis were intended to establish Hobbes's second conclusion, namely, that any given Christian is subject to only one authority, in both civil and religious matters. Taking himself already to have demonstrated his first conclusion, that one ought to profess and practice religion as the appropriate authority over religion dictates, Hobbes needs only to show who that appropriate authority is, that is, who it is that has sovereignty, in order to specify the "duty to God" exemption in his proposed principle of political obligation in a way that allows the principle both to respect people's interest in fulfilling their duties to God, and to be effective in maintaining social order. Thus, the final step in his project of redescribing his readers' transcendent interest in fulfilling their duties to God is to establish that it is the national civil sovereign, as opposed to the pope or any other church official, who has sovereignty over all matters, including the interpretation and teaching of religion.

Conclusion (3)

Hobbes supposes that he has already proved that any church official who is not also a civil sovereign cannot have any sovereignty at all, by his scriptural argument from the function of ecclesiastics as commissioned only to convert people to belief and so as devoid of coercive authority (an essential right and necessary condition of sovereignty). This means that only a church official who is the *sole* representative of a people can have sovereignty, and this entails that ecclesiastics *within* a national state, where subjects are represented by a civil sovereign, cannot themselves be sovereigns, and are, in fact, subject to that civil sovereign who represents everyone within his jurisdiction. Thus, the only person other than the head of each national state who can have a claim to sovereignty over Christian subjects is the pope as the vicar of Christ and representative of a universal commonwealth of Christians.

Hobbes reinforces this conclusion with another argument, conceptual rather than scriptural, starting from his earlier contentions that only a public authority can issue commands concerning religion that have the force of law, and that a public authority must be "a person," that is, the authorized representative of a people. A multitude of people can only be understood as a unity, as having a will, when they are represented by a single entity capable of judging, willing, commanding, and so on. A public authority must be able to command, will, judge, and the like; these are personal qualities, and in this sense it is a "person." The only candidates for public authority (that is, sovereign over all matters, secular and religious) are the church and the national civil sovereign. Now, if the church is not one person (if it is not a single entity, the sole representative of a people), then it cannot have any authority, because commanding, willing, and so on are personal qualities (can only be done by persons). If the church is a person, then it is equivalent to a commonwealth of Christians: "[A] commonwealth which (to define it) is one person, of whose acts a great multitude . . . have made themselves every one the author" (88). If the whole number of Christians is *not* contained in one commonwealth, then they are not one person (because they do not all have the same representative), and there is no universal church to have sovereign authority. If the whole number of Christians *is* contained in one commonwealth, then there is a universal church, and all Christian monarchs and states are *private* persons, subject to the authority of one universal sovereign of Christendom. So the question of who holds sovereignty is reduced to the question of whether Christian kings are sovereign under God in their own territories, or rather are subjects of a sovereign of the universal church.

These arguments, if successful, would rule out the possibility that it is the head of the national church or of some other religious faction within a nation that has sovereignty in matters of religion, and would thus put Hobbes's readers in the position of having to admit either the pope or the national civil sovereign as the appropriate authority over religion and everything else. If he had been able to convince his readers of his conclusions thus far, Hobbes would hardly have needed to present the next and final stage of his argument, for only a small minority of his fellow Englishmen would have been willing to relinquish their national autonomy to the so-called Antichrist.[34] Nevertheless, Hobbes proceeds to argue at length, in the form of a reply to Cardinal Bellarmine's *De Summo Pontifice,* for his third conclusion: that it is not the pope but, rather, the head of each national state who has complete sovereignty. Some of the evidence he musters for this conclusion *directly* supports the claim of kings to sovereignty, and so serves not only to undermine the pope's claim but also to reinforce his argument against the claims of lesser church officials to any sovereignty.

Hobbes advances two major arguments against the claims of popes to sovereignty. In the first, Hobbes repeats his contention that ecclesiastics *can't* derive sovereignty from their religious function (since that function, of trying to effect belief, neither requires nor entitles one to coercive authority, which is an indispensable condition for the possession of sovereignty), and points out what is undeniably true, that they *don't* claim sovereignty from either express or tacit consent of the people. But, Hobbes argues repeatedly, consent is the *only* possible source of sovereign authority; because all people are by nature – that is, inherently – free from political subjection, no one can become bound to obey another except through an act of his own (or an omission, e.g., by just living openly in a commonwealth, thus tacitly accepting the protection of its laws). All political obligation, even that of the Israelites to God during the Old Covenant, requires the consent of the people. Moreover, as a purely practical point, sovereign *power* requires obedience, but because no man is sufficiently powerful to impose his will on others by sheer force, the obedience that makes for power ultimately depends on having elicited the consent of those governed. Popes assert that they have supreme temporal authority in the dominions of other Christian kings *indirectly*, that is, as a consequence of their pastoral authority, because, as they claim, they could not effectively exercise the latter without also having the former.[35] But this claim, as Hobbes has argued is false: The pastoral function of teaching and preaching does *not* involve sovereign powers. It is true that popes couldn't exercise *authority* over doctrine (because authority involves a right of coercing behavior) without having authority in other spheres as well – such is the connection among the essential rights of sovereignty; but because popes *have* no authority (doctrinally or otherwise), this fact about sovereign rights has no implications. Although authority over the teaching of doctrine is an essential right of sovereignty, and so possession of sovereign authority entails authority over doctrines, a mere pastoral commission does not even imply *authority* over doctrine, let alone the other aspects of sovereign authority. Because popes do not claim to have sovereignty by consent, there is no remaining ground for such a claim. Moreover, even if they were to allege sovereignty by consent, that allegation would be manifestly implausible; in a place such as England, where others are clearly running the country, and Catholic doctrine is explicitly rejected by the majority of subjects, the case for even the weakest sort of consent, namely, tacit consent, would be preposterous.

In a like vein, Hobbes's second argument exploits the implausibility of a claim that all Christians are members of a single commonwealth. The contention that "kings and popes, clergy and laity make but one common-wealth, that is to say, but one church" is a "grosse errour," "for it is evident that France is one common-wealth, Spain another, and Venice a third, &c. And these consist of Christians; and therefore also are severall bodies of Christians, that is to say, severall churches: And their severall soverains represent them" (316). Prima facie, the case for a universal commonwealth is weak; and Hobbes has already argued against the possible buttresses of universal consent to the pope's rule, and administration of a present spiritual kingdom or realm.

But loath to rely on this empirical fact because, as he points out elsewhere, actual practice neither proves nor refutes normative arguments (107), Hobbes presents a further conceptual support for his position that there is no universal Christian commonwealth: He has also already made the case that a church, if it is to be capable of having any authority – of doing anything – must be a "person," that is, it must be capable of acting as a unity; but only if it is a *lawful* congregation can a church be a person, because "without authority from a lawful congregation, whatsoever act be done in a concourse of people, it is the particular act of every one of those that were present and gave their aid to the performance of it, and not the act of them all in grosse, as of one body; much lesse the act of them that were absent, or that being present, were not willing it should be done."[36] But because a congregation in any commonwealth that has forbidden it is unlawful, any church without warrant from the national civil sovereign is unlawful, and so, not a person, and therefore can have no authority. Because there is no single person (including the pope) who can determine the *legality* of all the various churches assembled in various commonwealths, there cannot be any universal church, and there is no one who can represent or have authority over all Christians. "And therefore a church, such a one as is capable to command, to judge, absolve, condemn, or do any other act, is the same thing with a civil commonwealth, consisting of Christian men; and is called a civill state for that the subjects of it are men, and a church, for that the subjects thereof are Christians" (248). This puzzling argument was probably more effective against Hobbes's opponents than we might suppose, since even they would have conceded that *legality* depends on the dictates of each national civil sovereign, while relying on a distinction between legality and moral defensibility to make their case; but this distinction, even if Hobbes accepted it, would not undermine his argument here.

Once a church is conceded to be illegal, it follows (from Hobbes's analysis) that it cannot be a person, and from this, that it cannot have any authority.

Hobbes supplements these two arguments with three further points:

1. Sovereign power includes the authority to choose one's successor, which national civil sovereigns (whatever their form) possess[37] but popes lack;

2. Because Christ himself had no magisterial authority, his kingdom being yet to come, and because he did not take away but, rather, confirmed the authority of civil sovereigns, then neither did the apostles have any magisterial authority, and neither can the pope. So if any church official, including the pope, has any jurisdiction at all, he holds it by appointment from, and at the pleasure of, the civil sovereign. The civil sovereign may, if he wishes, entrust the religious teaching and counseling of his subjects to the pope, but the pope does not thereby gain any independent authority, let alone sovereignty. Even in this case, a civil sovereign delegates the teaching of his subjects at his own peril, for God will hold him alone responsible for what they are taught.

3. Lastly, Hobbes says we can know by natural reason that we should obey as sovereign the head of our commonwealth. He does not make an explicit argument here, but he seems to think that we can know by our reason that sovereignty must be unitary, that is, that sovereign powers cannot be divided, and we can infer from the civil sovereign's having some of the sovereign powers (legislation, adjudication, taxation, etc.) that he must have all of the sovereign powers (including interpretation and teaching of doctrines). Why doesn't this "all or nothing" argument cut both ways, supporting the pope's claims as well as the civil sovereign's? Although in principle it could, Hobbes has already argued that popes possess *none* of the rights of sovereignty. Moreover, and perhaps more importantly, natural reason tells us that we ought not (both prudentially and morally) to act in bad faith, a species of which is refusing to obey one whom we've consented, even tacitly, to obey. Assuming, as Hobbes

does, that in living openly in a commonwealth, or in receiving the protection of its laws, a person has tacitly consented to obey the civil sovereign of that commonwealth (391), and assuming, as Hobbes does, that his readers have actually sworn allegiance to their sovereign (*B* 190–1), one would be acting in bad faith to withhold obedience from the civil sovereign in favor of the pope or anyone else.

Civil sovereigns, then, have supreme authority in their dominions, and although they will have acquired their authority by consent of the governed, both the laws of nature and the Scriptures stand behind their authority. It is in this sense that national civil sovereigns rule by divine right: Although God has not given in advance his seal of approval to *particular* rulers, as author of the laws of nature he confirms the authority of *whomever* the laws of nature require subjects to obey. "All pastors, except the supreme, execute their charges ... *jure civili*. But the King, and every other soveraign, executeth his office of supreme pastor, by immediate authority from God, that is to say, in Gods right, or *jure divino*" (296). There is no incompatibility, in Hobbes's view, between having authority by consent of the governed, and ruling by divine right.

Despite his presentation of these many arguments to support the rights of kings against the claims of popes, Hobbes appears not to feel confident of having convinced his opponents of his conclusion, and ends his discussion by insisting on the somewhat weaker (yet more firmly established) conclusion that all Christian kings ought *either* to accept the pope's claim that he is sovereign over kings, and renounce all claim to civil as well as religious government, or else take the position of head of the church in their own territories.[38] Even if Hobbes cannot demonstrate his desired conclusion, this weaker conclusion is really all that Hobbes needs to establish, given his audience. As noted earlier, very few Englishmen (indeed, no sort of Protestant, no matter what his nationality, or even many English Catholics) would have been willing to relinquish their national autonomy to any foreign power, and in the case of Protestants, least of all to the pope. So although the arguments of this section may not fully succeed in establishing the authority of kings against that of popes, to the extent that they provide additional support for Hobbes's attack on claims to religious sovereignty of lesser or independent ecclesiastics, it is worthwhile for Hobbes to include them.

Let us now review the course of this portion of Hobbes's argument, presented in Part 3 of *Leviathan*. The problem Hobbes faced was that of specifying the "duty to God" exemption in his proposed principle of political obligation in such a way that all of his readers would accept the specification as adequately capturing their transcendent interest in fulfilling their duties to God, while ensuring that the principle thus specified would not exempt large numbers of people from political obedience to their extant effective political authority. The task of identifying an effective principle of political obligation that everyone could have sufficient reason to affirm seemed a forbidding one because to the extent that people affirm divergent descriptions of their transcendent interests, any specification of the principle that excluded some affirmed descriptions would make that principle unacceptable to some people, and any specification of it that allowed all descriptions would justify a perilous amount of resistance to the extant sovereign power. As we saw, Hobbes's strategy for solving this problem was to transform the question of what particular doctrines and practices constitute one's duty to God into that of whose specifications God requires us to take as specifications of our duty to God – from one of what our duties are, to one of whom we should acknowledge as authoritative in such matters – thus redescribing the transcendent interest in fulfilling one's duties to God as a formal interest in whichever doctrines and practices the appropriate religious authority dictates. This appropriate religious authority was then shown to be the civil authority as well, and was identified as the national civil sovereign.

Hobbes began by examining what can be known of our duties to God by means of unaided natural reason, and concluded that there are no grounds based on natural reason for people either to affirm divergent descriptions of their transcendent interest in fulfilling their duties to God, or to prefer any particular practices over and against any that the sovereign power may stipulate. He next tried to establish that people have no reason to affirm divergent descriptions on the basis of the alleged personal revelations of others because those revelations both need not and ought not to be taken seriously by anyone other than him whose revelations they are, *unless* they are underwritten by the appropriate religious authority. Finally, Hobbes argued that Scripture supports the claim that one ought to take for the proper description of one's duty to God whatever the civil sovereign, who is the appropriate authority in all matters, both secular and religious, stipulates. Hobbes concluded that for most people (excepting only those who believe themselves divinely inspired) there is no reason not to accept, as accurately capturing their interest in fulfilling their duties to God, the characterization of that interest as an interest in practicing and professing religion as the extant effective political authority dictates. Moreover, natural reason and the Scriptures indicate that this is the proper description of their transcendent interest.

If Hobbes has given adequate arguments for this conclusion, then he will have shown his principle of political obligation to be both acceptable to the people for whom it is intended to hold and effective in maintaining social order. That is, he will have succeeded both in satisfactorically specifying the principle – so that it can be seen to be one that really could, if followed, maintain perpetual domestic stability – and in providing his readers with a reason from religious duty to adhere to that principle. That principle, when fully specified, would read: One is to obey one's extant effective political authority in all of its commands not repugnant to one's duty to God as specified by that same political authority. Under this description, the "duty to God" clause of the principle has, for all practical purposes, no exemptive force whatsoever; it virtually never justifies disobedience to one's effective political authority. The only case it will rule out is that of obedience to a political authority who declares what one's duties to God are, and then proceeds to command one to violate those duties; but this is an exceedingly unlikely prospect, which one would want, in any event, to rule out. So if Hobbes can get people to accept this description of their duty to God, he can insert it into the principle of political obligation (which they can now, finally, see themselves as having prudential reason to accept, since they now know it would be capable of ensuring effective social order), thereby specifying that principle in such a way that there is no reason why it should not be acceptable to virtually everyone.

In the course of Hobbes's argument that none of the political authority's commands can conflict with one's duty to God, and thus that adherence to the principle of political obligation cannot conflict with pursuit of one's transcendent moral or religious interests, Hobbes claims that one actually has a duty *to God* to obey one's extant effective political authority in all of its commands. Anyone, then, who has an interest in fulfilling his duties to God will have a religious reason for adhering to Hobbes's principle.

PRUDENCE AND SPECIAL PRUDENCE

In the final chapter of Part 3 of *Leviathan*, Hobbes attempts to derive a transcendent interest in obeying the extant effective political authority – in adhering to Hobbes's principle – from a transcendent form of *self*-interest, namely, the interest in salvation. Note that this argument is quite distinct from his "duty to God" argument. The desire to fulfill one's duty to God (which includes one's moral duties toward other people) need not be at all self-interested – one might wish to do one's duty to God just for its own sake, and not because one expects to receive any benefit or avoid any harm for it, just as one might have an interest in acting justly or benevolently, not because one thinks one will gain by it, but because one has an interest in the welfare of others or in simply "doing the right thing." Up to this point in his argument, Hobbes has not claimed that people ought to obey the sovereign for fear of God's wrath, but here, with his salvation argument, Hobbes explicitly links political obedience with the longest-run, supremely rational *self*-referring interest in salvation ("eternal felicity"). It is true that Hobbes earlier offered an argument to link adherence to his principle with people's self-interest, but that link was with self-interest *narrowly* construed, as an interest in physical survival and commodious living, and so could not establish the existence of a transcendent self-interest in political obedience. For example, those natural "punishments" that are consequent to the breach of laws of nature are not expressions of God's wrath but are mere descriptions of the natural causal effects of various actions given the way the world is constituted, and thus provide prudential indications of how men ought to act in order to secure their self-interest narrowly construed in their natural lifetime. And Hobbes's demonstration that people who want security and a commodious life have a rational reason, other things equal, for affirming his principle of political obligation, namely, that their prospects for security and prosperity are generally best secured within an enduringly stable state, and that Hobbes's principle alone can ensure such a state, does not yet even show that it is *always* in one's overall self-interest narrowly construed to follow it, let alone that one has reason to risk one's preservation in defense of it. Hobbes's salvation argument thus signals a distinct reason for affirming his principle of political obligation: It is in one's transcendent self-interest in salvation to act on this principle.

Perhaps it will seem surprising that Hobbes has not offered such an argument earlier. Given his interest in displaying the *rationality* of his principle, and given his belief that the use of punishments and rewards can be of some help in securing social order, one might have expected him to bring out the heavy artillery of salvation before, or even instead of, his "duty to God" argument. But, of course, what Hobbes's readers were primarily concerned with was fulfilling their duties to God; as I remarked in Chapter 1, they were concerned to do this even though they were predestinarians and did not believe they could affect their own salvation. And Hobbes's salvation argument is both weaker and more controversial than his "duty to God" argument and so is better deployed in a supplemental capacity. It is weaker in the sense that it requires more premises – not only that obedience to one's political authority is part of one's duty to God, but also that fulfilling one's duty to God is a necessary condition of salvation – and it is more controversial because the last of these premises is one his readers would have found questionable. With the Reformation came the notion of salvation through faith alone, that actions are either inessential or useless for procuring salvation. So Hobbes already would have to have established that obedience to one's political authority is in fact part of one's duty to God, in order even to make out his salvation argument; and to make that argument convincing, he would have further to convince his readers that actions can affect salvation, a task not easily done.

He lessens the "popish" appearance of his dual-aspect theory of the requirements of salvation by arguing that the unfeigned endeavor to obey God's laws itself counts as an action, and that this is the only sort of action he is claiming to be a requirement of salvation. God takes the will or the attempt for the deed, so the only actions that can jeopardize salvation are those done "with a seared conscience," or in bad faith. Doing, or attempting to do, what one believes to be wrong bespeaks a will to disobey God's laws, and this, says Hobbes, is sin. Sin is disobedience to God's laws, and because God takes the will for the deed, the willingness, intention, or attempt to disobey God's laws – to do what one knows or believes to be wrong – is also sin.

We can see, argues Hobbes, that nothing beyond faith and a will to obey God's laws is required for salvation, because salvation is to be denied only to sinners. If we were originally guiltless, a constant genuine attempt to obey God's laws would be sufficient for salvation. But because everyone is guilty of Adam's original sin, faith in Christ is an indispensable condition of salvation. The reward of our faith in Christ is the remission of sin, and only those whose sins have been remitted will be saved. Sinners that we are, we cannot be received into the kingdom of God unless we have faith. Nevertheless, Hobbes asserts, one must also endeavor to obey God's laws. Repentance, charity, love, and righteousness are all different ways of signifying the attempt or willingness to obey God. One renders all the obedience necessary for one's salvation if one either truly repents one's transgressions of God's laws, or truly desires to fulfill God's commands, or loves God completely and one's neighbor as oneself.[39]

Being repentant, righteous, and so on are *ways of rendering obedience* but, of course, the laws to which we are to be obedient are the laws of nature (*qua* laws of God), the political authority's positive laws, and the precepts contained in the Bible (when these are made law by the political authority). Hobbes has argued throughout that the latter two sorts of laws are underwritten by the first: The laws of nature (which are God's laws, laws of morality, and rules of prudence) dictate obedience to one's extant political authority (making civil obedience part of obedience to God) and so indirectly dictate obedience to those precepts of the Bible which the civil authority commands to be taken for law.[40]

Because a will to obey God's laws is a requirement of salvation, and God's laws dictate obedience to one's political authority, the intention or effort to obey one's sovereign is a requirement of one's salvation, and anyone who has a transcendent interest in salvation will also have (by transitivity) a transcendent interest in obeying his civil authority. Such a person can be sufficiently motivated to risk his preservation in defense of the commonwealth if his political authority commands him to. The demands of salvation give him both a transcendent interest in *following* Hobbes's *principle* (that is, in acting on the principle that one ought to obey one's extant effective political authority in all of its commands, which just amounts to obeying the political authority), and, in cases where the sovereign has commanded him to bear arms to defend the commonwealth, a transcendent interest in defending the commonwealth. This is all

Hobbes needs to complete his scheme for a stable social order. If people can have sufficient reason, and sufficient motivation, to uphold his principle of political obligation, even when it involves risking themselves, they will be able to ensure so far as is humanly possible the maintenance of effective social order.[41]

How, precisely, would adherence to the principle ensure the maintenance of effective social order? Hobbes cannot demonstrate that it is always narrowly imprudent to disobey any of the political authority's commands. But the success of his scheme for securing social order does not depend on this. He can show that it would be irrational for a person to expect to gain (in terms of his self-interest narrowly construed) by *overthrowing* the existing effective political authority, because that process will very likely involve either a war or the lapse for a time of any effective social order. Either eventuality presents a real threat to everyone's preservation, including his own: "For of them that are the first movers in the disturbance of common-wealth . . . very few are left alive long enough to see their new designes established: so that the benefit of their crimes redoundeth to posterity, and such as would least have wished it: which argues they were not so wise as they thought they were" (154). Moreover, even if he survives the conflict unscathed, there is no guarantee that his side will win, and if it doesn't, he can expect to suffer serious punishment for his part in the rebellion.

Disobedience as a means to reforms (what we would call "civil disobedience"), because it opens the way for social collapse, or at least disorder, is also too dangerous to be rationally undertaken. Hobbes writes, "They that go about by disobedience to doe no more than reforme the commonwealth, shall find they do thereby destroy it; like the foolish daughters of Peleus (in the fable;) which desiring to renew the youth of their decrepit father, did by the councell of Medea, cut him into pieces, and boyle him, together with strange herbs, but made not of him a new man" (177).

As for violating isolated laws, the prospect of detection and punishment (especially where there is an effective system of law enforcement, the need for which Hobbes repeatedly stresses) will make disobedience to most laws irrational most of the time. Of course, when one's disobedience would contribute significantly to the disruption of social order – say, in cases of organizing tax evasion or draft resistance – it might be even more irrational to disobey.

Nevertheless, there will undoubtedly be some instances in which a person can rationally expect to profit by disobedience, and in such cases there is no reason from self-interest narrowly construed to refrain. However, Hobbes's salvation argument shows that people may nonetheless have prudential reason to refrain because, as he argues, obedience to one's political authority is a necessary condition of salvation. Moreover, if one cares about acting morally or about fulfilling one's duties to God, one will also have moral and religious reasons for refraining from disobedience to one's extant effective political authority. There is thus a convergence of reasons – prudential, moral, and religious – for adhering to Hobbes's principle. In a society with effective law enforcement, there will arise very few opportunities for profitable disobedience, and when moral and religious interests are taken into account, there will be even fewer cases in which people will find it in their interest to disobey. Those few who do can be expected to have a negligible effect on social order.

Thus, the fact that Hobbes cannot demonstrate that it is *always* in one's self-interest narrowly construed to obey one's extant effective political authority does not affect the viability of his political project. Hobbes wants to ensure the maintenance of effective social order, and although I have been describing his strategy for doing so as one of providing *everyone* with a sufficient reason for adhering to his principle (and Hobbes proceeds as if this were his strategy), his project is a success if he can provide *most* people with a sufficient reason to adhere to the principle most of the time. Given the ways in which real human beings are actually motivated, virtually everyone can be expected to be sufficiently motivated to follow the principle. Thus, we see that far from evidencing a debased, narrowly egoistic conception of human nature, Hobbes's political project grapples with the problems that arise when people have interests that *override* their narrowly self-interested concerns, and, in fact, relies for its success on the fact that people can and do possess and act upon moral and religious interests.

Nevertheless, to affirm this principle of political obligation – to see oneself as having sufficient reason to adhere to it – is one thing; to risk life and limb defending it is another. Hobbes recognizes that there are likely always to be some people who will not see that they have reason for following it, or who will fail to act on the reasons they have, and who will attempt to replace the extant regime, or to create social disorder, for their own purposes. Be they internal or external to the commonwealth, these disruptive forces may necessitate not only a passive affirmation of the principle, but an active defense of the commonwealth. Hobbes believes that in general, mere passive obedience to the extant political authority will be sufficient to foil the designs of enemies internal to the commonwealth. Virtually all internal strife can be avoided if people will simply refuse to disobey the extant political authority; under such conditions would-be rebels will not be able to garner the support, in money, arms, soldiers, and sympathies, needed to pose any real threat to the current regime. Even so, there may be some occasions (certainly when foreign forces are involved) when people must take up arms to maintain their commonwealth.

If a stable social order is to be maintained, it is necessary that at least some people can be sufficiently motivated to risk their preservation in defense of the commonwealth. But the sacrifice of one's self-interest (narrowly construed) generally requires the intervention of a transcendent interest.[42] If people are to be willing to act on Hobbes's principle in the face of anticipated mortal danger, they need actually to have a transcendent interest in upholding that principle. This is part of the reason why the arguments in support of Hobbes's principle – in support of unconditional obedience to an effective sovereign – from people's potentially transcendent interests are so crucial to Hobbes's project.

Chapter 4

Hobbes's mechanism for the reproduction of social stability

> B. For aught I see, all the states of Christendom will be subject to these fits of rebellion, as long as the world lasteth.
> A. Like enough; and yet the fault, as I have said, may be easily mended, by mending the universities.
> – Hobbes (*B* 90)

We have so far discussed the major part of Hobbes's strategy for solving the problem of social disorder. Hobbes was aiming first, to identify a principle of political obligation that could, if followed, ensure the perpetual maintenance of domestic peace; and second, to provide his readers with what they could accept as a sufficient reason to adhere to that principle. If Hobbes's principle can do what Hobbes thinks it can do, and if he can persuade people to follow it, then we ought to get order. But Hobbes is concerned to ensure the continuation of order *perpetually*. This will require that not only some of Hobbes's contemporaries, but many of his contemporaries and future generations as well, be brought to the view that they have sufficient reason to adhere to Hobbes's principle. It is not enough that the people who pick up *Leviathan* be persuaded by Hobbes's argument; the insights it contains must be very widely disseminated, and reproduced perpetually, if Hobbes is to succeed in his practical political project. Part of this task will involve reproducing acceptance of Hobbes's argument for his principle – his "science of politics" – and part will consist in reproducing those interests that, when properly conceived, provide peo-

158

ple with reasons for adhering to the principle. And, of course, it will be crucial to prevent the reproduction of improperly conceived interests, interests of the sort that disrupt social order.

How are these things to be done? They are to be done through an aggressive process of education.[1] Political obedience is in virtually everyone's narrow self-interest, and it is a part of everyone's moral, and (if Hobbes's redescription argument is correct) every Christian's religious, duty; yet people have come to believe, indeed have been taught to believe, that political obedience is in many cases contrary to all of these. As we've seen, Hobbes thinks that people are powerfully moved by moral and religious interests, and that a proper conception of these interests is *essential* to the maintenance of civil order. This is because the *misconception* of these sorts of potentially transcendent interests, particularly religious interests, is primarily responsible for civil strife. Pursuing a process of socialization, or of moral education, will encourage the formation of *properly conceived* interests, and instill in people a desire to do what the satisfaction of these interests requires. A solid education of this sort will, Hobbes thinks, eliminate both the discontent and the "pretense of right" that are, in his view, necessary conditions of rebellion.[2] This makes reeducation *necessary* to Hobbes's project of building a perpetually stable social order.

A sovereign's job is to procure the safety of the people, which "is intended should be done . . . by a generall providence, contained in *publique instruction*, both of doctrine, and example" (175, emphasis added). Recall that Hobbes thought that the protection of subjects, because it is the aim of all people in subjecting themselves to commonwealths, was the definitive function of a commonwealth. This idea played a crucial role in Hobbes's argument about membership in a commonwealth, and exemption from obedience to it, in our Chapter 2, and an equally central role in his argument, presented in our Chapter 3, that the kind of "spiritual protection" the church may claim to afford subjects by means of its powers over princes is illusory. Sovereigns fail in their duty if they do not protect their subjects, and this includes protection from the evils caused by faulty socialization. Thus,

> it is against his duty to let the people be ignorant, or misinformed of the grounds, and reasons of those his essential rights, because thereby men are easie to be seduced, and drawn to resist him, when the common-wealth shall require their use and exercise. And the grounds of these rights, have the rather need to be diligently, and truly taught, because they cannot be maintained by any civill law, or terrour of legal punishment. (175)

It is the sovereign's duty to protect his subjects, but social disorder undermines his capacity to do so, and, as we would suspect, it is Hobbes's view that virtually all social disorder is the result of bad education. For example, crime is largely caused "by false teachers, that either misinterpret the law of nature, making it thereby repugnant to the law civill; or by teaching for lawes such doctrines of their own, or traditions of former times, as are inconsistent with the duty of a subject" (153). So also is the disorder that may arise upon the death of a monarch the result of negligent education, for "such inconvenience (if it happen) is to be attributed, not to the monarchy, but to the ambition and injustice of the subjects, which in all kinds of government, where the people are not well instructed in their duty, and the rights of soveraignty, is the same" (97).

Because rebellion is largely owing to faulty education, it is the educators themselves, and those by whose authority they teach what they do, who are to be held responsible for the resulting disturbances to the commonwealth: "The punishment of the leaders, and teachers in a commotion; not the poore seduced people, when they are punished, can profit the common-wealth by their example. To be severe with the people, is to punish that ignorance, which may in great part be imputed to the soveraign, whose fault it was, they were no better instructed" (183).

Although the sovereign bears ultimate responsibility for what his subjects are taught, the immediate fault lies with the universities, for the

greatest part of Man-kind . . . received the notions of their duty
chiefly from Divines in the pulpit, and partly from such of
their neighbours, or familiar acquaintance, as having the faculty of discoursing readily and plausibly, seem wiser and better learned in cases of law, and conscience than themselves.
And the Divines, and such others as make shew of learning,
derive their knowledge from the Universities, and from the
Schooles of law, or from the books, which by men eminent
in those Schooles, and universities have been published. It is
therefore manifest, that the instruction of the people dependeth wholly on the right teaching of Youth in the universities.
But are not (some man may say) the Universities of England
learned enough already to do that? or is it you [who] will
undertake to teach the Universities? Hard questions. Yet to
the first, I doubt not to answer . . . that though the Universities
were not authors of those false doctrines [which they taught],
yet they knew not how to plant the true. . . . But to the latter
question, it is not fit, nor needfull for me to say either I, or
No: for any man that sees what I am doing, may easily perceive
what I think. (179–80)

Reforming the universities so that they will teach the truth
is necessary to the maintenance of perpetual stability.

But not only is proper education *necessary* if social stability
is to be maintained: Hobbes comes very close to suggesting
that it may also be *sufficient*. Given his belief that faulty education is the root of most evil, we can understand why
Hobbes speaks as if he thought that the *mere teaching* of his
political doctrine, founded on "morall philosophy" and the
"science of naturall justice" would be sufficient to secure
social order. Having

> put into order, and sufficiently, or probably proved all the
> theoremes of morall doctrine, that men may learn thereby,
> both how to govern, and how to obey, I recover some hope,
> that one time or other, this writing of mine may fall into the
> hands of a soveraign who will . . . by the exercise of entire
> soveraignty, in protecting the publique teaching of it, convert
> this truth of speculation into the utility of practice. (194)[3]

Education in subjects' moral and civil duty will be enough
to ensure the maintenance of social order because human

beings are, in Hobbes's view, quite malleable. Our Chapter 7 examines many passages detailing the plasticity of human nature, but here we may notice Hobbes's conception of humans as tabula rasa in his reply to the suggestion that the vulgar are incapable of learning civic virtue. Hobbes writes,

> I should be glad that the rich, and potent subjects of a king-dome, or those that are accounted the most learned, were no lesse incapable than they . . . the common-peoples minds, un-less they be tainted with dependance on the potent, or scrib-bled over with the opinions of their Doctors, are like clean paper, fit to receive whatsoever by publique authority shall be imprinted in them. Shall whole nations be brought to ac-quiesce in the great mysteries of Christian religion, which are above reason . . . and shall not men be able, by their teaching, protected by the law, to make that received which is so con-sonant to reason that any unprejudicated man needs no more to learn it, than to hear it? (176–7)[4]

Education involves for Hobbes not the mere *presentation* of ideas, but also their *inculcation,* or what we might call more broadly a process of socialization. This is clear in the Review and Conclusion of *Leviathan,* where Hobbes writes: "To the Laws of Nature, declared in the 15. chapter, I would have this added, *that every man is bound by nature, as much as in him lieth to protect in Warre the Authority, by which he is himself protected in time of Peace.* . . . And though this law may be drawn by consequence, from some of those that are there already mentioned, yet the times require to have it *inculcated, and remembred"* (390, last emphasis added).

What is particularly interesting about this passage is Hobbes's assertion that this duty needs to be "inculcated" in people, even though it can be known by natural reason. This is only one of many passages in *Leviathan* where Hobbes stresses the need to educate people in their moral and civil duty, and to *instill* in them a *disposition* to do what they ought to do. Thus, although mere natural reason allows people to "see" or to know what their duties are, the *desire* to do their duty and to give it priority over other considerations (what we have been calling a transcendent interest in doing their duty) must be inculcated in them through a process of moral education.

In general, all of the passions, our desires or appetites and aversions, can be affected through education (e.g., "the difference of passions proceedeth partly from the different constitution of the body, and partly from *different education* . . . [difference of wits] proceeds therefore from the passions, which are different, not onely from the differences of mens complexions, but also from their difference of customes, and *education*" [35, emphasis added]). As we shall see in Chapter 7, many of the passions contain cognitive components in such a way that altering the beliefs involved can alter the passions themselves. And, of course, many passions may be brought into play, or rendered inappropriate, depending on what beliefs we instill in people. Through either of these mechanisms, education can have a profound impact on the passions that motivate action.

Hobbes's belief that people can be taught properly to conceive their moral and religious interests, and to regard these interests as overriding, and can develop a disposition to give them priority over all of their other interests, accounts for his optimism about the prospect of securing a stable social order. Hobbes is attempting to persuade his readers that they have sufficient reason to follow, and to encourage others to follow, his principle of political obligation, but the most important goal of this attempt is to get people to *teach* his principle of civil duty – from the pulpits, in the schools, and in the family – in order to instill in their contemporaries and in future generations a disposition to act on that principle, and to develop in them a *transcendent* interest in acting on it.

Experience itself is something of a teacher, but it is not enough. Because of the civil war, Hobbes says, people now realize that the rights of sovereignty must not be divided, and they will continue to acknowledge this only "till all their miseries are forgotten, and no longer, except the vulgar be better taught than they have hitherto been" (93). For this reason, speaking of his political doctrine, Hobbes writes,

> Therefore I think it may be profitably printed, and more profitably taught in the Universities. . . . For seeing the universities are the fountains of civill, and morall doctrine, from whence the preachers, and the gentry, drawing such water as they find, use to sprinkle the same (both from the pulpit, and in their conversation) upon the people, there ought certainly to be great care taken, to have it pure. . . . And by that means the most men, knowing their duties, will be the less subject to serve the ambition of a few discontented persons in their purposes against the state; and be the lesse grieved with the contributions necessary for their peace and defence; and the governours themselves have the lesse cause to maintain at the common charge any greater army than is necessary to make good the publique liberty against the invasions and encroachments of forraign enemies. (395)

Experience must be supplemented with the teaching of moral and political virtue, "For God disposeth men to piety, justice, mercy, truth, faith, and all manner of vertue, both morall, and intellectual, by doctrine, example, and by severall occasions, naturall, and ordinary" (228), speaking, even to many of His prophets, "onely in such manner as naturally he inclineth men to piety, to beleef, to righteousnesse, and to other vertues all other Christian men. Which way, though it consist in constitution, *instruction, education,* and the occasions and invitements men have to Christian vertues, yet it is truly attributed to the operation of the spirit of God. . . . For there is no good inclination, that is not of the operation of God. But these operations are not alwaies supernaturall" (229, emphasis added).

God has made human beings in such a way that education and experience are the two major determinants of their opinions, from which proceed their actions. It is true that for Hobbes, the passions influence action; but opinions, as we shall see, can both modify existing passions and themselves give rise to passions. This is why education can have such a powerful effect on action. And the content of the teaching is of paramount importance. People must be taught to recognize that "it is annexed to the soveraignty to be judge of what opinions and doctrines are averse, and what conducing, to peace. . . . For the actions of men proceed from their opinions; and in the wel governing of opinions, consisteth the well governing of mens actions, in order to their peace, and concord" (91). For this reason, a political authority ought not to alienate his authority over religious and moral teaching to anyone else, "for that were to deprive himself of the civill power, *which depending on the opinion men have of their duty to him and the fear they have of punishment in another world,* would depend also on the skill and loyalty of Doctors, who are no lesse subject, not only to ambition, but also to ignorance, than any other sort of men" (296, emphasis added). We can do all we need to do toward ensuring perpetual stability by systematically and aggressively socializing people in stability-reinforcing beliefs, interests, and motives.

Hobbes concludes that human beings are perfectly capable both of affirming his principle of political obligation (his principle of civil duty) and of being sufficiently motivated to adhere to it:

> From the contrariety of some of the naturall faculties of the mind, one to another, as also of one passion to another, and from their reference to conversation, there has been an argument taken to inferre an impossibility that any one man should be sufficiently disposed to all sorts of civill duty. . . . And to consider the contrariety of mens opinions, and manners in generall, it is they say, impossible to entertain a constant civill amity with all those with whom the business of the world constrains us to converse. . . . To which I answer, that these are indeed great difficulties, but not impossibilities: *For by education, and discipline,* they may bee, and are sometimes reconciled. . . . There is therefore no such inconsistence of humane nature with civill duties as some think. (389–90, emphasis added)

Education is, then, the primary mechanism Hobbes proposes for disseminating, consolidating, and perpetuating the fruits of his theoretical and religious analyses. People are to be taught Hobbes's principle, the grounds and reasons for it, and a proper understanding of their religious and moral duties, and are to have inculcated in them a concern to act on these interests that can be buttressed – indeed, made transcendent – by constructive use of the passions. And if Hobbes's principle of political obligation is, as he has argued, one that people have prudential, moral, and religious reasons for accepting, and if he is right to think that people could be given sufficient reason and, through education, sufficient motivation to follow his principle of political obligation, then he will have succeeded in providing an ingenious theoretical solution to the problem of disorder, even when that problem is conceived as one of transcendent interests.

Hobbes's painstaking discussion of Christian doctrine in Part 3 of *Leviathan* suggests that he did in fact understand transcendent religious interests to be a primary cause of disorder, and in Chapter 6 I shall present evidence that corroborates this hypothesis. But first, I want to examine the argument Hobbes presents in Part 4 of *Leviathan* – one portion of his resolutive analysis of disorder – in which he advances his project of reproducing a proper, stability-supporting conception of religious duty by explaining to his readers how religious understandings have gone so far astray, and how to prevent the like corruption of religion from recurring in the future.

Chapter 5

Hobbes's resolutive analysis, phase two: Part 4 of *Leviathan*

> If it be lawfull then for subjects to resist the King when he commands anything that is against the Scripture, that is contrary to the commands of God, and to be judge of the meaning of Scripture, it is impossible that . . . the peace of any Christian kingdom can be long secure. It is this doctrine that divides a kingdom within itself . . .
>
> – Hobbes (*B* 63–4)

We saw in Chapter 2 that the two most important implications of Hobbes's principle of political obligation were that sovereignty must not be divided and that it must not be limited. We saw in Chapter 3 that Hobbes was particularly concerned about one special form of division or limitation: the division of the rights of sovereignty between civil and religious authorities, and the limitation of civil authority by religious authority (either individual, as in the case of private conscience and private interpretation of Scripture, or collective, as in the case of authority exercised by churches conceived as independent of the state). Indeed, as I shall argue, Hobbes took the primary source of social disorder to be divisions of or limitations on civil authority of precisely this sort. It was crucial for Hobbes to persuade his readers that civil sovereignty included supreme religious authority, for "if that were not, but kings should command one thing upon pain of death, and priests another upon pain of damnation, it would be *impossible* that peace and religion should stand together" (*EL* 2.7.10, emphasis added). And this would spell disaster, because Hobbes's audience is religious (in Hobbes's view people will always be religious), and so may expect continuing disorder:

> When therefore these two powers oppose one another, the common-wealth cannot but be in great danger of civill warre, and dissolution. For the civill authority being more visible, and standing in the cleerer light of naturall reason cannot choose but draw to it in all times a very considerable part of the people: And the spirituall, though it stand in the darknesse of schoole distinctions, and hard words; yet because the fear of darknesse, and ghosts, is greater than other fears, cannot want a party sufficient to trouble, and sometimes to destroy a common-wealth. (L 171–2)

Division between civil and religious authorities, or religious limitations on civil authority, are inimical to the maintenance of social order. But a right understanding of religion shows such division or limitation to be religiously unacceptable. Hobbes's task is to bring people to a proper understanding of religious duty, and to prevent them from backsliding. We saw Hobbes's attempt to correct religious misconceptions in Chapter 3. Chapter 4 discussed Hobbes's insistence on a vigorous program of *re*education to correct civil and religious error. His attempt to prevent backsliding rests on an analysis of how it is that people came to embrace an erroneous conception of religious duty, a conception that results in widespread, recurring social disorder. This is the second phase of Hobbes's resolutive analysis of disorder, and he presents it in Part 4 of *Leviathan.*

Part 4 contains Hobbes's account of the origin and explanation of the errors that had resulted in the formation of those religious transcendent interests inherently inimical to the maintenance of social order, and in the formation, in different factions, of competing transcendent interests. His account is primarily historical and sociological, and is intended to bolster his central philosophical analysis of disorder by offering a plausible explanation of how Christians came to embrace the erroneous views that undermine order. Whereas in Part 3 Hobbes concentrates on showing *that* certain views are wrong, in Part 4 he aims to show where these errors came from. Were they brought into Christian religion, or simply left in it? And by whom were they brought or left, and for what purpose? Hobbes thinks, not implausibly, that if he can show that these errors have unsavory origins, people's allegiance to the erroneous views themselves will be further diminished.

We may suppose that Hobbes thought his readers would find it particularly distasteful that these erroneous views had been incorporated into Christian religion for base purposes, and because this is exactly what Hobbes believed to have occurred, he frames his account of how such disruptive views came to be so widely accepted as a discussion of the designs and effects of the rulers of "the kingdom of Satan" (Matthew 12.26) or of "the darkness of this world" (Ephesians 6.12) mentioned in the Scripture. Hobbes interprets these scriptural passages as referring to "a confederacy of deceivers, that to obtain dominion over men in this present world, endeavour by dark, and erroneous doctrines, to extinguish in them the light both of nature and of the gospell; and so to dis-prepare them for the kingdome of God to come" (333). The aim of those who cultivate spiritual darkness is to gain or to maintain temporal power, and Hobbes's task is to show that the spiritual errors that disrupt order were either simply not purged from Christianity or alternatively imported anew into it, precisely to this end. His account is thus partly historical, showing how and at what point the errors crept in, and partly sociological, revealing in whose interest it was that they should be affirmed.

Hobbes begins by remarking that although those who do not believe in Jesus Christ are, of course, most in the dark, the warring, bickering, and petty jealousies among Christians attest to their spiritual darkness as well. "The enemy," writes Hobbes, "has been here in the night of our naturall ignorance, and sown the tares of spirituall errors" (334) by four mechanisms: the misinterpretation of Scripture, the introduction of imaginary beings into Christian religion by incorporating the superstitious demonology of the Greeks and

Jews, the incorporation into Christianity of Greek philosophy, especially Aristotle's, and the incorporation of false or
doubtful history and traditions, such as are the stories of the
lives of the saints, of ghosts, and old wives' tales.

MISINTERPRETATION OF SCRIPTURE

The primary means by which errors in Christian doctrine
come to be affirmed is the misinterpretation of Scripture. Absent this misinterpretation they would not be so prone to the
errors that result from mixing their religion with elements of
gentile religion, "vain" philosophy, and false stories, since a
right understanding of Scripture would compel them to reject
those ideas. But once the Scriptures have been misinterpreted
to yield certain doctrines, these sources can be exploited to
support those doctrines.

Hobbes identifies the three main abuses of Scripture as:

1. interpreting it to assert that the kingdom of God is the present
   church,
2. transforming consecration, the separation of ordinary objects to
   God's exclusive use, into conjuration or magic, and
3. interpreting such scriptural terms as "everlasting death" and
   "eternal life" so as to support the view that people have by their
   nature immortal souls separable from their bodies.

The first, and most important, of these abuses serves to establish ecclesiastical independence from civil jurisdiction,
and to secure to ecclesiastics a duplication of the essential
rights of sovereignty over Christians. If the kingdom of God
is a presently existing kingdom constituted by the present
church, then whoever heads the church must hold regal (including coercive) power under Christ. This doctrine causes
great social disruption for, as Hobbes writes, "this power
regal under Christ, being challenged, universally by the
Pope, and in particular common-wealths by assemblies of
the pastors of the place, (when the Scripture gives it to none
but to civil soveraigns,) comes to be so passionately disputed
that it putteth out the light of nature, and causeth so great

a darkness in mens understanding that they see not who it is to whom they have engaged their obedience" (335).

It followed from the pope's claim to sovereignty over all Christians that the pope and his bishops held authority over Christian kings, giving rise to such doctrines as that a Christian king, to be legitimate, must be crowned by a bishop, and that a pope can release a king's subjects from civil obedience under certain circumstances. (This second doctrine, Hobbes is careful to note, was an innovation of the Fourth Lateran Council, under Pope Innocent III.) The result of this doctrine is, says Hobbes, that

> as often as there is any repugnancy between the politicall designes of the Pope, and other Christian Princes, as there is very often, there ariseth such a mist among their subjects that they know not a stranger that thrusteth himself into the throne of their lawfull prince, from him whom they had themselves placed there; and in this darknesse of mind, are made to fight one against another, without discerning their enemies from their friends, under the conduct of another mans ambition.
> (335–6)

Not only does the doctrine that the kingdom of God is the present church allow ecclesiastics to assert authority over Christians, it enables them to gain independence of the civil state. By taking the name of clergy, pastors of the church asserted to themselves a right to the tithes and other taxes that had been paid to the Levites when the Jews were God's peculiar kingdom, "by which means," writes Hobbes, "the people every where were obliged to a double tribute; one to the state, another to the clergy; whereof that to the clergy, being the tenth of their revenue, is double to that which a king of Athens (esteemed a tyrant) exacted of his subjects for the defraying of all public charges" (336). In addition to securing their financial independence, the doctrine that the present church is the kingdom of God was used to justify the introduction of a distinct set of laws – canon laws – and the exemption of ecclesiastics from the civil laws, from civil taxes, and from the jurisdiction of civil courts. Thus was created a wholly independent clergy, which claimed authority over Christian kings as well as subjects, and which "in many places, bear so great a proportion to the common people, as if need were, there might be raised out of them alone an army sufficient for any warre the church militant should imploy them in, against their owne, or other princes" (337).

The second and third abuses of Scripture serve to maintain the independent authority of ecclesiastics, and to increase their power. The transformation of solemn consecration into magical incantation in Christian rites and sacraments increases the power of the clergy because they alone can make the magic necessary to the performance of these sacred ceremonies. This transformation presupposes the existence of phantasms and imaginary spirits that must be exorcised – from people in the case of baptism and visitation of the sick, from places in the case of consecration of churches and churchyards – and a supernatural power in the clergy to exorcise them. Among these misinterpretations of the sacraments, Hobbes is most distressed about construing the Lord's Supper, which ought, he thinks, to be merely a symbolic reminder to men of their redemption, as an event of transubstantiation. This doctrine, he argues, causes people to commit "most grosse idolatry." Worse than this, it in effect gives priests the most compelling power of all, the power to *make God*. But, as he argues, the doctrine of transubstantiation is a human invention not supported in Scripture,

> For [Christ] never said that of what bread soever, and priest whatsoever, should say, *This is my body*, or, *This is Christs body*, the same should presently be transubstantiated. Nor did the church of Rome ever establish this transubstantiation till the time of *Innocent* the third; which was not above 500 years agoe, when the power of popes was at the highest, and the darknesse of the time grown so great, as men discerned not the bread that was given them to eat, especially when it was stamped with the figure of Christ upon the crosse, as if they would have men beleeve it were transubstantiated, not onely

into the body of Christ, but also into the wood of his crosse, and that they did eat both together in the sacrament. (338)

The error of interpreting Scripture to support the doctrine that people have by their nature immortal souls separable from their bodies serves further to increase the power of ecclesiastics, by giving them coercive threats of great persuasive force. Chief among these is, of course, the threat of eternal damnation, understood as never-ending torture in the fires of hell. This error also tends to both the profit of the clergy and the people's dependence on them, for "this window it is that gives entrance to the dark doctrine, first of eternall torments, and afterwards of purgatory, and consequently of the walking abroad, especially in places consecrated, solitary, or dark, of the ghosts of men deceased; and thereby to the pretences of exorcisme and conjuration of phantasmes; as also of invocation of men dead; and to the doctrine of indulgences" (340).

Naturally, the first step in Hobbes's exposé must be to show that using Scripture to support these three views is indeed an abuse of Scripture. He thus systematically considers and reinterprets those passages of Scripture alleged in support of these views. How important this task is to Hobbes is evident from the fact that here in Part 4 he repeats and elaborates upon arguments he had already made in Part 3. He argues once again that the kingdom of God ended in the election of Saul and will not be reestablished until the Resurrection, and that at that time, the elect will be resurrected, body, brain, and mental life, to live forever, not by their natures but by God's promise. The damned will die a second death, after which they will never again exist. Hobbes scrupulously replies to all Scriptural objections to his position, which replies include an exceedingly imaginative account of how the eternal torment of the wicked is to be understood:

> The fire, or torments prepared for the wicked in Gehenna, Tophet, or in what place soever, may continue for ever; and there may never want wicked men to be tormented in them;

though not every, nor any one eternally. For the wicked being left in the estate they were in after Adams sin, may at the resurrection live as they did, marry, and give in marriage, and have grosse and corruptible bodies, as all mankind now have; and consequently may engender perpetually, after the resurrection, as they did before . . . which is an immortality of the kind, but not of the persons of men . . . to the reprobate there remaineth after the resurrection, a second, and eternall death: between which resurrection and their second, and eternall death, is but a time of punishment, and torment; and to last by succession of sinners thereunto, as long as the kind of man by propagation shall endure, which is eternally. (345–6)

By this sort of process Hobbes seeks to correct the errors that arise from misinterpretation of Scripture in its own terms.

DEMONOLOGY AND GENTILE RELIGION

But that done, Hobbes turns to show how these doctrines are *underwritten* by demonology and other remnants of gentile religion, by Greek philosophy, and by false stories, and to expose who it was that brought in, or allowed to stand, these errors that constitute the spiritual darkness of Christians. In Chapter 45, Hobbes explains that the demonology that supports the doctrine of independent immaterial souls, and the idolatry that in conjunction with it finds expression in magical ceremonies, worship of saints, and the use of images and relics, are elements of Gentile religion that became incorporated into Christianity. Demonology was spread from the Greeks, by colonization and conquest, to Asia, Egypt, and Italy, ultimately infecting the religion of the Jews, and was carried into Christianity with the conversion of the Jews. Idolatry, which was explicitly forbidden in Judaism, came into Christianity through the conversion of the Gentiles.

Hobbes argues that the demonology and idolatry of the Greeks were rooted in a misunderstanding of the mechanism of visual perception. His account of sense perception and imagination, sketched in Chapters 2 and 3 of *Leviathan* and used in Part 3 to undermine claims to personal revelation, is here employed to discredit demonology. After reminding us of his, proper, account of sense perception, Hobbes writes:

> This nature of sight having never been discovered by the an-
> cient pretenders to naturall knowledge . . . it was hard for men
> to conceive of those images in the fancy, and in the sense,
> otherwise than of things really without us; which some (be-
> cause they vanish away, they know not whither, nor how,)
> will have to be absolutely incorporeall, that is to say imma-
> teriall, or formes without matter; colour and figure, without
> any coloured or figured body; and that they can put on aiery
> bodies (as a garment) to make them visible when they will to
> our bodily eyes; and others say, are bodies, and living crea-
> tures, but made of air, or other more subtile and aethereall
> matter, which is, then, when they will be seen, condensed.
> But both of them agree on one generall appellation of them,
> DAEMONS. As if the dead of whom they dreamed were not
> inhabitants of their own brain, but of the air, or of heaven, or
> hell . . . and by that means have feared them, as things of an
> unknown, that is, of an unlimited power to doe them good,
> or harme. (352–3)[1]

The demonology of the Gentiles was absorbed into Jewish religion, providing an account of evil, illness, madness, and prophecy as possession by good or evil spirits. Although Scripture does not support the claim that immaterial spirits exist, as Hobbes attempts at length to show, this doctrine was nonetheless incorporated into Christianity and used to support the practice of exorcism and, in the early church, healing and speaking in tongues.[2] Demonology reappears in the doctrine of purgatory, as well as of exorcism:

> For men being generally possessed before the time of our
> Saviour, by contagion of the demonology of the Greeks, of an
> opinion that the souls of men were substances distinct from
> their bodies, and therefore that when the body was dead, the
> soule of every man, whether godly or wicked, must subsist
> somewhere by vertue of its own nature, without acknowl-
> edging therein any supernaturall gift of Gods; the doctors of
> the church doubted a long time, what was the place which
> they were to abide in, till they should be re-united to their

bodies in the resurrection; supposing for a while, they lay under the altars; but afterward the church of Rome found it more profitable, to build for them this place of purgatory. (340)

Thus the demonology of the Greeks when incorporated into Christianity functioned to support the third misinterpretation of Scripture, namely, that people have immortal immaterial souls, with its associated doctrines of purgatory and exorcism, and gave sense to the use of incantation in the sacraments and ceremonies of the church.

The second relic of gentilism Hobbes identifies is idolatry, which is not brought into the church by mediation of the Jews, but left in during the Christianizing of the Gentiles. The worship of images involves either the belief that God, or some other spirit, is present in the physical object worshiped (which is why Hobbes takes belief in transubstantiation to be idolatrous), or that the idol represents something that although taken for a god, is in fact merely a figment of the imagination. Understood in either of these ways idolatry depends on demonology. But its effects are more specific than those of belief in demonology generally. Idolatry appears in the form of worship of saints, and the use of relics and images in worship, and in many of the idolatrous ceremonies of the Greeks and Romans whose name, but not substance, was altered under Christianity. Hobbes writes,

> The heathens had also their aqua lustralis, that is to say, holy water. The church of Rome imitates them also in their holy dayes. They had their bacchanalia; and we have our wakes, answering to them: they their saturnalia, and we our carnevalls, and shrove-tuesdays liberty of servants: They their procession of Priapus; wee our fetching in, erection, and dancing about may-poles; and dancing is one kind of worship: They had their procession called ambarvalia; and we our procession about the fields in the rogation week. Nor do I think that these are all the ceremonies that have been left in the church from the first conversion of the gentiles. (366)

The most interesting effect of idolatry, and, Hobbes thought, the reason why Scripture prohibits it, is that it leads to social disorder by encouraging the exercise of *private judgment*. He writes that

> if the people had been permitted to worship and pray to im-
> ages (which are representations of their own fancies,) they
> had had no farther dependence on the true God, of whom
> there can be no similitude; nor on his prime ministers, Moses,
> and the high priests; *but every man had governed himself according*
> *to his own appetite, to the utter eversion of the common-wealth, and*
> *their own destruction for want of union.* And therefore the first
> law of God was, "They should not take for gods 'alienos
> deos' " . . . and the second was, that "they should not make
> to themselves any image to worship, of their own invention."
> For it is the same deposing of a king to submit to another
> king, whether he be set up by a neighbour nation, or by our
> selves. (356–7, emphasis added)

Although the Scripture strongly inveighs against idolatry –
and, indeed, the reformed church had purged many of these
ceremonies and images and relics from its worship – the early
church's failure to demand the destruction of all idols had
allowed idolatry to creep into Christianity. Hobbes suggests
that the idols themselves were much admired and very
costly, and that converted Gentiles, being loath to destroy
them, simply renamed the images for New Testament figures, and kept them as symbols of their honor. From this
beginning, writes Hobbes,

> and as worldly ambition creeping by degrees into the pastors,
> drew them to an endeavour of pleasing the new made Chris-
> tians; and also to a liking of this kind of honour, which they
> also might hope for after their decease, as well as those that
> had already gained it: so the worshipping of the images of
> Christ and his apostles grew more and more idolatrous; save
> that somewhat after the time of Constantine, divers emperors,
> and bishops, and generall councells observed and opposed
> the unlawfulnesse thereof; but too late, or too weakly. (364)

Among other ancient customs left in Christianity with the
conversion of the Romans was the canonization of saints, a
process that involved giving public testimony of the sanctity

of someone after his death. Processions in which images or shrines are carried about were another, "just as at this day the popes are carried by switzers under a canopie" (365). The use of candles and torches in divine worship, as the Romans worshiped their emperors, was likewise incorporated into Christianity, and "in processe of time, the devout, but ignorant people, did many times honor their bishops with the like pompe of wax candles, and the images of our Saviour, and the saints, constantly, in the church it self. And thus came in the use of wax candles" (366).

Finally, from gentile religion came the title by which popes claim sovereignty in religion, "pontifex maximus":

> This was the name of him that in the ancient common-wealth of Rome had the supreme authority under the senate and people of regulating all ceremonies and doctrines concerning their religion: And when Augustus Cesar changed the state into a monarchy, he took to himselfe no more but this office, and that of tribune of the people (that is to say, the supreme power both in state, and religion;) and the succeeding emperors enjoyed the same. But when the Emperour Constantine lived, who was the first that professed and authorized Christian religion, it was consonant to his profession to cause religion to be regulated (under his authority) by the Bishop of Rome: though it doe not appear they had so soon the name of Pontifex; but rather, that the succeeding bishops took it of themselves, to countenance the power they exercised over the bishops of the Roman provinces. For it is not any priviledge of St. Peter, but the priviledge of the city of Rome, which the emperors were alwaies willing to uphold, that gave them such authority over other bishops; as may be evidently seen by that, that the Bishop of Constantinople, when the Emperour made that city the seat of the empire, pretended to bee equall to the Bishop of Rome; though at last, not without contention, the Pope carryed it, and became the Pontifex Maximus. (365)

VAIN PHILOSOPHY

The errors incorporated into Christianity from "vain philosophy" are of two sorts. The practice of philosophy, as it

historically developed, encouraged and institutionalized
what Hobbes took to be an impertinent disputing of religion,
with the effect of legitimizing the exercise of private judgment in religion, and fostering division into competing religious factions. Numerous mistaken philosophical views
were mingled with scriptural interpretations to support and
to elaborate erroneous doctrine.

Philosophy, according to Hobbes, requires leisure for its
development, and thus first emerges only with the establishment of secure states or cities. Its development in Greece
began after prolonged warfare had made possible the construction and prosperity of great city-states. There philosophers would hold discussions each in some particular place,
spending time "in teaching or in disputing of their opinions"
with young followers. Thus arose various sects, or schools
of philosophy, and like schools, Hobbes tells us, spread all
over Europe and into Africa.

Unfortunately, Hobbes claims, these schools did not employ proper philosophical method, with the consequence
that they set philosophy back more than they advanced it:

> The naturall philosophy of those schools was rather a dream
> than science, and set forth in senselesse and insignificant lan-
> guage.... Their morall philosophy is but a description of their
> own passions . . . they make the rules of good and bad by their
> own liking and disliking: By which means, in so great diversity
> of taste, there is nothing generally agreed on; but every one
> doth (as far as he dares) whatsoever seemeth good in his owne
> eyes, to the subversion of common-wealth. (369–70)

The schools of the Jews were likewise unprofitable, ush-
ering in private judgment and breeding dissension, and

> they corrupted the text of the law with their false commen-
> taries, and vain traditions.... So that by their lectures and
> disputations in their synagogues, they turned the doctrine of
> their law into a phantasticall kind of philosophy, concerning
> the incomprehensible nature of God and of spirits; which they
> compounded of the vain philosophy and theology of the Grae-
> cians, mingled with their own fancies, drawn from the ob-

scurer places of the Scripture, and which might most easily bee wrested to their purpose; and from the fabulous traditions of their ancestors. (370)

From the ancient schools grew universities, which Hobbes defines as the entity created when a number of public schools within a territory are incorporated under a single government. These universities were founded for the study of Roman law, medicine, and Roman religion (in the service of which philosophy also was studied). School divinity, Hobbes tells us, was the product of mixing Greek philosophy, primarily Aristotle's, with scriptural interpretation, and it was through school divinity that the errors of vain philosophy came to be incorporated into Christianity.

From Aristotle's metaphysics came the ideas of abstract essences and substantial forms incorporated into church theology to support the immortality of the soul, purgatory, hell, exorcism, the mystification of the sacraments, and the church's account of the nature of God and of spirits. Hobbes's discussion here of the mistakes involved in positing separated essences rests on the accounts of speech, reason, and science he gave in Chapters 4 and 5 of *Leviathan*. He repeats his argument, already outlined in those early chapters, that the doctrine of separated essences stems from a misuse of language. Hobbes views it as crucial to his political task that he undermine this doctrine, because belief in it has terrible effects:

> But to what purpose (some man may say) is such subtilty in a work of this nature, where I pretend to nothing but what is necessary to the doctrine of government and obedience? It is to this purpose, that men may no longer suffer themselves to be abused by them, that by this doctrine of separated essences, built on the vain philosophy of Aristotle, would fright them from obeying the laws of their countrey with empty names. . . . For it is upon this ground, that when a man is dead and buried, they say his soule (that is his life) can walk separated from his body [and] that the figure, and colour, and tast of a peece of bread has a being, there, where they say there is no bread [and] that faith, and wisdome, and other

vertues are sometimes powred into a man, sometimes blown into him from heaven; as if the vertuous, and their vertues could be asunder; and a great many other things that serve to lessen the dependance of subjects on the soveraign power of their countrey. For who will endeavour to obey the laws if he expect obedience to be powred or blown into him? Or who will not obey a priest, that can make God, rather than his soveraign; nay than God himselfe? Or who, that is in fear of ghosts, will not bear great respect to those that can make the holy water that drives them from him? (373)

From Aristotle's *Physics*, the schools formulate those accounts of the secondary causes of natural events that underwrite such doctrines as the infusion of souls into bodies and free will. The schools set back natural science by embracing causal accounts that are not in fact explanatory: according to them, the cause of an act of willing is men's capacity to will; the cause of sense experience is our sensing of sensible species; the cause of contingent events is fortune, or the occult qualities of objects; the reason why objects fall is that they are heavy: "But if you ask what they mean by 'heavinesse,' they will define it to bee an endeavour to goe to the center of the earth: so that the cause why things sink downward, is an endeavour to be below: which is as much as to say, that bodies descend, or ascend, because they doe" (375). Not only do the schools' accounts fail to advance natural philosophy, but they disguise the inadequacy, and repugnance to reason, of their theological doctrines.

Ancient moral philosophy provides fertile ground for further errors:

Aristotle, and other heathen philosophers define good and evil by the appetite of men. . . . But in a common-wealth, this measure is false. . . . And yet is this doctrine still practised; and men judge the goodnesse, or wickednesse of their own, and of other mens actions, and of the actions of the common-wealth itself, by their own passions; and no man calleth good or evil, but that which is so in his own eyes. . . . *And this private measure of good, is a doctrine, not onely vain, but also pernicious to the publique state.* (376, emphasis added)

181

Its encouragement of the use of *private judgment* in evaluating the laws, policies, and actions of the state is, perhaps, the greatest ethical error of vain philosophy, but others have more direct ill effects. The school divines deny marriage to the clergy on the ground that it is unchaste and incontinent, and that it involves activities too impure for those who attend the altar, an argument that Hobbes rejects for the reason that either it makes all marriage vice (which is absurd) or it implies that no person whosoever can be fit for the altar (again absurd), since everyone must engage in natural and necessary activities that are much more unclean. In reality, says Hobbes, this doctrine was adopted because of "the designe of the Popes and priests of after times to make themselves the clergy, that is to say, sole heirs of the kingdome of God in this world; to which it was necessary to take from them the use of marriage, because our Saviour saith, that at the coming of his kingdome the children of God 'shall neither marry nor bee given in marriage, but shall bee as the angels in heaven' " (377). And its effect, in addition to supporting the clergy's claim to administer a present kingdom of God, was to make it impossible for civil sovereigns to be priests, unless they were willing to forgo having hereditary heirs.

From Aristotle's *Politics* the school divines embraced two ancient errors and formulated two erroneous doctrines of their own. Hobbes blames Aristotle for the view that all government is tyranny, an error that encourages and glorifies the use of private judgment: "And that which offendeth the people, is no other thing but that they are governed, not as every one of them would himselfe, but as the publique representant, be it one man, or an assembly of men, thinks fit; that is, by an arbitrary government; for which they give evill names to their superiors, never knowing (till perhaps a little after a civill warre) that without such arbitrary government, such warre must be perpetuall" (377).

The second "pernicious error" out of Aristotle's *Politics* is that government should be of laws and not of men. Quite apart from the fact that laws must be made and interpreted by men, and so, of course, law is merely a means by which men rule, no law can have an effect unless people support those who would enforce the law. People can say they will be governed by the law, but "it is men and arms" to enforce the law and to deter violations of it, and "not words and promises" to obey the law "that make the force and power of the laws" (377). If people reserve to themselves a right of *private judgment* over how the laws are to be interpreted, over whether the state is adhering to them, over whether or not they will support their enforcement, and over whether or not they will obey the laws, then there will be no unified public judgment, no peaceful mechanism for resolving disputes, and no recourse in the face of disagreement but to war. People must allow, perhaps even help, their sovereign to enforce the law:

> What man, that has his naturall senses, though he can neither write nor read, does not find himself governed by them he fears, and beleeves can kill or hurt him when he obeyeth not? or that beleeves the law can hurt him; that is, words and paper, without the hands and swords of Men? And this is of the number of pernicious errors: for they induce men, as oft as they like not their governours, to adhaere to those that call them tyrants, and to think it lawfull to raise warre against them: And yet they are many times cherished from the pulpit by the clergy. (377–8)

The divines themselves contribute further philosophical errors bearing on politics, among these, that the law constrains not only people's actions but also their inner thoughts and consciences, and that it is permissible for people to interpret law themselves, particularly divine law contained in the Scriptures. Obedience to the law in speech and action is all that people can require of one another, and the only ultimate authority on what the law requires is the person who makes the law into law:

> For a private man, without the authority of the commonwealth, that is to say, without permission from the representant thereof, to interpret the law by his own spirit, is another error in the politiques... for none of them deny but that in

the power of making laws is comprehended also the power of explaining them when there is need. And are not the Scriptures, in all places where they are law, made law by the authority of the common-wealth, and consequently, a part of the civill law? (378)

All of these errors from vain philosophy tend to the disruption of social order by setting up some authority, whether that of the church or that of private individuals, counterposed to the civil sovereign. They can thus be used to justify disobedience to the state. False philosophy compounds old errors, introduces new ones, and insulates both from detection, using sophisticated philosophical argument in the impenetrable language of the school divines, "which insignificancy of language, though I cannot note it for false philosophy; yet it hath a quality not only to hide the truth, but also to make men think they have it, and desist from further search" (379). Indeed, Hobbes complains, not only have the writings of divines discouraged the pursuit of truth, but those few people who have continued to search for it have been actively punished by ecclesiastics. "But," asks Hobbes, "what reason is there for it? Is it because such opinions are contrary to true religion? That cannot be, if they be true. Let therefore the truth be first examined by competent judges, or confuted by them that pretend to know the contrary" (380).

FALSE TRADITIONS

The final source of spiritual darkness is the importation of legends and tall tales into Christianity. The tales of miracles told in the biographies of saints, and of visitation by spirits and ghosts, have lent credence to the unwarranted doctrines of purgatory, hell, and exorcism. There is, however, no reason to believe these tales, taken only on the testimony of others, and we ought thus to wonder why the Roman church allowed their perpetuation.

Hobbes's sociological explanation of why all of these errors – from misinterpretation of Scripture, from demonology, vain philosophy, and false traditions – were embraced is that it was in someone's interest that they should be embraced. In particular, having them believed was a means by which someone was enabled to gain and to maintain temporal power. Hobbes's discussion of who these "rulers of the kingdom of darkness" might be employs a very simple test. He asks "Cui bono?" or to whom did the benefit of having these doctrines believed redound? – "For amongst praesumptions, there is none that so evidently declareth the author, as doth the benefit of the action" (381).

CUI BONO?

The benefit of having it believed that the present church is the kingdom of God manifestly redounds to ecclesiastics; it entitles them to govern the church, and this, in a Christian commonwealth, gives them a claim on civil government as well. This doctrine gave the clergy not only independency of the civil state (as with the Church of England), but often supremacy:

> By this title it is that the Pope prevailed with the subjects of all christian princes to beleeve that to disobey him, was to disobey Christ himself; and in all differences between him and other princes . . . to abandon their lawfull soveraigns; which is in effect an universall monarchy over all christendome. . . . This benefit of an universall monarchy (considering the desire of men to bear rule) is a sufficient presumption, that the popes that pretended to it, and for a long time enjoyed it, were the authors of the doctrine by which it was obtained. (381)[3]

Although the Presbyterian clergy renounced many Catholic doctrines, they retained this claim to rule a presently existing kingdom. "The authors therefore of this darknesse in religion are the Romane, and the Presbyterian clergy" (382).

The Catholic clergy further asserted civil sovereignty by taking the name of sacerdotes, which title, says Hobbes, comprehends civil as well as religious sovereignty. The canonization of saints and the declaration of martyrs express the church's authority over the standing of Christians, serving to assure its power over and against the civil sovereign, whose subjects can be incited to disobedience by the church's simple act of declaring him excommunicate. Likewise, the Catholic clergy can be presumed authors of the doctrines that they "make Christ" (in Communion), have the power to retain or remit sins, and can ordain penance: All of these doctrines increase the people's fear of them and dependence on them, to the disadvantage of civil sovereigns. Their demonology and use of exorcism do the same, serving to keep the people "more in awe of their power" (383).

The doctrine that bishops receive their authority from the pope is another error authored by the Roman church, for the purpose, says Hobbes, of providing popes with loyal agents in the territories of civil sovereigns whom they can use to raise civil war against uncooperative or disobedient kings. The practice of auricular confession allows the pope's agents to gain valuable inside information. By these means popes strive to maintain their power. The pope's claim to infallibility also serves to maintain his power, "For who is there that beleeving this to be true, will not readily obey him in whatsoever he commands?" (382).

The claim that the clergy is exempt from civil laws is an invention of the Catholic clergy designed to remove any ground they have to fear the civil sovereign, while assuring them the benefits of protection of the laws and exemption from taxes. Catholic doctrines of purgatory, of justification by works, and of indulgences (not to mention tithes) give the clergy financial independence and enrich them.

The pope maintains his ecclesiastical and especially his usurped civil authority by giving others to believe such doctrines as that priests can't marry, and that marriage is a sacrament:

> The teaching that matrimony is a sacrament giveth to the clergy the judging of the lawfulnesse of marriages, and thereby, of what children are legitimate; and consequently, of the right of succession to haereditary kingdomes . . . the denial of marriage to priests, serveth to assure this power of the pope over kings. For if a king be a priest, he cannot marry and transmit his kingdome to his posterity; if he be not a priest

then the Pope pretendeth this authority ecclesiasticall over him and over his people. (383)

Finally, the absurdities of school divinity can be laid at the door of popes as well, for "the metaphysiques, ethiques, and politiques of Aristotle, the frivolous distinctions, barbarous terms, and obscure language of the schoolmen, taught in the universities (which have been all erected and regulated by the Popes authority,) serve them to keep these errors from being detected, and to make men mistake the *ignis fatuus* of vain philosophy for the light of the Gospell" (383).[4]

The authors, then, of the spiritual darkness of Christians – the rulers of the kingdom of Satan in this world – are the pope, the Catholic clergy, and any who also affirm these mistaken doctrines, including the Presbyterian clergy, and to a lesser extent, officials of the Church of England.[5] Ecclesiastics themselves are to blame for that spiritual darkness that disrupts social order and demolishes commonwealths, contrary both to the material interests and to the religious and moral duties of Christians; for "the ecclesiastiques take from young men the use of reason, by certain charms compounded of metaphysiques, and miracles, and traditions, and abused Scripture, whereby they are good for nothing else, but to execute what they command them" (386). And although England has overthrown the pope's authority, and has thus far withstood Presbyterian attempts to impose the like disruptive doctrines, it cannot be safe until people recognize, and remember, and transmit to their posterity, that they must ever be vigilant against the designs of those who would usurp authority in the name of God. For "who knows," asks Hobbes,

> that this spirit of Rome, now gone out, and walking by missions through the dry places of China, Japan, and the Indies, that yeeld him little fruit, may not return, or rather an assembly of spirits worse than he, enter, and inhabit this clean swept house, and make the end thereof worse than the beginning? For it is not the Romane clergy onely, that pretends the kingdome of God to be of this world, and thereby to have a power therein, distinct from that of the civill state. (388)

The key to social order must be to prevent these false doctrines from resurfacing. But how is this to be done? Hobbes's answer is, as we saw, ordinary, elegant, and powerful. It is to educate people in true religion, and in the principles of civil and moral duty. We have, at this point, a good start on understanding Hobbes's theory; its basic components are in place. It remains for us finally to assemble all of the pieces of the Hobbesian puzzle, including, importantly, integrating the first phase of Hobbes's resolutive analysis of disorder (presented in Part 1 of *Leviathan*) into the overall theory. But before we embark on this final stage of our project, it may be desirable to see if we can assure ourselves that we are on the right track.

Chapter 6

Theory in practice:
Leviathan and *Behemoth*

How we can have peace while this is our religion, I cannot
tell . . .
— Hobbes (*B* 73)

We have thus far constructed, by means of a close textual
analysis of Parts 2, 3, and 4 of *Leviathan*, an interpretation of
Hobbes's political philosophy quite markedly different from
the widely received standard philosophical interpretation.
Our interpretation takes Hobbes to be addressing the problem of order posed by diversity of judgment; in particular,
the problem of order that arises when factions within a society affirm and act upon competing judgments about, or
conceptions of, their transcendent interests, especially religious interests. What we have argued to be Hobbes's solution
to the problem of order so conceived, is to redescribe competing transcendent interests in such a way that they become
both mutually reconcilable, and corroborative of the affirmation of a principle of political obligation argued to be max-
imally effective in ensuring the perpetual maintenance of
peaceful social order. (And, of course, to demonstrate that
adherence to this principle is instrumentally linked to the
satisfaction of people's various other interests as well.) Both
the principle and the redescription of transcendent interests
are then to be reinforced, and allegiance to them to be reproduced, by means of an aggressive system of education.
The strategy Hobbes employs in developing this solution is
to provide enough people, at any given time, with sufficient

reason to adhere to his principle of political obligation, that peaceful social order may be maintained perpetually.

Before we go on to investigate the implications of this interpretation for an understanding of Hobbes's central doctrines, most importantly his absolutism, and of the way *Leviathan* is structured, it may perhaps be useful to see what, if any, confirmation our interpretation receives from sources external to the text itself. If there is evidence that Hobbes did conceive the problem of order, and its solution, in the manner just described, it may serve to reassure the reader that our subsequent investigation of the implications of this interpretation merits the effort we shall expend upon it.

Most fortunately for Hobbes interpreters, we have ready to hand Hobbes's own history of that particular period of social disorder he asserts to have occasioned his writing of *Leviathan*. Although we should expect *Behemoth*, given its advertisement as a historical, rather than a philosophical, treatment of disorder, to be significantly less theoretical than *Leviathan*, we ought not therefore to suppose that it cannot shed important light on Hobbes's conception of the problem of order. Whatever one's interpretation of Hobbes's philosophical analysis of disorder, it must not be incompatible with Hobbes's analysis of a concrete instance of disorder, unless one is willing to attribute to Hobbes a most extreme incapacity to apply his own theory, or to form reasonable generalizations on the basis of particular cases.

More to the point, Hobbes's express purpose in writing his history seems further to collapse the distance between a theoretical and a historical analysis of disorder. Hobbes subtitles *Behemoth* "a history of the *causes* of the civil wars of England" (emphasis added). That Hobbes's primary concern is with the causes of the English disorder is made explicit by the remark of B, the interlocutor, (who speaks in the dialogue, as does A, in Hobbes's own voice for the most part) that

> your purpose was, to acquaint me with the history, not so much of those actions that passed in the time of the late trou-

bles, as of their causes, and of the councils and artifice by which they were brought to pass. There be divers men that have written the history, out of whom I might have learned what they did, and somewhat also of the contrivance; but I find little in them of what I would ask. (58)

A history of the causes of a particular disorder, and a general analysis of disorder occasioned by that same particular disorder, may reasonably be expected to share underlying assumptions about human nature, motivation, interests, and the like. It is precisely these assumptions that form the basis for philosophical interpretations of Hobbes's political theory, and differences among the interpreters' characterizations of these that generate differing interpretations.

Should any doubts remain about the propriety of using Hobbes's historical work to aid in the confirmation or disconfirmation of an interpretation of his philosophical work, we have, again to our great good fortune, Hobbes's own view of the aim and function of a history – his directions, as it were, for how to read a history – explicitly set down in his introduction to his translation of Thucydides's *History of the Peloponnesian War*. In this work Hobbes tells us that "the principal and proper work of history" is "to instruct and enable men, by the knowledge of actions past, to bear themselves prudently in the present and providently toward the future" (6). Histories are useful, "having in them profitable instruction for noblemen, and such as may come to have the managing of great and weighty actions," because "in history, actions of honour and dishonour do appear plainly and distinctly, which are which; but in the present age they are so disguised, that few there be, and those very careful, that be not grossly mistaken in them" (4). A good history is a history that teaches moral and civic virtue by placing the reader in the position of a spectator, as if to add a further experience to his own life, from which he may draw out lessons to himself. The more profitable to posterity in this respect, the better the history. And those histories which best instruct are those which take for their topic some calamity that men have brought upon themselves, for "men profit more by looking on adverse events, than on prosperity," and "their miseries do better instruct, than their good success" (20). With remarks such as these Hobbes makes it clear that he thinks the purpose of a history of some particular event is to enable men to abstract more general principles and lessons, which they may then apply to the specific circumstances with which they are confronted. A good history, one that fulfills this function, will have to give, or at least imply, a general analysis of the problem with which, in some concrete instantiation, it is concerned; otherwise, its lessons could not be applied to circumstances differing in any respect. We can be fairly confident that Hobbes's views on the function of a history remained constant between the times of his articulation of them, and of the composition of his own history, because *Behemoth* adheres quite scrupulously to the canons for historical work laid down in Hobbes's introduction to his *Thucydides*. Assuming, then, that Hobbes wished to write a good history, we are warranted in thinking that *Behemoth* can profitably be used to illuminate Hobbes's concerns in *Leviathan*, and to evaluate the plausibility of differing interpretations of Hobbes's political philosophy.

BEHEMOTH

Behemoth is a history of the causes of those struggles which brought about a more or less continual shifting of political power from one body to another between the years 1640 and 1660. In his most brief summary, Hobbes traces the seat of ruling power from Charles I through the Long Parliament, the Rump, Oliver Cromwell, Richard Cromwell, the Rump, the Long Parliament again, and finally to Charles II. In addition to these major successions Hobbes discusses the Council of State, Barebone's Parliament, the Committee of Safety, and a brief period in which, as he writes, "the sovereignty was nowhere." His account is quite orthodox and of no particular interest to us. What is of interest is that he actually *reduces* each major phase to the dominance of one or another religious faction. For Hobbes, the English Civil War is first and foremost a religious war.

The *people* who were primarily responsible for the Civil War were, in Hobbes's view, the Presbyterian ministers. Hobbes is quite emphatic about this:

> The mischief proceeded wholly from the Presbyterian preachers, who, by a long practised histrionic faculty, preached up the rebellion powerfully . . . to the end that the State becoming popular, the Church might be so too, and governed by an assembly; and by consequence, as they thought, seeing politics are subservient to religion, they might govern. . . . (201) Our late King, the best King perhaps that ever was, you know, was murdered, having been first persecuted by war, at the incitement of Presbyterian ministers; who are therefore guilty of the death of all that fell in that war. (120)

According to Hobbes, the Presbyterian ministers instigated the collapse of social order in two ways: They sought by their preaching to weaken the king and the established church in hopes of effecting the abolition of episcopacy; and they preached doctrines that, as an unintended consequence, led to the formation of many competing religious factions. Their preaching produced both of these disruptive effects because *what* they preached was a set of doctrines that impugned the right of the king, and of his established church, to govern in matters of religion, and they were able to *persuade* subjects to follow them.

Some of these doctrines challenged the civil power directly, others, indirectly. Central among doctrines of the first sort was the view that the state must be subordinate to the church in spiritual matters. Speaking of the Scots' rejection of the Rump's plan to unite England, Ireland, and Scotland into a single commonwealth, Hobbes writes:

> A. The cause why they refused the union, rendered by the Presbyterians themselves, was this: that it drew with it a subordination of the Church to the civil state in things of Christ.
> B. This is a downright declaration to all kings and commonwealths in general, that a Presbyterian minister will be the

true subject to none of them in the things of Christ; *which things what they are, they will be judges themselves.* (217, emphasis added)

This doctrine – that the state is not to be obeyed whenever it issues a command that conflicts, in the judgment of the church, with God's commands (that is, that passive disobedience to the state is permissible when the church judges it so) – was, according to Hobbes, affirmed by Presbyterians, papists, Anglicans, and various Independent sects alike. These groups differed in their views as to who constituted the relevant church, but all agreed on this basic principle, one implication of which is that the state *qua* state does not have legitimate ultimate jurisdiction in matters of religion. Because it directly challenges the civil power's authority in matters of religion, this principle is inimical to the preservation of social order, no matter the other allegiances of the group that affirms it:

> If it be lawful then for subjects to resist the King, when he commands anything that is against the Scripture, that is, contrary to the command of God, *and to be judge of the meaning of the Scripture,* it is *impossible* that the life of any King, or the peace of any Christian kingdom, can be long secure. It is this doctrine that divides a kingdom within itself, whatsoever the men be, loyal or rebels, that write or preach it publicly. (63–4, emphasis added)

To allow the church the right to resist when *it judges* resistance justified undermines stability. Although the most obvious, this is only one of the doctrines that weakens the authority of the civil sovereign. Others do so indirectly, either by dividing the commonwealth into multitudinous religious factions, whose differing religious judgments and interests then oppose one another, or by so obscuring religious truth that men feel they must rely on the judgment of "experts" for knowledge of their religious duties, or by implying the existence of a present spiritual kingdom of God, obedience to the governors of which takes priority over any temporal obligations. Speaking of university-educated men who set out to use their private judgment in interpreting the Scriptures, Hobbes writes:

> These are therefore they, that praetermitting the easy places which teach them their duty, fall to scanning only of the mysteries of religion. Such as are: How it may be made out with wit, that there be three that bear rule in heaven, and those three but one? How the Deity could be made flesh? How that flesh could be really present in many places at once? Where is the place, and what the torments, of hell? And other metaphysical doctrines: Whether the will of man be free, or governed by the will of God? Whether sanctity comes by inspiration or education? By whom Christ now speaks to us, whether by the King, or by the clergy, or by the Bible, to every man that reads it and interprets it to himself, or by a private spirit to every private man? These and the like points are the study of the curious, and the cause of all our late mischief, and the cause that makes the plainer sort of men, whom the Scripture had taught belief in Christ, love towards God, obedience to the King, and sobriety of behavior, forget it all, *and place their religion in the disputable doctrines of these your wise men*. (70, emphasis added)

Disputation over such doctrinal details has no positive value, for affirmation of these points is not essential to the fulfilling of one's duty to God. Hobbes continues, "I do not think these men fit to interpret the Scripture to the rest, nor do I say that the rest ought to take their interpretation for the word of God. Whatsoever is necessary for them to know is so easy, as not to need interpretation: whatsoever is more, does them no good" (70–1). More importantly, this sort of disputation breeds dissension, factionalism, and, ultimately, civil unrest. If people rely on the judgment of so-called experts for their religion, and the experts disagree, diversity in judgment will lead to religious conflict and so social instability. Thus, we see that some doctrines are inherently disruptive, whereas others are disruptive only as a consequence of the contingent fact that other factions affirm conflicting doctrines.

Certain of these various disruptive doctrines concerning

religion were also held by "Papists and diverse congregationalist sects." For this reason one might suppose that
Hobbes would spread the blame for civil strife among all of
these groups. In the opening paragraphs of *Behemoth*, he lists
the various "seducers of the people" whose activities corrupted the general population, thereby effecting a collapse
of social order, and the first three groups he names are Presbyterians, papists, and various other groups – Independents,
Adamites, Quakers, Fifth Monarchy Men, and Anabaptists
(listed, it would seem from the ensuing discussion, in order
of importance). All these groups are potentially seditious
because all may attempt to counterpose some pretended spiritual authority to the civil authority, but the Presbyterians
are most at fault, for two reasons: It is their preaching that
was responsible for the formation of those many "fanatic"
sects whose differences in religious judgment led common
folk to confusion and conflict; and while proponents of the
"Romish" religion were "less quiet than they ought to have
been," they could cause relatively little direct harm in a commonwealth so committedly reformed. Indeed, for Hobbes,
Presbyterians and papists are reverse sides of the same coin:
Both contend that the kingdom of God presently exists;[1] both
counterpose temporal and spiritual government, asserting
the latter to have primacy; both engage in what Hobbes sees
as esoteric and dangerous doctrinal disputes; and each takes
itself to be the only true church. In Hobbes's view, excepting
their commendable attack on popish superstition, Presbyterians are just as bad as Catholics – and much more dangerous given English commitments, because much more
influential. Hobbes is quite explicit about this, saying of the
Presbyterians, for example, "What have we then gotten by
our deliverance from the Pope's tyranny, if these petty men
succeed in the place of it, that have nothing in them that can
be beneficial to the public, except their silence?" (217).

Now these disruptive doctrines were the result partly of
the private interpretation of Scripture, and partly of an inheritance of Catholic church doctrine and tradition, perpetuated through the universities. The universities play a pivotal

role in the dissemination of pernicious doctrines because they affect the views of those men who will have the most influence on the population at large, namely, all varieties of preachers as well as men who will share in the administration of government in one or another capacity. Hobbes holds a decidedly trickle-down theory of education and influence. Both of these groups may be expected to attempt to implement the normative views they have acquired at university, and they will be in an excellent position to do so – to persuade others to their views from the pulpit, or to legislate, adjudicate, advise, grant or withold subsidies, and to sway public opinion by publishing their documents (e.g., most notably, the Grand Remonstrance) in ways that will further their ends.[2] Any fault in the university will be magnified a thousandfold in the society.

According to Hobbes, the particular education men received in the universities of his day (education in divinity and classics) was a tremendously destabilizing force. Because university men engaged in heated doctrinal disputes and detailed scriptural interpretation, and published their disputes, the universities became the source of widespread religious dissension. Because they regarded these points of doctrine as essential to Christian faith (in Hobbes's view problematically conflating religion with divinity), university divines served to increase the power of the clergy relative to the civil power, encouraging the belief that they were experts in religion and were to be taken as authorities on the duties of Christians. Furthermore, as a result of the Roman church's incorporation of the doctrines of Aristotle and other ancients into church theology, university men studied those authors, and came to admire their "democratical principles" and to desire a less hierarchical political organization. Hobbes insisted that Greek and Roman ideas of republicanism and liberty, as these came forth from the universities, were important contributors to rebellion, especially against monarchs.[3] Most importantly, the universities perpetuated those doctrinal remnants of the Roman church that *indirectly* create conflict between church and civil government, including, for example, the views that men have eternal souls, that the kingdom of God presently exists, that church officials have their authority directly from God, and the like.

In Hobbes's view, these faults in the educational system affect everyone who passes through it, including those who become Anglican clergy. He discusses this at some length, arguing that if Presbyterians were to be judged by the official principles of Episcopalians, they would have to be found not guilty of sedition against the civil government. Nevertheless, although Episcopalians harbor doctrinal beliefs that are potentially disruptive, it was not their activities which directly precipitated the collapse of social order.

The universities play such a pivotal role in reproducing and disseminating disruptive ideological commitments that it is, perhaps, worth our while to examine a lengthy passage in which Hobbes traces their history and influence. He asserts that the universities were originally erected in order to advance the pope's authority:

> There they learned to dispute for him, and with unintelligible distinctions to blind men's eyes, whilst they encroached upon the rights of kings. And it was an evident argument of that design, that they fell in hand with the work so quickly. For the first Rector of the University of Paris, as I have read somewhere, was Peter Lombard, who first brought in them the learning called School-divinity; and was seconded by John Scot of Duns, who lived in, or near the same time; whom any ingenious reader, not knowing what was the design, would judge to have been two of the most egregious blockheads in the world, so obscure and senseless are their writings. And from these the schoolmen that succeeded, learnt the trick of imposing what they list upon their readers, and declining the force of true reason by verbal forks; I mean, distinctions that signify nothing, but serve only to astonish the multitude of ignorant men . . . these schoolmen were to make good all the articles of faith, which the Popes from time to time should command to be believed: amongst which, there were very many inconsistent with the rights of kings, and other civil sovereigns, as asserting to the Pope all authority whatsoever they should declare to be necessary . . . in order to religion.

From the Universities also it was, that all preachers proceeded, and were poured out into city and country, to terrify
the people into an absolute obedience to the Pope's cannons
and commands. . . .

From the Universities it was, that the philosophy of Aristotle
was made an ingredient in religion, as serving for a salve to
a great many absurd articles, concerning the nature of Christ's
body, and the estate of angels and saints in heaven; which
articles they thought fit to have believed, because they bring,
some of them profit, and others reverence to the clergy. . . .

[I]n the doctrine of Aristotle, they made use of many points;
as first, the doctrine of separated essences . . . in questions
concerning the estate of man's soul after death, in heaven,
hell, and purgatory; by which you and every man know, how
great obedience, and how much money they gain from the
common people. . . .

[Aristotle's politics] has, I think, done them no good, though
it has done us here much hurt by accident. For men, grown
weary at last of the insolence of the priests, and examining
the truth of these doctrines that were put upon them, began
to search the sense of the Scriptures, as they are in the learned
languages; and consequently studying Greek and Latin, became acquainted with the democratical principles of Aristotle
and Cicero, and from the love of their eloquence fell in love
with their politics, and that more and more, till it grew into
the rebellion we now talk of. (52–6)

Despite the Reformation, the English universities have retained many of the features and activities that produce grad-
uates attached to disruptive ideas, including the learning of
Aristotle, esoteric scholarly disputation over church doctrine,
and affirmation of the primacy of clerical authority in matters
of religion. The produce of the universities are faction, disaffection to monarchy, and clerical self-conceit. In sum,
writes Hobbes, "the Universities have been to this nation,
as the wooden horse was to the Trojans" (51).[4]

A second, though related, source of the disruptive activity
of the Presbyterian ministers was the private interpretation
of Scripture, the deadly introduction of private judgment
into matters of religion. Hobbes tells us that the Reformation

controversy had occasioned the translation of the Scriptures into vulgar languages, in order that people might read the Scriptures and decide for themselves which party to the controversy was in the right. But direct access to the Scriptures was bound to lead, as it did, to the (impertinent) use of private judgment, to the development of many *differing* interpretations of Scripture, and to the (prideful) presumption by each interpreter that his interpretation was correct. The Presbyterians were at once products of the private interpretation of Scripture, and, through both their example and their preaching of the doctrine "that men were to be assured of their salvation by the testimony of their own private spirit," the cause of further factionalism dividing along interpretively demarcated lines. Hobbes writes that "this licence of interpreting the Scripture was the cause of so many several sects, as have lain hid till the beginning of the late King's reign, and did then appear to the disturbance of the commonwealth" (29), that no sooner had the Presbyterians gained power than "they were defeated again by the other sects, which, by the preaching of the Presbyterians and private interpretation of Scripture, were grown numerous" (29); and this, understandably, "insomuch as there was no so dangerous an enemy to the Presbyterians, as this brood of their own hatching" (171).

Although the Reformation seemed to require it, the translation of the Scriptures into vulgar languages was, in Hobbes's view, a disaster for any sort of unity within the reformed church, precisely because it tended to corrode the authority of *any* established church, to the temptation of *any* aspiring church. The translation of the Scriptures amounted, albeit inadvertently, to a license for individual interpretation,

> whereas before, the translation of them was not allowed, nor any man to read them but such as had express license so to do. For the Pope did concerning the Scriptures the same that Moses did concerning Mount Sinai. Moses suffered no man to go up to it to hear God speak or gaze upon him, but such as he himself took with him; and the Pope suffered none to

speak with God in the Scriptures, that had not some part of the Pope's spirit in him, for which he might be trusted.

B. Certainly Moses did therein very wisely, and according to God's own commandment.

A. No doubt of it, and the event itself hath made it appear so. For after the Bible was translated into English, every man, nay, every boy and wench, that could read English, thought they spoke with God Almighty, and understood what he said, when by a certain number of chapters a day they had read the Scriptures once or twice over. The reverence and obedience due to the Reformed Church here, and to the bishops and pastors therein, was cast off, and every man became a judge of religion, and an interpreter of the Scriptures to himself. (28)[5]

Thus we see Hobbes claim that private interpretation of Scripture carries with it the same disruptive consequences as a university education: factionalism, diminution of established church authority, and an increase in the possibility of resistance to the civil sovereign justified by reference to God's will (now identified by private individuals rather than by divines). Private interpretation of Scripture leads to private judgment in religion; and, as a consequence, to *differing* characterizations of Christian duty, from which may be expected to proceed conflict, struggle, and social collapse.

Both university education and private interpretation of Scripture tend, in Hobbes's view, to produce prideful and ambitious men. A university education made those who received it confident they knew more than others about true religion or civil government; it encouraged them to view themselves as experts in these fields of study. This attitude both fostered and expressed a certain pridefulness. That the population at large also regarded these men as wiser and more knowledgeable than themselves reinforced their self-conception. More importantly, the fact that a university education could be expected to unlock doors to positions of power and influence tended to the self-selection of ambitious men; and that university men did in fact find themselves in positions of influence made for increased ambition in proportion to their increased prospects for success in obtaining their desired ends.

Likewise, the private interpretation of Scripture tended to produce men who believed they knew what God's will was, and were willing to take their private judgment as authoritative. Again, this attitude both encouraged and expressed a kind of prideful self-conceit, particularly since these people were willing to affirm their own private judgments about religion over and against those put forward by the constituted church. Once more, their prideful self-conceptions gave rise to ambition, for, as Hobbes writes,

> they that are of a condition and age fit to examine the sense of what they read, and that take a delight in searching out the grounds of their duty, certainly cannot choose but by their reading of the Scriptures come to such a sense of their duty, as not only to obey the laws themselves, *but also to induce others to do the same.* For commonly men of age and quality are followed by their inferior neighbours, that look more upon the example of those men whom they reverence, and whom they are unwilling to displease, than upon precepts and laws. (69, emphasis added)

It is in the nature of the beast, in Hobbes's view, that commitment to a religious view involves a desire that others should share it, or at least not offend against it.[6] A person with a religious commitment must be ambitious; not, perhaps, for himself, but for his religion. This is why incompatibilities among religious views have such potentially explosive social consequences. And this is why the faction-engendering disputation of university divines, and the private interpretation of Scripture with its resulting heterogeneity are like a torch to a powder keg.

As we have seen, it is Hobbes's view that the Presbyterian ministers had primary responsibility for the bloodshed and chaos of the English Civil War. For Hobbes they epitomize the worst that university education and private interpretation have to offer; they are excessively prideful and excessively ambitious. Some of them believe they are in direct communication with God, "and give themselves out for prophets by extraordinary inspiration. But the rest pretend only, for their advancement to benefices and charge of souls, a greater skill in the Scriptures than other men have, by reason of their breeding in the Universities" (114). A prideful certainty that they alone know God's will, and a limitless ambition to impose their opinions, are, in Hobbes's view, a fundamental characteristic of Presbyterians: "Presbyterians are everywhere the same: they would fain be absolute governors of all they converse with; and have nothing to plead for it, but that where they reign, it is God that reigns, and nowhere else" (210–11). Moreover, the doctrine they disseminate is wholly pernicious. Hobbes writes,

> To believe in Christ is nothing with them, unless you believe as they bid you. Charity is nothing with them, unless it be charity and liberality to them, and partaking with them in faction. How we can have peace while this is our religion, I cannot tell. . . . The seditious doctrine of the Presbyterians has been stuck so hard in the people's heads and memories, (I cannot say into their hearts; for they understand nothing in it, but that they may lawfully rebel), that I fear the commonwealth will never be cured. (73)

Presbyterian *doctrine* has corrupted the people and subverted order; and *Presbyterians* have spread the doctrine.[7] In so doing they have exhibited pride and ambition. Presbyterian ministers have made a fundamental error:

> A minister ought not to think that his skill in the Latin, Greek, or Hebrew tongues, if he have any, gives him a privilege to impose upon all his fellow subjects his own sense, or what he pretends to be his sense, of every obscure place of Scripture: nor ought he, as oft as he hath found out some fine interpretation, not before thought on by others, to think he had it by inspiration: for he cannot be assured of that; no, nor that his interpretation, as fine as he thinks it, is not false: and then all his stubbornness and contumacy towards the King and his laws, is nothing but pride of heart and ambition, or else imposture. (68)

This last passage brings us to the great distinction in terms of which Hobbes organizes his entire analysis of the attitudes behind the causes of the collapse of social order: pride versus imposture, self-conceit versus hypocrisy, folly versus iniquity, injustice, baseness, falsity. If the Presbyterian ministers *really believe* that they alone know God's will (which, in Hobbes's view, they cannot be warranted in believing), then their dissemination of disruptive doctrine and calls to action on it proceed from pride of heart and self-conceit; if they do *not* really believe what they preach but are acting merely from personal ambition, they are hypocrites. Likewise, if the parliamentarians who are resisting constituted authority genuinely believe their university education certifies them the wisest to rule, they are vainglorious; if they believe that their disruptive actions will conduce to the welfare of the people, they are fools; and if they *don't* believe these things, but are acting from personal ambition, they are iniquitous and unjust. In Hobbes's view, any activity that threatens the unity of the commonwealth is folly, but such acts of imprudence may be performed out of personal ambition, unfounded self-conceit, or simple ignorance of the consequences of one's act. Hobbes holds that although ignorance of consequences among those who *followed* the Presbyterian ministers and "democratical" members of Parliament *allowed* social order to collapse because it made them easy to be "seduced" and "corrupted" by those groups (that is, had the followers of those groups not been ignorant, those groups would not have had the support needed to be able to bring down the state), their ignorance did not *cause* the collapse; the cause of the Civil War was the promulgation of disruptive doctrine, moved by the pride, ambition, and injustice of the instigators of the rebellion. In the opening paragraph of *Behemoth* Hobbes writes:

> If in time, as in place, there were degrees of high and low, I verily believe that the highest of time would be that which passed between 1640 and 1660. For he that thence, as from the Devil's Mountain, should have looked upon the world

and observed the actions of men, especially in England, might have had a prospect of all kinds of injustice, and of all kinds of folly, that the world could afford, and how they were produced by their hypocrisy and self-conceit, whereof the one is double iniquity, and the other double folly. (3)

After a brief discussion of papacy and the rise of the universities, Hobbes introduces his discussion of the rise to power of the Presbyterians, suggesting that both they and their university fellows in Parliament acted from conceit-based ambition:

It was not their own art alone that did it, but they had the concurrence of a great many gentlemen, that did no less desire a popular government in the civil state than these ministers did in the Church. And as these did in the pulpit draw the people to their opinions, and to a dislike of the Church-government, Canons, and Common-prayerbook, so did the other make them in love with democracy by their harangues in the Parliament. . . . And as the Presbyterians brought with them into their churches their divinity from the universities, so did many of the gentlemen bring their politics from thence into the Parliament. . . . And though it be not likely that all of them did it out of malice, but many of them out of error, yet certainly the chief leaders were ambitious ministers and ambitious gentlemen; the ministers envying the authority of bishops, whom they thought less learned; and the gentlemen envying the privy-council . . . whom they thought less wise than themselves. For it is a hard matter for men, who do all think highly of their own wits, when they have also acquired the learning of the university, to be persuaded that they want any ability requisite for the government of a commonwealth. (30–1)

To summarize, then, Hobbes argues that the primary cause of the English Civil War was religious dissension created by the erroneous doctrines of Presbyterian ministers, whose divinity disputation and preaching against the state church caused further religious factionalism, and whose ambition expressed a prideful self-conceit resulting from their university education, private interpretation of Scripture, and pretense of divine inspiration. They were aided by members of

the Parliament (many themselves Presbyterians) who, in virtue of their university educations in the politics of the Ancients, thought themselves best qualified to govern and so
desired to increase their authority in relation to the crown;
some even attempted to bring about a popular government
so that they might invest themselves with the entire sovereign authority. These groups gained support for themselves,
and an ear for their harmful doctrines, by charging the king
and his government with the intention to restore the papacy,
to the horror of the general population; and this was the
most effective possible tool to achieve their aims.[8] Yet they
could not effect any stable alternative government because
they were themselves divided into competing religious factions that vied for power causing continuous upheaval and
shifting of authority. Moreover, in attempting to divide and
limit the former sovereign power, they endorsed and disseminated doctrines that undermined their *own* ability to
claim sovereign authority, because these doctrines were inimical to *all* sovereignty. In general, the actions of these
groups may be divided into those imprudent actions which
proceeded from self-conceit or naiveté, and those unjust,
hypocritical, or iniquitous actions which proceeded from personal ambition:

> I think you need not now have a catalogue, either of the vices,
> or of the crimes, or of the follies, of the greatest part of them
> that composed the Long Parliament; than which greater can-
> not be in the world. What greater vices than irreligion, hy-
> pocrisy, avarice and cruelty; which have appeared so
> eminently in the actions of Presbyterian members, and Pres-
> byterian ministers? What greater crimes than blaspheming and
> killing God's anointed; which was done by the hands of the
> Independents; but by the folly and first treason of the Pres-
> byterians who betrayed and sold him to his murderers? Nor
> was it a little folly in the Lords, not to see that by the taking
> away of the King's power they lost withal their own privileges;
> or to think themselves, either for number or judgment, any
> way a considerable assistance to the House of Commons. And
> for those men who had skill in the laws, it was no great sign

of understanding not to perceive that the laws of the land were made by the King, to oblige his subjects to peace and justice, and not to oblige himself that made them. And lastly and generally, all men are fools which pull down anything which does them good, before they have set up something better in its place. He that would set up democracy with an army, should have an army to maintain it; but these men did it, when those men had the army that were resolved to pull it down. To these follies I might add the folly of those fine men, which out of their reading of Tully, Seneca, or other anti-monarchics, think themselves sufficient politicians, and show their discontents when they are not called to the management of the state, and turn from one side to another upon every neglect they fancy from the King or his enemies. (195–6)

We have seen Hobbes's analysis of the causes of the English Civil War. What is his prescription for preventing the like social collapse in the future? The simple answer is, to reform the universities. We see this in an exchange between Hobbes's discussants:

B. For aught I see, all the states of Christendom will be subject to these fits of rebellion, as long as the world lasteth.
A. Like enough; and yet the fault, as I have said, may be easily mended, by mending the Universities. (90)

Any attempt by *force* permanently to suppress pernicious doctrines, or permanently to contain those who affirm them, is bound to fail; people must *give up* these disruptive doctrines. And that can only be done by reeducating the people, starting (as is required by Hobbes's trickle-down theory of education) with a reeducation of men in the universities.[9] The universities must be reformed so that they no longer produce men of influence who hold disruptive beliefs. This is because, as we've seen, the actions of men proceed from their opinions (L 91), and men with disruptive opinions *will* act disruptively, whenever they think they can further their ends.[10] Hobbes writes,

I despair of any lasting peace amongst ourselves, till the Universities here shall bend and direct their studies . . . to the teaching of absolute obedience to the laws of the King, and to his public edicts under the Great Seal of England. *For I make no doubt, but that solid reason, backed with the authority of so many learned men, will more prevail for the keeping of us in peace within ourselves, than any victory can do over the rebels.* (71, emphasis added)

Hobbes's program for reforming the universities is to teach in them the results of his "science of justice." What these conclusions are becomes evident a bit farther on in his discussion, where Hobbes gives what may be the clearest and most striking account by implication to appear in any of his writings of the mistaken beliefs that had caused disorder:

The core of rebellion, as you have seen by this, and read of other rebellions, are the Universities; which nevertheless are not to be cast away, but to be better disciplined: that is to say, that the politics there taught be made to be, as true politics should be, such as are fit to make men know, that it is their duty to obey all laws whatsoever that shall by the authority of the King be enacted, till by the same authority they shall be repealed; such as are fit to make men understand, that the civil laws are God's laws, as they that make them are by God appointed to make them, and to make men know, that the people and the Church are one thing, and have but one head, the King; and that no man has title to govern under him, that has it not from him; that the King owes his crown to God only, and to no man, ecclesiastic or other; and that the religion they teach there, be a quiet waiting for the coming again of our blessed Saviour, and in the mean time a resolution to obey the King's laws, which also are God's laws; to injure no man, to be in charity with all men, to cherish the poor and sick, and to live soberly and free from scandal; without mingling our religion with points of natural philosophy, as freedom of will, incorporeal substance, everlasting nows, ubiquities, hypostases, which the people understand not, nor will ever care for. When the Universities shall be thus disciplined, there will come out of them, from time to time, well-principled preachers, and they that are now ill-principled, from time to time fall away. (74–5)

In the passage immediately following this that I have just quoted, the interlocutor reiterates and underscores Hobbes's contention that it is necessary to the maintenance of peaceful social order that people be reeducated in religious, moral, and civic duty:

> I think it [reformation of the universities] a very good course, and perhaps the only one that can make our peace amongst ourselves constant. For if men know not their duty, what is there that can force them to obey the laws? An army, you will say. But what shall force the army? . . . I am therefore of your opinion, both that men may be brought to a love of obedience by preachers and gentlemen that imbibe good principles in their youth at the Universities, and also that *we never shall have a lasting peace, till the Universities themselves be in such manner, as you have said, reformed.* (75, emphasis added)

Given Hobbes's contention that the Presbyterian ministers' preaching produced widespread religious dissension, and resistance by religious factions to the crown, and so brought about social collapse, it is clear that the prevention of further disorder will require that people be *disabused of the doctrines* that the Presbyterians preached. These included, as we've seen, the claims that the religious and civil authority were distinct, and the latter subordinate to the former; that the kingdom of God presently exists; that disobedience is justified in the name of religion; and that men are to *decide for themselves* what God's will is, by the private interpretation of Scripture, and then to act according to their consciences, that is, according to their own *private judgment*. If people believe these things, then their religious interests, especially when these are transcendent, may move them to disruptive action. These false doctrines are to be eradicated by reforming the universities so that they teach what Hobbes has identified as true religion, and moral and political virtue.

What is crucial to note is that in Hobbes's view, *no amount of force nor any military victory will secure the peace until people give up these doctrines. Force alone cannot be sufficient. But it does have a role. The proper role of force is to rob would-be rebels and reformers of any hope of success.[11]

What will deter ambitious and prideful men from acting disruptively is a clear perception that they cannot succeed in their designs. So long as they think they have hope of success, they may be willing to risk their lives in pursuit of their ends. The prospect of personal harm, if it is for a good reason and will further their ends, will not deter them; but there is no advantage to risking personal harm when their actions will make no difference to their cause. Even transcendent interests will not motivate action that is perceived to be futile. The way to crush people's hopes of success is to take away their potential base of support, by reeducating in their duty those who might be tempted to follow them: "For ambition can do little without hands, and few hands it would have, if the common people were as diligently instructed in the true principles of their duty, as they are terrified and amazed by preachers, with fruitless and dangerous doctrines" (90).[12]

Of course, this reeducation will ultimately require a reformation of the universities, but some progress can be made, particularly in those periods immediately following social collapse when experience has "opened man's eyes," by publishing and publicizing true principles of moral and civic virtue (as Hobbes has done). But assuming that disruptive religious groups will resist any attempt to reform the universities, force will also be required to effect a reformation of the universities. The order of business, then, is first to muster enough power to bring about the reformation of the universities (enough force so that resisters can have no hope of preventing the reforms), and then to reeducate people so that they and future generations no longer affirm those doctrines action upon which causes the collapse of social order. This process becomes possible in the wake of social collapse, when the common people have suffered enough, and have become sufficiently disillusioned that they will passively support the reorganizational program of a strong state. Speaking of the diseased state of the commonwealth that has resulted from the seditious doctrine of the Presbyterians, Hobbes says:

The two great virtues, that were severally in Henry VII and Henry VIII, when they shall be jointly in one King, will easily cure it. That of Henry VII was, without much noise of the people to fill his coffers; that of Henry VIII was an early severity; but this without the former cannot be exercized. . . . I would have him [the king] have money enough readily to raise an army able to suppress any rebellion, *and to take from his enemies all hope of success, that they may not dare to trouble him in the reformation of the Universities;* but to put none to death without the actual committing such crimes as are already made capital by the laws. (73–4, emphasis added)

The primary role of force is to aid in the reformation of the universities. *This* is how force most contributes to social order. What is essential to lasting peace is that people cease to hold disruptive beliefs, or at minimum, that those few people who retain belief in disruptive doctrines be made to perceive clearly that they have no hope of success in imposing their religious (or political) conceptions on others. Both of these conditions necessary to lasting peace require an aggressive and extensive process of reeducation, the institution of which will rely, in part, on the exercise of force. Assuming that some people will possess ulterior motives for holding their disruptive views, which will make them unamenable to correction through rational and reasonable argument alone, force will be required to effect a reformation of the universities, and so will, in this sense, be a necessary condition of the establishment of conditions for the perpetual maintenance of social order. But force could never be sufficient to establish a stable social order; and it could never be sufficient to maintain peaceful social order. In Hobbes's view, not only is sheer might incapable of keeping down all of the people all of the time, but it is unlikely to keep down *anyone* who affirms a disruptive belief when he sees a possibility that his actions will further his transcendent interests. It is not might that makes order but, rather, education according to sound principles. Poor education is the cause of the disease of social disorder; education in the principles of true religion and right reason is the cure. The sword has a role to play, but it requires Hobbes's science as its scabbard, in order not to be always unsheathed.[13]

IMPLICATIONS FOR INTERPRETATION

We have seen the analysis Hobbes gives in *Behemoth* of the causes of the English Civil War, and his prescription for the establishment and maintenance of peace. What light does this analysis shed on Hobbes's political philosophy? And to what extent does it confirm our interpretation of that political philosophy? To the first question, we shall answer that it justifies our contention that *Behemoth* is indeed a concrete instantiation of the philosophical problem and solution presented in *Leviathan*, and thus can be used to determine the proper emphasis of Hobbes's political theory, including such questions as the relative importance of its various premises, and the proper role and scope of particular arguments within the theory.

Behemoth and *Leviathan* give parallel analyses of disorder and its remedy, but in differing degrees of specificity. For example, the causes of social collapse articulated as general principles in *Leviathan* appear in *Behemoth* as concretely specified causes of the English Civil War: the disruptive inclination toward imitation of neighbors (*L* 170) and the evils of the excessive greatness of a town (*L* 174) are manifested in the activities of the city of London and other great towns of trade (*B* 6); the ill effect of the imitation of the Greeks and Romans (*L* 170) appears in the actions of the university-educated members of the House of Commons (*B* 6); the disruptive doctrine of absolute property (*L* 169) was held by the general population who hated taxation (*B* 7); the disruptive doctrine of distinct spiritual and temporal governments (*L* 171–2) was affirmed by Presbyterians and papists (*B* 5); the disruptive doctrines that faith and sanctity are gotten by supernatural inspiration (*L* 169), and that action against one's conscience is sin (*L* 168), were held by various Congregationalist sects (*B* 5) and Presbyterians (*B* passim); the ill effect of the popularity of a potent subject (*L* 173) can be seen in the events surrounding Cromwell (*B* 189ff.); the disruption caused by the liberty of disputing against sovereign power (*L* 174), by the effects of the Parliamentary debates, petitions, and remonstrances (*B* 103ff.); the disruptive opinion that the sovereign is subject to the civil laws, to be judged and punished by others according to them (*L* 169), is instantiated in the actions of the members of Parliament and the army (especially at the king's trial) (*B* 193ff.); and on and on. All of these disruptive doctrines and circumstances either bring about or express a division of or limitation on sovereign power (*L* 89, 168–70, 172), that is, an absence of absolute power (*L* 167), the common denominator and summary cause of the dissolution of social order generally, and of the collapse that occurred in the English case particularly (*B* passim).

This relationship of instantiation is so striking, it is doubtful that any central feature of Hobbes's political theory will fail to appear in *Behemoth*, or that crucial features of the historical analysis will fail to figure prominently in *Leviathan*. Of course, this is a relationship of *instantiation* and not of *equivalence*. It would be a mistake to assume that we can equate the fields of operation of the two works, or that they must be saying precisely the same thing, for *Leviathan* was published under the Commonwealth, whereas *Behemoth* was unpublishable under the Restoration. Although we have some reason to believe that Hobbes generally spoke his mind, and that *if* he were attempting diplomatically to avoid espousing offensive views, he was singularly unsuccessful, we cannot be positive that he did not selectively censor himself, perhaps with an eye to achieving publication. For this reason, we cannot be certain that Hobbes wrote all and only what he genuinely believed to be true in each of these works; some additions or omissions may have seemed reasonable to him in the differing historical circumstances surrounding the composition and attempted publication of the two works. We cannot, then, require of an interpretation of Hobbes's political theory in *Leviathan* that it map precisely onto *Behemoth*. But given their relationship of instantiation, we *can*

require substantial overlap, and the absence of major dis-
crepancies in the explanatory components of the two accounts of disorder.

Now, here is the striking fact. The fact is that none –
not one – of the concepts alleged by the standard philosophical interpreters to be crucial to Hobbes's theory of
disorder appears in *Behemoth*. Neither psychological egoism
nor mechanistic materialism nor overriding fear of violent
death nor order by sheer might play any role whatsoever
in the *Behemoth* analysis. Neither scarcity nor competition
nor desire for power after power nor fear of invasion nor
preemptive aggression appear in any important capacity.
Nothing in *Behemoth* directly relies on Hobbes's natural science, yet the standard philosophical interpretation makes
psychological egoism, mechanistic materialism, and determinism central to the political theory; nearly everything in
Behemoth relies on religious particularism, yet the standard
philosophical interpretation largely dismisses the religious
half of *Leviathan* as inconsequential to the theory.[14] Of
course, the standard interpretation does give primary importance to the concept of divided sovereignty, but its analysis of *why* such division is problematic, and of what the
root of such division is, bears no relation to the account in
Behemoth. Let us examine the case against the standard
philosophical interpretation, and for our interpretation,
point by point.

The *Behemoth* analysis of disorder and its cure confirms
our interpretation in all important respects. First, it makes
explicit the centrality of *transcendent interests* to the problem
of order. Hobbes lays primary responsibility for social collapse at the door of Presbyterian ministers, who had an
interest in themselves fulfilling and in compelling others to
fulfill what they took to be men's duties to God, and who
were willing to pursue this interest even at risk to themselves. They were willing to engage in a war, jeopardizing
their freedom, their livelihoods, their lives, and the peace
of the commonwealth in order to secure this interest. Their
pride and ambition led them to believe they alone knew

God's will, and to attempt to impose their agenda on the commonwealth, even at serious risk to their self-preservation. This is a paradigm case of having a transcendent interest. Their followers, too, acted from a transcendent interest in fulfilling their religious duties. Moreover, pursuit of competing transcendent interests by Episcopalians, various Congregationalist sects, and even papists fueled and perpetuated social upheaval. Those parliamentarians who were passionately attached to an ideal of mixed monarchy or republicanism, or to a substantive conception of justice, may also be said to have acted on transcendent interests. In fact, it seems, of the major groups that instigated the collapse of social order, only the merchants acted from an interest (namely, a misguided calculation of self-interest) that was *not* transcendent. In contrast, the psychological egoism and mechanistic materialism assumptions of the standard philosophical interpretation preclude its even formulating the concept of a transcendent interest.

Second, Hobbes's historical analysis shows that he took the collapse of order to be the result of (1) a transcendent commitment to certain *inherently* disruptive doctrines, and (2) the transcendent commitment by different groups to *competing* doctrines. The doctrines of the first sort identified in *Behemoth* are precisely the same doctrines that Hobbes attacks in Chapter 29 (entitled "of those things that Weaken, or tend to the Dissolution of a Commonwealth"), and in various chapters of Parts 3 and 4 of *Leviathan:* that "every private man is judge of good and evil actions," that "whatsoever a man does against his conscience is sinne," that "faith and sanctity are not to be attained by study and reason, but by supernaturall inspiration or infusion," that "the present church now militant on earth is the kingdom of God," and that ecclesiastics hold their authority immediately from God. The relevance of these doctrines to social disorder could not be made more explicit, and our interpretation gives them appropriate emphasis. As for the affirmation of competing characterizations of religious duty – the factionalism with which Hobbes was so concerned in *Behemoth* – this issue is at the center of what our interpretation identifies as Hobbes's project of redescribing transcendent interests in such a way that they become mutually reconcilable. The careful scriptural exegesis of Part 3 of *Leviathan* is designed to settle particular doctrinal disputes, and to settle the question of who ought to be acknowledged as authoritative in matters of religion; Hobbes's argument for the insignificance of form of worship is a crucial step toward weakening particularist allegiances; his attempt to minimize the number of articles necessary to Christian belief is an attempt to ferret out the lowest common denominator for religious agreement, and to eliminate the variables on which faction depends. In contrast, the standard interpretation neither reflects nor can accommodate the massive, detailed, religious argumentation of Hobbes's political theory in *Leviathan*.

Moreover, the analysis of *Behemoth* confirms our emphasis on differences in who is believed, and on private judgment, as at the root of competing transcendent interests. In *Behemoth*, Hobbes writes that the Presbyterian ministers went out preaching in the market towns of England as the preaching friars had done, and that "neither the preaching of the friars nor monks, nor of parochial priests, tended to teach men what, but whom to believe" (22). That what one believes is a function of whom one believes is, as we've seen, a crucial premise in what our interpretation identifies as Hobbes's argument for the redescription of transcendent interests. As we would expect, much of that argument is echoed in his remarks in *Behemoth*:

> It is true, that the law of God receives no evidence from the laws of men. But because men can never by their own wisdom come to the knowledge of what God hath spoken and commanded to be observed, nor be obliged to obey the laws whose author they know not, they are to acquiesce in some human authority or other. So that the question will be, whether a man ought in matter of religion, that is to say, when there is question of his duty to God and the King, to rely upon the

preaching of his fellow-subjects or of a stranger, or upon the
voice of the law? (*B* 59)

The *Behemoth* answer to this question also parallels Hobbes's
more developed *Leviathan* argument as to who ought to be
obeyed:

> Can any minister now say, that he hath immediately from
> God's own mouth received a command to disobey the King,
> or know otherwise than by the Scripture, that any command
> of the King, that hath the form and nature of a law, is against
> the law of God, which in divers places, directly and evidently,
> commandeth to obey him in all things? . . . where the King is
> head of the Church, and by consequence (to omit that the
> Scripture itself was not received but by the authority of Kings
> and States) chief judge of the rectitude of all interpretations
> of the Scripture, to obey the King's laws and public edicts, is
> not to disobey, but to obey God. (*B* 67–8)

Likewise, Hobbes's attack on private judgment in religion
(including his skepticism about divine inspiration and his
attack on private interpretation of Scripture) is central in his
Behemoth analysis of disorder, as our interpretation of the
political theory would predict. Where does this notion appear
in the standard philosophical interpretation's account of
disorder?

In general, the prominence in the *Behemoth* analysis of disorder of transcendent interests, inherently disruptive doctrines or the disruptiveness of competing doctrines, private
judgment in religion, and the issue of whose judgment in
religion is to be taken as authoritative, confirm not only certain details of our interpretation but our insistence that Parts
3 and 4 of *Leviathan* are essential, working pieces of Hobbes's
political theory. Any alternative interpretation that either
cannot accommodate or does not require these notions of
Parts 3 and 4 will be undermined by the argument of *Behemoth*. The standard interpretation neither needs nor allows
for these notions, since it cannot admit that these are important sources of disorder while maintaining that sheer

might – the threat of bodily harm – can so "change the pay-offs" as to remedy disorder. Brute force will not serve when transcendent interests are at work.

Third, Hobbes's historical analysis of disorder confirms our interpretation of *Leviathan* in respect of the contention that force alone cannot maintain social order because fear of death, wounds, or imprisonment is quite often not the strongest motivating passion. This would seem not even to require saying, since *Behemoth* is, after all, the history of the causes of a *war*, in which people knowingly risked their lives and fought and died and were imprisoned, and so on. But because the standard interpretation, even though it holds that fear of violent death is the overriding motivational factor, has room for the possibility of risking immediate personal harm in order to minimize the probability of future personal harm (e.g., preemptive aggression), the mere fact of war is not sufficient to show that fear of personal harm is not of overriding motivational force. Nevertheless, on Hobbes's account, the instigators of the war were not engaged in defensive aggression, and so their actions were not foresighted maneuvers motivated by fear of death; moreover, Hobbes gives example after example of loyalist uprisings and counterattacks by people who clearly could have expected to be safer by obeying and affiliating with the new regime. More pointedly, however, Hobbes argues that stable social order cannot be established by any victory over the rebels, clearly indicating that threat of force alone is insufficient to deter rebellion. This does not mean that anyone who has a minority transcendent interest will act so as to disrupt social order, because, as Hobbes writes, "It happens many times that men live honestly for fear, who, if they had power, would live according to their own opinions; that is, if their opinions be not right, unrighteously" (B 60). Without power, that is, without support, one will have no chance of succeeding in imposing his private judgments on others, and so may see no benefit in sacrificing himself for his cause. However, "men that are once possessed of an opinion that their obedience to the soveraign power will bee more hurtfull to them than their disobedience, *will disobey* the laws, and thereby over-throw the common-wealth, and introduce confusion and civ-ill war" (*L* 295). For Hobbes, the frustration of one's moral, religious, or other-regarding interests counts as a harm to oneself, and the expectation of such harm may move one to disobedience, even in the face of threatened punishment. In contrast, the standard interpretation asserts that for Hobbes, might makes order, and this because fear of personal harm is the strongest motivating passion in any normal human being.

Fourth, the analysis of *Behemoth* supports our emphasis on education as the key to the maintenance of social order. Nothing is more central to Hobbes's theory than his contention that "the actions of men proceed from their opinions; and in the well governing of opinions, consisteth the well governing of mens actions, in order to their peace and concord" (91). But men's opinions are the result of their experience and education. The way we educate men has a profound impact on their opinions, and so on their actions. Reeducation is required if disruptive opinions are to be eradicated; reeducation is required if socially stabilizing opinions are to be cultivated in their place; and this reeducation must be far-reaching and *uniform* if it is to foster a reconciliation of opinions and to produce *consensus in judgment*. The far-reachingness requirement is to be satisfied in Hobbes's program by universal mandatory education from the pulpit. The uniformity requirement can only be met, in Hobbes's view, by state regulation of what is to be taught, and who is to teach it.

This puts reformation of the universities right at the heart of Hobbes's agenda. We saw in *Behemoth* that Hobbes traced the particular disorders of his day back to the universities, and so declared the need for a reformed educational system. In Chapter 30 of *Leviathan*, Hobbes offers an expanded version of his trickle-down analysis:

> As for the means, and conduits, by which the people may receive this [correct] instruction, wee are to search, by what

means so many opinions, contrary to the peace of man-kind, upon weak and false principles, have neverthelesse been so deeply rooted in them. . . . They whom necessity, or covetousnesse keepeth attent on their trades, and labour; and they, on the other side, whom superfluity, or sloth carrieth after their sensuall pleasures, (which two sorts of men take up the greatest part of man-kind,) being diverted from the deep meditation, which the learning of truth . . . necessarily requireth, receive the notions of their duty, chiefly from divines in the pulpit, and partly from such of their neighbors, or familiar acquaintance, as having the faculty of discoursing readily, and plausibly, seem wiser and better learned in cases of law and conscience than themselves. And the divines, and such others as make shew of learning, derive their knowledge from the universities, and from the schooles of law, or from the books, which by men eminent in those schooles and universities have been published. It is therefore manifest, that the instruction of the people, dependeth wholly on the right teaching of youth in the universities. (L 179–80)

This is why strenuous attacks on the universities occur in both works (beginning in *Leviathan* as early as page 4), and why the importance of education is a running theme through both (the first mention of it in *Leviathan* appearing in the Introduction).

This process of reeducation will not only teach men truths and form their opinions, it will also affect their dispositions; it will instill in them a *desire* to do what they ought to do – creating in them transcendent *attachments* to socially beneficial opinions. Men are passionate creatures, inclined to form transcendent attachments, to have transcendent interests – but the *content* of these interests, the *objects* of passionate attachment, can be affected by education. Hobbes writes that the passions among men are sufficiently similar that introspection into the operation of one's own mind can give one some insight into what makes other men tick. But one cannot by this means discover the objects of other men's passions,

for the similitude of the thoughts, and passions of one man, to the thoughts, and passions of another, whosoever looketh into himself, and considereth what he doth, when he does think, opine, reason, hope, feare, &c, and upon what grounds; he shall thereby read and know, what are the thoughts, and passions of all other men, upon the like occasions. I say the similitude of passions, which are the same in all men, desire, feare, hope, &c; not the similitude of the objects of the passions, which are the things desired, feared, hoped, &c: for these the constitution individuall, and particular education do so vary, and they are so easie to be kept from our knowledge, that the characters of mans heart . . . are legible only to him that searcheth hearts. (*L* 2)

Men will always be passionate creatures, capable of passionate attachments to ideals. They will always be capable of caring more about such things as fulfilling their duty to God, and living honorably, than they do about their physical well-being; but their passions can be directed in ways that reinforce, rather than undermine, social stability. The key is to see that the passions have proper objects, and this is accomplished through education.

A further important consideration is that our interpretation allows us to see the relationship between consensus in judgment and unitary sovereignty, and the respective roles of these notions within Hobbes's theory. Division of power and authority per se do not cause social disorder; if there were complete *agreement* among the various possessors of rights and powers, and their followers, there would be no barrier to peace and cooperation. *Diversity in judgment* is the key variable in Hobbes's equation for social order. Where there is diversity in judgment, *no* concentration of power will be sufficient to maintain order; where there is perfect agreement in judgment, no concentrated power is *necessary* to maintain order.

Thus, it would seem that the question of division of sovereignty is of only secondary or derivative importance to Hobbes's theory. Yet Hobbes puts this question at the center of his analysis, and our interpretation can explain why this should be so. Because undivided sovereignty is required in order to *produce*, through education, uniform judgment, it is a necessary condition of stable social order. *The most important function of unified authority is to produce unanimity in opinion or uniformity in judgment,* because it is differences in these things that cause disruption, even in the face of previously undivided power. Given this relationship between consensus in judgment and unified sovereignty, it is perfectly obvious why a concern with the former should take the form of an argument for the latter. Moreover, it makes sense that the most devastating form that division of sovereignty can take is that of a division between temporal and spiritual authority, for if the sovereign "give away the government of doctrines, men will be frighted into rebellion with the feare of spirits" (*L* 93). As we have seen, Hobbes wrote in *Leviathan* that the most frequent pretext of sedition in Christian states is a perceived conflict between duty to God and duty to man; and this perception can only arise on a societywide scale when the civil and religious authorities are distinct. Of the essential rights of sovereignty, the rights of determining doctrine and administering education are the most essential: "For the points of doctrine concerning the kingdome [of] God have so great influence on the kingdome of man, as not to be determined but by them that under God have the sovraign power" (241–2).

We are now in a position to appreciate the relationship between the concepts of power and authority in Hobbes's political theory – a relationship that the standard philosophical interpreters have difficulty seeing because of their view that power per se is the necessary and sufficient condition of social order. Hobbes uses the term 'sovereignty' to signify the possession of both supreme authority and supreme power. But authority is the primary notion. The power of a human ruler is nothing more than the combined power of the individual people who support him; power consists in support, and is not distinguishable from it.[15] In authorizing a person, we agree to support him. Someone who is recognized as having authority will have supporters, and it is in his supporters that his power consists.[16] This is the meaning of Hobbes's insistence that "the power of the mighty

hath no foundation but in the opinion and belief of the people" (*B* 22). Divided authority, which both produces and
expresses a division in the opinions and judgments of supporters, entails division of power. Because what one believes
is a function of whom one believes, multiple authorities will
produce multiple judgments; and differences in judgment
are then expressed by allegiance to different authorities.
Thus, the power of a ruler is simply a by-product of his
authority; the foundation of supreme power is supreme authority, which both reflects and conditions consensus in
judgment.[17]

What is crucial is that subjects regard their sovereign as
having authority, meaning only that they *view themselves* as
having authorized him. Subjects must have a certain *attitude*
toward their sovereign, *"as if* every man should say to every
man, I authorise and give up my right of governing my selfe,
to this man, or to this assembly of men, on this condition,
that thou give up thy right to him, and authorise all his
actions in like manner" (*L* 87, my emphasis). This is why the
notion of authorization is so prominent in Hobbes's political
theory. Subjects must regard themselves as having submitted
their private judgment to the public authority, and it is their
so regarding themselves that confers power on that authority. The critical point to see is that the sovereign's continued
power depends on their *continuing* to regard themselves as
having authorized him. Far from having any *independent*
power with which to *hold* people to some past authorization
of him, his authority must be continuously reaffirmed if he
is to have any power at all, for "it is not the right of the
sovereign, though granted to him by every man's express
consent, that can enable him to do his office; it is the obedience of the subject, that must do that. For what good is it
to promise allegiance and then by and by to cry out, as some
ministers did in the pulpit, To your tents, O Israel!?" (*B* 181).
Peace requires a *uniform and continuous affirmation* of the authority of a single entity. And only uniformity in judgment
can produce this result.

Because authority is the central concept around which

Hobbes's discussion of judgment revolves, the problem of discrepancy in judgment takes the form of a problem of division of authority. As we've seen, the most problematic sort of division of authority is division between authority over opinions and authority over actions, or, more precisely expressed for the case that particularly concerned Hobbes, division between authority over the civil subject, and authority over the Christian (*L* 248). This is because opinion is the main determinant of action. When men are asked to serve two masters, the outcome of competing internal forces will differ among individuals. Men will be divided into factions, based on whom they recognize as having authority; power will divide, and chaos will ensue.

Hobbes's concern with *this* division – between church and state, God and man, the Christian subject and the civil subject – is so perfectly and pointedly symbolized in the frontispiece of *Leviathan* that it would not even bear comment, had we not so long been persuaded by the standard philosophical interpretation that Hobbes's theory really had nothing to do with religion. The anonymous engraving Hobbes commissioned summarily to depict the content of his book affords as graphic a confirmation of our interpretation as we could wish. What this book is about is the social instability created by that counterposition of spiritual and temporal interests which occurs when civil and religious authority are divided. Look carefully at the engraving reproduced in Figure 1.

Certainly everyone has noticed that the large figure of the king is wearing armor composed of many small subjects, signifying that the sovereign's power consists in the combined strength of his subjects, and that he holds the civil sword in his right hand, and the church staff in his left. Above him is written a quotation from Job 41.33, "Upon earth there is not his like" (citation to the Vulgate).

But what has not, I think, been sufficiently attended to is the significance of the two sets of smaller drawings on either side of the title banner. These, I suggest, represent the division of authority with which the book is primarily concerned, the counterposition of the ways and means of

Figure 1. Frontispiece of *Leviathan*

225

temporal versus spiritual rule. The first counterposition depicts the seat of power, the temporal castle on the left, and
the spiritual church on the right. The person in whom authority is vested, the representative of the people, is signified
by the crown on the temporal side, and the bishop's hat on
the spiritual. The third set of drawings contrasts the type of
force exercised in temporal rule – physical force, as symbolized by the cannon – with the wrath of God, the threat of
excommunication and damnation, symbolized by lightning
bolts. The fourth set of pictures takes as its subject the weapons and equipment of war; temporal rule uses guns, bayo-
nets, standards, drums, and the like; spiritual warfare is
conducted by means of arguments and distinctions. The far
left figure in the spiritual frame has the word 'syllogisme'
written on it, divided into three parts, perhaps to correspond
to the structure of a syllogism. The next three figures are
"verbal forks." Recall that verbal forks are "distinctions that
signify nothing, but serve only to astonish the multitude of
ignorant men," which the schoolmen use for "imposing what
they list upon their readers, and declining the force of true
reason" (*B* 52: cf. *L* 171). The verbal forks depicted here
include the temporal–spiritual distinction (the most important of the church's weapons, which "makes men see double,
and mistake their lawfull soveraign"), the direct–indirect distinction (which, as we saw, was used to assert the church's
power over those civil matters thought to affect spiritual matters), and the *esse reale* versus *esse intentionale* distinction (the
distinction between the object itself and the object in/of con-
sciousness), which underwrites claims to personal revelation
and demonology. In the bottom of the frame we have
Hobbes's wry editorial comment on these distinctions;
Hobbes has labeled a set of *horns* from which the temporal–
spiritual distinction springs "Di-lem-ma." The final set of
scenes depicts the battlefield on which each side struggles –
the site of its conquests. The temporal frame shows an ordinary battlefield, with soldiers engaged in combat. The spiritual frame is a scene from a university disputation among
divines.

Close attention to the frontispiece of *Leviathan* might have given us enough of a clue to the interpretation of the political theory that we would not have needed the guidance of *Behemoth*. But certainly now that we have the help of the historical analysis, we can see the frontispiece for what it is: a symbolic representation of Hobbes's theory of social disorder.

In addition, the *Behemoth* analysis clearly confirms our contention that Hobbes employs arguments from *both* prudence *and* duty, as distinct, but each *necessary*, parts of his solution to the problem of social disorder. As we saw, Hobbes organizes his *Behemoth* analysis in terms of folly on the one hand, iniquity on the other. The actions that proceed from ignorance, pride, and self-conceit are imprudent; those from hypocrisy, injustice, personal ambition, baseness, and falsity are iniquitous. Here the prudence–duty distinction is explicitly articulated but not clearly visible in the macrostructure of the work; in *Leviathan* the converse is true: The first two parts of the book are devoted primarily, though by no means exclusively, to considerations of prudence, and the latter half primarily to considerations of duty, although these governing concepts are not explicitly distinguished.[18] But the *Behemoth* analysis confirms our view that the considerations advanced from prudence and from duty are distinct parts of a *single* argument. Political obedience *is* prudent, and it is also dictated by the natural duties and one's Christian duty. "To obey the laws is justice and equity, which is the law of nature. . . . *Likewise*, to obey the laws is the prudence of a subject," writes Hobbes (*B* 57, emphasis added). Both of these arguments must be made. The duty argument is crucial to Hobbes's project, but this does not mean that the prudence argument is dispensable. Hobbes is aiming at a confluence of reasons for electing always to obey the government under which one lives; this is the form that his project of providing everyone with a sufficient reason for rendering political obedience takes. *Leviathan* is not two hundred pages of political theory and two hundred pages of inconsequential addendum; it is a rationally planned, masterfully constructed, immensely sophisticated *single* argument. Any interpretation that fails to reflect this fact should be rejected.

Finally, the *Behemoth* analysis shows that the concept of pride is indeed indispensable to Hobbes's analysis of disorder. It is the pride expressed in contentiously asserting the superiority of one's private judgments, particularly in such areas as religious duty – this unwarranted self-conceit – that causes decent men to rebel. Hobbes, to his credit, does not hold a conspiracy theory of disorder; it is not, by and large, the machinations of unjust hypocrites that provoke social collapse; it is the bumbling of men blinded by self-conceit. Not that such hubris is blameless, but this sort of self-deception is a form of ignorance, and amenable to significant modification by education. It is pride that makes one take one's private judgments for right reason, and hold them over and against those of the public authority. And when one has a transcendent interest in acting as one's judgments dictate – when they are passionately held opinions – one will attempt to gain enough support to impose those judgments on others, even at risk of death. As we have seen, this disruptive pride appears primarily in the form of religious judgments.[19]

The pivotal role of pride in Hobbes's political theory should come as no surprise to anyone who has read *Leviathan*; it occurs among the causes of conflict listed in his discussion of the state of nature, it is a dominant motif of the book as a whole, and, of course, the book is titled for the "king of the proud." At the end of Chapter 28, Hobbes writes:

> Hitherto I have set forth the nature of man, (whose pride and other passions have compelled him to submit himselfe to government;) together with the great power of his governour, whom I compared to Leviathan, taking that comparison out of the two last verses of the one and fortieth of Job; where God having set forth the great power of Leviathan, called him King of the Proud. "There is nothing," saith he, "on earth to be compared with him. He is made so as not to be afraid. Hee seeth every high thing below him; and is king of all the children of pride." (166–7)

Although the reason why Hobbes is concerned with pride – the question of what sort of pride he is concerned about – is not evident from this passage, we can divine that the sort of pride Hobbes was primarily concerned with was religious pride, not only (as we have shown) from the content of *Leviathan*, but also from the significance of the book of Job from which *Leviathan*'s title is taken.

The book of Job addresses the question of why good men suffer. Simply (and no doubt oversimply) stated, Job maintains that the suffering God has allowed to be inflicted upon him is not a merited punishment for sin, for he is confident that he has lived righteously. Job's friends insist that in his justice, God does not inflict suffering on any who are sinless, and so, that Job must have sinned and should admit it. Job calls God to account for Job's sufferings, and God responds with the question "Who are you to question me?" God is greater than man, and his purposes may be beyond human comprehension. It is only human pride that induces men to insist on diminishing God to a size small enough to fit within their conceptions. Job has no knowledge and no understanding of God, and neither do Job's friends. But whereas Job's friends refuse to allow for the possibility that God is beyond their comprehension, insisting that God would not do anything that *they* would regard as unjust, at least Job calls upon God to explain himself. God points to this distinction, asserting that Job's friends have not spoken rightly of Him, as Job has. Both Job and his friends are guilty of pride; Job for thinking that God owes him an explanation, and his friends for thinking that they know God's nature and purposes. But the latter form of pride is the more objectionable.[20] Hobbes understood the Book of Job to be about men's limited access to knowledge of God and their unwarranted pride in the face of this fact. This is why he names his political treatise for the king of the proud. Both of these themes of Job, human pride and human ignorance, are, as we've seen, central themes of Hobbes's own writings.

Now, Leo Strauss sees that *Leviathan* is importantly concerned with pride (in fact, he claims to have been the first to have seen this) but fails to realize that Hobbes was concerned with a particular sort of pride – religious pride – and, more generally, the pride expressed in one's normative private judgments. Strauss prefaces his partial quotation of the *Leviathan* passage I just quoted with the remark, "At the end of *the most important part* of this work [Leviathan], he says . . ."[21] But, of course, the implication of this remark is that most of the work of *Leviathan* has been completed by the end of Chapter 28, before Hobbes has even discussed the kingdom of God by nature, let alone the scriptural half of the book. This would seem to indicate that Strauss did not understand the role that the concept of pride actually plays in Hobbes's theory. The discussions of pride in the early chapters of Part 1 (like most all of the concepts introduced in Part 1, as we shall see in the next chapter) are included simply to lay the foundation for the crucial arguments Hobbes makes in the religious half of the book. Strauss does not see this but, rather, takes pride to be simply an undirected evil feature of fundamental human nature. He appropriately terms the concept he has in mind "vanity," and claims that, in the end, men's natural but "unjust" vanity is overcome by man's natural but "just" fear, saying that "the moral and humanist antithesis of fundamentally unjust vanity and fundamentally just fear of violent death is the basis of Hobbes's political philosophy."[22] Driven by vanity, each man attempts to extort from others a recognition of his superiority, and finds himself engaged in a violent physical struggle for triumph. "Fear for his life, which came upon the man in his struggle for triumph, moderates, even kills, the will to triumph, and makes him ready to submit, to leave triumph to the enemy, in order that he may save his own life."[23] This is Strauss's explanation of sovereignty by conquest. Sovereignty by institution "arises when the two opponents are both seized with fear for their lives, overcome their vanity and shame of confessing their fear, and recognize as their real enemy not the rival, but 'that terrible enemy of nature, death.' "[24] According to Strauss, natural undirected vanity causes antisocial behavior, but fear of violent death completely overrides vanity. Presumably, once a state is settled, so long as the government keeps fear of violent death vividly before men's eyes, all will live peacefully thereafter. Once again, fear of violent death overrides all other passions and interests. Thus, we see that Strauss's recognition that pride is one of Hobbes's central concepts fails to advance his interpretation beyond the standard philosophical interpretation. Not only does he retain the standard interpretation's pseudosolution to the problem of order, but his novel analysis of the problem of order is, if anything, less plausible than that of the standard interpretation. Our interpretation, in contrast, reflects the centrality of religious pride to Hobbes's political theory.

In sum, *Behemoth* confirms our interpretation in all important respects. It confirms our analysis of the structure of Hobbes's argument in *Leviathan,* and it justifies our insistence on the centrality of such notions as private judgment, transcendent interest, pride, and education. Correlatively, *Behemoth* undermines the standard interpretation in a number of essential respects. The standard interpretation asserts that fear of violent death, and more immediately, fear of punishment, is sufficient to motivate political obedience. This would be required if it were true that Hobbes thought supremacy of sheer might was the key to social order. But Hobbes did not think that might makes order. Hobbes's theory does not need to make the empirically false assumption that fear of personal harm is the strongest motivating passion, but the standard interpreters' does; not only is it required for their alleged solution to work, but it is implied by their interpretation of the mechanistic materialism–based psychological egoism assumption they attribute to Hobbes. Given that assumption, it necessarily follows that fear of personal harm must be the strongest motivating passion in any properly functioning human being; such a person could have no transcendent interests. And the alleged solution, if it could work at all, could only work on properly functioning human beings.

All of the central assumptions of the standard philosophical interpretation stand or fall together; but if disruption is because of transcendent interests, then sheer might cannot make order, and so fear of personal harm cannot be the strongest motivating passion; thus men must not be narrow egoists as they would have to be if mechanistic materialism were true. What seemed to be an impressive unity and systematicity in the standard interpretation turns out merely to express the completeness of its mischaracterization of Hobbes's theory.

Interestingly, Watkins alone among the standard philosophical interpreters correctly identifies the problem of order as Hobbes conceived it. He recognizes that Hobbes was concerned with normative, and primarily religious, conflict. Although Hobbes's political theory prescribes "a universal cure for all revolution and civil war," its analysis of disorder conforms to Hobbes's more particular analysis of the English Civil War. Watkins writes:

> [Hobbes] attributed the deterioration [i.e., "what caused an established political system to crack up"] to *ideas* – to wrong ideas, and especially to bad theology and bad philosophy. (Few men have been more impressed by the practical importance of ideas.) For him the main cause of the Puritan Rebellion was Puritan ideology. . . . Civil war due to divided authority, and divided authority due to ideological disputes – that, in brief, was Hobbes's reading of the Puritan Rebellion.[25]

Nevertheless, according to Watkins (*Hobbes's System of Ideas*), Hobbes "regarded aversion to violent death as men's overriding passion" (Watkins 93); "the avoidance of wounds and destruction is an egocentric end dictated by a man's biological-cum-psychological make-up" (Watkins 83), and "aversion to death is not just one of various dispositions which the individual tries to satisfy. . . . It overrides the rest; its demands have priority over all others" (Watkins 116–17). Thus, according to Watkins, once men see that their natural propensity to use normative terms subjectively creates a condition that threatens their preservation, their overriding fear of death will motivate them to give up, once and for all, their private judgment to a sovereign who will define good and bad, and enforce his own arbitrary definitions with the death penalty if necessary. It's as simple as that. Men are incapable of having any passion or interest that cannot be squelched by the prospect of death.

But we are now in a position to see that for Hobbes, it's not as simple as that, and Watkins himself goes on to criticize Hobbes's system for depending on the "key principle that men have an overriding fear of violent death," which principle, Watkins asserts, it seems "has been falsified, and not just by stray counter-examples."[26] What is worth noting, is that Watkins's interpretation arrives at the same old standard "solution" – a solution that, as we have seen, cannot solve (or even speak to) the problem of order properly conceived.

Watkins remains a standard interpreter, despite his insightful recognition of what Hobbes took the problem of order to be, precisely because he retains an orthodox interpretation of the individual pieces of Hobbes's system. In his preface, Watkins asserts that his "accounts of the individual pieces of the Hobbesian jigsaw are fairly orthodox," and certainly the centerpiece of Watkins's interpretation, the "overriding fear of death" principle, is entirely orthodox, as are the moral subjectivism, materialism, and egoism assumptions he attributes to Hobbes. But these traditionally understood components have implications and mutual connections such that a commitment to any of these orthodox components commits one to much of the rest of the standard interpretation, including its pseudosolution. Watkins could not but have arrived at the standard interpretation, given his acceptance of some of the standard interpretation's central assumptions.

If an orthodox interpretation of the individual components of Hobbes's theory entails the attribution to Hobbes of a solution that was not in fact Hobbes's solution, and an analysis of the problem that was not in fact Hobbes's analysis, then we should expect that our interpretation of Hobbes's problem and solution will involve a revised understanding of the individual pieces of his theory. And so it does.

Chapter 7

Hobbes's resolutive analysis, phase one:
design and detail

Any man that sees what I am doing, may easily perceive what
I think.

– Hobbes (L 180)

As we've seen, the standard philosophical interpretation assigns a prominent role in Hobbes's political theory to the
notions of mechanistic materialism, an egoistic conception of
human psychology that is preservation-centered, moral subjectivism or personal relativism, and coercive force; and dis-
counts the importance to the theory of such notions as moral
and religious interest and duty. This orthodox understanding
of the components of Hobbes's theory is quite naturally suggested by the text of *Leviathan*, provided that attention is
focused primarily on Part 1, and that examined through the
lens of our contemporary concerns. Certainly in Part 1
Hobbes issues pronouncements and makes remarks that,
considered singly, seem fairly straightforward statements of
egoism, moral subjectivism, and the like. But the standard
emphasis on these notions is no part of our interpretation of
Hobbes's political theory, and the precision criterion for adequate interpretations requires that we provide a plausible
alternative to the orthodox understanding of these particular
remarks. I propose to do that in this chapter and, in the
process, to provide a general account of the function and
content of Part 1, thereby rounding out my own interpretation of *Leviathan* and offering a view of how the book is
structured.

The account I present of each set of remarks from which the standard philosophical interpretation compiles one of the orthodox categories proceeds from the idea that the best way to discover what Hobbes thinks – what he means by his remarks – is to analyze what he is doing – how, and toward what end, he is using those remarks. We ought thus to begin by examining Hobbes's method – the "resolutive–compositive" method we've alluded to throughout – to see what it is that Hobbes is attempting to do.

HOBBES'S METHOD

Our discussion began from Hobbes's conception of the problem of social disorder, and traced a solution that both speaks to Hobbes's problem and finds support in the text. Neither the problem nor the solution is, on this interpretation, to be understood as deriving from a physical-scientific account of fundamental human nature; rather, Hobbes analyzes actual existing social practice, identifying the sources of social disruption, and then argues for changes in social practice to prevent the like disruption in future. In the course of this project Hobbes must, naturally, offer some at least partial account of human motivation, and some account of the formation of human interests, desires, beliefs, and attachments. But the direction of Hobbes's explanation is from social fact to social fact, via certain accounts – derived primarily from ordinary observation of human beings – of individual traits; not from individual traits to the social arrangements that respect or best exploit them.

We can better understand what this involves by noticing that on this account, the resolutive component of Hobbes's resolutive–compositive method does far more work in Hobbes's theory than is generally supposed. On standard views, the resolution is completed in one easy step: A society is composed of individual persons, therefore we start by examining the properties of isolated individuals. On our view, resolution is more complicated; it involves first determining what is causing social disorder within a state – for example, determining that particular practices and institutions produce people with religious interests of a certain specific sort that when acted on cause disruption – then isolating the genesis of these practices and institutions, that is, the interests they serve, the operations by which they are established, and the tendencies to make the errors on which they rest; and, finally, considering people with those interests and tendencies starting from scratch. Only after all of this work has been done is Hobbes in a position to describe how a society might be recomposed in such a way that it would not produce practices and institutions that generate disruptive activity.

The metaphor for a commonwealth that Hobbes most heavily relies on is that of a human body, and the use of this particular metaphor is telling. One first examines an ailing organism, analyzing symptoms and tracing as far as possible both the causes of these symptoms and the way a human body generally functions. When the source of the problem is isolated, the part or process responsible is *altered,* and only then is a new healthy whole reconstituted. The point here is that the whole is not simply broken down into its component parts and then put back together, perhaps in a different pattern but using the very same components (as might be the case in disassembling and reassembling a clock); rather, the components themselves must be altered if the whole is to function properly. Not only must the diseased parts be altered, but the causes of the disease must be addressed. Healthy cells become cancerous under certain environmental influences – continued health will require not only that the cancerous cells be destroyed but also that the bad influences to which healthy cells are naturally subject be eliminated. Likewise, the matter of a commonwealth, the people of which it is composed, is not given, fully determined and immutable; the matter itself is transformed through social processes, and undesirable transformations may be altered or avoided through the imposition of alternative social processes. Resolution thus most fruitfully begins from a thorough analysis of a diseased and defective commonwealth, one on the eve or in the wake of civil war, which identifies how and where its components have gone awry; and recomposition will be performed on components, that although now corrected, are naturally prone to corruption or alteration under social processes. We don't begin as natural men, we begin as beings formed by social institutions. And so, for us, the resolutive–compositive method, when resolution is taken seriously, is bound to be more profitable than any pristine deductive method beginning from a purely physical-scientific account of the nature of individual human beings.

That Hobbes is serious about the resolutive component of his method, and correspondingly that it is an error to dismiss this component as a fancy way of saying that we start from fundamental human nature and derive a necessary form of political organization from that, can be quite clearly seen by examining the chart of the sciences Hobbes presents in Chapter 9 of *Leviathan* (see Figure 2). According to that chart, civil philosophy, that is, the science of politics, is a distinct branch of philosophy *not connected* to the study of bodies, including men, and their natural properties. Civil philosophy is not a branch of, nor is it deducible from, the philosophy of human nature. Rather, the political rights and duties of subjects and sovereigns are implications of the institution of states, and this must reflect the essential properties of commonwealths. This is why our compositive reconstruction in Chapter 2 began, as Hobbes began Part 2, from the concept of a commonwealth. Political philosophy proceeds from an analysis of the essential properties of commonwealths, and an analysis of the ways in which existing practice does or does not respect these properties, to the dispositions of socially formed individual persons, to superior social practices that can, taking into account known human dispositions, preserve the integrity and stability of commonwealths.

The well-known fact that Hobbes declared his intention to complete a three-part project made up of the sciences of body, of man, and of government, has led some commentators to suppose that Hobbes intended the first two parts

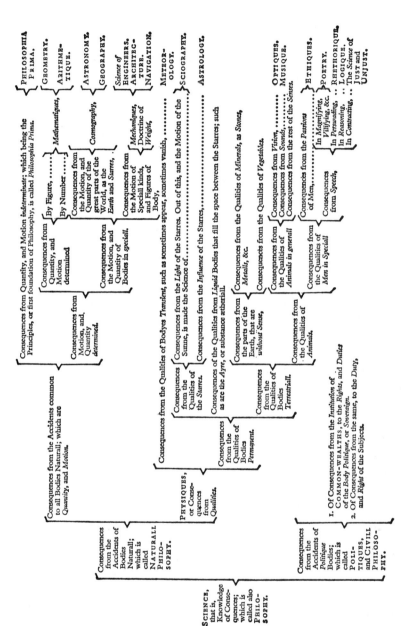

Figure 2. Hobbes's chart of the sciences

238

of his project to provide a *deductive* ground for the third. Hobbes's chart of the sciences shows this assumption to be false because it shows civil philosophy not even to be a branch of natural philosophy, let alone deductively grounded in it. (Note, though, that even prima facie there is no reason to suppose that the various parts of Hobbes's projects should be deductively related: We do not, for example, assume that the various parts of Hobbes's examination of the sources of religious knowledge – natural reason, personal revelation, and Scripture – must be internally related in any particular way; nor that the two parts of the kingdom of God – God's natural kingdom and his prophetic kingdom – must involve deducing features of the latter from features of the former.)

What, then, is going on in Part 1 of *Leviathan,* the part entitled "Of Man"? If it does not lay out a physical-scientific conception of human nature from which will be derived conclusions about the required form of political institutions, what is its function? It contains a seemingly peculiar mix of chapters: Chapters 1 through 3 and Chapter 6 appear to give a more or less physical scientific account of the inner workings of human beings; Chapters 4, 5, and 7 through 11 seem to present lots of observations about the use of language, definitions and stipulations of terms, and categorizations of things – virtues, vices, sciences, modes of knowledge or belief; suddenly there's a chapter on religion; then a chapter on natural characteristics that incline people to quarrel; two chapters on natural law; and, finally, a chapter on persons, authors, actors, and representatives. This motley assortment of chapters does not seem to follow any coherent method – it isn't systematic natural science, it doesn't follow a geometrical method, some discussions are of isolated individuals while others are of social conventions and practices, and discussions of God, Scripture, school divines, and the teachings of the universities keep appearing. Nonetheless, there it is, first in the order of Hobbes's exposition, even though according to Hobbes's chart of the sciences, he ought to be beginning from a discussion of commonwealths. Surely, one might suppose, if Hobbes put it first, it must contain the building blocks of Hobbes's theory, from which he will derive his political conclusions.

Nonetheless, this supposition is false. There is a superior alternative account of Part 1, which explains both why it is presented first and why it contains the seemingly odd assortment of topics it does, and which fits with both Hobbes's resolutive–compositive method, and his chart of the sciences. Part 1 contains a catalog of all of the root sources of disorder in Hobbes's commonwealth – a distillation of the results of his resolutive analysis – and a first pass at correcting disruptive errors at their source. Not all errors stem from bad natural science, but some do; hence an early four chapters on errors grounded in faulty science. Numerous other disruptive errors rely on mistakes about the use of language, and a failure to distinguish distinct ideas; hence another seven chapters on errors from the abuse of language. Religious errors are a major source of disorder; so Hobbes includes a preliminary corrective discussion of religion. Other sources of disruption are not *errors,* or the result of *mis*understanding reality, but are "natural," that is, built-in traits of character; hence a discussion of the circumstances in which these traits will cause disruption. A misunderstanding of the most basic norms of social life causes people to offend one another and to advance contentious moral claims, so Hobbes devotes two chapters to clarifying these norms. A misunderstanding of persons, authors, and the like leads subjects to resist their public representative, sometimes on the ground that they will be held responsible for doing the sinful actions he commands, other times on the ground that they have not authorized the powers he exercises; hence Hobbes includes a corrective chapter on authorization.

These are most of the primary sources of disorder, as revealed by application of the resolutive method from the social practice of socially formed human beings to the causes of disruption. (The remainder of the sources of disorder are presented in the completion of Hobbes's resolutive analysis in Part 4, where he discusses the root causes of those religious errors that most severely threaten order.) Part 1 is entitled

"Of Man" because these are the errors into which men are naturally prone to fall – errors from faulty science, inconstant speech, pre-prophetic religious errors, moral errors, and errors from the exercise of private judgment – but it does not describe a full conception of human nature. Hobbes begins from the fruits of resolution, enumerating them and providing a preliminary corrective discussion in Part 1, to the task of recomposition, partially and generally in Part 2, then fully and specifically in Part 3, with Part 4 completing the resolutive analysis by identifying further sources of erroneous and disruptive religious views – a task that could not be completed until Hobbes had established (in Part 3) what true religion properly involves. Nothing in Part 1 stands on its own, nor is anything strictly speaking derived from it.[1] Everything in Part 1 is developed, applied, and integrated into the theory in subsequent portions of the book.

In contrast, the standard philosophical interpretation takes Hobbes to be presenting in Part 1 a physical-scientific account of man as matter in motion, from which is (ideally at least) supposed to follow an egoistic, preservation-centered conception of human nature, moral subjectivism or personal relativism, a complete account of disorder, and a set of political institutions needed to establish and maintain social order. This set of entailments is then complemented by the attribution to Hobbes of full-blown atheism, or at least of a skeptical argument designed to undermine what would otherwise appear as a purely prudential interest in meeting religious requirements. Let us look at each component of the standard philosophical view, beginning with the alleged foundation of Hobbes's system, natural science.

SCIENCE

If, as Hobbes's chart indicates, a science of politics is not connected to a science of natural bodies, then obviously Hobbes's natural science cannot ground his political argument. Even if natural science were in principle a possible foundation for social science, it would have in practice to give us something to build our social science on – a knowledge of human nature. Yet Hobbes explicitly denies that it can do this: "For it is supposed that in this naturall kingdome of God, there is no other way to know any thing, but by naturall reason; that is, from the principles of naturall science; which are so farre from teaching us any thing of Gods nature, *as they cannot teach us our own nature*, nor the nature of the smallest creature living" (191, emphasis added).[2] Science may tell us what we're made of, and sketch a general picture of the mechanisms by which we operate – it may tell us what it is to want something, or to believe something – but it cannot tell us *what* we want, or *what* we believe. For these we must look to our experience, through observation or introspection, because these are largely social products. And even then it is a tricky matter to discover the objects of men's passions, "for these the constitution individuall, and particular education do so vary, and they are so easie to be kept from our knowledge, that the characters of mans heart . . . are legible only to him that searcheth hearts" (2).

Moreover, if the function of Part 1 is to identify and begin to correct the errors that most undermine social order, as these have been determined by previous resolution, then we should expect the science to allude to these particular errors, to have a less than fully systematic, pick-and-choose kind of quality, and to be discussed only insofar as it applies to disorder; certainly not what one would expect if the science were to form the deductive ground of Hobbes's system. In fact, Hobbes's natural science is abandoned after four chapters; and in each of these chapters, Hobbes explicitly states how a given scientific error leads to a socially disruptive error.

The function of Hobbes's "scientific" remarks in the early chapters of Part 1 is to provide alternative accounts of the phenomena that have historically led people to embrace disruptive religious views. His scientific remarks serve to undermine claims to personal revelation in religion, and to undermine the demonology that supports disruptive religious doctrines. They delegitimize troublesome substantive conceptions of God, and challenge the problematic doctrines of venerated authorities. They serve to explain why certain argumentative strategies are unprofitable, and how serious political errors come to be affirmed. Hobbes's "scientific" discussion sets the stage for his later, crucial, arguments concerning religion, by exposing the dependence of certain disruptive religious views on faulty natural science. It is there for the purpose of supporting these arguments, and has no independent role in his political project.

Hobbes remarks in his Chapter 1 that "to know the naturall cause of sense is not very necessary to the business now in hand"; nonetheless, he briefly sketches an account of perception according to which perception depends on physical action on our sensory organs. He then goes on, for the final quarter of the chapter, to use his account to criticize the schools' doctrine of intelligible and sensible species. He remarks, almost offhandedly, that this criticism is not meant as a general attack on the usefulness of the universities, "but because I am to speak hereafter of their office in a commonwealth, I must let you see on all occasions by the way, what things would be amended in them; amongst which the frequency of insignificant speech is one" (4). It is not until later, in Parts 3 and 4, that we see why he objects to this particular form of insignificant speech: The (Aristotelian) doctrine of species supports the ecclesiastic claims that qualities can be "powred in" to a person, that in transubstantiation the sight and taste of a piece of bread can be present "there where they say there is no bread," and that apparitions have an independent existence, apart from any physical bodies, a view that supports demonology. Chapter 1 merely sets the stage for his later attacks on disruptive scholastic doctrine.

The same is true of, and even more evident in, his discussion of imagination in Chapter 2. The decaying remnants of sense perception constitute memory, and are the components of dreams and visions. Hobbes offers an entirely naturalistic account of dreams and visions, in terms of motion communicated from sensory organs to "the internall parts of a man." With this account, Hobbes is able to explain why it is that dreams are sometimes clearer and more vivid than waking experience. And he argues that visions are most often simply dreams that occur as one slides, without noticing it, in and out of sleep.

But what is the purpose of this discussion? It is to undermine claims to personal revelation (Chapter 32), and religious beliefs and practices that depend on the doctrine of incorporeal substance (Chapter 46), as becomes evident in the last third or so of Chapter 2. Hobbes's account shows how it is quite possible that one might mistakenly think oneself to have had a vision. "And this is no very rare accident: for even they that be perfectly awake, if they be timorous, and superstitious, possessed with fearfull tales, and alone in the dark, are subject to the like fancies, and believe they see spirits and dead mens ghosts walking in church-yards" (7). People oughtn't to suppose that they have seen supernatural beings, for there is a perfectly *natural* alternative account of their experience. Demonology (Chapter 45) is the result of a simple error:

> From this ignorance of how to distinguish dreams, and other strong fancies, from vision and sense, did arise the greatest part of the religion of the gentiles in time past . . . and now adayes the opinion that rude people have of fayries, ghosts and goblins, and of the power of witches. . . . And for fayries, and walking ghosts, the opinion of them has I think been on purpose either taught, or not confuted, to keep in credit the use of exorcisme, or crosses, or holy water, and other such inventions of ghostly men. . . . *If this superstitious fear of spirits were taken away, and with it, prognostiques from dreams, false prophecies, and many other things depending thereon, by which crafty ambitious persons abuse the simple people, men would be much more fitted than they are for civill obedience.*
>
> *And this ought to be the work of the schooles: but they rather nourish such doctrine.* (7–8, emphasis added)[3]

As we've seen, these arguments are developed and incorporated into Hobbes's broader project in Parts 3 and 4. They are not intended to undermine Christian faith generally but only to discredit the unnecessary and disruptive doctrines socially incorporated as a matter of historical fact into Christianity.[4] They are to be seen as attacks on the schools, not on Christianity, for "there is no doubt but God can make unnaturall apparitions: But that he does it so often, as men need to feare such things, more than they feare the stay, or change, of the course of nature, which he also can stay and change, is no point of Christian faith. But evill men under pretext that God can do any thing, are so bold as to say any thing when it serves their turn" (7).

Chapter 3 contains Hobbes's discussion of trains of thought, in terms of which he explains both prudence and experience. At the end of this chapter Hobbes discusses the limits of what we can imagine, and these, tellingly, entail our inability to conceive of God, or of souls and other putatively immaterial substances:

> Whatsoever we imagine is finite. Therefore there is no idea, or conception of anything we call infinite. . . . And therefore the name of God is used, not to make us conceive him (for he is incomprehensible, and his greatnesse and power are unconceivable); but that we may honour him. Also because whatsoever . . . we conceive has been perceived first by sense . . . a man can have no thought representing any thing not subject to sense. No man can therefore conceive any thing, but he must conceive it in some place . . . nor that any thing is all in this place and all in another place at the same time; nor that two or more things can be in one and the same place at once: For none of these things ever have, or can be, incident to sense; but are absurd speeches, taken upon credit . . . from deceived philosophers, and deceived, or deceiving schoolemen. (11)

Hobbes elaborates in Chapter 12 on this argument that God cannot be conceived of, but not until Part 3 does he show his readers the implications of God's incomprehensibility for ecclesiastics' claims about religious duty and practice. The argument sketched here that one cannot conceive of any object but in some determinate place that it exclusively occupies, comes into play in the argument of Parts 3 and 4 against the existence of immaterial substances – souls, spirits, demons. Lastly, this passage introduces Hobbes's more concerted attack on the authority of the schools, a theme further developed in Chapter 4, and pursued with great vigor throughout Parts 3 and 4.

The purpose of Chapters 4 and 5 is to undermine the authority of the schools, by exposing errors that arise from the misuse of language, either in naming or in carrying out reasoning.[5] Hobbes has scarcely begun Chapter 4 when he remarks that although God taught Adam to name things, there is absolutely no evidence that God taught him such words as " 'entity,' 'intentionality,' 'quiddity,' and other insignificant words of the school" (12). Words are to be used to mark our thoughts to ourselves, and to serve as signs of our thoughts to others, to register the causes and effects of things, to counsel and teach others, to make our wills known to others, and to amuse ourselves. But language is frequently abused, to the disruption of commonwealths: People deceive themselves by using words to stand for things they've never conceived of (like incorporeal substance), they deceive others by using words metaphorically (like 'circumscriptive' and 'definitive' place) and by lying, and they use speech to wound one another. Abuse of speech undermines reasoning, for correct reasoning, or truth, is nothing more than "the right ordering of names in our affirmations" (14).

This is why it is imperative "for any man that aspires to true knowledge to examine the definitions of former authors," because

> in the right definition of names, lyes the first use of speech ... and in wrong, or no definitions, lyes the first abuse; *from which proceed all false and senselesse tenets;* which make those men that take their instruction from the authority of books, and not from their own meditation, to be as much below the condition of ignorant men, as men endued with true science are above it. ... For words are wise mens counters, they do but reckon by them: but they are the money of fooles, that value them by the authority of an Aristotle, a Cicero, or a Thomas, or any other doctor whatsoever, if but a man. (15, emphasis added)

Reliance on former authors, particularly, as we've seen, these authors, leads people into error.[6] These errors stem from two different sorts of misuse of words:

> One, when they are new, and yet their meaning not explained by definition; whereof there have been aboundance coyned by schoole-men and pusled philosophers. Another, when men make a name of two names whose significations are contradictory, and inconsistent; as this name, an 'incorporeall body,' or (which is all one) an 'incorporeall substance' . . . so likewise if it be false to say that vertue can be powred, or blown up and down; the words 'in-powred vertue,' 'in-blown vertue,' are as absurd and insignificant as a 'round quadrangle.' (17)

In Chapter 5 of *Leviathan*, Hobbes traces reasoning that results in absurd conclusions (such as are those which he takes to disrupt order) to the misuse of language. The "priviledge" of absurdity belongs only to human beings, "and of men, those are of all most subject to it, that professe philosophy. . . . And the reason is manifest. For there is not one of them that begins his ratiocination from the definitions, or explications of the names they are to use" (20). Problem in definition is the first cause of absurd (and ultimately disruptive) conclusions, but there are numerous others as well, not the least of which are "names that signifie nothing; but are taken up, and learned by rote from the schooles, as 'hypostatical,' 'transubstantiate,' 'consubstantiate,' 'eternal-now,' and the like canting of schoolemen" (20–1). The effect of these abuses, and the reason for avoiding them (and so the purpose of Hobbes's discussion here) is precisely that they cause social disorder: "To conclude, the light of humane minds is perspicuous words, but by exact definitions first snuffed and purged of ambiguity . . . and on the contrary, metaphors, and senslesse and ambiguous words, are like ignes fatui; and reasoning upon them is wandering amongst innumerable absurdities: *and their end, contention, and sedition, or contempt*" (21–2, emphasis added). If we want to avoid disorder, we must reason aright; and this requires that we cease to rest our views of religious and civil duty on the authority of the church divines, and ancient philosophers.[7]

Finally, in Chapter 6, the last of the chapters that could be characterized as at least partially physical-scientific, Hobbes discusses the passions. As we've seen, people's passionate attachments can be a profound source of disorder, depending on the content of those attachments. Here Hobbes explains how it can be that there is so much disagreement over what things are desirable, and why people use words like 'good' and 'evil' differently. This turns out to be important for Hobbes's argument that we cannot begin any fruitful science of politics from assertions of what is good, right, just, or righteous (an argument I recount presently, and which is crucial for a proper understanding of Hobbes's moral theory).

He also offers in this chapter a catalog of the passions, for instance, benevolence is the desire of good to another, ambition is the desire of office or precedence, magnanimity is the contempt of little helps, and valor is magnanimity in the face of danger of death or other physical harm. One of the most striking points Hobbes makes in this chapter is that passions contain cognitive components, and are differentiated by the beliefs or opinions that accompany them: Indignation is composed of anger (a passion) conjoined with the *opinion* that another has been *wrongly* injured. And it matters for the purpose of identifying the passion whether the opinion that in part comprises it is true: Fear of invisible powers, *"when the power we imagine is truly so,"* is true religion; otherwise it is mere superstition. This distinction, as we've seen, becomes important in Hobbes's attack on those disruptive religious beliefs that stem from superstitious belief in such imaginary objects as immaterial substances. Because passions depend on beliefs, it is not surprising to learn, as we do in Chapter 7, that "the difference of passions proceedeth partly from . . . different education" and the passions "are different, not onely from the difference of mens complexions, but also from their difference of customes, and education" (35).

The point of all this discussion of the passions? In the next chapter Hobbes explains that the passions, when conjoined with wrong opinions, or when overvehement, can inspire rebellion: "Though wee perceive no great unquietnesse, in one, or two men; yet we may be well assured, that their singular passions are parts of the seditious roaring of a troubled nation" (36). And because the passions are formed by education, and conjoined with opinions also learned, bad education can result in disruptive passionate attachments. Here in Chapter 6, Hobbes begins to correct the disruption that is related to misconceptions about the passions by suggesting, first, that our use of terms of praise and approval often reflect merely our own desires and opinions; second, that beliefs (very often false) play a crucial role in the formation of (often disruptive) passions; and third, that many problematic scholastic accounts rest on a misunderstanding of the operations of the passions (for example, the schoolmen's doctrine of free will rests on a misunderstanding of deliberation, and their doctrine of "poured in virtue" wrongly views people's motives or qualities as separated from them, rather than as a kind of motion within them).

When we examine these six chapters, we see that far from presenting an unadulterated, systematic physical science, they contain targeted piecemeal attacks on the erroneous views (mostly religious views) that stem from particular scientific and linguistic errors. Bad science and improper use of language either give rise to, or are used to support, demonology, transubstantiation, claims to personal revelation, intelligible and sensible species, immaterial substances, positive conceptions of God, infusion of qualities, free will, and other disruptive doctrines. And scientific ignorance has a more general, deeply disruptive consequence: "Want of science, that is, ignorance of causes, disposeth, or rather constraineth a man to rely on the advise and authority of others" (49). But, as Hobbes repeatedly stresses, reliance on authorities usually results in absurd and seditious conclusions.

In sum, consideration of Hobbes's self-proclaimed method, his chart of the sciences, the context of his "scientific" discussions, and the actual content of those discussions, all discredit the idea that Hobbes is intending to derive a conception of human nature, or any other general conception, from a general physical-scientific account of man as matter in motion. There is no such general scientific account in *Leviathan*. Rather, Part 1 presents a selective preliminary discussion of certain of the errors that underlie disruptive beliefs and practices – errors that have been identified by a previous process of resolution from a social analysis of Hobbes's own commonwealth – a preliminary discussion that serves as the basis for the more detailed and systematic treatment of these very same topics farther along in the book.[8] And if there is not a general scientific account in *Leviathan*, then the first link of the standard philosophical interpretation's account of Hobbes's system – the derivation from systematic mechanistic materialism to a self-preservation-centered conception of human nature – becomes suspect.

But perhaps, even though science does not serve as the ground of derivation of such a conception of human nature, there is other support for the claim that Hobbes held a self-preservation-centered, or even egoistic, conception of human nature. What is Hobbes's conception of human nature?

HUMAN NATURE

One thing is sure. Whatever Hobbes's full and considered conception of fundamental human nature is, it does not appear in Part 1 of *Leviathan*. Why not? Because Part 1, to the extent that it discusses human qualities (as opposed to errors men make) at all, contains discussions of only those human qualities that play a role in social disorder (hence any conception gathered from there must be merely partial), and because those qualities are largely formed and altered through the particular social processes that affected Hobbes's contemporaries (hence the conception cannot be fundamental). This isn't to say that Hobbes hasn't got a conception of human nature, but what it is must be gleaned and compiled from remarks throughout the whole of *Leviathan*.

What do we know about people from Hobbes's remarks? We know that people are profoundly *malleable* through education and socialization. Even their passions are formed by culture and education, not to mention the objects of their passions, their religious beliefs, and their opinions (on which "the power of the mighty" depends). Common people's minds "unlesse they be tainted with dependence on the potent, or scribbled over with the opinions of their doctors, are like clean paper, fit to receive whatsoever by public authority shall be imprinted in them" (176). People begin as tabula rasa, but once education has formed their opinions, they can become quite intractable, such that no amount of force, but only a slow and steady reeducation, can change their opinions (*L* 384, *EL* 2.9.8, *B* 80). Education or, more broadly, socialization, is the greatest determinant of people's aptitude to peaceful cohabitation.

We know that people are *credulous*, and hence quite easily manipulated: "So easie are men to be drawn to believe any thing, from such men as have gotten credit with them; and can with gentleness, and dexterity, take hold of their fear and ignorance" (56). "For such is the ignorance, and aptitude to error of all men . . . as by innumerable and easie tricks to be abused" (236).

We also know that people want *dominion*, that there is a widespread desire to rule, as can be seen from fragments of Hobbes's remarks: "The finall cause, end, or designe of men, (who naturally love liberty and *dominion over others*)" (85, emphasis added); "This benefit of an universall monarchy, (*considering the desire of men to bear rule*)" (381, emphasis added); "For considering the love of power naturally implanted in mankind" (313). People want to govern others, "that is to say, to rule, and reign over them; which is a thing, that all men naturally desire" (230). Hobbes explains this desire to rule as at least partly a quite reasonable desire to use the power of others (their strength, influence, riches) in securing one's own ends.[9] And although there are some people who do not aspire to rule others, most everyone would prefer not to be ruled by others, "for there are very few so foolish, that had not rather governe themselves than be governed by others" (77). People would prefer to live only according to their own private judgment (and would be happiest if others would also defer to their judgment [*L* 61, *B* 69, *EL* 2.6.13]), and it is a difficult matter to induce people to give this up. But they may sometimes be induced to give it up by appeal to their interest in security or in fulfilling their religious or moral duties, when and only when these interests and the conditions of their satisfaction are properly understood.

We know further that people are *prideful*. They are apt to take their own reason for right reason, they are apt to insist that their own judgment is authoritative, they are prone to believe themselves in direct communication with God, they are liable to think themselves wiser or better fit to rule than others, and they are inclined to see their own interests, concerns, and opinions as more important and pressing than other people's. They care deeply for their reputations, and will war with one another over any perceived sign of undervaluing or insult. "Glory [maketh men invade] for reputation . . . for trifles, as a word, a smile, a different opinion, and any other signe of undervalue, either direct in their persons, or by reflexion in their kindred, their friends, their nation, their profession, or their name" (62). Many people would rather risk their lives than be dishonored, as evidenced by the fact that they engage in duels (45, 159); and *"most* men choose rather to hazard their life, than not to be revenged" for signs of contempt or hatred from others (76, emphasis added).

We know that people are prone to develop *religious* beliefs. The natural seeds of religion, Hobbes writes, "can never be so abolished out of humane nature, but that new religions may againe be made to spring out of them, by the culture of such men as for such purpose are in reputation" (58). There are even natural routes to belief in the one true God. Moreover, religious beliefs tend to have an enormous motivational force; they can motivate obedience to the state (57), and they can motivate rebellion against the state, overriding interests in peace, security, and self-preservation (321, 384,

295). Because religion will likely be a part of the life of any society, and because it will have a profound effect on people's attitudes toward civil obedience, no useful political theory can fail to address religious beliefs; hence Hobbes's own theory cannot be atheistic.[10] People will always have religious interests. And religious interests can be, and often are, transcendent.

But how can this be if people desire self-preservation above all else, if self-preservation is "an egocentric end dictated by a man's biological-cum-psychological make-up" which "overrides the rest" (Watkins, *Hobbes's System of Ideas*, pp. 83, 116–17)? Well, the evidence above doesn't support the claim that Hobbes thought it was. The passages that are often cited to support it (70, 72, 75, 78, 97) say only that men strive to act for their own benefit, and are to be interpreted, in light of Hobbes's general theory, as making the observation that human beings will do what seems to them best for themselves given their interests, whatever those may be, self-interested, moral, religious, or affectionate. This is why the opinions and doctrines that affect their interests have to be carefully managed; and "the right of judging what doctrines are . . . to be taught the subjects, is . . . inseparably annexed . . . to the soveraign power civill . . . for . . . men that are once possessed of an opinion that their obedience to the soveraign power will bee more hurtfull to them, than their disobedience, will disobey the laws, and thereby overthrow the commonwealth, and introduce confusion, and civill war" (295).

It may be that the primary *reason* people in general, disregarding their religious interests, have for submitting to the rule of others is that they expect thereby to be better able to preserve their lives – it may be that increased security is the primary reason for which people do in fact submit to government – but this is quite a different point than the claim that self-preservation is people's overriding concern. Desire for security is what usually induces people to *submit* to government; but discontent along with "pretense of right," primarily stemming from their beliefs about their religious duties and interests, is what *usually* causes them to *rebel* against government. There is no incompatibility between holding on the one hand that people will do what they think best, and that the reason why they allow constraints on their right of private judgment, when they do, is that they see it as a means to their self-preservation, and holding, on the other hand, that people do often willingly jeopardize or sacrifice their preservation for the sake of realizing their religious interests. Neither is there any contradiction between holding, on the one hand, that "the passion to be reckoned upon [to hold men to the performance of their covenants] is fear" (70), and asserting, on the other hand that the rights of sovereignty "cannot be maintained by any civill law, or terrour of legal punishment" (175), or asking, "If men know not their duty, what is there that can force them to obey the laws?" (*B* 75). Fear may be a more dependable motivating factor than pride (the other possibility Hobbes discusses) without being sufficient.[11] *Nowhere in* Leviathan *does Hobbes say that fear of death is the dominant and overriding passion of human beings.* And there is no reason, particularly in light of his analysis of social disorder, to suppose that he thought it was.[12] Thus, the second component of the standard philosophical interpretation – the attribution to Hobbes of a preservation-centered conception of human psychology – is discredited.

SUBJECTIVISM AND RELATIVISM

The second link in the standard philosophical interpretation is between the ideas of a preservation-centered conception of human psychology and moral subjectivism or personal relativism. Does Hobbes think that people are capable of moral virtue, or of being moved to act by moral considerations at all? There is no prima facie reason to think that he does not, since he seems not to have held the preservation-centered mechanical conception of human nature that could have provided grounds for thinking that people cannot be moved by anything but a concern for their own survival. He may have held quite an ordinary view – that people are sometimes moved to act by moral considerations, that certain kinds of actions are morally good, and that certain qualities of character are morally admirable. Let us begin with the question of whether Hobbes espouses any familiar formal moral theory.

Some commentators have thought that Hobbes was a moral subjectivist; others, that he was a personal relativist. Either of these moral theories would be attractive to one who was looking to interpret Hobbes's remarks about good and evil in line with a preservation-centered mechanism. But the text does not actually support the claim that Hobbes held moral subjectivism or personal relativism. The passage commentators generally cite as evidence for their claim should be construed, not as establishing subjectivism or relativism, but rather as an observation about linguistic usage, a description of how people in fact tend to use, though mistakenly, evaluative terms. Let us carefully examine the alternatives. The passage in question is this:

> whatsoever is the object of any mans appetite or desire, that is it, which he for his part *calleth* good: and the object of his hate, and aversion, evill; and of his contempt, vile and inconsiderable. For *these words* of good, evill, and contemptible, *are ever used* with relation to the person that useth them: there being nothing simply and absolutely so; nor any *common rule* of good and evill, to be taken from the nature of the objects themselves; but from the person of the man . . . or (in a commonwealth) from the person that representeth it, or from an arbitrator or judge, whom men disagreeing shall by consent set up, and make his sentence the rule thereof. (24, emphasis added)

Is Hobbes asserting here that evaluative utterances have no truth value (subjectivism), or alternatively, that one person's statement that something is good and another person's statement that the very same thing is evil can be simultaneously true (personal relativism)? Or is he, rather, making an observation about how people tend to use evaluative terms, without endorsing such a use of them, for a purpose not yet revealed?

It is unlikely that Hobbes is asserting that there is no fact of the matter about what things are good or evil, because if there weren't, then things couldn't be *misrepresented* to people as good or evil; but in fact Hobbes lists as one of the reasons people have difficulty living sociably with one another that "some men can represent to others that which *is good* in the likeness of evill, and evill, in the likeness of good" (87). Moreover, people can err in their judgments of good and evil, which should not be possible if evaluative utterances have no truth values. Hobbes writes, "Another doctrine repugnant to civill society is that 'whatsoever a man does against his conscience is sinne'; and it dependeth on the presumption of making himself judge of good and evill. For a mans conscience, and his judgement is the same thing, *and as the judgement, so also the conscience may be erroneous*" (168, emphasis added). If people can err in their judgment of good and evil, then utterances that express those judgments must have a truth value. But clearly, all people, even sovereigns, may err: "There is no judge subordinate, nor soveraign, but may erre in a judgement of equity" (144). There must be some fact of the matter about moral rightness if moral error is to be possible, and if it is to be possible to "discern" between good and evil, as Hobbes evidently thinks it is by his remark that one of the inconveniences of monarchy is "that the soveraigntie may descend upon an infant, or one that cannot discerne between good and evill" (97). Subjectivism is thus ruled out.

But perhaps, although evaluative utterances have truth values, their truth is relative to the attitudes of the speaker. " 'Good' and 'evill' " writes Hobbes, "are names that signifie our appetites and aversions" (79), thus perhaps the truth of evaluative statements depends solely on *correct reporting* of our appetites and aversions. This would be a peculiar view for Hobbes to hold, since he often claims that errors in judgment have to do with corruptive influences such as overvehement passions, false beliefs, mistakes about causal connections, and partiality, rather than with making a mistake about, or misreporting, what one is feeling. (This alone may be sufficient ground for dismissing the claim that Hobbes was a personal relativist. But let us suppose for a moment that this problem could be overcome.) That Hobbes took some evaluative statements to be universally true is no evidence against the claim that he held personal relativism, because to say that evaluative statements may be universally true might be only to say that people universally hold the same attitude toward the thing in question. Thus, evaluative statements could be personally relative even though "all men agree on this, that peace is good, and therefore also the way or means of peace . . . are good; this is to say morall vertues; and their contrarie vices, evill" (80).

Personal relativism is a thesis about the *truth conditions* for evaluative statements, rather than a thesis about what people regard as correct, treat as if it were authoritative, or agree to be bound by whether true or not. If Hobbes really were to hold that the *truth* of an evaluative statement were relative to the attitudes of the speaker, there would arise a tremendous puzzle about the relationship between Hobbes's personal relativism and his no less well documented "sovereign relativism." If sovereign relativism is also a thesis about the truth conditions for evaluative statements, then the two theses are incompatible (supposing that it is not the case that each subject is literally identical with his sovereign), and cannot be held simultaneously. Nor can these theses be held consecutively unless we are willing to countenance abrupt changes in truth conditions, or in the structure of moral reality. (Picture Hobbes declaring to his contemporaries, "Of course the laws of physics are sovereign-independent, and the laws of nature are sovereign-independent, but the truth about good and evil is whatever the sovereign likes, unless of course there is no sovereign, in which case the truth about good and evil is whatever each of you likes, but at any rate it is your duty to obey the sovereign in whatever he commands." It is not likely they would have found such a position plausible, or an argument built on it persuasive.)

But if sovereign relativism is not a thesis about the truth conditions for evaluative statements – if it is, rather, a thesis about, say, whose judgment we ought to defer to in evaluative questions – then it would seem to be undermined by

personal relativism. Why ought I to defer to the sovereign's
judgments when those judgments are false (that is, when
we disagree in appetite)? What is the force of this "ought"?
If I judge it bad to defer to the sovereign's judgment – if I
have an aversion to doing this – then it is, truly, bad. Why
ought I to do what I'm averse to doing? Because it's truly
good? But it isn't, if I am averse to it, because what's truly
good is whatever I have an appetite for. Unless there is no
connection between what I ought to do, and what is good
or evil – maybe I ought to do what's truly evil. If this were
Hobbes's view, it would be quite puzzling. And it won't help
to say here that what's *really* good is whatever conduces to
one's preservation, and so that one ought to defer to the
sovereign's judgment of good and evil because refusing to
defer threatens preservation, since this conception of moral
goodness conflicts with personal relativism. If we take
Hobbes to be a personal relativist, then we arrive at a view
that is inconsistent, implausible, or deeply puzzling, depending upon how we interpret his apparent sovereign relativism.

But if Hobbes isn't a personal relativist, then what is he
doing in that passage that so looks like an assertion of relativism? I would argue that he is making an *observation* about
people's tendency to *use* evaluative terms as synonyms for
their own appetites. Why? Because this practice is an important source of disorder. He writes that "divers men differ
[in their judgment] of what is conformable, or disagreeable
to reason in the actions of common life. Nay the same man,
in divers times, differs from himself, and one time praiseth,
that is, calleth good, what another time he dispraiseth, and
calleth evil: *From whence arise disputes, controversies, and at last
war*" (79, emphasis added).

People in fact tend to use evaluative terms to stand for
their attitudes, and this causes disruption. This use of evaluative terms is one instantiation of a more general tendency
to use words inconstantly: "Men give different names to one
and the same thing, from the difference of their own passions: As they that approve a private opinion call it opinion,
but they that mislike it, heresie: and yet heresie signifies no

more than private opinion; but has onely a greater tincture of choler" (50). Moral terms are virtually always used as synonyms for people's appetites and aversions, thus not only causing disorder, but also precluding the possibility that any fruitful, consensus-generating argument can begin from so-called assertions of moral fact:

> The names of such things as affect us, that is, which please, and displease us, because all men be not alike affected with the same thing, nor the same man at all times, are in the common discourses of men, of inconstant signification. . . . *For though the nature of that we conceive be the same;* yet the diversity of our reception of it, in respect of different constitutions of body, and prejudices of opinion, gives everything a tincture of our different passions. And therefore in reasoning, a man must take heed of words, which besides the signification of what we imagine of their nature, have a signification also of the nature, disposition, and interest of the speaker; *such as are the names of vertues and vices. . . . And therefore such names can never be true grounds of any ratiocination.* (17, emphasis added)

People use words inconstantly, not only using moral terms to stand for their passions, but selectively alternating between appeals to reason and appeals to practice according to what best serves their interests: "Which is the cause, that the doctrine of right and wrong is perpetually disputed, both by the pen and the sword" (50). If the doctrine of right and wrong is perpetually disputed (as Hobbes has documented that it is, and moreover explained why this phenomenon occurs), then clearly we cannot begin our argument from moral assertions. *This is why Hobbes does not do so.* Such an argumentative strategy cannot be expected to be persuasive. Therefore, nothing should be inferred about Hobbes's own moral theory, or about the proper role of moral argument in his theory, from the fact that he begins the compositive portion of his argument with the consideration of the purely prudential grounds for accepting his principle of political obligation. These are separate questions, to be decided on the basis of the textual evidence throughout *Leviathan.*

Supposing that Hobbes is making an observation about

how people tend in fact to use moral terms, we may still ask, Does he approve of this usage? The answer is quite clearly no. In Chapter 46, entitled "Of Darknesse from Vain Philosophy and Fabulous Traditions," he discusses why the schools of the Grecians were unprofitable, listing this among the reasons:

> Their morall philosophy is but a description of their own passions. For the rule of manners, without civill government, is the Law of Nature; and in it, the law civill; that determineth what is honest, and dishonest, what is just, and unjust; and generally what is good and evill: whereas they make the rules of good and bad by their own liking and disliking: By which means, in so great diversity of taste, there is nothing generally agreed on; but every one doth (as far as he dares) whatsoever seemeth good in his owne eyes, to the subversion of commonwealth. (369–70)

It is *incorrect* to suppose that private appetite is the measure of good and evil. In a state of nature the proper measure of good and evil is the law of nature, and in a commonwealth, the proper measure of good and evil is the civil law, because the law of nature requires us to take it for such. We may observe that in a state of nature, private appetite is in fact used as the measure of good and evil (partly because there are difficulties in applying and enforcing the laws of nature); but even there, it is *not* the correct measure. It is *never* the correct measure. Hobbes thus rejects personal relativism.

THE STATE OF NATURE

Now if, as I've suggested, the misuse of words to stand for our appetites (especially this misuse of evaluative terms) is such an important cause of disorder, why doesn't Hobbes set off – highlight – his discussion of it, as he does for other central sources of disorder, such as religion? He does. In the passage I've quoted above, where Hobbes asserts that from inconstant use of the terms 'good' and 'evill' arise "disputes, controversy, and at last war," he continues, "And therefore so long a man is in the condition of mere nature, (which is a condition of war,) as private appetite is the measure of good and evill: . . . " (80). Note carefully that this passage does *not* say that *so long as* people are in the condition of mere nature, their private appetites *are* the measure of good and evil; what it says is that so long as private appetite is *the measure* of good and evil, people will remain in the condition of mere nature (which is a state of war). What it *is* to be in a condition of mere nature is to be every man measuring good and evil by his own private appetite. Government by individual appetite – private judgment of good and evil – is the *defining* characteristic of a state of nature. The state of nature is not defined by the absence of government; it is defined by the absence of a public judgment – of a public measure of good and evil – which is provided in a commonwealth by the government. To be in a state of nature is to be governed every one, by his own private judgment – and this state can be present not only in the absence of any government, or before the institution of government, but also in the presence of a government if there is another authority (say, a church) that challenges its authority in such a way that each individual must use his own private judgment in deciding which, if either, authority he will obey; or in the presence of an unopposed government so long as individuals retain their own private judgment as to whether to obey its commands at all. This is why even though Hobbes believes that a state of nature "was never generally so, over all the world," he asserts that it may be perceived what a state of nature is like "by the manner of life, which men that have formerly lived under a peacefull government, use to degenerate into, in a civill warre" (63). In a civil war, an existing public judgment is challenged, and people are guided to support one side or the other, or to fend for themselves, by their own private judgments.

A state of nature just is a state of unbridled private judgment. The state of nature, writes Hobbes, is a condition "in which every one is governed by his own reason" (64); "that every private man is judge of good and evill actions . . . is true in the condition of meer nature" (168); in the state of

nature, "all men are equall, and judges of the justnesse of
their own fears" (68); "in the condition of nature, where
every man is judge, there is no place for accusation" (70).
So what is the problem? Hobbes anticipates our question,
saying, "it is true that certain living creatures . . . live sociably
one with another . . . and yet have no other direction than
their particular judgments and appetites . . . and therefore
some man may perhaps desire to know why man-kind cannot do the same" (86). The underlying theme of his answer
is that we cannot do so because we *disagree.* We disagree
about everything – about what's ours, about what honor
we're due, about what is good and evil, about religion, about
whether natural laws have been violated. Given this disagreement, no matter how many people there are, "if their
actions be directed according to their particular judgements,
and particular appetites, they can expect thereby no defence,
nor protection, neither against a common enemy, nor against
the injuries of one another" (86); and "as long as every man
holdeth this right of doing any thing he liketh; so long are
all men in the condition of warre" (65). The remedy to this
war is "to appoint one man . . . to beare their person . . . and
therein to submit their wills, every one, to his will, and their
judgements, to his judgment" (87). The subordination of
private judgment to public judgment is the means to peace.
   And once people have done this, what can disturb their
peace? One cause of disruption is "the weak and false principle" that "men shall judge of what is lawfull and unlawfull
. . . by their own private judgements," another that "subjects
sinne in obeying the commands of the common-wealth unlesse they themselves have first judged them to be lawfull"
(179). For "in such diversity as there is of private consciences,
which are but private opinions, the commonwealth must
needs be distracted, and no man dare to obey the soveraign
power, farther than it shall seem good in his own eyes" (169).
We disrupt the commonwealth by taking our own inspiration
for the rule of our action, "And thus wee fall again into the
fault of taking upon us to judge of good and evill; or to make
judges of it, such private men as pretend to be supernaturally

inspired, *to the dissolution of all civill government"* (169, emphasis added).

These uses of private judgment completely undermine the commonwealth, for "shall a private man judge, when the question is of his own obedience?" (330). It is imprudent to exercise private judgment, it is against the laws of nature to do so, and it is explicitly prohibited by God's positive laws as revealed in Scripture, for "the Scripture teacheth [that] it belongeth... to the soveraigne to bee judge, and to preascribe the rules of discerning good and evill" (105–6):

> For the cognisance of judicature of good and evill, being forbidden by the name of the fruit of the tree of knowledge, as a triall of Adams obedience; The Divel to enflame the ambition of the woman... told her that by tasting it, they should be as Gods, knowing good and evill. Whereupon having both eaten, they did indeed take upon them Gods office, which is judicature of good and evill, but acquired no new ability to distinguish them aright... it was then they first judged their nakednesse (wherein it was Gods will to create them) to be uncomely; and by being ashamed, did tacitly censure God himselfe. And thereupon God saith, "Hast thou eaten, &c." as if he should say, does thou that owest me obedience take upon thee to judge of my commandements? Whereby it is cleerly (though allegorically) signified, that the commands of them that have the right to command, are not by their subjects to be censured, nor disputed. (106)

If what a state of nature is, is a state wherein people make their own private appetites the measure of good and evil, then we know precisely where to look for Hobbes's special, set-off discussion of the disruption caused by private judgment: Chapter 13, on the catastrophic consequences of a state of nature. Modern Hobbes interpreters have, without exception, taken Chapter 13 to be the centerpiece of Hobbes's theory. But none of them has seen it for what it is – a *reductio of private judgment*, a brutal, graphic depiction of the intolerable consequences of unbridled private judgment over absolutely everything.

In Chapter 13, Hobbes lists the three principal *natural*

causes of quarrel – that is, the three main causes of disorder that are *not* the result of errors or of faulty social practices – as competition, diffidence, and glory. He writes:

> The first maketh men invade for gain; the second, for safety; and the third, for reputation. The first use violence to make themselves masters of other mens persons, wives, children, and cattell; the second, to defend them; the third, for trifles, as a word, a smile, a different opinion, and any other signe of undervalue, either direct in their persons, or by reflexion in their kindred, their friends, their nation, their profession, or their name. (62)

The desires for a safe and comfortable life, and for the esteem of our fellows, are natural desires. The problem arises when each of us uses his own judgment and reason to determine what objects shall be his, what value others shall set on him, and what his safety requires. Because then controversies arise among people that cannot be settled except by force because "the difference between man and man is not so considerable, as that one man can thereupon claim to himselfe any benefit, to which another may not pretend as well as he" (60). The desires themselves are not inherently disruptive – in a commonwealth people have and act on these very same desires without ill effects – but in the absence of a public judgment that can assign property and distinctions of honor, adjudicate disputes, and enforce its judgments, people's attempts to gratify these desires will result in a disastrous state of insecurity and misery. Private judgment is the culprit.

As I noted earlier, commentators have gravitated toward Chapter 13 as if it were the stone for deciphering the hieroglyphic of Hobbes's theory, often banishing the majority of Part 1 to the shadows as they spotlight these six pages of Hobbes's text. What is it about Chapter 13 that elicits this reaction? It isn't that Chapter 13 houses Hobbes's entire analysis of social disorder, for all it contains is his discussion of one among many sources of disorder – the disorder that arises from people's natural desires for safety, comfort, and esteem when they make private judgment the rule of their actions – rather than the disorder that arises from errors about science, errors about religion, errors from a misunderstanding of the concept of authorization, or any other sort of error. That's why it's located there in the midst of a whole catalog of various sources of disorder, after his discussion of natural religion and before his account of natural law, without special demarcation or emphasis.

But there is something special about Chapter 13. It focuses our attention on the concept of private judgment, which concept can be used to give a *blanket* account of what goes wrong in a host of disruptive activities: the use of private judgment in religion, the use of private judgment in questions of honor, in questions of property, in questions of good and evil, in questions of obedience. Chapter 13 is also unique in that the cause of disorder it isolates is not the result of any error or any misperception of reality, or at least it needn't be. The truth is, we ought to regard our sovereign's judgment as authoritative – natural reason, whether in the form of the precepts of prudence or the laws of God, requires us to do so – but if we don't have a sovereign, then we aren't making any *error* in relying on our own private judgments, because although the laws of nature are the true measure of good and evil, we must exercise private judgment in deciding whether we have followed them or others have violated them. We simply have no feasible alternative. It is in our nature to exercise our private judgments when we have no public judgment to appeal to; and unfortunately, it is in our nature to revert to the use of private judgment even when we do. If we think it permissible to use our private judgment despite the fact that we have a sovereign, then we are making an error; but if one has no sovereign, there is no choice but for each to act "according as his judgement, and reason shall dictate unto him" (64).

MORAL THEORY

If my alternative interpretation of Hobbes's remarks about the use of evaluative terms is right, then there is no reason to attribute moral subjectivism or personal relativism to Hobbes, especially considering that this causes difficulties or inconsistencies in his theory, and is not required by anything in Hobbes's conception of human nature. Does Hobbes hold some other sort of moral theory? I'm inclined to think that he does not have anything answering to our notion of a metaethical theory. He has very little to say about the status of moral statements or the conditions for their truth. He discusses the meanings of moral terms on a case-by-case basis, defining a few terms, such as 'just,' but never offers a general theoretical account of rightness or goodness. He treats the laws of nature, which he claims are both the eternal and immutable laws of God and precepts of rational prudence, as articulating a set of natural duties. And he holds the view that there can be no such thing as a dilemma of practical reason, a view I call his doctrine of the unity of practical reason, and will discuss in the next chapter. Far from thinking that moral considerations cannot motivate action, Hobbes also insists that an extremely important sort of action – namely, rebellion – cannot occur *without* the presence of a moral consideration: "To dispose men to sedition three things concur. . . . The second is pretence of right; for though a man be discontented, yet if in his own opinion there be no just cause of stirring against, or resisting the government established . . . he will never show it. . . . Without these three . . . there can be no rebellion" (*EL* 2.8.1.). But all in all, Hobbes seems to offer no systematic metaethical theory.

What he does offer is, first, a reasonably well developed ideal of virtuous character, and, second, an irritatingly elliptical argument for our primary moral duty, obedience to our existing sovereign. I shall not discuss the first of these because it has already been elegantly documented by Keith Thomas,[13] but because philosophers have found the second puzzling, I shall briefly remind the reader of how I think Hobbes intends this argument to go.

Our primary moral duty is to obey our existing sovereign in all of his commands not repugnant to our duty to God, and Hobbes declares that this duty is an implication of our natural duties enumerated in the laws of nature. It might be derived in a number of ways,[14] but two of the simplest routes of derivation are from the tenth law of nature (against arrogance) and the third (against injustice). The tenth law forbids us to reserve to ourselves any right we would not be willing to have others retain as well. We cannot be willing to have others retain a right of private judgment as to whether to obey whatever sovereign exists, because if they did, it is likely that social order would collapse, leaving us in the wholly undesirable situation of a state of nature. But if we are not willing to have others reserve this right, then we have a duty not to retain it ourselves.[15]

The third law of nature forbids us to violate faith once given, and thus forbids us to disobey the sovereign once we have consented to his rule. And *have* we consented to the sovereign's rule? Yes: "Every subject in a commonwealth hath covenanted to obey the civill law" (138), either tacitly, if we but live openly under the protection of the government;[16] or expressly, if we have taken one of the oaths of obedience common in Hobbes's day.[17]

It is somewhat surprising that Hobbes should not have made more explicit his argument for a moral duty to obey one's sovereign (as opposed to a religious duty, the argument for which is totally explicit in *Leviathan*), since it would seem that such an argument must be central to his theory. But it becomes less surprising when we consider both Hobbes's strategy and the complexity of his overall argument. Hobbes is intending to provide people with reasons – with considerations that they, given their interests and allegiances, can regard as reasons – for adhering to the principle that one is to obey one's existing effective political authority unconditionally (given how the "duty to God" exemption is specified). He offers a number of different reasons, none of which should be taken as *the* central argument. Hobbes argues that the Scriptures require us – that it is part of our duty to God – to adhere to his principle, and this is one reason (for his Christian audience) to do so. On the same ground he argues that obedience is a necessary condition for salvation, providing a second reason. He also argues that we have a natural duty to do so (given in the way I specified by the law of nature against arrogance), and this provides a third reason. Moreover, the natural duty argument relies on a prudential consideration (because the premise that one cannot be willing to have others reserve a right of private judgment concerning political obedience depends on Hobbes's argument that a state of unrestricted private judgment – a state of nature – frustrates the satisfaction of our narrowly self-interested desires), hence this prudential argument can be considered separately as providing a fourth reason for adhering to Hobbes's principle. And Hobbes offers us yet a fifth distinct reason for doing so by his argument that we have an *obligation* – a self-imposed moral duty arising out of our own act – (in virtue of our tacit or express promise to obey), which obligation is underwritten by our natural duty of fidelity. These are five distinct reasons, all of them useful in Hobbes's project of persuading people to political obedience, none of them primary, or foundational. Unless we separate them out, we are bound to find "the" argument for obedience elliptical, and "its" presentation from passage to passage inconsistent. But once we understand Hobbes's argumentative strategy, and acknowledge how complex his argument for obedience is, the impression of gaps and contradictions vanishes.

So much for Hobbes's strategy, his method, his science, his conception of human nature, his alleged atheism, his moral theory, and his analysis of disorder. We have provided interpretations of all of these components of his system that fall squarely in line with our analysis of the problem Hobbes was tackling, and the solution he proposed. I said at the end of the last chapter that standard philosophical interpreters have failed to grasp Hobbes's remedy to the problem of social disorder (even in the rare instances, as with Watkins, when they have understood his conception of the problem) because their characterization of the individual components of Hobbes's system has led them inexorably to a false conclusion. The internal logic of the standard philosophical interpretation is so powerful that any false move pretty well forces one to another false conclusion, and another, and yet another. The standard interpretation takes Hobbes to be attempting to move, by a deductive method (though with gaps and errors) from a physical scientific account of man as matter in motion to a preservation-centered conception of human nature (which precludes the motivational efficacy of religious concerns per se, or even self-interested religious concerns that might involve the death of one's present physical body, thus making theism inconsequential to the theory), to moral subjectivism or personal relativism, to a coordination problem account of disorder, to a "changing the payoffs," might-makes-order solution. But we have seen that each step in this progression involves a misinterpretation of Hobbes's position. His method is not deductive but is, rather, resolutive–compositive, where the fruits of resolution presented in Part 1 cannot serve as a deductive ground for the subsequent positive theory. His scant physical science serves not as a basis for a conception of human nature but rather as a partial and conjectural alternative to those scientific views that give rise to particular disruptive religious doctrines.[18] His conception of human nature is emphatically not preservation-centered but is, rather, brimming with overriding concerns for honor, for power, and for fulfilling religious duties. He is not a moral subjectivist or personal relativist, but rather a vigorous critic of such uses of moral terms, and herald of their disruptive consequences. His analysis of social disorder is not a primitive game-theoretic account to be reconstructed from six pages of his text, but is, instead, a rich, complex system of identifications of interconnected errors and social practices that requires more than two hundred pages just to introduce. And his solution to social disorder, as we've come to see, is much more than that we see to it that the state credibly threatens to punish disobedience; rather, it involves the correction of scientific errors, linguistic errors, religious errors, moral errors, the development of a rationalizing redescription of Christianity, massive reeducation, and persuading people that they have sufficient reasons – by means of arguments from duty, from prudence, from obligation, and from Christian religion – for rendering obedience. No defining part nor any central link of the standard philosophical interpretation survives a close scrutiny of Hobbes's text. That interpretation dissolves before our very eyes.

Chapter 8

The treatment of transcendent interests

May I not rather die if I think fit?

— Hobbes (*EW* 5:180)

According to our interpretation, Hobbes took social disorder to be primarily the result of action on transcendent interests, where these interests reflect differing private judgments. Recall that transcendent interests are interests that may override one's interest in self-preservation, or in one's own "commodious living," or any other concern of narrow self-interest. It is for the sake of satisfying their transcendent interests that people will rebel, risking punishment, civil war, and their own death.

Hobbes's primary concern is with those transcendent interests that can be *systematically* disruptive, so although, for example, one's concern for the welfare of one's loved ones may be transcendent, and might have caused a person here or there to resist the state in Hobbes's day, this interest was not a systematic cause of disorder and thus receives very little attention from Hobbes. Hobbes understood the lion's share of disorder in his own time to stem from transcendent religious interests, thus most of the argumentation of *Leviathan* is directed toward correcting the linguistic, scientific, moral, and scriptural errors on which disruptive characterizations of religious duty and interest rest. But he recognized as well two further types of potentially transcendent, potentially disruptive, interest — the interest in liberty and the interest in justice — and does accordingly devote a small share of his discussion to these. In this chapter I briefly sketch Hobbes's discussion of these additional potentially transcendent kinds of interest; but first, let me make a couple of bird's-eye observations about Hobbes's treatment of transcendent religious interests.

Two things about Hobbes's treatment of religion are remarkable for how alien they are to our own practice. The first is that Hobbes attempts to *rationalize*, rather than to cast doubt on, or to refute, Christian religion.[1] The second is that Hobbes pitches for authoritarianism in religion, rather than toleration. In each case, he chooses what may seem to us the harder row to hoe. Why?

There are a number of possible explanations for why Hobbes attempts to rationalize Christian religion rather than to attack it as a fiction, or to undermine belief in it, among which three seem to me jointly to form the correct explanation. The first is that Hobbes believed in the truth of the basic doctrines of the Judeo-Christian tradition. He speaks throughout *Leviathan* as if he thought they were true, and Aubrey provides us with evidence that he was a Christian believer.

The second is that Hobbes did not take religion to be inherently, or necessarily, subversive of order but instead to be disruptive only when it was not authoritatively regulated by the state, and so he was concerned not to abolish religious beliefs but only to show them to be properly under civil jurisdiction. Far from being inherently disruptive, religion has often provided a mechanism for *sustaining* social order, as Hobbes argues at length in Chapter 12.[2] And in a Christian commonwealth, a sovereign's civil power depends "on the opinion men have of their duty to him, and the fear they have of punishment in another world" (296). The fear of God's punishment, when the civil sovereign is taken to have authority in religion, *helps* to maintain civil obedience. So long as the civil state is acknowledged as having authority in religion, it is *better* that a people have some religion than that they do not; and it is better for people to espouse (a properly conceived) true religion (namely, Christianity) than to embrace a false religion, because then civil obedience will be further urged by the prophetic word of God contained in the Scriptures, which explicitly enjoin civil obedience. Order is more easily maintained in a population that holds true religious beliefs, than in one that holds no religious beliefs. So it is preferable, from the point of view of maintaining order, to rationalize true religion than to discredit religion altogether.

In addition to his believing Christianity to be true, and a properly conceived Christianity to be invaluable in procuring civil obedience, Hobbes also recognized that *his readers* believed Christianity to be true, and thus he had a third reason for attempting to rationalize, rather than to discredit, Christian belief: Hobbes could *never* have hoped to succeed in persuading his audience to *give up* Christianity, so to have made an argument whose success depended upon their doing this would have been utterly vain. Had Hobbes tried to delegitimize Christianity itself, he would likely have been summarily dismissed and his theory ignored. Even as it was, Hobbes's attempt merely to rationalize religion brought charges of atheism down upon him. (Although how much of this was mere abusive name-calling and how much authentic assessment, we cannot be sure.) But he was *not* summarily dismissed; he was regarded as a force to be reckoned with, as is eloquently attested by the voluminous critical commentary of his contemporaries, including many of the luminaries of his day. It would have been intellectual suicide to propound a theory requiring the outright rejection of Christianity, and Hobbes, more than anything, it would seem, wanted his theory to have a practical impact on the world.

It is important to understanding Hobbes's project that we recognize he was concerned to rationalize rather than to reject Christianity; otherwise, we lose sight of the historical specificity of his project, of his strategy of giving what his readers can accept as reasons for obedience, and of the point of the bulk of his argument in Part 3. It is particularly easy to mistake Hobbes as attempting to undermine Christianity altogether if one fixates on Part 4 without due attention to Part 3, and fails to see that Part 4 is designed to isolate the origins of *errors* within Christianity rather than to expose some alleged error *of* Christianity.[3]

The second interesting feature of Hobbes's treatment of religion is that he argues for authoritarianism in religion rather than for toleration. One might suppose that disagreement in religion is more easily handled by tolerating differences than by attempting to achieve uniformity (after all, that's the way we do it).

There can be no doubt that Hobbes found toleration a tempting possibility, and he may even have thought it best, other things equal; nevertheless, he did not believe that the people of his time could really live with religious differences, and if they could not, a theory that depended on tolerating such differences would be bound to fail. In Chapter 47, Hobbes writes:

> And so we are reduced to the independency of the primitive Christians to follow Paul, or Cephas, or Apollos, every man as he liketh best: Which, *if it be without contention,* and without measuring the doctrine of Christ, by our affection to the person of his minister . . . *is perhaps the best:* First, because there ought to be no power over the consciences of men, but of the word it selfe, working faith in every one . . . according to the purpose . . . of God himself . . . and secondly, because it is unreasonable in them, who teach there is such danger in every little errour, to require of a man endued with reason of his own, to follow the reason of any other man. (385, emphasis added)

But although Hobbes thought a policy of toleration would be best if people could really avoid religious contention, he was not at all confident that they could. There was virtual consensus in Hobbes's England that toleration ought *not* to be extended to Catholics, and there was nothing close to consensus on whether or not it should be extended even to all varieties of Protestant.[4] People were in disagreement about acceptable religious profession and practice, and many espoused religious views that required uniformity. There was as yet no settled "agreement to disagree" in matters of religion. Moreover, Hobbes thought that people's tendency to take their private judgments as authoritative, and their pride, would likely always preclude a peaceful toleration of others' religious views: "But the truth is apparent, by continual experience, that men seek not only liberty of conscience, but of their actions; nor that only, but a farther liberty of persuading others to their opinions, nor that only, *for every man desireth, that the sovereign authority should admit no other opinions to be maintained but such as he himself holdeth*" (EL 2.6.13, emphasis added). From where Hobbes stood, experience – both the personal experience of Hobbes's contemporaries in England and on the Continent, and the historical experience of Christians, particularly of the wars of religion – taught quite clearly that Christians had difficulty maintaining peace in the face of religious differences, and so that any expectation of toleration without contention would be unwarrantedly optimistic. Hobbes thought, perhaps not unreasonably, that authoritarianism in religion would better conduce to a stable peace than would toleration. And, remember, Hobbes also thought it was *true* that the civil state had authority in religion, true that the dictates of prudence, the moral laws, the eternal laws of God, and God's positive laws revealed in Scripture gave authority in matters of religious doctrine, profession, and practice to the civil sovereign. It is not surprising, then, that he should have come out in favor of authoritarianism in religion.

This allows us to note an interesting feature of the way Hobbes tackles the problem of social disorder, a feature most evident if we examine the difference between Hobbes's approach to the problem of political philosophy he faced, and the contemporary liberal approach to the problem of political philosophy we face. His problem was one of establishing and maintaining social order; ours, in developed Western democracies, is one of establishing and maintaining justice in the institutions that regulate our social and personal lives. Both problems arise when people within a society disagree in values, interests, and ends, and either cannot or will not allow everyone free reign to act on their own conceptions.

(In the latter case, this disagreement is part of the subjective circumstances of justice.) Hobbes's problem was generated by a pair of facts that may be most generally characterized as follows:

1. The fact of diversity – a collapse of consensus – among people in their values, interests, and ends (particularly concerning religion).
2. The fact of people's unwillingness to allow members of society to pursue competing values, interests, and ends, and their willingness to use state power to enforce their own values, interests, and ends.

Hobbes's strategy for resolving his problem of order is to overcome (1) by reconciling through redescription and the elimination of error competing conceptions of what's valuable, good, useful, and worthy. The liberal solution to our problem of justice focuses, rather, on overcoming, or limiting the scope of, (2) by promoting liberty, toleration, and individuality as independent values, by separating church and state, value and fact, and private and public realms, and by this means protecting the pursuit of competing conceptions. The liberal strategy has certain virtues, particularly once disagreement in values becomes intractable.

But given Hobbes's problem, there was a genuine advantage to Hobbes's strategy of tackling (1) rather than (2). If such a reconciliation as he attempted could be successful, the prospects for a settled, stable peace, as opposed to a mere modus vivendi or contingent balance of power among competing religious factions, were vastly better. People would support the existing political arrangements, not just because it was the best they could hope for at the moment given the relative balance of forces, but because those arrangements respected and furthered their values. And Hobbes's strategy for overcoming the fact of diversity – namely, rational persuasion by means of argument, redescription, reinterpretation of Scripture, and reeducation – was not vulnerable to the objection that the means employed in overcoming (1) were more objectionable than (1) itself (as, say, the use of force in overcoming diversity might be). Hobbes thought that the fact of diversity could be changed without the oppressive use of state power, and, as we've seen, he did not even think state coercion an effective *possible* means to overcoming diversity.

On the one hand, Hobbes thought there was a broad enough base for religious agreement that agreement could be reached, and such agreement could form the basis for a principled, stable peace. On the other hand, he judged (2) to be nearly impossible to overcome; for although there were some political or religious factions (Levellers, Independents, and Politiques, for example) who were willing to allow and to protect diverse public practice, their willingness to do so could have little effect in the face of competing factions who were *not* willing to do so. Moreover, for many in this period, their stance against toleration was itself a matter of principle, generated by the content of their religious views, and so not to be compromised. The content of the religious views of some factions actually required uniformity in profession and practice; whereas the content of the views of others (Congregationalists, for example) mandated that degree of toleration necessary to preserve the required autonomy and independence of various congregations. But where stances on toleration are held in a principled fashion by factions whose stances are opposed, any policy on the matter will necessarily represent a mere balance of power. A settled and stable policy will require the elimination of the principled differences that arise from differing conceptions of religious duty and interest. In light of these considerations, Hobbes's decision to focus his attention on reconciling religious differences appears quite sensible. Had we been in his place, we might very well have chosen to do the same.

In order to appreciate Hobbes's argument for absolutism, and to evaluate its plausibility and power, we will need to keep very much in mind the features of his circumstances that made his treatment of religion not unreasonable. The facts about Hobbes's world in the main – the profound, unshakable belief in the truth of Christian religion, the uniformity-requiring character of many religious views, and the dominance, or overriding importance, of religious concerns – all affect the viability of his argument for absolutism, as we shall see in Chapter 9. So, too, does the degree of people's commitment to liberty and justice, and their understanding of these notions, affect the viability of Hobbes's argument for absolutism. Thus, before we turn to that argument, a preliminary look at Hobbes's treatment of these two potentially transcendent interests is in order.

Although liberty and justice are of secondary importance for Hobbes (for a reason that I will discuss at some length in the next chapter), he recognized the potential transcendence of interests in justice and in liberty. Some of Hobbes's contemporaries did in fact urge resistance to the crown on the grounds of its infringement of liberty and its injustice, and so, as part and parcel of his effort to provide everyone with a sufficient reason for adhering to his principle of political obligation, Hobbes offered a brief treatment of each of these topics.

Hobbes's treatment of the two issues is not only much less prolonged and scrupulous than his treatment of religion, but it is also of a very different kind. In part, this is because discussion of these interests (unlike that of religion) does not involve extrarational sources of knowledge, and the settling of these issues does not require a process of reconciliation through redescription, or reinterpretation of Scripture. But the quality of his treatment of them is different also because he regarded the issues of liberty and justice as straightforward matters of fact. Hobbes believed that to advance one's interest in liberty or in justice as a justification for civil disobedience is to commit a *simple error*, and this is, interestingly, a consequence of what we might call Hobbes's doctrine of the unity of practical reason. Perhaps more than any other of his views, Hobbes's doctrine of the unity of practical reason attests to his genuine (though, as he insisted, not superstitious) belief in God.

The doctrine of the unity of practical reason consists in the view that all normative truths are perfectly compatible. There is no such thing, on Hobbes's view, as a dilemma of practical reason. The set of rules of natural duty, of natural religion, and of prudence are perfectly coextensive, and are presented each under the name of the laws of nature. Hobbes argues in the famous fool passage (whatever you may think of the power of that argument) that unjust action can never be justified by considerations of prudence. Obligations cannot conflict with natural duties, for any vow, or any obligation undertaken in violation of the laws of nature, is void, "and therefore they that vow any thing contrary to any law of nature, vow in vain; as being a thing unjust to pay such vow" (69), and "a covenant, if lawfull, binds in the sight of God . . . if unlawfull, bindeth not at all" (71). God's positive laws as revealed in the holy books of the true religion are perfectly compatible with the requirements of natural reason, "for though there be many things in Gods Word above reason . . . yet there is nothing contrary to it; but when it seemeth so, the fault is either in our unskilfull interpretation, or erroneous ratiocination" (195); and in general, "there is no law of natural reason, that can be against the law divine, for God Almighty hath given reason to a man to be a light unto him" (*EL* 19.12). The doctrine of the unity of practical reason explains why the five distinct reasons for political obedience Hobbes offers – reasons from revealed religion concerning both religious duty and special prudence, natural duty, narrow prudence, and obligation – all direct us to the same result, constituting a confluence of reasons for adhering to Hobbes's principle of political obligation. The doctrine of the unity of practical reason implies that if adherence to Hobbes's principle of political obligation is religiously required, or prudentially required, or morally required, then it is ipso facto compatible with liberty and justice, when these are properly understood.

The unity of practical reason is a consequence of God's activity. Because God has created the world and set it in motion, it all hangs together in a perfectly coherent way. God does not contradict himself, and God does not make mistakes or change his mind. (To think otherwise would be to think less of God than we might possibly.) The hand of God is conspicuous in the orderly design of the world (51). All normative requirements are designed to set us on the road to peace with one another, and reconciliation with God, and this is so because, as we must suppose, God cares for our well-being (190).[5] Thus, the fact of the matter about our religious, moral, and prudential duties – the truth about what we ought to do – is singular and unified and given by the requirements of peace, for "doctrine repugnant to peace can no more be true, than peace and concord can be against the law of nature" (91). Hobbes viewed it as his great achievement that he had seen what it is that unifies the norms of human life – namely, the requirements of peace, and reconciliation with God – and the attraction of his view is apparent once we consider how irreverent it would be to suppose that a perfectly good God has created us just to watch us destroy one another, and deprive ourselves of eternal bliss.[6]

Because the laws of nature, of prudence, and of God (both natural and prophetic) enjoin unconditional obedience to an existing effective political authority in any realm in which it can in principle be effective, it simply cannot be the case that such unconditional obedience involves objectionable constraints on liberty, or compels us to suffer injustice. If it seems so to us, it is because we are embracing mistaken conceptions of liberty and justice. It is Hobbes's job to disabuse us of our erroneous conceptions.

Hobbes deals, then, with disruptive conceptions of liberty and of justice as if they involved clear-cut errors. He feels he must deal with them because (as we have seen, and will further consider later), if people are to be able to see themselves as having reason to give their obedience, political obedience must be linked to what people actually care about. Because they do care about liberty and justice, Hobbes's "sufficient reason" strategy requires him to address himself to these concerns.

LIBERTY

The fact is that affirmation of a mistaken conception of liberty can produce rebellion. Hobbes writes that "it is an easy thing, for men to be deceived, by the specious name of liberty; and for want of judgement to distinguish, mistake that for their private inheritance, and birth right, which is the right of the publique only. And when the same errour is confirmed by the authority of men in reputation for their writings in this subject, it is no wonder if it produce sedition, and change of government" (110).

In particular, Hobbes believed that the conception of liberty embedded in the ancient republican tradition, and disseminated in his day in the universities, fueled social disorder. He identified the commitment to this conception as an independent, albeit secondary, source of disruption as early as the *Elements,* and discussed it again in both *De Cive* and *Leviathan.* Although many of Hobbes's contemporaries agreed that considerations of liberty inspired rebellion, not all accepted Hobbes's claim that the fault lay with the doctrines of ancient authors.[7] Still, Hobbes thought that a certain mistaken conception of liberty caused rebellion, and so undertook to correct this misconception, replacing it with a proper conception of his own that would reinforce stability.

Hobbes seeks to show that the only sense of liberty in which people can reasonably have an interest is what we might call practical liberty, and then to show that the degree of practical liberty one possesses is generally directly proportional to the degree of social stability, and inversely proportional to the social scope of private judgment. One's instrumental interest in practical liberty cannot be furthered by constraining sovereign authority.

Hobbes first distinguishes between two sorts of liberty, which we shall call metaphysical liberty and practical liberty. Metaphysical liberty is the capacity to frame one's own will, or to will as one chooses (freedom of the will). Practical liberty is freedom from external impediments to action: "Liberty, or freedome," writes Hobbes, "signifieth (properly) the absence of opposition; (by opposition, I mean externall impediments of motion). . . . And so of all living creatures, whilest they are imprisoned, or restrained with walls or chayns . . . we use to say, they are not at liberty to move in such manner as without those externall impediments they would" (107). So, for example (presuming one wants to do these things), one does not have practical liberty to leave the room if one is locked in, one does not have practical liberty to eat a particular apple if someone else has seized it, and one does not have practical liberty to enter one's house if others are blocking one's way. This is the only kind of liberty in which, according to Hobbes, people can have an interest. Why? Because there is no such thing as metaphysical freedom: "A free-man is he that in those things which by his strength and wit he is able to do, is not hindred to doe what he has a will to . . . from the use of the word freewill, no liberty can be inferred to the will, desire, or inclination, but the liberty of the man; which consisteth in this, that he finds no stop in doing what he has the will, desire, or inclination to doe" (108). Metaphysical freedom is impossible because everything that happens is ultimately determined by God. But this does not undermine the possibility of practical freedom:

> Liberty and necessity are consistent: As in the water, that hath not only liberty, but a necessity of descending by the channel; so likewise in the actions which men voluntarily doe; which (because they proceed from their will) proceed from liberty; and yet because every act of a mans will, and every desire proceedeth from some cause, and that from another cause, which causes in a continuall chaine (whose first link in the hand of God the first of all causes) proceed from necessity. . . . And therefore God, that seeth, and disposeth all things, seeth also that the liberty of man in doing what he will, is accompanied with the necessity of doing that which God will, & no more, nor lesse. (108)[8]

The only sort of liberty that people can reasonably desire is practical liberty, and the desire for self-determination (expressed, for example, in Patrick Henry's famous declaration "Give me liberty or give me death") is, in Hobbes's view, a desire for practical liberty – it is a desire to act, without impediment, according to one's private judgment. Practical liberty, according to Hobbes, signifies the absence of *external* impediments, as opposed to internal obstacles – contrary desires or inclinations (such as an extreme fear that would have to be overcome) – to doing what one wants to do. Practical liberty is good, not in itself but as a means to doing, or getting, whatever one wants to do or to get. We care about obstacles to our doing what we want to do only because (and insofar as) they hinder our doing as we wish. And correlatively, our interest in removing, or preventing the erection of, obstacles to action, is derived from, and extends no farther than, our interest in achieving our ends. The value of practical liberty is derivative, a mere reflection of its instrumental connection to the successful performance of actions.

What follows from this, according to Hobbes, is that one cannot expect to increase one's practical liberty by limiting the authority of the government. This first conclusion relies on the observation that the fewer the external impediments, the greater one's practical freedom, and because the actions of others may create obstacles to one's doing what one wants to do (as in the cases of the apple and the house already mentioned), one's own practical freedom is roughly inversely proportional to the freedom of others. This means that in what Hobbes calls a state of license (like the state of nature), where all behavior occurs according to private judgment, there is virtually no practical freedom. Men in unregulated pursuit of their desires will pose impediments to the similar pursuits of others, particularly (though not only) under conditions of moderate scarcity. And the greater the number of men acting according only to their private judgments, the narrower the practical freedom of each.[9]

It is on this basis that Hobbes argues that the greater the sphere of private judgment, the lesser the practical liberty of all subjects. It would be paradoxical to limit the government in an attempt to gain greater freedom, because to limit the government is to increase the sphere of private judgment, and so to increase dramatically the number of people whose actions can pose impediments to one's own. In an unlimited regime, only the sovereign power can (if it wishes to) impede one's actions, but in a limited regime, everyone can (with respect to some range of actions) impede one's actions. This is clearest if we consider Hobbes's own self-preservation case. The impediments to securing one's self-preservation posed by a thousand men of roughly equal one's strength and wit, each acting according to his own private judgment, can be expected to be many times greater than the impediments posed by a single sovereign (even if a thousand times more powerful than oneself), because in the latter case there is only one entity which can impede one, and the likelihood of its deciding to do so is smaller than the likelihood that many among the one thousand will (either by accident or by design) impede one.[10] In society, says Hobbes, men do have practical liberty: "For if wee take liberty in the proper sense, for corporall liberty, that is to say, freedom from chains, and prison, it were very absurd for men to clamor as they doe for the liberty they so manifestly enjoy. Againe, if we take liberty for an exemption from lawes, it is no lesse absurd, for men to demand as they doe, that liberty by which all other men may be masters of their lives" (109).

In fact, in Hobbes's view, one's political authority usually does not limit one's practical freedom *at all*. This is because laws do not limit, but actually increase, practical freedom![11] Hobbes writes that "generally all actions which men doe in commonwealths for feare of the law, [are] actions which the doers had liberty to omit" (108), and "Again, the consent of a subject to sovraign power, is contained in these words 'I authorise, or take upon me, all his actions'; in which there is *no restriction at all* of his own former naturall liberty" (112, emphasis added). A law does not reduce people's practical freedom, because a law constrains action, not by erecting *external* impediments to action but, rather, by framing a person's *will*. Recognition that some proposed course of action is illegal (usually) makes people *decide* not to do it. The law does not impede their doing what they have decided to do; the law comes into decisions about *what* to do. It serves as a mechanism for coordinating private judgment. The same is true, in Hobbes's view, of moral and religious requirements; they affect what it is that people want to do, rather than create an obstacle to people's doing what they want to do. It is the physical actions of others, and physical features of the world, that diminish one's practical liberty. So, for example, a restraining order doesn't diminish practical liberty, but if one decides to approach the person for whose protection the order was issued, the bodyguard or the locked door do. This is how Hobbes is able to say that practical freedom is compatible with the rule of law, and that an effort to increase practical freedom by restricting the scope of the rule of law is self-defeating.[12]

Thus, Hobbes's argument against the claim that one might have an interest in liberty capable of providing one with a reason for political disobedience is that (1) there are two senses of liberty: (2) liberty in its metaphysical sense is illusory, and so one cannot have any reason for political disobedience (or for anything else) from it; and (3) liberty in its practical sense is not decreased, but is instead enhanced, by political obedience.

No doubt this will strike many people as a somewhat odd, and not entirely satisfactory, argument. But it is perfectly predictable, given Hobbes's view on the role of private judgment in social disruption. Hobbes's argument here is fully compatible with the rest of his theory, and it is not, in itself, absurd. Even we can see how, for example, laws regulating property reduce the conflict that would interfere with our doing many things that we want to do.[13] But those who are still dissatisfied with it will be relieved to find that very little hangs on the success of this argument. As we shall see in the following chapter, Hobbes could have reasonably dispensed with this argument altogether.

JUSTICE

Hobbes's treatment of justice is even more perfunctory than his treatment of liberty. He asserts that virtually no injury done to a subject by his political authority can be rightly construed as an act of injustice. Hobbes argues simply that justice is nothing more than the rendering to another of what is due him by covenant. Where there is no covenant to be broken, there can be no injustice. The political authority is not to be understood as having made any covenant with subjects (since their obligation to obey is unconditional), and so can do them no injustice; whereas subjects are understood to have (if not explicitly then) tacitly covenanted with one another to obey their political authority (signified by their having accepted the benefits of one another's obedience by living openly in the commonwealth), and so their disobedience is an injustice to one another. Furthermore, Christian subjects have it on scriptural authority that they owe it to God to obey their civil authority in all of its commands, and thus violate their baptismal covenant to obey God (hence acting unjustly) if they refuse to render civil obedience. (Christian sovereigns owe it to God not to violate the laws of nature, but this duty is to God only, who alone may hold them accountable for violations. That is, Christian sovereigns may act unjustly, but only toward God and never toward subjects.) Thus, subjects are simply mistaken if they think that the political authority has done them an injustice, and, in fact, themselves do an injustice both to God and to one another by withholding their obedience. Injustice, then, is a very specific notion that cannot be made use of in supporting a claim against one's civil authority.

Hobbes's attenuated treatment of justice may strike us as insufficient, but again, it is in keeping with his concern to restrain the scope of private judgment, and might well not have appeared so inadequate from within a seventeenth-century perspective. His seemingly impoverished, formalistic, treatment of justice is rendered more reasonable by an acknowledgment of the seventeenth-century phenomenon of the subordination of secular moral concerns (such as a concern for justice) to religious concerns. And its length relative to the treatment of religion is explicable in terms of its degree of subordination. The subordinate place of justice within Christian religion is made vividly explicit by Christian religion itself. Sin is the violation of God's law, and is injustice in one who has covenanted by his baptism to obey God; but, as Hobbes points out, "if God should require perfect innocence, there could no flesh be saved" (322). We ought not to place so much weight on the claims of justice, because, in justice, we all deserve damnation. Moreover, even if we were to reject Hobbes's analysis of justice, and to retain our own mistaken conception, it would still be true that we are too shortsighted to be able accurately to judge the justice of anything, because knowledge of the events of the afterlife might well alter our perceptions of justice. And, of course, to refuse to obey *God's* commandment that we obey our civil authority on the grounds that that authority is, in *our* judgment, unjust, is the most extreme form of hubris imaginable.

The potential transcendence of interests in liberty and justice positions these concerns as possible impediments to the acceptance and implementation of Hobbes's political theory, and so he offers a preemptory treatment of these concerns. I have already reproduced his actual arguments on each of these topics. But the warrant for Hobbes's thinking his treatment of these topics adequate to his purpose is intimately tied to his reasons for thinking he has established the necessity for – indeed, the justifiability of – absolutism. In order to determine whether he is warranted in discussing these topics so cursorily, we must examine his argument for absolutism. Is Hobbes right to think that he has established absolutism? Is his argument for it valid? Is it sound? Does he actually succeed in justifying absolutism? We shall now attempt to answer these questions, through an investigation of Hobbes's most infamous claim, namely, that his political theory entails, and indeed justifies, absolutism.

Chapter 9

Hobbes's absolutism

The sovereign power is not to be resisted.
                              – Hobbes (*EL* 8.6)

Hobbes evidently thought he had in his political theory demonstrated both the necessity and the desirability of political absolutism. He took himself to have provided a solid argument for rendering absolute obedience to any existing effective political authority – an argument that could justify such unconditional obedience. The standard philosophical interpreters have typically disagreed with Hobbes's assessment of his success in this endeavor. Given the standard interpreters' accounts of Hobbes's analysis of social disorder, of his conception of human nature, and of his conception of individual rationality, those interpreters have convincingly argued that absolutism simply does not follow from Hobbes's argument.[1] Some have argued that Hobbes failed to establish his claim that the only alternative to political absolutism is anarchy, thus failing to establish the need for political absolutism; and that because there is a more appealing intermediate possibility, he failed also to establish the desirability of absolutism.[2] Others have argued that Hobbes's conception of human nature makes it impossible for him to offer any alternative to anarchy at all, because although it's true that only submission to an absolute state could increase the security of Hobbesian men, they are not sufficiently tractable for it to be possible for them so to submit themselves.[3] So even if Hobbes has

289

shown in some abstract sense the necessity and desirability
of political absolutism, the impossibility of it undermines
the success of his argument for absolutism. Still others have
argued that, as Watkins puts it, "if men were wolves, it is
sometimes said, a Hobbesian sovereign would be the only
remedy; fortunately, men are better than wolves."[4] Here it
is conceded that absolutism is both necessary and desirable
for Hobbesian human beings. But because real human
beings are *not* as Hobbes characterizes them, nothing follows from Hobbes's argument about the *actual* necessity or
desirability of absolutism. So again, Hobbes's argument for
absolutism fails. On the standard philosophical interpretation, absolutism is either impossible to establish, or unnecessary. Nonetheless, Hobbes insisted that absolutism
was entailed by his argument. And because he did, we
have reason, other things equal, to prefer an interpretation
of his theory according to which this assertion is true.

Perhaps the single most interesting implication of our interpretation of Hobbes's theory is that Hobbes turns out to have
been correct in arriving at absolutism. His absolutism follows
by a valid argument from premises that are by no means
obviously false, absurd, unreasonable, or implausible.[5]

TWO SENSES OF ABSOLUTISM

To see the truth of Hobbes's contention, we must distinguish
between two senses in which a theory can be said to be
absolutist or to entail absolutism. The first is that the theory
asserts the necessity of an absolutist *form of government;* the
second is that the theory entails an *absolute obligation* to obey
the government, regardless of the form or features of that
government. An absolutist form of government is a form in
which the powers of government are neither divided nor
limited, a form in which, in Kavka's words, there is "total
concentration of the power to select exercisers of unlimited
powers."[6]

What is distinctive about an absolutist form of government
can best be seen in terms of H.L.A. Hart's distinction be-

tween the primary and secondary rules of a social structure.[7] Primary rules are rules of obligation that regulate the conduct of citizens, for example, criminal laws, contract laws, tax laws, and the like. Secondary rules are rules about the primary rules of the system that "specify the ways in which the primary rules may be conclusively ascertained, introduced, eliminated, varied, and the fact of their violation conclusively determined."[8] Most important among these secondary rules is the rule of recognition, which identifies what is, and what is not, to count as a valid legal rule in the system. Using Hart's classification, we may say that if the rule of recognition contains no substantive restriction on what primary rules can count as valid legal rules in the system when those rules are made by a single body, then the system is absolutist. Substantive restrictions would include not only such stipulations as that the primary rules not infringe on some private sphere (that is to say, not abridge free speech, freedom of religion, and so on), but also such stipulations as that the primary rules be made according to certain procedures, that they be made with the consent of, or be approved by, other bodies, that they be universally applicable, that they be permanent standing rules, or that they be consistent with the existing primary rules of the system. We may say, roughly, that a system in which the rule of recognition substantively restricts the *ways* in which primary rules can be made (one that, for example, requires that primary rules be approved by other bodies) is a system of divided sovereignty;[9] a system in which the rule of recognition contains restrictions on the *content* of primary rules is a system of limited sovereignty. An absolutist system is one in which the rule of recognition contains neither sort of restriction on primary rules.[10]

Although, as we'll see presently, it would not be incorrect to view Hobbes's theory as endorsing absolutism in this first sense, his theory is more properly conceived as absolutist in the second sense distinguished above – namely, that it entails an absolute obligation to obey one's effective government whatever the form or policies of the government.[11] Hobbes's absolutism falls out of his principle of political obligation, a principle that admits no exemptions from obedience to an effective government, no matter what the form or policies of that government. To say that the principle contains no exceptions that would allow disobedience to an effective government is just to say that the principle requires that subjects obey the effective government of the commonwealth of which they are members unconditionally – absolutely. There are no grounds upon which one might legitimately refuse to obey an effective government.[12]

The question of form of government is, for Hobbes, subordinate to his primary argument that people have an unconditional obligation to obey their existing effective government, whatever its form. This is clear enough in the case of differing forms of unlimited and undivided sovereignty, such as monarchy, aristocracy, and democracy. Hobbes writes that "of the three sorts, which is the best, is not to be disputed, where any one of them is already established; but the present ought alwaies to be preferred, maintained, and accounted best; because it is against both the law of nature, and the divine positive law, to doe any thing tending to the subversion thereof" (301). This is so even though an assembly may disagree with itself, "and that to such a height, as may produce a civill warre" (96); and "in a democracy, or aristocracy, the publique prosperity conferres not so much to the private fortune of one that is corrupt, or ambitious, as doth many times...a civill warre" (96). Even though Hobbes sees great danger of dissolution in democratic and aristocratic forms of government, he insists nonetheless that we have a duty of unconditional obedience to *any* existing effective government, regardless of its form. This shows that his primary concern is to defend his principle of political obligation, rather than any particular form of government. In this case, the considerations he advances in support of monarchy over alternative forms of government are purely practical. As a purely practical matter, the most stable form of government (and so the best form) will be the one that gives the least scope to private judgment – namely, monarchy. It is preferable that the unified sovereign be a single natural person (a monarch) rather than an assembly, since an assembly is compiled of distinct individuals whose differences in private judgment may allow for dissension or stalemate among them. But if one's existing effective government is an aristocracy, the fact that monarchy is preferable can provide no justification for resisting, or attempting to alter, existing arrangements. And, needless to say, this consideration of the scope of private judgment removes the ground for even preferring, let alone justifying resisting an existing effective government in order to obtain, democracy.

What about Hobbes's preference for undivided and unlimited sovereignty over mixed or limited forms of government? Is this preference also subordinate to his concern that people give unconditional obedience to any existing effective government, and is this preference, too, a purely practical matter? It would seem so. Hobbes does *not* hold that only an absolute government has a claim on subjects' obedience, or that subjects could be justified in resisting the commands of a mixed or limited government. And this indicates that establishing an absolutist form of government is indeed less central to Hobbes's project than is establishing an unconditional obligation to obey any effective government, no matter what its form. Hobbes's argument does not make political obedience conditional on the form of government at all. Scripture tells us that we must obey the existing government, period. In fact, all of the reasons for obedience Hobbes offers us – from prudence, from natural duty, and from Christian religion – will apply to *any* effective government, regardless of its form. If a government is not effective, we lose our prudential and moral reasons for obeying it. But so long as it is effective, these reasons for obedience kick in as strongly for a limited or mixed form as for an absolute one. So if Hobbes were to have held that we can be obligated to obey only an absolute form (which he did not), this could only have been because only such a form can be effective. But then, the reason for preferring an absolute form of government *would be* purely practical, a matter of its degree of aptitude to produce peace. Hobbes does indeed think an absolutist *form* of government is, for practical reasons, preferable to any other, but I don't believe he thought that *only* an unlimited and undivided government could be effective (England had, for example, had periods of effective government). The question is one, not of effectiveness at a time, or *simpliciter*, but of long-term stability. Governments can be more or less enduringly effective, depending in part on the degree of free reign given to private judgment by the form itself,[13] and in part on the *content* of the private judgments that the possessors of sovereign rights actually make.[14] A divided form will *not* be problematic unless the possessors of the various rights of sovereignty *disagree* in their particular judgments about what is to be done. Nor will a limited form become unstable unless the government and the limiting power (the people, or whatever) *disagree* in their actual judgments as to whether the government has exceeded its authority. Some forms of government may give less reign to private judgment than others, and to this extent they will tend to be more stable, and hence more enduringly effective. But governments in all their forms and manifestations are ultimately to be judged solely by their position on a continuum of effectiveness. What is crucial, as a theoretical task, is that people be made to see that they have sufficient reason to obey any effective government unconditionally. What is crucial is that they renounce the use of private judgment, that they embrace a commitment to absolute subjection.

Hobbes's reasons for preferring an absolute government can all be understood in terms of the idea of the scope of private judgment: that form of government which gives least scope to private judgment – to the possibilities of dissension and stalemate generated by differing private judgments – is, for the practical purpose of maintaining social order, to be preferred. Thus, it is preferable that sovereignty be unified rather than divided (as in, say, "mixed monarchy") because when sovereignty is divided the possibility arises that the many possessors of various sovereign powers may be led by differing private judgments to adopt incompatible ends or policies. Hobbes writes that "in the kingdome of God, there may be three persons independent, without breach of unity in God that reigneth, but where men reign, *that be subject to diversity of opinions,* it cannot be so" (172, emphasis added). Likewise, an unlimited sovereign is to be preferred over a constitutional, or limited, regime because a regime of this latter sort fosters the false belief that one's obligation to obey the state is contingent upon the state's respecting traditional or constitutional limits, and encourages the use of what must be private judgment to determine whether or not the state has overstepped these limits. As a practical matter, it is dangerous to stability to institutionalize norms of governmental conduct, since people will almost certainly be misled into thinking that their obedience is conditional upon the government's satisfaction of those norms. Once people have these expectations, they will think they can legitimately impose their expectations on the government, which, if it disappoints them, may then be resisted according to their own private judgments. But in each case, the considerations advanced are considerations of efficiency or expediency, directly tied to the scope of private (and hence potentially variable) judgment. The difference between an absolute monarchy and a constitutional democracy with separation of powers is that the former can better ensure social stability because it minimizes the disruptive effects of variable private judgment among subjects, even in the best case, when all are acting in good faith. Hobbes's most central theoretical conclusion is that people's obligation in each instance is equally stringent, equally absolute, provided only that both governments are effective. The form of government is irrelevant to political obligations. What is crucial is that subjects have the proper *attitude* toward the government, whatever its form: "In those nations, whose commonwealths have been long lived, and not been destroyed but by forraign warre, the subjects never did dispute of the sovereign power" (107).

Nonetheless, there *is* one principled difference between absolutist forms of government and limited or divided forms, and this difference accounts for Hobbes's insistence on the importance of unlimited and undivided sovereignty, and cor-

respondingly on his insistence on the importance of unconditional obedience. Limited and divided states build in –
institutionalize – room for the exercise of private judgment.
Their very structure allows for, and invites, the use of private
judgment. This feature of the structure of limited and divided
governments is a defect that can be avoided. We can build
states that do not suffer from this inherent weakness. In
contrast, the room allowed for the exercise of private judgment in a sovereign assembly is not the result of any *structural*
feature. In an assembly, the majority (either simply, or by
some margin or determinate number) rules – there is a procedure that allows an assembly to act as a single, unlimited,
sovereign entity. When it fails to do so, it is not because of
any built-in weakness but is, rather, because individual members are defying the majority, or usurping power, or acting
as renegades. Thus, although a sovereign assembly may become paralyzed by the use of private judgment, this is to be
attributed to abuses of power rather than to some inherent
– and remediable – defect in the structure of government.
Hobbes's preference for an absolutist form of government *is*
practical, but it is not merely practical. It is also a principled
preference. Nonetheless, the most crucial feature of Hobbes's
position – and the one that captures his principled preference
– is his insistence that subjects adhere to a principle of unconditional obedience, no matter what the form of their
government.

Thus, Hobbes's absolutism is really absolutism of the most
powerful form precisely because it takes the form or policies
of government to be irrelevant from the standpoint of political obligation; on, for instance, Locke's scheme, one could
(under certain circumstances) have a moral right to disobey
even a mixed regime in which the legislative power is shared,
but in Hobbes's scheme one has a duty to obey any regime
absolutely. Thus, on our interpretation, Hobbes's absolutism
will not turn out to be defensible merely because it is a weak-
ened, or derivative, form of absolutism. The kind of absolutism I'll argue Hobbes did establish is actually stronger than

the sort of absolutism that the standard philosophical interpreters claim Hobbes failed to establish.

Let us remind ourselves of the way in which Hobbes settled
on his principle of political obligation. He began from the
concept of a commonwealth as a great multitude united into
a single person who may use the strength and means of them
all as he, in his own single judgment, shall think expedient
for their peace and common defense. Hobbes defended each
clause of this definition by showing its relation to ensuring
the end of commonwealths, that is, peace and security. In
the process, he spun out from this definition various rules
of reason for the construction of an indestructible commonwealth. The contraries of these rules were translated into
grounds for disobedience to an effective government, and
compiled into two alternative principles of political obligation
– one a principle of divided sovereignty, and one a principle
of limited sovereignty – both of which were then argued to
be incapable of ensuring a perpetually stable commonwealth.
As we saw, this argument involved showing that the increased play given to potentially variable private judgment
by each of the alternative principles undermined their ability
to guarantee a perpetually stable commonwealth.

Hobbes's argument for this conclusion was particularly
compelling given the way human beings were characterized
– as prideful people partial to their own interests, desirous
of power and eminence, easily offended, gullible and man-
ipulable, whose differing passions, experience, and education lead them to form differing judgments. It was plain to
see that private judgment really would pose extreme problems for people so characterized; and that characterization
of human beings was compiled from Hobbes's analysis of
the causes of his own society's disorder (presented in Part
1), and defended by appeal to people's social experience.
Hobbes went on to argue that each of his readers should
recognize himself as having prudential reason to opt for a
principle of political obligation that gave the least play to
private judgment, and this because the variability of private

judgment was at the root of that social disorder which threatened the self-preservation and commodious living of each. And once the narrowly prudential undesirability of unrestricted private judgment had been shown, the (arguably more powerful) argument from natural duty in support of Hobbes's principle could be made out.

In establishing his principle of political obligation (in both identifying that principle and in providing reasons for adhering to it), Hobbes was intending to undermine the possibility of satisfying two of the three conditions necessary for social disorder. Recall that in his clearest statement of the conditions for rebellion Hobbes named (1) discontent, (2) pretense of right, and (3) hope of success.[15] Hobbes's principle of political obligation – which, when fully specified, admits no grounds on which one could legitimately disobey one's effective government – would, if people could be brought to accept it, eliminate the possibility that (2) could ever be satisfied. It denies all claims of right against the government, and thus, if people see they have sufficient reason to accept this principle, one of the conditions necessary to motivate them to rebel will become impossible to meet. In addition, the narrowly prudential considerations that compose one part of Hobbes's reasons argument for his principle ought to remove much of the discontent that is a precondition of rebellion; once they see that they stand to fare better in some important material respects – security, property possession, and liberty – by following Hobbes's principle, people should experience significantly less discontent. And the superimposed argument from natural duty works to deny people some grounds for pretense of right.

But it is essential to notice that not every ground for discontent or for pretense of right is neutralized by the early portion of Hobbes's argument. Indeed the most important ground for both – the one Hobbes took to be the major cause of disorder in his own time – is left completely untouched. Religious interests – competing transcendent (often uniformity-requiring) religious interests – constituted a paramount source of both discontent and pretense of right. If obedience to the government would require one to violate one's duties to God as these are stipulated by revealed true religion, then one has every right to resist the government; and if obedience would jeopardize one's salvation, one has every reason for discontent of the most powerful sort. If the satisfaction of religious interests is taken to have priority, then we are still at square one; narrowly prudential and secular moral interests be damned. Obviously, the possibility of establishing an absolutist doctrine depends on a skillful handling of these religious interests, and if absolutism is entailed by Hobbes's theory, this will be so because of some feature of Hobbes's argument from revealed religion.

HOBBES'S ARGUMENTS FOR ABSOLUTISM

Hobbes provides two different arguments for absolutism, both of which depend on the *content* of his readers' religious views. The first, more general, argument is that people have a sufficient reason (that is, a reason not overridden by contrary reasons) to adhere to Hobbes's principle of political obligation, which is, as we've seen, an absolutist principle. The principle is a principle of unconditional obedience to an effective sovereign, so if people can see that they have a sufficient reason to adhere to it, then absolutism (of the strongest sort I have already distinguished) will have been justified to them. If Hobbes establishes his argument that people have prudential reasons from their interest in security and commodious living, and moral reasons from both natural duty and obligation, for adhering to his absolutist principle, and no religious reason not to adhere to it (given a proper understanding of the requirements of true religion), then, concluding that these collectively constitute a sufficient reason for adhering to the principle, unconditional obedience to the sovereign will have been justified. It is obviously crucial to this "sufficient reasons" justification that religion not provide any reason for refusing to adhere to the absolutist principle, and this will, of course, depend on the content of his readers' religious views.

The second, and perhaps less attractive although in some ways stronger, argument for absolutism also depends crucially on Hobbes's claims about not only the content but also the *status* of his readers' religious interests. The form of the second of Hobbes's arguments of absolutism is so simple that the argument is easy to miss. The argument is simply:

P1: There can be no justification for refusing to fulfill one's duty to God.
P2: Adherence to Hobbes's principle of political obligation (which requires unconditional obedience to one's effective sovereign) is a part of one's duty to God.
C: There can be no justification for refusing to adhere to Hobbes's principle of political obligation (i.e., for refusing to give unconditional obedience to one's effective sovereign).

This argument could also be framed in terms of an overriding positive duty to fulfill one's duty to God, of which unconditional political obedience is a part. Whichever way the argument is viewed, we can see that its aim is to undermine the "pretense of right" condition on rebellion. Because the argument makes no reference to the form or policies of one's government, it is properly understood as an argument for the stronger sort of absolutism I have described. I will say something in what follows about Hobbes's reasons for thinking the first premise (P1) acceptable. But first, let us begin by reminding ourselves of how Hobbes set up his argument for P2.

As we saw, Hobbes's principle of political obligation contained two formal restrictions on obedience to one's government, both dictated by the concept of a commonwealth. The condition on obedience was that the government be effective in preserving its members. The reason for this condition was that the end of a commonwealth is protection, and so nothing that does not protect its members can be a commonwealth, and anyone who is not protected by a particular commonwealth is not to be accounted a member of it. The exemption from obedience was that subjects may disobey their sovereign in those of its commands that would require them to violate their duties to God, which also was dictated by the end for which commonwealths are created. Commonwealths cannot protect their members from what may be the disastrous consequences of disobeying God, and so cannot insist on obedience in this particular realm, even though they are due obedience in all other matters.

Although the "duty to God" exemption was formally derived from the concept of a commonwealth, there was an additional reason why Hobbes had to include it. Many of his readers had a transcendent interest in fulfilling their duties to God, and would flatly have rejected any principle that did not include this exemption. But the exemption was itself problematic: It left open the possibility that massive numbers of subjects would exempt themselves from political obedience, to the disruption of the commonwealth. This possibility would have undermined Hobbes's project of providing people with a sufficient reason for adhering to a principle of political obligation that really could, if widely followed, ensure a perpetually stable commonwealth.

Hobbes's redescription argument was designed to remove any possibility that his readers might see themselves as having religious grounds for disobeying their effective government. He argued that God requires us to acknowledge the civil sovereign's judgment as authoritative in matters of religion, with the result that a situation in which the sovereign could command something repugnant to our duty to God becomes, for all practical purposes, impossible (rendering Hobbes's exemption from political obligation inconsequential). The beauty of that argument was that it not only purported to show that Christians could have no *religious* grounds for violating Hobbes's principle, but it also had the indirect consequence of establishing that for any Christian who had a transcendent interest in fulfilling his duties to God, there could be *no* grounds *whatsoever* for violating the principle. Both of these results were due to the particular character of Hobbes's readers' religious interest.

The possibility that people could have religious grounds for rejecting Hobbes's principle was ruled out by Hobbes's demonstration that (a) there are no grounds given by the dictates of natural reason or the personal revelations of others for affirming any particular substantive description of one's interest in fulfilling one's duties to God over and against any substantive description one's political authority might dictate, and (b) the Scriptures tell us that God requires us to obey our civil authority in all of its commands. The first consideration entails that people have no religious reason for refusing to obey the sovereign; the second entails that people have religious reason for obeying the sovereign. This latter consideration, that one owes it to God to obey one's political authority unconditionally, is what supports Hobbes's absolutist principle: Once it has been established that disobedience to the sovereign *is* disobedience to God, one cannot have any religious grounds for disobeying one's political authority. The possibility of a religious justification of disobedience is shown to be illusory. Thus, one has a narrowly prudential reason and a special prudential reason, two moral reasons (from natural duty and from obligation), and a religious reason to adhere to Hobbes's principle, and if one's religious interest is transcendent, one can be sufficiently motivated even to sacrifice one's preservation in defense of the political authority, overriding even the effectiveness condition on political obedience, and, less dramatically, to refrain from free riding in those very few cases where the possibility of profitable disobedience seems to arise.

As to the second point, the extremely powerful indirect effect that Hobbes's demonstration deprives people with transcendent religious interests of any grounds whatsoever for withholding political obedience, this is a consequence of the peculiarity of Judeo-Christian religious views generally. One who has a transcendent religious interest of this sort will see the fulfillment of one's religious duties as *the most important thing*. This observation about the *status* of religious interests will be used to support premise one in Hobbes's argument for absolutism.

That one who has a transcendent Judeo-Christian religious interest will see the fulfillment of one's religious duties as the most important thing reflects an ordering of potentially conflicting transcendent interests. Any transcendent interest will (according to our definition) trump concerns of narrow self-interest, overriding a person's interest in his own preservation and flourishing. But a person may have a number of transcendent interests, which circumstances bring into conflict and so which cannot all be satisfied. For example, a person might have a transcendent interest in the preservation of his children (an interest that overrides his interest in his own preservation and flourishing), which he might nonetheless refrain from pursuing if the satisfaction of that interest conflicted with another transcendent interest – say, an interest in liberty or justice, or in putting an end to genocide. If I am the leader of a fifth column in Nazi Germany, I might well allow the enemy to kill my hostage child rather than betray my cause, even though I would trade my own life for my child's if I could. Conversely, one might under some conditions resign oneself to a life of oppression, refusing to act on one's transcendent interest in liberty or justice, rather than risk some harm that might come to one's children as a result of one's resistance. It is clearly possible for one to have conflicting transcendent interests, and one's actions will depend on what one takes to matter most.

But the peculiarity of transcendent Judeo-Christian religious interests is that although one might conceivably find oneself psychologically unable to do that which one understood to be religiously required, one cannot feel that one is *justified* in violating one's religious duties. For one who holds (Judeo-Christian) religious beliefs, it makes no sense to say, "I know I have a duty to God to do this, but I am justified in (have legitimate grounds for) refusing to do my duty." On certain conceptions of God it might be possible for one to see oneself as being justified in one's disobedience (for example, on the conception of the gods in Greek religion); the idea of justifiably "defying the gods" is not in all cases conceptually incoherent.[16] On such conceptions, and particularly if one's religious interests were purely prudential, it could be conceptually consistent to decide that one ought, on the whole, to disobey the deity. But a transcendent religious interest of the sort Hobbes's readers held precludes this possibility. Their transcendent interest in doing their duties to God involved a certain view about, so to speak, who God is – God ought to be obeyed because God is the supremely good, all-knowing, all-powerful creator – and given this view about God's goodness, omniscience, and power one cannot think oneself in any position justifiably to refuse to submit one's judgment to God's.[17] Consideration of the story of Abraham and Isaac shows that even other transcendent interests must give way to fulfilling one's duties to God. So if one has a transcendent interest in fulfilling one's duties to God when God is so conceived, then one will view the satisfaction of that interest as the most important thing, and (supposing that one believes one owes it to God to obey one's political authority unconditionally) this will deprive one of any grounds whatsoever for refusing to obey the state. There will be *no* possibility of "pretense of right." This is made perfectly clear in the book of Job, from which *Leviathan* takes its title. God is greater than men, his purposes are his own, and men must subordinate their private judgment to God's. It is not up to men to judge God (as they would be doing if they refused to fulfill their duty to God to obey their sovereign on the ground that justice requires disobedience), and a recognition of this fact is entailed by the acknowledgment of God as God.

It is this, I think, which explains why Hobbes gives so relatively little attention to other potentially transcendent interests – interests, for example, in liberty or in some substantive conception of justice. Virtually all of Hobbes's readers were deeply religious: If, as seemed to be the case, their religious interests were transcendent, then a demonstration of the religious grounds for obedience would give them a sufficient reason for obeying, because it would *override* all of their interests, including other transcendent interests; if, per chance, their religious interest were *not* transcendent, then, Hobbes thought, it was unlikely they would have any transcendent interests at all.

This latter thought may strike us as implausible, but, I think, it did not seem so to Hobbes, nor in fact *is* it implausible when predicated of Hobbes's contemporaries. Of an age when religion was so powerful, so nearly universal, and so pervasive, it is hard to imagine how human beings (who are – it is clear that Hobbes was right about this – prone to believe there are things greater than themselves, to see these things as giving their lives meaning, and to care passionately about them), could fail to have a transcendent interest in doing God's will. Even setting aside the natural needs that religion seems well suited to meet (which Hobbes took to be a natural and ineradicable feature of human beings, the seeds of natural religion being something "that can never be so abolished out of humane nature but that new religions may againe be made to spring out of them" [58]), the whole cultural history of Hobbes's contemporaries, the social and psychological pressures on them, and what must have been their enormous psychic investment given the recent wars of religion, must have made a transcendent interest in religion nearly inescapable. In fact, it seems quite reasonable to suppose that the absence of a transcendent religious interest, *in a believer,* would signal a defect of courage and character, a small, self-regarding pettiness (perhaps a sign of that same natural weakness that makes men so susceptible to sin) that would make such people incapable of any transcendent interests at all. On what basis could a Christian too small to be willing to die in God's service have the courage of his convictions for anything else? For us it may be easier to have transcendent moral interests in the absence of transcendent religious interests, but when this is so, it is (arguably) so because we have no religious interests at all.[18] For many in the modern age, moral interests have taken the place of religious interests, and for the remainder, moral interests are seen as a part of religious interests. In Hobbes's day, the latter was certainly true, but, I think, Hobbes was warranted in believing that the former was unlikely. It is not surprising then, that, as we noted in Chapter 8, Hobbes gave so little attention to those interests we hold so dear, the potentially transcendent interests in liberty and justice.

Now, suppose for a moment that Hobbes's redescription argument works.[19] Suppose, that is, (1) that Hobbes really has captured his readers' transcendent interest, both its status and its content, and (2) that Scripture really does support his claims, and thus that his readers really could accept his redescription of their transcendent interests. *Then his absolutism follows.*[20] If Hobbes's argument that revealed religion requires adherence to his principle of political obligation works, there can be no grounds for denying unconditional obedience to the state – no pretense of right whatsoever. Absolutism falls out of Hobbes's principle of political obligation, a principle allowing no exemptions from political obedience, and underwritten by the primary and overriding transcendent interest of his readers.

How can this argument for absolutism work? The reason why it works (if it works, that is, if his readers will accept the assumptions and intermediate conclusions of his valid redescription argument) is that disagreement in religious interests is revealed to be only an illusion. Recall that Hobbes's project was to transform what looked for all the world like competing (often uniformity-requiring) transcendent religious interests into a uniform transcendent interest whose realization was connected with obedience to the state in such a way that all in the society could see themselves as having sufficient reason to obey the state unconditionally. This transformation was effected through a process of redescription (described in Chapter 3), which was possible only because differing descriptions reflected only apparent differences: Although people affirmed divergent descriptions of their transcendent interest, they could, Hobbes thought, be brought to agree about what their interest really amounted to – about what really mattered – and this allowed for a redescription of their interest that they should all be able to affirm. Hobbes thought that behind the appearance of diversity stood the fact of unity. The state would embody this unity, and because of this genuine consensus, everyone would be able to see himself as having reason to support an effective state unconditionally. Absolutism would turn out to be something that all could agree to, and could agree to in a principled way, as an expression of their most deeply held convictions. Hobbes's principle would be supported by their most profound interest.

We can more clearly appreciate this point by seeing what would be the status of dissenters in Hobbes's scheme. A dissenter is a person who is in error. The same process of investigation and reflection designed to bring Hobbes's readers to see that it was part of their duty to God to give their complete obedience to the state can also be used to show that dissenters are making an error, and even, at least in principle if not in practice, to bring dissenters themselves to see that they are in error. The state, and the citizenry, reject their claims as errors. Why ought the state to respect false claims (particularly when those making them could be brought to see that they are false), especially when to honor them would be to allow the dissenter to threaten society's pursuit of what its members regard as the most important thing? Dissenters can be very dangerous: They can lead men astray, they can undermine men's confidence in the true religion, they can cause disruptive faction, and they can sell men out. And, of course, dissent is particularly dangerous when people's interests are uniformity-requiring. When religious interests are regarded as of fundamental and overriding importance, from what basis are people to be able to allow claims against those interests? They have every reason *not* to admit such claims. Thus, we see that in Hobbes's view dissent does not express legitimate differences that would undermine the justification of an absolute obligation to the state; and the state, in requiring uniformity, is merely refusing to embrace error, preventing the spread of error, and, we may suppose, if possible, correcting error. Once a right of private judgment is conceived in this way, as a right to resist the state in defense of an *error* – an error, moreover, that can be shown to be an error, and that when acted on threatens the social pursuit of men's overriding interest – the refusal to extend such a right makes sense.

In a nutshell, then, absolutism follows (provided the redescription argument works) in virtue of two features of Hobbes's readers' religious interest: First, an aspect of the *content* of that interest, namely, that one has a duty to God to obey the sovereign unconditionally, and hence that disobedience to the sovereign *is* disobedience to God; and second, the status of their religious interest, namely, that their interest in fulfilling their duties to God is their paramount transcendent interest – it overrides all other interests. Together, these two features of Hobbes's readers' religious interest determine the absolutist character of Hobbes's conclusion. Given these features, a right against the state cannot be defended. *Hobbes is correct to arrive at absolutism.*

Now, as we saw, on the standard philosophical interpretation's analysis of Hobbes's problem and his solution, absolutism does not follow. This is because (depending on the particular standard interpreter) either it can't be gotten, or it isn't needed. And it is true enough that *if* one takes Hobbes to be attempting to provide a purely narrowly prudential argument for absolutism from a conception of fundamental human nature in which fear of death is the overriding motivational force, then the argument fails. But this is not what Hobbes was doing. The primary root of social disorder on Hobbes's analysis was competing (characterizations, based on differing private judgments, of) religious interests, where these interests were transcendent, in most cases uniformity-requiring, and with a very particular content and status. And given *this* analysis of disorder, absolutism becomes not only a possible solution, but the necessary solution. The character of the disruptive interests both allowed for, and required, an absolutist solution.

THE STATUS OF HOBBES'S ARGUMENTS
FOR ABSOLUTISM

If what I've said is true, then it looks as if the success of Hobbes's arguments for absolutism is historically contingent. His reasoning is correct, *given his premises,* but the premises articulate a particular, historically contingent, view of what God requires, and a particular, historically contingent, claim about the overriding importance of doing what God requires. So, far from having demonstrated the necessity of absolutism for all times and places, Hobbes has at most provided us with an account of the conditions under which absolutism could be justified, and it turns out that these conditions may or may not hold.[21]

This is indeed the implication of my argument. The success of Hobbes's arguments for absolutism is historically contingent. And because it is, my interpretation becomes immediately subject to two objections. The first is that if I am right, Hobbes's theory loses its interest and his work is reduced to the status of a mere historical curiosity, of no continuing use or value. If this is what Hobbes is doing, his work simply isn't important or interesting. (And from here one might mount the transcendental argument that Hobbes's work is clearly of enduring interest; a precondition of its being so is that it contain a trans-historically applicable analysis; and that because my interpretation allegedly implies that it has no such analysis my interpretation must be wrong.) The second objection is that Hobbes obviously intended to provide, and thought he had provided, a universally valid analysis of and remedy for disorder – a *science* of politics – and thus that we ought to prefer an interpretation of his theory according to which (unlike mine, the objection would go) Hobbes turns out, at least in theory, to have done so.

The answer to both objections depends on seeing how it is that Hobbes's theory can simultaneously be historically specific and provide a general account. Hobbes does provide us with a trans-historically applicable *method* for analyzing and remedying disorder. It is this that makes Hobbes's work of enduring usefulness and interest. But the employment of Hobbes's method yields, in each instance of its application, historically specific conclusions. And far from being a defect, it is this feature of Hobbes's achievement that makes his work important, and affords us the most profound insights into the practice of political philosophy, and the constraints on fruitful work in this field.

Hobbes's method for approaching the problem of social disorder is conceptually to resolve an ailing society into its component parts, the problematic pieces – the interests and attachments, based on doctrines, beliefs, and sometimes simple errors – that bring members of society into seemingly irresoluble conflict. The strategy for regaining order is to begin from the interests that people actually claim as their own, and provide people with reasons linked to these interests for adhering to the most stable principle of political obligation they could be brought to affirm given the limiting constraints their interests impose. The most stable principle of political obligation in any particular case will the one that gives the least play to private judgment over the range of contended issues; but how far private judgment can be restricted (on what matters, and by what means) will depend on the content of the interests at issue. Thus, the particular principle that Hobbes's theory generates will be contingent on the specific data (the content of disruptive interests) plugged into the theory. Nonetheless, the theory does not just spit out whatever is plugged in. The content of people's disruptive interests is not perfectly fixed; interests will be malleable to some degree, by reflection on the beliefs, attachments, and doctrines that ground them. In order to recompose an ailing society into the most orderly and stable whole it can be (given what will turn out to be very real constraints imposed by people's reconsidered interests), the problematic interests themselves, and the beliefs and doctrines on which they depend, must be altered. The tactic for altering the problematic components revealed by resolution is twofold: *rationalizing beliefs* and *redescribing interests*. These tasks involve purging the errors underlying disruptive interests that arise from bad theory, poor reasoning, and improper use of language; and paring apparently competing interests down to their lowest common denominators and then elaborating them using only methods that are acceptable to all the contending parties. These are the major tasks of the compositive portion of Hobbes's theory. How far any particular interest can be altered by these means will depend on the actual content and character of that interest. Some apparent interests will turn out to have no hold at all on those who had formerly affirmed them, while others may be quite intractable. So again, where one gets by using Hobbes's method will be contingent upon where one starts. The method is general, but in every instance of its application, the conclusions it yields will be historically specific.

Schematically, we can present the form of Hobbes's theory as follows: Part 1 presents the fruits of a resolutive analysis of a particular society's disorder, systematically enumerating, and offering a preliminary corrective discussion of, the errors, dispositions, doctrines, and genuine interests on which disruptive characterizations of interest rest. Part 2 begins the compositive portion of the argument, starting from the ends and features of political association, employing only natural knowledge; those disruptive characterizations of interest that can be altered through a process of natural reason are corrected; and the most promising candidate for a stable principle of political obligation is identified and then linked to people's (now reformulated) interests. Because both prudence and morality are accessible to natural reason, the recomposition of Part 2 should provide people with at least prima facie reasons for adhering to the principle of political obligation from both narrow self-interest and natural duty. Now, if disruptive interests make *no* appeal to nonnatural sources of knowledge – if, say, none of the disruptive characterizations of interest depend on claims about the requirements of revealed religion – then the project ends with Part 2. But if there are any interests at issue that cannot be settled solely by appeal to natural reason, third and fourth parts will be needed. Part 3 redescribes competing or problematic characterizations of the disruptive interest, using acceptable methods for interpreting the nonnatural source of knowledge taken to be authoritative in such questions. Part 4 then completes the argument by providing a sociological and historical account of how the errors that underwrote the disruptive characterization of interest in Part 3 arose, attempting thereby to delegitimize, once and for all, the problematic conception of interest.

When the conditions that give rise to disorder differ, the content of Parts 1, 3, and 4 will vary. The *features* of these parts will remain largely the same – Part 1 will identify sources of disorder, Part 3 will redscribe and rationalize competing or problematic revelation-based characterizations of interest, Part 4 will give a natural account of the sources of error that discredits the disruptive characterizations, and so on – but the *particular sources* of disorder they enumerate, redescribe, or account for will differ from case to case. (Of course, the content of Part 2 will also differ somewhat from case to case, reflecting the differing Part 1 analyses of disorder, according to what restrictions on obedience the proposed principle of political obligation is required by the particular disruptive interests to include. For example, if Hobbes's readers had had no problematic commitment to religious interests, the principle of political obligation defended in *Leviathan* would not have had to include an exemption from obedience to commands that would require one to violate one's duty to God.) The arguments of Parts 1 and 2 will proceed on the basis of natural reason alone; Parts 3 and 4 will discuss the contribution to instability of transcendent interests based on supernatural or extranatural sources of knowledge or belief. There may often be a Part 3 and Part 4, because often the most seriously destabilizing sorts of transcendent interests rely on nonnatural sources of knowledge or belief. But there *needn't* be any Parts 3 or 4; we can, for example, imagine a case in which disorder is generated by competing substantive conceptions of justice, where justice is taken to be entirely accessible to natural reason. In such a case, no Part 3 will be necessary, although an account of a Part 4 sort, to explain the errors that contribute to disorder enumerated in Part 1, might still form a useful part of the theory. (The justice problem, if it can be solved, will be dealt with in Parts 1 and 2 by rationalizing beliefs and redescribing interests.)

What is crucial to note is that how "absolutist" the principle of political obligation formulated in Part 2 can be will depend on what the causes of disorder, in each particular case, are taken to be. If people are resisting the state on the grounds that it is requiring them to violate their duties to God as these are given to them by revelation, then the principle of political obligation will have to allow a corresponding exemption from obedience, if people are to be able to accept the principle. If the disruptive consequences of allowing this exemption are to be contained or overcome, it will have to be on the basis of considerations that come from within revealed religion itself. And what can be achieved in this respect on the basis of revealed religion will depend on the particular content of revealed religion. In Hobbes's case, Scripture itself (when properly interpreted, Hobbes argues) requires Christians to *reject* the exemption from obedience – revealed religion deprives Christians of any religious grounds for disobeying their sovereign. That Hobbes is able to reach this conclusion depends on the peculiarity of the Judeo-Christian Scriptures. If the analogous problem arose among Moslems, then the Koran would be the relevant authoritative nonnatural source of knowledge; and the identification and defense of an appropriate principle of political obligation would depend on the content of the Koran.[22] It is an open question whether or not an absolutist principle of political obligation could be defended. More clearly, if the primary source of disorder within a society were competing uniformity-requiring religious interests among religious factions that made appeal to *differing* authoritative texts or bodies of doctrine, the content of both sources would affect the principle that could be reached, and the principle that resulted might leave significantly more room for the exercise of private judgment in matters of religion than the one that Hobbes defends in the case he is considering. In short, the possibility of an absolutist solution to disorder depends on the particular content of the interests that give rise to disorder. Indeed, there is no way of knowing in advance whether *any* stable solution is possible at all. What Hobbes gives us is a method for discovering whether, and what sort of, a remedy to social disorder is possible in any particular case. And by advocating social arrangements that minimize the formation of differing private judgments, Hobbes suggests a way in which future disorder might be minimized.

Hobbes's method is thus *perfectly general;* but at various points it requires that historically specific information be provided, with the result that the outcome it generates will have only limited applicability. Nonetheless, selecting the particular information to be inserted into the theory isn't a wholly haphazard process. Hobbes's analysis tells us what *kinds* of information to look for – the major headings under which will fall the particular, historically contingent facts to be inserted. The idea of differing private judgments about what is to be done, particularly those that result in competing interests that are transcendent (worth risking preservation to satisfy) and uniformity-requiring, can serve as the general catchall category of the relevant historical facts. These differing private judgments will be rooted in trans-historically applicable features of human nature and circumstance – in the human tendency to make errors in reasoning, in basic human passions such as pride and the desire for power, and the tendency to partiality and shortsightedness, in our disposition to use language inconstantly, in our natural inclination toward religion, in the material conditions of relative scarcity that condition cooperation in most societies, and so on. These are the kinds of things Hobbes's theory requires us to look for, and to make appeal to, in the forms in which they actually appear in any particular case of disorder, in applying his method.

Hobbes is not offering an argument for the universal necessity of absolutism, and we can see this clearly by noticing that according to Hobbes's own analysis, absolutism cannot be in principle universally necessary. As we've already seen, for

Hobbes, consensus in judgment is the key to the maintenance of social order. Thus if there were a period in which people achieved perfect agreement in judgment, no political institutions at all would be required in that period. Alternatively, if there were a situation in which disagreement did not lead to disorder, then again, no political institutions at all would be required for the duration of that situation. It is merely contingently true (if true at all) at any given time that people do not have consensus in judgment, or that their disagreement results in disorder. Although it may be more likely than not that people will disagree, and in ways that threaten order, an absolutist solution may not be necessary – and, depending on the particular form their disagreements take, it may not be possible. Whether Hobbes's method will yield an absolutist theory, then, will depend on the particular character of the interests that disrupt order in any particular case.

There are also certain conditions on the application of Hobbes's method that may or may not be met, depending on the particular historical circumstances. For Hobbes's method to be fruitful, members of the disrupted society must have a good deal of common ground from which to work. They must affirm common criteria for evidence and argument, and they must share a number of interests and beliefs. In many circumstances, these conditions will be met. But in some cases, they won't; and in those cases, Hobbes's method of reestablishing order will be of little use.

The power and cohesiveness of Hobbes's view is quite impressive. What Hobbes has done here is to provide us with a statement of the conditions under which absolutism is justifiable. It seems that absolutism cannot be justified to us, but the reasons why this is so stand out in sharp relief against the background of Hobbes's philosophy. Absolutism would be difficult to justify to us because we do not have consensus in values (and so cannot agree on which claims may be rejected as errors), nor do we see our society as having as its purpose the furthering of some shared transcendent interest of overriding importance which interest the state embodies and promotes. Our conceptions of the good are arguably too far apart for it to be possible to redescribe them into a single substantive description acceptable to all. And the Hobbesian move to substitute a purely formal description (a description that makes reference to an authority) for our differing substantive descriptions is not, it seems, available to us, because we agree neither on who such an authority might be, nor even on the question of whether there could be such an authority. This is why Hobbes's absolutist solution to his problem of order cannot be straightforwardly applied to the political problems we now face, and it explains how Hobbes could be correct in arriving at absolutism even though we may well not.

This is one of the things Hobbes's work allows us to see. But it suggests other things to us as well, things that account, I think, for the enduring interest and importance of Hobbes's work. Let us close, as most commentaries on Hobbes do, by considering some of these lessons by Hobbes.

CONCLUSION

Hobbes's work allows us to appreciate some important points about the very enterprise of political philosophy, and the constraints on fruitful work in this field. In this respect, perhaps more than any other political theorist, Hobbes has "written truth perspicuously," and has "set us in a better way to find it out ourselves" (395).

Some of what we learn from Hobbes is a result of what he taught, the rest a result of our own reflections on his methods and the place of his work in the sequence of political thought that engages us. Almost all of what we learn should strike us as simple and straightforward, despite the fact that we frequently proceed as if it didn't.

Political philosophy is often occasioned by particular historical developments, by the problems that arise when shared social understandings break down, and established systems of institutions and practices crack up. In these cases, the task of political philosophy is essentially practical: It is to mediate – in thought – these sorts of conflicts. We want to resolve such conflicts in a principled and, if possible, peaceful way, rather than to leave their resolution to the morally undiscerning turn of events or to brute force. Political philosophy is normative rather than purely descriptive, but as a practical enterprise it must be about and for human beings, if not as they actually are, at least as they realistically might be.

Because political philosophy is often occasioned by concrete historical developments, it is not surprising that the tasks of political philosophy should differ over time and circumstance. Hobbes was concerned to provide a basis for stable social order in the face of apparently competing transcendent religious interests; Locke intended to justify rebellion against the crown within a mixed constitution when it was abusing prerogative; Marx addressed the question of the unfreedom and exploitation caused by capitalism, and of how these could be overcome by a democratic socialist revolution of the working class; contemporary Western political philosophers are concerned to mediate conflicting demands of liberty, equality, and community, and to settle, in a principled way, competing claims on common social institutions. Although political philosophy speaks to human concerns of limited scope – those involved with socially and politically regulated interaction and cooperation – the character of those concerns is shaped by the particular circumstances in which persons find themselves. A failure to recognize this diversity of the tasks of political philosophy, and the sort of tunnel vision that compels us to interpret the work of our predecessors in terms of our own project, has, I think, resulted not only in a tremendous amount of distortion of the work of others, but in an obfuscation of some obvious and important constraints on fruitful work in political philosophy. This is where Hobbes can help us.

Hobbes recognized that government – indeed, any social institution or practice – must always be ultimately self-imposed and self-sustained. This is obvious, but it is easy to lose sight of. And it entails, for example (in conjunction with certain other uncontroversial assumptions), the perhaps less obvious propositions that government by laws alone, a complete remedy to arbitrary government, is impossible; that government completely by coercion is strictly speaking impossible; that no government can be settled once and for all; and that a mere modus vivendi – a mere balance of power – can never be expected to be stable. Hobbes reminds us that laws can never apply themselves, and that "it is men and arms, not words and promises, that make the force and power of the laws" (377). "What man," asks Hobbes, "does not find himself governed by them he fears, and beleeves can kill or hurt him when he obeyeth not? or that beleeves the law can hurt him; that is, words and paper, without the hands and swords of men?" (377–8). But this does *not* mean that government by coercion all the way down is possible, which again Hobbes points out with the question "If men know not their duty, what is there that can force them to obey the laws? An army you will say. But what shall force the army?" (*B* 75). The exercise of government requires the uncoerced cooperation of a significant number of the governed. Because government is always government by and for people, many of whom must be freely cooperating, there can be no such thing as government settled once and for all. Both governors and governed change their opinions and allegiances, grow old and die, and are replaced by new people who also change their opinions and allegiances. A state is, as Hobbes maintained, a living organism that can be upset not only by external violence but, more importantly, by "intestine disorder" (167). The "living body" metaphor that recurs consistently throughout Hobbes's work is a particularly apt expression of the idea that states must be viewed as ever changing. But once we recognize this, we see that there are good reasons for thinking that a mere modus vivendi – a mere balance of power among competing social factions – cannot be stable. Interests change, their perceived urgency changes, populations change, and such changes can be expected to bring changes in social forces, which may in turn induce cycles of rebellion and repression. All of these considerations represent *constraints* on successful political philosophy – any theory that ignores them ceases to be capable of fulfilling its practical task – and they are explicitly and forcefully set out in Hobbes's work.

What do these constraints suggest about the proper focus of political philosophy? Arguably, it is that political philosophy must give a prominent place to the concept of *consensus in judgment*. The constraints on political philosophy suggest that for law to have force, for force to be exercisable, and for states to remain stable over time, some certain minimal threshold of consensus in judgment must be met. The realization that government must ultimately be self-imposed and self-sustained involves recognizing the importance of the problems posed by incompatible judgments, and the need for consensus in judgment. And this means that the factors that go into individual judgment – interests, values, beliefs, and the like – must be taken seriously by political philosophy.

Hobbes's philosophy provides us with an example of a political philosophy that takes the components of judgment seriously. In particular, I would argue, Hobbes shows us what it means to take people's values seriously. It means that any process of justification of a political conception will have to begin from the particular values any given group actually holds, and demonstrate a positive connection between those values and the conception to be justified: It will have to give people reasons linked to what they actually care about. If we are ever to achieve anything more than a fragile modus vivendi among competing interests and conceptions of the good, we must be able to provide people with reasons of this sort. If political philosophy is to accomplish its practical tasks, it must begin from what particular people in particular periods under particular conditions actually care about. This does not mean that no criticism is possible, but it means that even criticism must begin from where people are.

What follows from this is that in a society like ours, where pluralism is a fact and can be expected to remain so, the kinds of reasons offered to different groups will likely be very different. We cannot hope to reach thorough agreement, by a single route, on all of the substantive issues that concern us, but we can strive by a variety of arguments to achieve at least partial agreement on at least the most basic terms of our collective social life.[23] We can aim to justify a limited political conception to most of the people to whom it is supposed to apply.

But what can *count* as justification will depend on the peculiarities of of the conception from which justification is to proceed. We should thus expect any political conception, no matter how it is originally generated, to be justified in many different ways, according to the character of the values held by the different groups to whom the conception is to be justified. This means that the justification of a political conception cannot be given in advance of an investigation into what various groups take really to matter; we cannot even determine whether such justification is possible until we do that work. From some sets of values it may be impossible to justify a given conception; Hobbes's principle of political obligation, as he thought suitable for his own audience, could not, I think, be justified to us. But *Leviathan* provides us with what, so far as I know, is the best example of the kind of *detailed* work that the justification of a political conception requires. A general sketch will not advance the projects of political philosophy; we need detailed working drawings for each particular structure of justification. As Hobbes writes, even men who "desire with all their hearts, to conforme themselves into one firme and lasting edifice . . . cannot without the help of a very able architect, be compiled into any other than a crasie building, such as hardly lasting out their own time, must assuredly fall upon the heads of their posterity" (167). If we are to be such architects, we must confront the problems of political philosophy as they are, in all of their complexity and messy particularity. We cannot expect to make headway if we begin our political philosophy from some timeless and faceless account of "man" or "society," let alone from an abstract conception of Reason. But this does not mean that we must surrender to a quicksand of moral or speculative relativism or subjectivism, or abandon our quest for a political science – for a useful general theory to address our political concerns. Hobbes's work shows us that there is a middle ground. And it just may be that this is the most useful thing Hobbes teaches us.

Notes

INTRODUCTION

1 For excellent treatments of Hobbes's political philosophy that are more historical and contextual than the interpretation I offer here, see Richard Tuck, *Hobbes* (Oxford: Oxford University Press, 1989); Deborah Baumgold, *Hobbes's Political Theory* (Cambridge: Cambridge University Press, 1988); and Quentin Skinner, "The Ideological Context of Hobbes's Political Thought," *Historical Journal* 9, No. 3 (1966).

CHAPTER 1. THE STANDARD PHILOSOPHICAL
INTERPRETATION

1 David Gauthier, *The Logic of Leviathan* (Oxford: Oxford University Press, 1969); J. W. N. Watkins, *Hobbes's System of Ideas* (London : Hutchinson, 1965); J. W. N. Watkins, "Philosophy and Politics in Hobbes," in K. C. Brown, ed., *Hobbes Studies* (Cambridge, Mass.: Harvard University Press, 1965); C. B. Macpherson, *The Political Theory of Possessive Individualism; Hobbes to Locke* (Oxford: Clarendon Press, 1962); Thomas Nagel, "Hobbes's Concept of Obligation," *Philosophical Review* 68 (January 1959); John Plamenatz, "Mr. Warrender's Hobbes," in *Hobbes Studies;* Skinner, "The Ideological Context of Hobbes's Political Thought"; Gregory S. Kavka, *Hobbesian Moral and Political Theory* (Princeton, N.J.: Princeton University Press, 1986).
    It should be said that Kavka aims not so much to give an interpretation of Hobbes as to construct a defensible moral and political theory using what he understands to be Hobbesian methods and insights. Nonetheless I shall take issue with his

claims as to which insights are Hobbesian. Jean Hampton's interpretation in *Hobbes and the Social Contract Tradition* (Cambridge: Cambridge University Press, 1986) contains many elements of the standard philosophical view, presented (like Kavka's and Gauthier's) using game-theoretic analysis. Because Hampton is primarily concerned to situate Hobbes's philosophy within the broader social contract tradition, I do not discuss her version of the standard philosophical view.

2   A. E. Taylor, "The Ethical Doctrine of Hobbes," in Brown, ed., *Hobbes Studies;* Howard Warrender, *The Political Philosophy of Hobbes* (Oxford: Oxford University Press, 1957); Howard Warrender, "A Reply to Mr. Plamenatz," in *Hobbes Studies;* Francis C. Hood, *The Divine Politics of Thomas Hobbes* (Oxford: Clarendon Press, 1964); Brian Barry, "Warrender and His Critics," *Philosophy* 42, no. 164 (April 1968); Michael Oakeshott, Introduction to Hobbes's *Leviathan,* edited by Oakeshott (Oxford: Basil Blackwell, 1957); David Johnston, *The Rhetoric of Leviathan* (Princeton: Princeton University Press, 1986).

There is a further approach to Hobbes interpretation that I shall not say much about, not because it is unimportant (it is not), but because it is less familiar to the analytic philosophical tradition with which I hope to engage. This is the "contextualist" approach to writing on the history of political theory associated with Quentin Skinner, Richard Tuck, and Deborah Baumgold (in the case of writings on Hobbes), and more generally with John Dunne, John Pocock, Richard Ashcraft, and Jim Tully. This "contextualist" approach to interpretation emphasizes the idea that understanding the meaning of a view involves situating it in the intellectual–political–discursive context in which it was developed and advanced. Although I shall make important use of the issues that *occasioned* Hobbes's political writing, I shall neither argue nor assume that the content or meaning of Hobbes's theory ought to be *reduced* to a response to these occasioning events. I am grateful to Josh Cohen for having clarified my thinking on this contrast.

3   According to Watkins, Hobbes is attempting "to discover what men are, and what the state ought to be consistent with their nature"(*Hobbes's System of Ideas,* p. 77), and to reconstruct "the kind of civil society which alone is consistent with human nature" (J. W. N. Watkins, "Philosophy and Politics in Hobbes," in Brown, ed., *Hobbes Studies,* p. 261).

C. B. Macpherson distinguishes between fundamental and actual human nature for purposes of constructing his variant of the standard philosophical interpretation (in which he argues that Hobbes was a bourgeois thinker): The conception of the person presented in the state of nature is not a description of essential human nature, it is a description of the "behavior to which men as they now are, men who live in civilized societies and have the desires of civilized men, would be led if all law and contract enforcement... were removed" (Macpherson, *The Political Theory of Possessive Individualism*, p. 22). This distinction makes no difference for our purposes. The point is that the standard interpretation claims that Hobbes is attempting to derive the need for an absolute sovereign from what he offers as a *description* of the way people *really are*. Whether his description is universally accurate or accurate only to a historically specified mode of production is a further question, the answer to which does not affect a description of the content of his argument (although it may, of course, affect the plausibility of that argument).

4 C. B. Macpherson, "Hobbes's Bourgeois Man," in Brown, ed., *Hobbes Studies*, pp. 181–2.

5 C. B. Macpherson's Introduction to Macpherson, ed., *Leviathan* (New York: Penguin, 1968), pp. 43–4.

6 For example, David P. Gauthier writes, "Note the primary role which Hobbes assigns to fear. The two methods for erecting civil society differ primarily in the object of the motivating fear" (*The Logic of Leviathan*, p. 113). He continues, "Fear, indeed, is the common ground of all human relationships, the basic differentiation being between fear among equals – the relation of men in the state of nature, and fear among unequals. As a species of the latter, the relation of child to parent is comparable with that of servant to master and that of subject to sovereign" (ibid., p. 118). And Watkins writes that for Hobbes, "a man's fear of violent death is stronger than any other fear, and it overrides any competing desire for pleasure" (Watkins, *Hobbes's System of Ideas*, p. 164).

7 For a compelling argument that Hobbes was not in fact a psychological egoist, see Bernard Gert, "Hobbes and Psychological Egoism," *Journal of the History of Ideas*, 28 (1967): 503–20. In subsequent chapters I present evidence that corroborates Gert's view.

8   John Plamenatz writes that in Hobbes's theory "we may have an interest where we have no duty, but it can never be our duty to do what is not, in the long run, to our advantage. For we necessarily choose our greatest advantage when we see it, and 'I ought' implies for Hobbes, 'I can'" (Plamenatz, "Mr. Warrender's Hobbes," in Brown, ed., *Hobbes Studies*, p. 76).

9   This point is suggested by Thomas Nagel's description of "the Hobbesian man's malady": "He can never perform *any* action unless he believes it to be in his own best interest.... He is susceptible only to selfish motivation and is therefore incapable of any action which could be clearly labeled moral. He might, in fact, be best described as a man without a moral sense" (Nagel, "Hobbes's Concept of Obligation," p. 74).

10 Wrongly, in my view. (Kavka agrees.) See Kavka, *Hobbesian Moral and Political Theory*, pp. 47–8.

11 Watkins makes explicit the alleged link between mechanism and egoism, and between egoism and the impossibility of purely moral motivation: From Hobbes's mechanistic account of man as matter in motion, it follows that "since the vital motions of the heart can only be excited by the prospect of some bodily change *in its owner*, all motivation is essentially egocentric; merely moral considerations unrelated to such a change cannot affect behavior" (Watkins, "Philosophy and Politics in Hobbes," p. 252).

12 Gauthier, *The Logic of Leviathan*, p. 7.

13 Gauthier holds the view that theism is inessential to Hobbes's political theory; Stephen and Plamenatz, that theism causes inconsistencies and difficulties in the theory; and Strauss, that Hobbes's theory actually requires an atheistic society. For a discussion of these views, see Ronald Hepburn, "Hobbes on the Knowledge of God," in Maurice Cranston and Richard Peters, eds., *Hobbes and Rousseau: A Collection of Critical Essays* (New York: Doubleday, Anchor, 1972), pp. 85ff. For the argument that Hobbes was not an atheist, see Willis B. Glover, "God and Thomas Hobbes," in Brown, ed., *Hobbes Studies*, pp. 141–68.

14 However, subjectivism dominates the picture only in the absence of a sovereign authority; where a sovereign authority exists, its judgments are the true measure of good and evil. According to the standard interpretation, in a state of nature, private judgment is the measure of good and evil, which are

conceived as subjective, there being no fact of the matter about them; in society, there is a fact of the matter about what is good and what is evil, and it is sovereign-relative. In neither situation are there any objectively true evaluative propositions.

15 Taylor and Warrender focused attention on the various passages, both in *Leviathan* and in earlier versions of Hobbes's political theory, in which Hobbes draws a distinction between duty and self-interest. For example, "More clearly therefore I say thus: that a man is obliged by his contracts, that is, that he ought to perform them for his promise sake; but that the law . . . compels him to make good his promise for fear of the punishment appointed by the law" (*EW* 2:185), and "Although a man should order all his actions so much as belongs to external obedience just as the law commands, but not for the law's sake, but by reason of some punishment annexed to it, or out of vain glory; yet is he unjust" (*EW* 2:ch. 4, 21); "Or if the apostles wanted temporall forces to depose Nero, was it therefore necessary for them in their epistles to the new made Christians to teach them (as they did) to obey the powers constituted over them . . . and that they ought to obey them, not for fear of their wrath, but for conscience sake? . . . It is not therefore for want of strength, but for conscience sake, that Christians are to tolerate their heathen princes" (*L*, 318).

16 Plamenatz, "Mr. Warrender's Hobbes," in Brown, ed., *Hobbes Studies*, pp. 87, 83.

17 David Johnston has a nice discussion of the peculiarity of Hobbes's religious views in his book *The Rhetoric of Leviathan*. For an example of Hobbes's contemporaries' outraged reaction, see Samuel I. Mintz, *The Hunting of Leviathan* (New York: Cambridge University Press, 1962).

18 David Johnston notices this, and tries to avoid the difficulty by arguing that the narrow egoism Hobbes refers to (with the primacy of bodily self-preservation) is intended normatively or prescriptively, rather than descriptively. I suggest in Chapter 7 that we needn't resort to so roundabout and speculative an explanation of the seemingly egoistic passages in Hobbes's book.

19 One even less promising explanation of the second half of *Leviathan*, seemingly suggested by David Johnston's interpretation, is that Hobbes was trying to persuade his readers to *give up* their foundational Christian beliefs, such as their belief

in the possibility of salvation. We will show the implausibility of this possible explanation when we come to examine the actual course of Hobbes's arguments concerning religion.

20 The Epistle Dedicatory to *Leviathan* (emphasis added).

21 Leslie Stephen, *Hobbes* (London, 1928), p. 152.

22 Watkins criticizes Hobbes for resting his theory on the assumption of psychological egoism, which assumption Watkins (rightly) thinks implausible. Kavka also rejects what he takes to be Hobbes's assumption of egoism. Kavka (see *Hobbesian Moral and Political Theory*, ch. 3) argues further that Hobbes's argument that the state of nature is a war of all against all is unsound as it stands, and takes great care to fill in the gaps and to reconstruct a sound argument. Watkins thinks that Hobbes's argument against divided or limited sovereignty is unsound (see the conclusion of *Hobbes's System of Ideas*); and, I think it is fair to say that Kavka agrees (see Kavka, *Hobbesian Moral and Political Theory*, ch. 12.2, 10, 11). All of the standard interpreters agree in thinking that Hobbes's argument for the desirability of absolutism is flawed, all reject his argument that absolutism is necessary. The standard interpreters seem to think that Hobbes's absolutist solution is too extreme – that his state of nature describes a cooperation problem easily solved by more moderate measures. Kavka's article is primarily devoted to proving just this point, and Gauthier's unfavorable assessment of the success of Hobbes's theory rests on his view that Hobbes's unrealistic psychology sets up a false dichotomy between the state of nature and unlimited sovereignty. He writes, "We need not avoid anarchy by acquiescing in what, despite Hobbes's dislike of the term, we may call tyranny. Both are extremes . . . they limit, but do not represent, the actual condition of man. Between them, within the limits set by man's actual tractability and by the existent threats to human survival, we may choose" (Gauthier, *The Logic of Leviathan*, p. 169). And he argues further that given Hobbes's conception of human nature, absolutism would be impossible to establish even if it were (by a set of plausible assumptions demonstrated to be) necessary. Gauthier writes, "Given Hobbes's account of man, and his view of how power may be concentrated, he is not really able to offer any alternative to anarchy – not even what his critics consider tyranny. When we examine the internal structure of the mighty Leviathan, we find that on

327

Hobbes's premisses it will not work. The sovereignty necessary for security is not attainable" (ibid., p. 170).

23 Watkins, *Hobbes's System of Ideas*, pp. 169, 163.
24 Gauthier, *The Logic of Leviathan*, p. 133.
25 Ibid., p. 170.
26 Ibid., p. 17.
27 Ibid., p. 18.
28 Obviously, if the unfavorable conditions cannot be sufficiently altered, the problem of order is insoluble. If, for example, scarcity is real (absolute) and extreme, rather than a problem of cooperation only, the existence of laws against the disruptive pursuit of necessities, and the threat of punishment for violations of such laws, will not succeed in modifying behavior. Indeed, Hobbes allows, as justified, violations of the laws motivated by need (*L*, 157), and further recognizes that when faced with threats to their self-preservation, men will respond to the more immediate threat – say, starvation or exposure – rather than the possibility of capture and punishment for their crime. Thus, those standard interpreters who would have the disorderly character of the state of nature to be the result of rational considerations, rather than perturbations of reason, must also hold that the problem is one of cooperation only, if the problem of order is to be soluble, that is, if what they identify as Hobbes's solution to the problem of order is to be in principle capable of success.
29 This solution is affirmed by all standard interpretations, regardless of whether they hold that the sovereign's coercive rule serves to make rational sociable conduct that was formerly irrational, or, rather, that it serves to remedy the otherwise ill effects of men's nearsightedness in calculating their rational self-interest.
30 Nagel, "Hobbes's Concept of Obligation," p. 82.
31 Gauthier, *The Logic of Leviathan*, pp. 18–19.
32 Kavka, *Hobbesian Moral and Political Theory*, p. 310.
33 Changing the payoffs might work, depending upon whether or not Hobbesian men's psychological makeup allowed for the possibility that they could submit themselves to a power that could change the payoffs. In his observations about Hobbesian men's "intractability," Gauthier expresses doubts about their psychological capacity to do this.
34 The Scottish invasion provided an occasion for Englishmen

to raise issues that provoked conflict among Englishmen, but it did not in itself bring about the collapse of order in England.

35 See Deborah Baumgold's instructive discussion of Hobbes's concerns, in her *Hobbes's Political Theory*.

36 Some other variable must have come into play. This other variable would then be the explanation of why order collapses. But it is not at all clear what this variable could be on the standard philosophical interpretation. We have already raised problems with a couple of likely candidates.

One further possibility available to the standard interpreter could be to attribute to Hobbes the view that subjects *rebel* whenever public officials are "lax" in their enforcement of the law. But this would be such an implausible account of recurrent disorder, I shall simply assume that the standard interpreters would not wish to offer it. I am grateful to Paul Weithman for having suggested (without endorsing) this possibility to me.

37 In ch. 6.3 of his book, Kavka discusses the possibility that irrational behavior plays a large though by no means sufficient role in explaining how revolution is possible. In that discussion on the paradox of revolution Kavka argues that *both* rational and irrational motives must be appealed to in explaining the occurrence of revolutions. This position seems to me in itself the most plausible account of disorder, but problematic for the proponent of the standard philosophical interpretation because it is subject to *both* sorts of objections I raise here.

38 As Paul Weithman has pointed out to me, it is possible *in principle* that ever escalating threats might overcome disruptive passion. The idea is that threats would escalate from imprisonment, through torture, to death, to death (with torture), of oneself, then of one's family, and so on. Although this is not conceptually impossible, there is no evidence that Hobbes held this view. No where does Hobbes make this sort of suggestion; but he does often suggest that there are some passions, notably pride, that systematically trump fear.

39 And, as I argue further on, Hobbes thinks this is as it should be. He rejects psychological egoism both as a descriptive theory and as a normative theory. Egoism is no more part of Hobbes's cure for social disorder than it is part of his diagnosis. For the contrary view, see Johnston, *The Rhetoric of Leviathan*.

40 Kavka acknowledges that religious beliefs could account for disorder among rational egoists: "Note that if we do not treat belief in divine punishments for nonparticipation (or divine rewards for participation) in revolution as irrational, we have a theological solution to the paradox of revolution in some cases. When God is on the rebels' side, participation maximizes one's expected payoffs over this life and the next" (*Hobbesian Moral and Political Theory*, p. 268n).

41 The standard interpreters recognize this fact, but they do not realize that Hobbes recognized it. Kavka writes, "And, most important of all, [Hobbes] fails to notice that even unlimited and undivided sovereign authority is no guarantee against internal strife. It cannot be a guarantee, because the physical powers of a monarch or a sovereign assembly are never great enough, in themselves, to deter violent opposition. Thus, all sovereigns depend upon the cooperation of others for the effective exercise of their authority, for their power. So serious civil strife . . . can and does occur even under absolute sovereigns. Life within Leviathan is not so tranquil as Hobbes would have us suppose" (ibid., p. 308). Likewise, Gauthier writes, "tractability is required not only among the general body of subjects but especially among the officials authorized by the sovereign. For the institutional arrangements which make any concentration of power possible depend for their effectiveness on the willingness of those who staff the institutions to cooperate in maintaining them, rather than only to compete in aggrandizing power. This co-operation cannot rest entirely on the fear of some further power. At some point, barring a Kafkaesque regress without limit, some degree of voluntary co-operation on the part of some persons is the condition of the continued working of all social and political bodies" (*The Logic of Leviathan*, p. 168).

42 Any person who believes that he "shall be damned to eternall and extreme torments, if he die in a false opinion concerning an article of Christian faith," will not *change* his opinion, no matter what coercion is used against him: "For who is there, that knowing there is so great danger in an error, whom the naturall care of himself, compelleth not to hazard his soule upon his own judgement, rather than that of any other man that is unconcerned in his damnation?" (378).

CHAPTER 2. HOBBES'S COMPOSITIVE
RECONSTRUCTION, PHASE ONE

1 For example, in his introduction to the Pelican edition of *Leviathan*, C. B. Macpherson writes, "his central concern was peace, as ours is coming to be. True, Hobbes gave little thought to war between nations. His overriding concern was with civil war; its avoidance was for him the main purpose of political inquiry" (p. 9).

2 Although this statement of the principle would seem to ignore the fact that Hobbes does allow disobedience in immediate self-defense, I argue further on that Hobbes's notion of membership in a commonwealth allows him to capture this condition in the principle as I've stated it.

3 I do not mean my discussion here to be taken as a thorough exposition of Hobbes's theory of the relationship among reasons, interests, and action. Hobbes does not just argue that people have reasons to obey his principle, and he recognizes that people must be provided with motives to act on the reasons they have, even reasons to act in ways that serve their perceived interests. Paul Weithman has alerted me to the danger of seeming by the brevity of my discussion here to attribute to Hobbes an overly simplistic view of these matters.

4 Cf. Gregory Kavka's *Hobbesian Moral and Political Theory*, pp. 383–4.

5 Hobbes presents his resolutive analysis of the sources of social disorder in Part 1 of *Leviathan* (where he discusses the sources of disorder accessible to unaided natural reason), and in Part 4 (about those sources of disorder whose identification as errors depends on revelation). I discuss the resolutive analysis in Chapters 5 and 7 below.

6 Hobbes writes that "the obligation a man may sometimes have, upon the command of the soveraign to execute any dangerous, or dishonourable office, dependeth not on the words of our submission; but on the intention; which is to be understood by the end thereof. When therefore our refusall to obey frustrates the end for which the soveraignty was ordained; then there is no liberty to refuse: otherwise there is. . . . And when the defence of the common-wealth, requireth at once the help of all that are able to bear arms, every one is obliged; because

otherwise the institution of the common-wealth, which they have not the purpose, or courage to preserve, was in vain" (112).

7 Hobbes writes: "To resist the sword of the common-wealth, in defence of another man, guilty, or innocent, no man hath liberty; because such liberty takes away from the soveraign the means of protecting us; and is therefore destructive of the very essence of government" (112).

8 Hobbes argues that nothing can be a commonwealth "unlesse it be of that power by its own number, or by other opportunities, as not to be subdued without the hazard of war. For where a number of men are manifestly too weak to defend themselves united, every one may use his own reason in time of danger, to save his own life, either by flight, or by submission to the enemy, as hee shall think best" (105).

9 A commonwealth cannot have two different representative authorities, "for that were to erect two soveraigns; and every man to have his person represented by two actors, that by opposing one another, must needs divide that power, which (if men will live in peace) is indivisible; and thereby reduce the multitude into the condition of warre, contrary to the end for which all soveraignty is instituted" (95).

10 Hobbes writes that some people "think there may be more soules, (that is, more soveraigns) than one in a common-wealth; and set up a supremacy against the soveraignty; canons against lawes; and a ghostly authority against the civill. ... Now seeing it is manifest, that the civill power, and the power of the common-wealth is the same thing; and that supremacy, and the power of making canons, and granting faculties, implyeth a common-wealth; it followeth, that where one is soveraign, another supreme; where one can make lawes, and another make canons; there must needs be two common-wealths, of one and the same subjects; which is a kingdome divided in it selfe, and cannot stand. For notwithstanding the insignificant distinction of temporall and ghostly, they are still two kingdomes, and every subject is subject to two masters [and] every subject must obey two masters, who both will have their commands be observed as law; which is impossible. ... When therefore these two powers oppose one another, the common-wealth cannot but be in great danger of civill warre, and dissolution" (171–2).

11 In *The Elements of Law*, Hobbes offers a nearly identical account
of why human beings cannot live peaceably in the absence of
a unifying public judgment. In this, his earliest formulation of
his political theory, he writes: "But contrary hereunto may be
objected, the experience we have of certain living creatures
irrational, that nevertheless continually live in such good order
and government, for their common benefit, and are so free
from sedition and war amongst themselves, that for peace,
profit, and defence, nothing more can be imaginable. . . . Why
therefore may not men, that foresee the benefit of concord,
continually maintain the same without compulsion, as well as
they? To which I answer, that amongst other living creatures,
there is no question of precedence in their own species, nor
strife about honour or acknowledgment of one another's wisdom, as there is amongst men; from whence arise envy and
hatred of one towards another, and from thence sedition and
war. Secondly, those living creatures aim every one at peace
and food common to them all; men aim at dominion, superiority, and private wealth, which are distinct in every man,
and breed contention. Thirdly, those living creatures that are
without reason, have not learning enough to espy, or to think
they espy, any defect in the government; and therefore are
contented therewith; but in a multitude of men, there are always some that think themselves wiser than the rest, and strive
to alter what they think amiss; and divers of them strive to
alter divers ways; and that causeth war. Fourthly, they want
speech, and are therefore unable to instigate one another to
faction, which men want not. Fifthly, they have no conception
of right and wrong, but only of pleasure and pain, and therefore also no censure of one another, nor of their commander,
as long as they are themselves at ease; whereas men that make
themselves judges of right and wrong, are then least at quiet,
when they are most at ease" (Part 1, ch. 19.5, p. 102).

12 Problems generated by differing individual judgments can
arise even within a single sovereign representative, if that sovereign is an assembly. Hobbes holds that a monarchy is preferable to an assembly for the purpose of maintaining peace
and security because "a monarch cannot disagree with himselfe, out of envy, or interest; but an assembly may; and that
to such a height, as may produce a civill warre" (96).

13 In the *Elements*, Hobbes uses the term 'unify' to express this

idea of reducing multiple judgments and wills into a single judgment and will. See *EL* 12.8, 19.6–10.

14 Paul Weithman has raised an interesting question about whether the mere receiving of protection can be wholly sufficient to determine membership, with an example of the following sort: Suppose the king of France prevents his generals (or, say, the king of Spain) from waging war against England, an action that has the effect of protecting English subjects. Why aren't English subjects then members of the French commonwealth? One might try to make out an answer that appealed to the distinction between necessary protection and redundant protection, or between the aimed at effects of an action and its side effects. Or one might try arguing that only those who belong to no commonwealth can become members of any commonwealth, or alternatively, that questionable cases are to be settled by determining who first provided protection, or who provides the most protection, or protection in the most important matters. Any of these lines of reply might be pursued, but the question loses much of its interest once Hobbes's argument against divided sovereignty is in place. At that point Hobbes can give the answer: because they are *already* members of the English commonwealth, and no one can be subject to more than one authority at a time.

15 The case of visitors in a foreign land is somewhat different because these are presumed already to be members of another commonwealth.

16 The effectiveness condition on obedience, which also entails a right to disobey any commands obedience to which would seriously jeopardize one's safety or well-being, turns out to have very broad implications. Not only does it permit one to disobey commands to kill, wound, or maim oneself or to abstain from the use of anything one needs in order to survive, and to resist those who attempt to harm one, but it also permits one to refuse to harm others "by whose condemnation a man falls into misery, as of a father, wife or benefactor" (70). More striking still, the right to disobey commands obedience to which threaten one's preservation or welfare even excuses disobedience to general laws when that disobedience is motivated by need: "When a man is destitute of food, or other thing necessary for his life, and cannot preserve himselfe any

other way but by some fact against the law, as if in a great famine he take the food by force or stealth which he cannot obtaine for mony nor charity, or in defence of his life snatch away another mans sword, he is totally excused . . . because no law can oblige a man to abandon his own preservation" (157). Notice also that although the effectiveness condition does allow resisting harm to oneself, it does not preclude allowing a political authority the right to harm others. Indeed, effectiveness requires that a political authority be permitted to harm others. This right falls under the clause of its definition of a commonwealth that the sovereign shall do whatever he thinks expedient for peace and common defense.

Hobbes offers a fairly full argument that it is not unreasonable for people to submit themselves to a political authority with the right to wound, imprison, or kill whomever it chooses. In the first place, a government must have coercive power in order to be effective; it increases individual security by means of regulating everyone's behavior through the enforcement of laws, by adjudicating disputes and enforcing decisions, and by preventing people from taking matters at controversy into their own hands. The execution of these roles requires coercive force. There are many ordinary conditions under which a government without coercive authority would be incapable of securing the safety of the people, and people can expect to be safer if their political authority has the right to kill or imprison whomever it thinks necessary than they would be if it didn't. This is so, in Hobbes's view, because strong passions and strong interests require strong threats to deter their expression, or tough measures to prevent their expression, and because, as Hobbes argues, there is no way to limit the political authority's coercive powers without dramatically undermining its effectiveness.

If people were to reserve to themselves an *exercisable* right not to be killed, then they would have to do one of two things: They could (1) set up a second power powerful enough to defend them against threats to their preservation from the first, by deterring and avenging killings perpetrated by the first, and a third to avenge, deter, and defend them against threats by the second, and so on. Such a multiplicity of coercive powers, in cases where disagreements arose among them, would raise the specter of civil war or a paralysis of effective government. Either contingency poses a greater threat to the security of each person than does concentration of unlimited coercive power in a single political authority. Retaining an exercisable right not to be killed against one's political authority, by means of the maintenance of a coercively empowered regulatory body, may be expected to undermine the effectiveness of government to such a degree that no increase in security would be gained. And, of course, there is no reason to place greater trust in any coercively empowered regulatory body than in the original political authority whose actions are to be regulated. Any body that possesses coercive power can present a threat to the preservation of others. The only way for people to ensure themselves of an enforceable right against being killed by their political authority would be (2) to divest that authority of all coercive powers. They would have to make sure that the political authority was unable to kill them by refusing to allow it an army, police force, or other coercive body strong enough to pose a threat to their preservation. But in such a case, again there would be no effective political authority. Hobbes observes that even a single person is strong and stealthy enough to be able to kill any other, so the political authority would have to be completely disempowered for people to ensure it could not kill them. But, of course, this would defeat the purpose of having a political authority at all, because without coercive powers it might not be capable of performing any of the functions required for effective government.

Hobbes argues that the relative danger of submitting to an unlimited coercive authority is low as compared with the danger posed by a state of license. This is partly because a state of license promises to be so catastrophic, and partly because the absolute level of danger within a commonwealth is, Hobbes thinks, pretty low. People have reason to think it unlikely that their political authority will gratuitously slaughter them, since it would be irrational for it to do so; and certainly it is less likely that they will die by its hand than that they would be killed in the absence of an effective political authority, where *everyone* is potentially a threat to the preservation of each.

Hobbes believes that because the observance of the laws of nature would tend to peace, it is, in fact, in the sovereign's own interest to enforce, and also to observe, them. To kill innocent, law-abiding subjects would be contrary to the laws of nature. Not to protect such subjects, by means of the promulgation and execution of punishments for the violation of laws, from others who threaten their preservation would also be contrary to the laws of nature. It is against the political authority's interest either to perpetrate acts of hostility against any subject who is not threatening the safety of the people, or to omit doing everything possible to deter and avenge (with an eye to deterrence) injuries done to the population by their fellow subjects or outsiders. (Note that the political authority in a settled state is not in that condition which might make it irrational for one to obey the laws of nature; he does not make himself "easy prey" by following them.)

Far from having warranted fears that their political authority will gratuitously attack them, people actually have some reason to expect that authority to further their interest, not only in order, but also in the general enforcement of the laws of nature. For example, of retributive justice Hobbes writes that the "severest punishments are to be inflicted for those crimes, that are of most danger to the Publique; such as are those which . . . spring from contempt of Justice; those that provoke indignation in the multitude; and those which unpunished, seem Authorised, as when they are committed by Sonnes, Servants, or Favorites of men in Authority. For indignation carrieth men, not onely against the Actors, and Authors of Injustice; but against all Power that is likely to protect them" (182–3).

The same is true of the other laws of nature; because they dictate actions that tend to peace, it is in the sovereign's interest to enforce them. For example, the fifth law of nature, Complaisance, requires that a person not "strive to retain those things which to himselfe are superfluous, and to others necessary. . . . For seeing every man . . . by necessity of nature, is supposed to endeavoure all he can, to obtain that which is necessary for his conservation; He that shall oppose himselfe against it, for things superfluous, is guilty of the warre that thereupon is to follow" (76). The sovereign is to enforce this law of nature by establishing a mandatory state charity. Hobbes writes, "And whereas many men, by accident unevitable, become unable to maintain themselves by their labour; they ought not to be left to the charity of private persons; but

337

to be provided for, (as farforth as the necessities of Nature require) by the lawes of the Common-wealth. For as it is un-charitablenesse in any man to neglect the impotent; so it is in the Sovereign of a Common-wealth, to expose them to the hazard of such uncertain charity" (181) Moreover, the *reason* why the sovereign ought to enforce the fifth law of nature is that it is in his interest to do so, "For the good of the Soveraign and People, cannot be separated. It is a weak Soveraign that has weak Subjects" (182), and the "riches, power, and honour of a Monarch arise onely from the riches, strength and repu-tation of his Subjects. For no King can be rich, nor glorious, nor secure whose Subjects are either poore, or contemptible, or too weak through want, or dissention, to maintain a war against their enemies" (96).

In general, it is in the political authority's rational self-interest to enforce, *and also to conform to*, the laws of nature. The requirements of people's passionate natures – justice, eq-uity, complaisance, and the like – must be respected if the political authority is to expect from them the obedience without which it cannot ensure either the commonwealth's safety or its own. Although it may be true that "Covenants without the sword are but words, and of no strength to secure a man at all" (85), that is, that the fulfillment of promises or agreements cannot be *ensured* without a coercively empowered guarantor, it is nevertheless the case that "the power of the mighty hath no foundation but in the opinion and belief of the people" (*B* 22), that is, that the very ability of the political authority to wield force depends upon the obedience of subjects. This, after all, is the problem motivating Hobbes's project of providing people with what they can regard as a sufficient reason to adhere to a principle of political obligation that if followed, would ensure perpetual domestic peace. No authority can have effective power unless the people obey it; and even if enough people obey it that it can exercise coercive power, sheer force alone will not be sufficient to compel the obedience of the others. Hobbes writes: "And the grounds of [the essential rights of sovereignty] have the rather need to be diligently, and truly taught; because they cannot be maintained by any Civill Law, or terrour of legal punishment. For a Civill Law, that shall forbid Rebellion, (and such is all resistance to the essentiall Rights of Soveraignty) is not (as a Civill Law) any obligation, but by vertue onely of the Law of Nature, that forbiddeth the violation of Faith; which naturall obligation if men know not, they cannot know the Right of any Law the Soveraign maketh. And for the punishment, they take it but for an act of Hostility; which when they think they have strength enough, they will endeavour by acts of Hostility, to avoyd" (175–6).

Subjects therefore have some reason to expect that the sovereign power will both enforce and itself conform to the prescriptions of the laws of nature, which, among other things, forbid the perpetration of hostile acts upon innocents. For all of these reasons, people ought not to be fearful of allowing commonwealths that coercive power over their members which is required for commonwealths to function as associations that procure the safety of their members. We shall see Hobbes's full argument against limiting the sovereign's right in any way a bit farther on.

17 Kavka has asked whether Hobbes can offer a principled defense of his willingness to allow this potentially dangerous exemption from obedience while disallowing other well-argued exemptions that could be socially inculcated. Hobbes would argue that the danger posed by admitting his exemption is inescapable because that exemption *follows* from the concept of a commonwealth. No other exemptions do so follow, thus they *needn't* be admitted; and because *any* exemption is dangerous to the point of being potentially catastrophic, we have good reason to reject proposals to include further exemptions from obedience in our principle of political obligation.

18 Although I don't discuss until the next section of this chapter the positive reasons Hobbes offers for accepting his principle of political obligation, I might just observe here that he attempts to coat the pill of rejecting the exemption contained in principle (B) with the argument we saw earlier, that people have reason to expect that their political authority will *not* carry on systematic violations of the laws of nature, of what they perceive as their rights and privileges, or of their expectations from the justice system, because such violations would likely arouse that discontent which can pose a threat both to the power, and to the preservation, of the political authority itself.

19 Strictly speaking, principle (C) is not formulated in a way that allows it to capture a doctrine of separation of powers. It is

formulated as a statement of the conditions under which one is permitted to disobey the extant effective political authority, that is, the government, and says that one may disobey those of the government's commands that conflict with the pronouncements of *other* legitimate authorities (external authorities). But in a case of separation of powers, the various possessors of authority are branches of a single government, collectively constituting the government, rather than other legitimate authorities external to the government. So it would seem that one could reject principle (C) while endorsing a system of separation of powers. Nevertheless, as we'll see, the arguments Hobbes makes against radical division of authority also apply to what we would call separation of powers; thus Hobbes's reason for rejecting (C) is also a reason for people to hope not to live under a government that has separation of powers (although, as Hobbes will argue, they have reason to obey whichever political authority exists, regardless of its form). Because the doctrine of separation of powers holds special interest for us, I include some discussion of how Hobbes's arguments against radical division of authority speak against it as well. In general, Hobbes disapproves of separation of powers on the ground that "this endangereth the commonwealth . . . for although few perceive that such government is not government, but division of the common-wealth into three factions . . . yet the truth is that it is not one independent common-wealth, but three independent factions; nor one representative person, but three" (172). He likens this affliction of the commonwealth to the condition of what we now call Siamese triplets, each of whom has a will of his own and can thwart the intended actions of his attached fellows. As it stands, Hobbes's argument is not designed to decide among *forms* of government, but among principles stating the conditions under which one is to obey an effective existing government whatever its form; this is why principle (C) does not really capture our system of separation of powers.

20 There is good reason to think this is what actually occurred during the period preceding the English Civil War. The notion of "King *in* Parliament" degenerated into a reality of "king *and* Parliament." The King in Parliament signified a single political authority possessing all of the essential rights of sovereignty, but once the members of Parliament stymied the king's deci-

sion to wage a war by refusing to grant him sufficient subsidies, both sides claimed sole possession of the rights required to carry out a declaration of war, including the right to raise an army and the right to tax in certain ways. In the absence of any agreed-upon and enforceable mechanism for settling their dispute, "King in Parliament" became "king and Parliament" – multiple overlapping authorities.

21 Again, this is not to say that a system of separation of powers *within* a government would be likely to paralyze a government and render it incapable of securing the public safety; each branch of such a government will lack certain of the "essential rights of sovereignty," but the government as a whole will possess all of these rights, and the rules governing the interaction of its various branches will stipulate a procedure for reaching a determinate resolution of any conflicts that may arise among the branches. We, for example, have in place mechanisms, such as impeachment, designed to resolve conflict among the branches of government, and Locke seems to have thought a dissolution of a troubled government and a constitutional convention to frame a new government a promising solution to conflict or paralysis. But the viability of systems that rely on these mechanisms or rules depends on everyone's following the rules. Can we certainly rule out the possibility that the possessors of various rights of sovereignty will refuse to follow the rules in the absence of a power to enforce the rules? Hobbes is not considering the case of rule-governed separation of powers, but what he is concerned about, and justifiably concerned about given the nature of the English Civil War, is the potential for stalemate, ultimately resoluble only through force, in cases where different authorities hold either overlapping or partial sets of essential rights in the *absence* of any agreed-upon procedure for resolving conflicts should they arise. He would, presumably, be just as concerned about such a division of powers whose interaction *was* rule-governed, so long as there was no power to ensure that people would follow the rules. The issue is one of ensuring cooperation among those who possess the various rights of sovereignty – rules of cooperation must be enforceable if they are to be useful, but where essential rights of sovereignty are divided, who is going to enforce the rules, and how?

22 Hobbes writes, "The office of the soveraign . . . consisteth in

the end, for which he was trusted with the soveraign power, namely, the procuration of the safety of the people. . . . But by safety here, is not meant a bare preservation, but also all other contentments of life, which every man by lawfull industry, without danger, or hurt to the commonwealth, shall acquire to himselfe" (175).

23 Hobbes presents a full argument to support his assertion that political subjection actually increases liberty. I discuss his argument in detail in Chapter 8.

24 This claim may seem too strong. The argument Hobbes offers for its truth, at least in the important cases, is assessed in Chapter 8.

25 Although the *arguments* from natural duty and obligation make use of the conclusion of the narrowly prudential argument, I argue in Chapter 7 that Hobbes does *not derive* the moral requirements themselves from the dictates of self-interest. In his book, Kavka shows how secular moral requirements might be viewed as derivative from self-interest by means of a kind of rule egoism. I am unsure as to whether or not he thinks Hobbes actually intended to do this.

Kavka does not think that Hobbes need prove morality and self-interest *always* coincident, although he does seem to think that Hobbes needs to show them coincident overall, or on the whole. See Kavka's Chapter 9 on rule egoism, in *Hobbesian Moral and Political Theory*, pp. 338–84.

CHAPTER 3. COMPOSITIVE RECONSTRUCTION, PHASE TWO

1 This is not to say that effective social order could not exist in the absence of a political authority or some sort of political organization; it is possible there could be effective social order based on family ties, widespread fellow feeling, natural superiority, or universal altruism. But Hobbes argued in Part 1 that if one wants to ensure so far as is humanly possible the perpetual maintenance of effective social order, one ought not to count on being able to maintain effective social order in the absence of political organization. We are speaking here only of the requirements for order by *political* means.

2 Kavka discusses the problems surrounding compliance by

coercion in Chapter 6.2, "On the Paradox of Perfect Tyranny," in *Hobbesian Moral and Political Theory,* pp. 254–65.

3 For example, the basic rule of morality (the sum of all of the rules of morality), which prohibits treating others in a manner that one wouldn't want others to treat oneself, specifies a subset of the duties delineated by the stronger Golden Rule of Christian religion, namely, that one treat others in a way that one would want to be treated; if Hobbes's principle is compatible with the Golden Rule, then it should also be compatible with the weaker rule.

4 He doesn't offer a separate general secular moral interest argument. It is probable that Hobbes himself did not see clearly any distinction between an objective secular morality and religious morality, because this distinction presupposes the possibility of conceiving a world in which there exist objectively true propositions the truth of which is not dependent on the way God has created the world. Hobbes thinks that *everything* is dependent on the way God has created the world – human nature, physical law, and the law of nature are all dependent on God's creation – even though knowledge of these things does not depend on knowledge of the existence of God. Regarding the belief that everything that is, is the result of God's creation, Hobbes was probably typical of his age; it is exceedingly difficult to determine whether there were any unbelievers at all in the seventeenth century. G. E. Aylmer explains this difficulty as "not due only to the legal and other inhibitions on the open expression of unbelief, but to the ambivalent, two-edged nature of scepticism and – above all – to the absence throughout of any concept corresponding to 'agnosticism,' and before the 1670s–80s of any clear distinction between atheism and deism" (Aylmer, "Unbelief in Seventeenth-Century England," in *Puritans and Revolutionaries* [Oxford: Clarendon Press, 1978]).

5 Moreover, it's doubtful that any of Hobbes's readers would have been willing to accept a principle that allowed people whom they believed to be holding mistaken views about one's duty to God to disobey the political authority on religious grounds. This is a further problem with the second reading of the "duty to God" clause, generated by the fact that transcendent interests may be *uniformity-requiring.* Uniformity-requiring

transcendent interests are particularly problematic and disruptive in Hobbes's view, as discussed later, in Chapter 6.

6 As we'll see in Chapter 6, this kind of struggle among religious
factions with competing transcendent interests was, in
Hobbes's view, the primary cause of the English Civil War. It
is understandable, then, that he is so concerned here with the
problem of how the exemption concerning duty to God is to
be specified.

7 This allows us to see that *Leviathan* is not a series of separate
arguments – it is not one argument for secular types and another for any religious types there might be – but is, rather, a
single, immensely complicated argument. I am not attributing
to Hobbes what might be termed a conjunction view ("All it
takes is one good reason; here are two"); Hobbes gives a number of reasons for supporting his principle, but not by means
of separable arguments. It is not until completion of the specification of the exemption in Hobbes's principles (carried out
in Part 3) that a narrowly prudential reason for adhering to
the principle can be fully established; and because the secular
moral interests argument offered in Part 2 is parasitic on the
narrow prudence argument, neither can it be firmly established
until the argument of Part 3 is completed. Once the entire
argument is presented, we can distinguish a number of distinct
kinds of reason (five, to be exact) for adhering to Hobbes's
principle. But until the entire argument is laid out, no reason
for obedience of any sort is established for anybody, not even
for amoral atheists. (Even an amoral atheist has reason to adhere to Hobbes's principle only if it really could increase his
prospects for survival and flourishing; but whether it can do
so depends in part on whether it leads others in his society,
acting in accordance with it, to refrain from disruptive behavior
– which it may not do if the exemption allows considerable
disruption – and in part on whether others in his society – say,
those who do have religious beliefs – can be brought to adhere
to it.)

8 Of course, to our minds there is a promising escape from this,
what we understand to be a false, dilemma. We claim that to
take people's religious interests seriously it is necessary to
remove them from the domain of state control, to refuse to
allow the state to make policies concerning the belief, profession, and practice of religion. *Once religion is regarded as a private*

matter, the problem of conflict between obedience to the state and the fulfillment of one's duty to God is largely alleviated, although, to be sure, there are numerous cases where the commands and prohibitions of the state cannot remain neutral among competing religious or moral stances, for example, in permitting abortion, medical intervention, and euthanasia; and there are cases where a state policy, though not by design, will conflict with the religious or moral views of some people, for example, in requiring citizens to participate in military service or in permitting the death penalty. But this solution depends on a good deal of consensus in viewing religion as a private matter, a widespread agreement to disagree, so to speak, while still maintaining social cooperation. The reason why this solution of removing religion from the domain of public jurisdiction is not open to Hobbes will become clear in Chapter 6. I mention it here only to head off at the pass the, perhaps natural, inclination to dismiss this portion of Hobbes's argument as the result of a mistake he's making.

9 Thus we shouldn't be misled by the term 'redescription' into thinking that Hobbes is *merely restating* each faction's views. Redescription may involve substantive revision of views depending on what is done with the component conjuncts of a given description of religious duty. We use the term 'redescription' in order to emphasize Hobbes's attempt to forge a link between the old descriptions and the new.

10 Although in such a case, it isn't clear that differences in transcendent religious interests would pose a threat to effective social order.

11 There is room for disagreement on this question because, as David Johnston points out, "The notion that there is or was an 'orthodox' or 'traditional' version of Christian doctrine on any issue should be treated with caution, since almost every conceivable doctrinal matter has been controversial at one time or another in Christian history" (Johnston, "Hobbes's Mortalism," *History of Political Thought* 10, no. 4 [Winter 1989]: 648, n. 7).

12 That nothing follows directly from this fact may be seen by considering how we could go about judging the merits of David Johnston's interpretation of Hobbes's religion argument as against my own interpretation. Johnston centrally interprets Hobbes as seeking to undermine the authority of the Scriptures

so as to undermine the fundamental Christian interest in achieving salvation, rather than (as I shall argue) seeking to redescribe interests such as this one so as to show them to be rational and compatible with Hobbes's own principle of political obligation. The reason Johnston attributes to Hobbes a desire to subvert rather than to rationalize Christian belief is that Johnston believes Hobbes aimed to secure order by getting people to act on fear of bodily death; if this could be achieved, the sovereign would be able to secure obedience by threat of punishment with death. To achieve that goal, according to Johnston, Hobbes adopted the strategy of undermining Christians' belief in salvation because that belief obviously can enable them to overcome their fear of bodily death and so renders impossible the securing of order by threat of bodily death. In short, Johnston thinks Hobbes was trying to persuade his readers to *give up* their interest in salvation so that they could become the psychological egoists they would need to be for the standard philosophical interpretation's solution to work.

Now, suppose we recognize that Hobbes is not very likely to have succeeded in convincing his seventeenth-century audience just to abandon (to "get over," as it were) their most deeply cherished religious beliefs and interests. Does the suggested "acceptability" criterion for the truth of interpretations enable us to decide between Johnston's interpretation of Hobbes as seeking to undermine Christian belief, and my alternative interpretation according to which he was seeking to rationalize it? Clearly not. That criterion asserts that for an interpretation to be true, it has to ascribe to Hobbes views that could have been accepted by his audience (where the test of acceptability is simply whether or not the views were in fact accepted). But because Hobbes's views were not accepted, neither interpretation (indeed, *no* interpretation) is true by this criterion. So we have no help in deciding between the alternatives, and the proposed criterion should be rejected as useless. If, however, we take the possibility in principle of persuasion merely as one consideration in favor of the plausibility of a proposed interpretation, then in this respect, a "rationalizing of religion" interpretation is to be preferred to a "subverting of religion" interpretation because Hobbes's seventeenth-century readers were religious and seemingly quite attached to their religious views.

13 The idea Hobbes employs here is not exactly that of *adiaphora*, or "things indifferent," most closely associated with Melanchthon, but it is fulfilling the similar function of decreasing people's attachment to particular practices so as to make uniform state-directed practice of religion acceptable.

14 He thinks, for example, that in showing how absurd it would be to believe that something that appears in every respect indistinguishable from a piece of bread is actually God, he has provided us with sufficient reason to reject the doctrine of transubstantiation, at least when there is an available alternative interpretation of Christ's reference to bread as his body that does not require us to disbelieve our senses and experience. He writes, "The Egyptian conjurers, that are said to have turned their rods to serpents, and the water into bloud, are thought but to have deluded the senses of the spectators by a false shew of things, yet are esteemed enchanters: But what should wee have thought of them if there had appeared in their rods nothing like a serpent, and in the water enchanted nothing like bloud, nor like any thing else but water, but that they had faced down the King, that they were serpents that looked like rods, and that it was bloud that seemed water? That had been both enchantment and lying. And yet in this daily act of the priest, they doe the very same, by turning the holy words into the manner of a charme, which produceth nothing new to the sense; but they face us down that it hath turned the bread into a man, nay more, into a God; and require men to worship it, as if it were our Saviour himself present God and Man, and thereby to commit most grosse idolatry" (337–8).

15 This contention is supported by Hobbes's detailed discussion in *Leviathan* Chapters 1 through 7 of sense, memory, reason, understanding, and opinion. See especially Chapters 1, 2, 5, and 7. I discuss these connections at length in this volume's Chapter 7, in examining the function of Part 1 of *Leviathan*.

16 Hobbes writes, "For if a man pretend to me that God hath spoken to him supernaturally, and immediately, and I make doubt of it, I cannot easily perceive what argument he can produce, to oblige me to beleeve it. It is true that if he be my

347

soveraign, he may oblige me to obedience, so as not by act or word to declare I beleeve him not; but not to think any otherwise then my reason perswades me. But if one that hath not such authority over me, shall pretend the same, there is nothing that exacteth either beleefe, or obedience" (196).

17 Hobbes lays the groundwork for this argument in Chapter 1 of *Leviathan*, pp. 6–8, where he discusses dreams and hallucinations. From that passage, it is clear that what has been taken to be a purely scientific discussion there is included in order to make plausible this crucial argument about revelation. I present further evidence in support of this claim in Chapter 7.

18 Of course, there may seem to be something grandly circular about this process of discovering our duties to God: We decide which alleged revelations to acknowledge using criteria set out in the Scriptures, which are themselves just the accumulated revelations of the true prophets. But this appearance is importantly misleading. Hobbes's readers share some important basic judgments concerning their religion that they would not be willing to revise, for example, that the information contained in the canonical books of Scripture is true. There may certainly be dispute over how, precisely, that information is to be interpreted (and this is the general problem Hobbes is going to have to solve), but not every saying in Scripture will arouse such interpretive disputation. In fact, some points in Scripture will bear so evident a sense that they will be the objects of unshakable judgments. The scriptural passages Hobbes cites in his argument here are, I think, of the sort about which there is no interpretive controversy. Thus, we shouldn't worry that his attempt to identify the marks of a true prophet by appeal to Scripture won't get him anywhere; this mode of argument is perfectly acceptable to the people whom he is addressing.

19 Of course, the reference here is to the traditions of Judeo-Christian religion. *Once* people have acknowledged "the one true God," each true prophet is taken further to specify the content of "true religion," and anyone who attempts to "roll back," as opposed to reinterpret, the previously established body of doctrine, will fail to meet this criterion for true prophets.

20 Hobbes writes, "For as in naturall things, men of judgement

348

require naturall signes and arguments; so in supernaturall things, they require signes supernaturall (which are miracles), before they consent inwardly, and from their hearts" (59).

21 Hobbes emphasizes that he is not voiding his earlier distinction between what we believe and how we should act: "A private man has alwaies the liberty, (because thought is free) to beleeve, or not beleeve in his heart, those acts that have been given out for miracles, according as he shall see what benefit can accrew by men's belief, to those that pretend, or countenance them, and thereby conjecture, whether they be miracles, or lies. But when it comes to confession of that faith, the private reason must submit to the public, that is to say, to Gods lieutenant" (238).

22 It is interesting to note that Hobbes views his scriptural argument for his principle as stronger than his argument from natural reason, in the sense that if his scriptural argument is accepted, the argument from natural reason is dispensable, whereas the converse is not true. Hobbes allows that even if he is wrong to think that his theory is demonstrated by principles of reason, it is certainly demonstrated by principles in Scripture: "Long . . . after men have begun to constitute commonwealths, imperfect, and apt to relapse into disorder, there may principles of reason be found out . . . to make their constitution (excepting by externall violence) everlasting. And such are those which I have in this discourse set forth . . . But supposing that these of mine are not such principles of reason; yet I am sure they are principles from authority of Scripture" (176).

23 Hobbes's official view on the canonical status of Scriptures is that unless God has spoken to one directly, one cannot know what God commands except through natural reason, which tells one to obey one's public authority. So one can have no obligation to acknowledge as canonical any Scriptures not declared canonical by that public authority, and one is obligated to recognize as canon those books which the public authority stipulates. But Hobbes needn't rest anything on his official view because his readers are not in disagreement about what books of Scripture are to be regarded as canonical, and so he can take his argument from sources acceptable to all.

24 I have indicated in passing that for Hobbes the laws of nature have a triple status. God has constructed human beings in

such a way that ingratitude, iniquity, pride, truculence, intemperance, and so on will have harmful consequences for them. Thus, violation of these laws *qua* laws of nature is imprudent, and mere common sense allows us to recognize this. Second, the laws of nature are the laws of morality; they enumerate the things one morally ought not to do to another (since one wouldn't want to be so treated oneself). These are moral facts, which do not stand in need of anything to back them up, and which human beings are capable of recognizing. Thus, a violation of these laws, which condemn acts of iniquity, pride, and so on, *qua* laws of morality, is immoral. Now, human beings who believe in the existence and benevolence of God believe that God created them, and cares for them, and accordingly that he wants them not to harm one another. Thus, the violation of these same laws, *qua* laws of God, is sinful, and the mere possession of "natural" religion (belief in God) allows us to recognize this. It is in all of these senses (but in the latter particularly) that the laws of nature or God oblige in conscience; we know perfectly well that we ought not to violate them, both for prudential and for moral and religious reasons, on the basis of natural reason alone (because even the existence of God is discoverable by unaided natural reason). They do not need to be "made laws" by anyone (i.e., they do not have to be the commands of a person whom we've authorized in order to be laws) because they will hold for human beings just in virtue of the nature of the world. Moreover, there is no epistemological problem about them – we just naturally grasp them, much as we naturally perceive objects in a spatiotemporal array – in contrast to those positive laws, the knowledge of which requires that we recognize the authority of the legislator.

25 Actually, Hobbes first offers a simple conceptual argument that there can only be one representative of a Christian people, and that it must be either the sovereign of a universal church of all Christians, or each national civil sovereign. If this conceptual argument were convincing, Hobbes could skip the arguments I'm about to present, and proceed immediately to his arguments for conclusion (3). But this conceptual argument is so unconvincing as it stands, that before he can go on, Hobbes has to present the arguments I'm about to discuss as replies to objections. I have reversed the order of presentation because

doing so makes his argument less confusing and more immediately plausible.

26 Paul Weithman has expressed to me (in a personal communication) his amazement at Hobbes's interpretation of the story of Saul's election, noting that it is very tendentious, though perhaps useful to Hobbes in robbing of its force one of the scriptural verses that might most powerfully have supported a divided-sovereignty argument, and one, moreover, in which civil authority is subordinate to ecclesiastical. Weithman says: "The story of Saul could be read, not as the abolition of God's civil government on earth, but as the *institution* of constitutionalism or of limited monarchy. After the coronation of Saul, God's prophet (in this case Samuel) retained the right to depose the king in God's name. This is exactly what Samuel did to Saul, as reported in I Samuel, Chapter 15, verse 28. David became king of Israel, and he was subject to God through the prophet Nathan (you might recall the story of David's sin against Uriah and of Nathan's consequent rebuke, recounted at Samuel, Chapters 11–12). David's son Solomon too was responsible to the prophets. High priests may have ceased to be magistrates, but prophets had a very important political role and acted in God's name *after* the coronation of Saul."

We shall see Hobbes's arguments for assigning to ecclesiastics a much less important role than they would have on Weithman's alternative interpretation a bit farther on. Here we may just note that in Hobbes's view, if Samuel and Nathan had rightfully possessed the authority to depose the kings, then they themselves would actually have been sovereign, and possessed all the actual rights of sovereignty, a conclusion Hobbes seems to imagine his readers will reject. If, alternatively, we understand the remarks of God's prophets as (strongly worded) admonition or exhortation – attempts to persuade, by the voice of conscience – then Hobbes's interpretation should seem somewhat more plausible.

27 Hobbes continues with examples from Scripture, concluding that "if by soule were meant a substance incorporeall, with an existence separated from the body, it might as well be inferred of any other living creature as of man" (340).

28 Hobbes writes, "For though we read plainly in holy Scripture, that God created Adam in an estate of living for ever, which was conditionall, that is to say, if he disobeyed not his com-

mandment, which was not essentiall to humane nature, but
consequent to the vertue of the Tree of Life, whereof he had
liberty to eat as long as hee had not sinned; and that hee was
thrust out of Paradise after he had sinned lest hee should eate
thereof, and live for ever; and that Christs passion is a dis-
charge of sin to all that beleeve on him; and by consequence,
a restitution of eternall life to all the faithfull, and to them
onely: yet the doctrine is now, and hath been a long time far
otherwise; namely, that every man hath eternity of life by
nature, in as much as his soul is immortall: So that the flaming
sword at the entrance of paradise, though it hinder a man from
coming to the tree of life, hinders him not from the immortality
which God took from him for his sin, nor makes him to need
the sacrificing of Christ for the recovering of the same; and
consequently, not onely the faithfull and righteous, but also
the wicked, and the heathen, shall enjoy eternall life, without
any death at all, much lesse a second, and everlasting death.
To salve this, it is said that by *second* and *everlasting death*, is
meant a second, and everlasting life, but in torments; a figure
never used, but in this very case" (339).

29 Hobbes acknowledges that the view of man here presented
is "novel," and goes on at great length to answer anticipated
objections to his interpretation. For example, in reply to the
objection that men must have eternal souls separated from
their earthly bodies in order for the damned to suffer the
eternal torments of hell, Hobbes argues that hell is simply a
metaphor for the destruction by fire of a neverending succession of individuals sentenced to the second (and final)
death rather than a place where living beings are eternally
tormented. He bases his interpretation on an analysis of
Scripture, arguing that hell must be a metaphor because some
of its alleged locations are conceptually impossible (e.g., a
bottomless pit in the earth), the locations indicated in the
Bible are mutually incompatible, and in every context the
interpretation of 'hell' as destruction makes sense. Likewise,
he argues that nothing in Scripture supports the idea that
the saints will ascend into heaven, or that there is such a
place as purgatory.

30 Weithman has pointed out that Hobbes seems here to be relying on a Calvinist conception of excommunication according
to which excommunication does not entail damnation, not or

not only because God has predestined some for salvation, but also because human determination of an excommunicant's eternal fate would be an insult to God's power. (Although, excommunication's being a sign of one's eternal fate, Calvin did regard it as both a social and spiritual sanction.) It is not surprising that Hobbes should have adopted the more Calvinist alternative to the Catholic conception of excommunication because on it excommunication poses no threat to the salvation of civil sovereigns, whose salvation is presumably brought about in the same way as anyone else's is.

31 In particular, excommunication cannot harm sovereigns in the relevant temporal social world. Hobbes writes that "if a sovreign prince, or assembly be excommunicate, the sentence is of no effect. For all subjects are bound to be in the company and presence of their own sovereign . . . nor can they lawfully expel him from any place of his own dominion, whether profane or holy; nor go out of his dominion, without his leave; much lesse . . . refuse to eat with him" (278). Again, excommunication, when it is without civil enforcement, as it is "when a Christian state, or prince is excommunicate by a forain authority, is without effect; and consequently ought to be without terrour" (279).

32 Hobbes writes, "[A Christian King] cannot oblige men to beleeve, though as a civill soveraign he may make laws suitable to his doctrine which may oblige men to certain actions, and sometimes to such as they would not otherwise do, and which he ought not to command; and yet when they are commanded, they are laws; and the external actions done in obedience to them, without the inward approbation, are the actions of the soveraign, and not of the subject, which is in that case but as an instrument, without any motion of his owne at all, because God hath commanded to obey them" (309).

This is one of many examples of Hobbes's general strategy of forcing a wedge between belief and action (liberty of conscience vs. liberty of action); thus divorced, the former can have no implications for the latter. This separation counterfeits the desirable consequences of regarding religion as a private matter, namely, preserving social order and social cooperation among persons whose religious beliefs differ. Hobbes hopes to persuade his readers that although one is required to profess and practice publicly as one's political authority dictates, in so doing one is in no way compromising one's faith, "For internall faith is in its own nature invisible, and consequently exempted from all humane jurisdiction; whereas the words and actions that proceed from it, as breaches of our civill obedience, are injustice both before God and man" (285).

Hobbes lays the groundwork for this argument in Chapter 16 of *Leviathan*, where he writes: "When the actor doth any thing against the law of nature by command of the author, if he be obliged by former covenant to obey him, not he, but the author breaketh the law of nature: for though the action be against the law of nature, yet it is not his; but contrarily, to refuse to do it is against the law of nature that forbiddeth breach of covenant" (81).

33 Hobbes goes on to offer the following argument for his position: "If any man shall accuse this doctrine as repugnant to true, and unfeigned Christianity, I ask him, in case there should be a subject in any Christian commonwealth, that should be inwardly in his heart of the Mahometan Religion, whether if his soveraign command him to bee present at the divine service of the Christian church, and that on pain of death, he think that Mahometan obliged in conscience to suffer death for that cause, rather than to obey that command of his lawful prince. If he say, he ought rather to suffer death, then he authorizeth all private men to disobey their princes in maintenance of their religion, true or false: if he say, he ought to be obedient, then he alloweth to himself that which hee denyeth to another, contrary to the words of our Saviour 'Whatsoever you would that men should doe unto you, that doe yee unto them', and contrary to the law of nature (which is the indubitable everlasting law of God) 'Do not to another that which thou wouldest not he should doe unto thee' " (271–2).

34 Hobbes categorically rejects, and vigorously attacks, the contention of many Protestants in his day that the pope was the Antichrist. On this point he was squarely in the camp of emerging Anglican thought against that of the Puritans (303–4).

35 "In the fift book he [Bellarmine] hath four conclusions. The first is, 'That the Pope is not Lord of all the world': The second, 'That the Pope is not Lord of all the Christian world': The

third, 'That the Pope (without his owne territory) has not any temporall jurisdiction DIRECTLY': These three conclusions are easily granted. The fourth is, 'That the Pope has (in the dominions of other princes) the supreme temporal power INDIRECTLY': which is denyed unlesse hee mean by 'indirectly', that he has gotten it by indirect means; then is that also granted. But I understand that when he saith he hath it indirectly, he means that such temporall jurisdiction belongeth to him of Right, but that this right is but a consequence of his pastorall authority, the which he could not exercise, unlesse he have the other with it" (314).

36 Pp. 247–8. This argument depends on Hobbes's analysis of various sorts of systems within a commonwealth, presented in Chapter 22, which in turn relies heavily on Hobbes's discussion of representation and personhood, given in Chapter 16.

37 Hobbes argues this in Chapter 19.

38 "I wish they [princes] would all resolve to be kings, or subjects. Men cannot serve two masters: They ought therefore to ease them, either by holding the reins of government wholly in their own hands; or by wholly delivering them into the hands of the Pope; that such men as are willing to be obedient, may be protected in their obedience" (315). Indeed, sovereigns have a natural duty to do so.

39 Hobbes gestured toward his views that charity is a kind of obedience, and that God takes the will for the deed, in an earlier passage where he asserts that subjects "are to be taught that not onely the unjust facts, but the designes and intentions to do them, (though by accident hindred,) are injustice, which consisteth in the pravity of the will, as well as in the irregularity of the act. And this is the intention of the tenth Commandement, and the summe of the Second Table; which is reduced all to this one commandement of mutuall charity, *Thou shalt love thy neighbor as thy selfe.*" (179). Hobbes first presented his view that an unfeigned effort to fulfill the law counts as fulfilling the law in Part 1, Chapter 15. The laws of nature "because they oblige onely to a desire and endeavour, I mean an unfeigned and constant endeavour, are easie to be observed. For in that they require nothing but endeavour, he that endeavoureth their performance, fulfilleth them; and he that fulfilleth the law, is just" (79).

40 We must be careful not to conflate Hobbes's identification here of which laws are God's (of which laws we must attempt to obey in order to fulfill our duty to God, and thereby to satisfy the obedience condition for salvation) with his accounts of how one becomes obligated to obey God, or of how one becomes obligated to obey a civil sovereign. A person becomes obligated in *fact* to obey God through an explicit promise of obedience, made at his baptism (made on his behalf by one who has dominion over him, which he later reaffirms, or by himself, if he is of age) or through some other ceremony of admission into God's kingdom (as in the Old Testament). He is said to be obligated in *conscience* to obey God if he believes that God exists and has made rules of conduct for human beings. Such a person will be doing what he believes to be wrong in attempting to disobey God's laws, and so acting with a "seared conscience." Lastly, even disbelievers are said to be *obliged by* God's power – that is, subject to God's power – just in virtue of their status as objects in the world, subject to the laws of nature. In this sense, all animals and even inanimate objects are subject to God's power. This is not a form of obligation at all, but it is a form of subjection.

One becomes obligated to obey a civil sovereign through promising, either expressly or tacitly, to obey him. This is the *only* way one can become obligated to obey a sovereign, indeed, the only way one can take on *any* obligation *in fact*. One doesn't become obligated to obey a civil sovereign by being antecedently obligated to obey God; but one does have an obligation to God (either in fact or in conscience) to honor the obligations one has undertaken, that is, not to break one's (even tacit) promises; and one has a natural duty not to disrupt the peace, not to act ungratefully, and more generally, not to do what natural reason tells one to be wrong. This is because the laws of nature, which have intrinsic authority, are simultaneously God's laws and the laws of morality (conceived as natural duties).

It is thus mistaken to think that having an obligation to obey one's civil sovereign depends on having an obligation to obey God. One has an obligation to obey one's political authority if and only if one has promised, expressly or tacitly, to obey him. One *just is* obligated to keep one's covenants. This is a moral fact, which human beings can know by their natural reason. It is true, according to Hobbes, that it is God who has constructed people to have a moral sense, and to be able to perceive moral truths, but knowledge of right and wrong does not depend on believing in the existence of God, and moral obligations do not depend on any prior obligation to obey God. Human beings know it is morally wrong to treat others as they wouldn't want themselves to be treated, and they know it is wrong to do what their natural reason tells them to be wrong, quite independently of any natural or prophetical knowledge of the existence of God.

41 A person who has *no* transcendent interests can never be sufficiently motivated to risk his preservation, even to preserve social order. He will still usually have reason to affirm Hobbes's principle, and himself to obey the extant effective political authority – since it is in his self-interest narrowly construed that there be social order, and failing to act on this principle contributes to disorder as well as possibly incurring punishment – but he will be unable to risk his preservation to defend it. A transcendent interest is always required if one's interest in self-preservation is to be overridden. Nevertheless, one needn't believe in God, or desire salvation, to have a transcendent interest; moral interests and other-regarding interests can also be transcendent. Thus, an atheist might risk his preservation in defense of the commonwealth because he believes it is his moral duty to defend it, or because he fears for the well-being of his children. Hobbes's salvation argument is not *required* in order to give people a transcendent interest in upholding his principle, but it is capable of giving believers an additional, self-referring transcendent interest in doing so.

42 But see Kavka's discussion at Chapter 11.2 of his book that two nontranscendent factors – "progressively limited options" and "training-habituation" – may sometimes motivate self-sacrificing acts in the service of national defense. Kavka does not maintain that these will be in every case, or even in most, sufficient to motivate risky behavior: rather, he suggests they may combine with "nonegoistic motives" (our possibly transcendent interests) and the consideration that there are "fates worse than death" (sometimes also transcendent) to sufficiently motivate subjects to fight in defense

of the commonwealth. Kavka acknowledges that all but the first factor are either irrational or nonrational motivations from the point of view of the predominant egoism he attributes to Hobbes (Kavka, *Hobbesian Moral and Political Theory*, pp. 424–33).

CHAPTER 4. HOBBES'S MECHANISM FOR THE REPRODUCTION OF SOCIAL STABILITY

1 Bernard Gert has stressed the key role of education in Hobbes's political philosophy in his Introduction to *Man and Citizen* (Garden City, N.Y.: Doubleday, Anchor, 1972).

2 In *The Elements of Law*, Hobbes writes: "To dispose men to sedition three things concur. The first is discontent; for as long as a man thinketh himself well, and that the present government standeth not in his way to hinder his proceeding from well to better; it is impossible for him to desire the change thereof. The second is pretence of right; for though a man be discontent, yet if in his own opinion there be no just cause of stirring against, or resisting the government established, nor any pretense to justify his resistance, and to procure aid, he will never show it. The third is hope of success; for it were madness to attempt without hope, when to fail is to die the death of a traitor. Without these three: discontent, pretence, and hope, there can be no rebellion; and when the same are all together, there wanteth nothing thereto, but a man of credit to set up the standard, and to blow the trumpet" (2.8.1).

3 Of course, this new system of education will have to be instituted, and assuming that certain social interest groups will have some motive for resisting the necessary revisions of the old system, force may be needed in order to carry out these reforms. In principle, proper teaching may be enough to secure order, but in practice, at least initially and in certain circumstances, force may be needed in order to reform the universities so that they teach properly. I discuss the role of force in Hobbes's theory in Chapter 6.

4 That Hobbes does not view human nature as fixed, or programmed in, comes out strikingly in a passage where Hobbes speaks of children as if they had no wills of their own but were rather formless beings to be shaped by adult hands: "Now those things whereof we make benefit, are either subject to

us, and the profit they yeeld, followeth the labour we bestow upon them as a naturall effect; or they are not subject to us, but answer our labour according to their own wills. In the first sense the labour bestowed on the earth is called culture; and *the education of children a culture of their mindes"* (188–9, emphasis added).

CHAPTER 5. HOBBES'S RESOLUTIVE ANALYSIS, PHASE TWO

1   This "opinion of powers invisible" was one of the seeds of natural religion enumerated by Hobbes in Chapter 12 (seeds "that can never be so abolished out of humane nature, but that new religions may againe be made to spring out of them" [58]), although the much more destructive view that these invisible powers – ghosts – were incorporeal substances turns out to have been a later refinement by school divines: "And for the matter, or substance of the invisible agents so fancied, they could not by naturall cogitation fall upon any other conceipt, but that it was the same with that of the soul of man; and that the soul of man was of the same substance, with that which appeareth in a dreame to one that sleepeth; or in a looking-glasse to one that is awake; which, men not knowing that such apparitions are nothing else but creatures of the fancy, think to be reall, and externall substances; and therefore call them ghosts. . . . But the opinion that such spirits were incorporeall, or immateriall, could never enter into the mind of any man by nature" (53).

2   Hobbes has an interesting conjecture as to why Christians are no longer able to heal, to speak in tongues, and to survive things usually fatal to people, interesting in part because he clearly believes that Christians were once able to do these things (a view almost as surprising as his belief that spirits actually exist, although they are not immaterial, nor are the reflections, dreams, and visions people commonly take for them): "But how it comes to passe that whereas heretofore the apostles, and after them for a time, the pastors of the church, did cure those singular diseases, which now they are not seen to doe; as likewise, why it is not in the power of every true beleever now, to doe all that the faithfull did then . . . is another question. And it is probable, that those extraordinary gifts were

given to the church, for no longer a time, than men trusted wholly to Christ, and looked for their felicity onely in his kingdome to come; and consequently, that when they sought authority, and riches, and trusted to their own subtilty for a kingdome of this world, these supernaturall gifts of God were again taken from them" (356).

3 The benefit to popes of claiming this authority over God's present kingdom cannot be overemphasized. In *Behemoth*, Hobbes writes: "I see that a Christian king, or state, how well soever provided he be of money and arms, where the church of Rome hath such authority, will have but a hard match of it, for want of men. For their subjects will hardly be drawn into the field and fight with courage against their consciences." But even supposing that subjects could be paid to fight against their consciences, "the great mischief done to kings upon pretence of religion is when the Pope gives power to one king to invade another" (*B* 23).

4 Not only do the universities churn out inherently disruptive doctrines, but school divines, by employing their private judgments in impertinently debating questions of theology, generate so much dissension that they foster the development of competing religious interests among subjects. In *Behemoth*, Hobbes writes that "certainly an university is an excellent servant to the clergy; and the clergy, if it be not carefully looked to, by their dissention in doctrines and by the advantage to publish their dissentions, is an excellent means to divide a kingdom into factions" (*B* 185).

5 Hobbes's entire discussion here is foreshadowed in Chapter 12. There Hobbes has written: "Lastly, amongst the points by the Church of Rome declared necessary for salvation, there be so many manifestly to the advantage of the Pope, and of his spirituall subjects residing in the territories of other Christian princes, that were it not for the mutuall emulation of those princes, they might without warre, or trouble, exclude all forraign authority, as easily as it has been excluded in England. For who is there that does not see, to whose benefit it conduceth, to have it believed, that a king hath not his authority from Christ, unlesse a bishop crown him? That a king, if he be a priest, cannot marry? That whether a prince be born in lawfull marriage, or not, must be judged by authority from Rome? That subjects may be freed from their alleageance, if

by the court of Rome, the king be judged an heretique? That
a king . . . may be deposed by a Pope . . . for no cause; and his
kingdome given to one of his subjects? [Etc.]" (60).

CHAPTER 6. THEORY IN PRACTICE

1 In *Leviathan*, Hobbes attacks both Bellarmine (316) and Beza
   (341) for holding this view.

2 "The people have one day in seven the leisure to hear instruction, and there are ministers appointed to teach them their
   duty. But how have those ministers performed their office? A
   great part of them, namely, the Presbyterian ministers,
   throughout the whole war, instigated the people against the
   King; so did also Independents and other fanatic ministers.
   The rest, contented with their livings, preached in their par-
   ishes points of controversy, to religion impertinent, but to the
   breach of charity among themselves very effectual" (200–1).

3 In our Chapter 4 we saw Hobbes's *Leviathan* discussion of this
   source of disorder in the context of his identification of the
   errors, disseminated in the universities, that have destabilized
   the state. Hobbes had already presented the ancient republican
   view of *libertas* as a significant threat to order in both the
   Elements of Law and *De Cive*. As we shall see in Chapter 8,
   Hobbes developed his own distinctive concept of liberty as a
   correction to what he perceived as a disruptive error.

4 Indeed, in Hobbes's view, the ill effects of the incorporation
   of Aristotelian philosophy into university divinity give new
   meaning to the old saw "Beware of Greeks bearing gifts."

5 Hobbes's language in *Leviathan* is strikingly similar: "No man
   ought in the interpretation of the Scripture to proceed further
   than the bounds which are set by their severall soveraigns.
   For the Scriptures since God now speaketh in them, are the
   Mount Sinai. . . . To look upon them and therein to behold the
   wondrous works of God, and learn to fear him is allowed; but
   to interpret them; that is, to pry into what God saith to him
   whom he appointeth to govern under him, and make themselves Judges whether he govern as God commandeth him,
   or not, is to transgresse the bounds God hath set us, and to
   gaze upon God irreverently" (L 252).

6 This view appears explicitly even in Hobbes's earliest political
   work: "But the truth is apparent, by continual experience, that

men seek not only liberty of conscience, but of their actions; nor that only, but a farther liberty of persuading others to their opinions; nor that only, for every man desireth, that the sovereign authority should admit no other opinions to be maintained but such as he himself holdeth" (*EL* 2.6.13).

7 This distinction is important. It is the *doctrine* that when widely accepted, threatens social order. It would have this effect no matter *who* affirmed it, as we saw Hobbes saying earlier. That ambitious elites seeking power put forward the doctrine is in itself of no special significance. Not just any power seeker, no matter how elite, can disrupt order.

Disruptive *doctrines* must be widely publicized and embraced. Of course, the powerful are in a better position to spread the ideas, but the guns they hand people have to be, so to speak, properly loaded. The fact that a group is elite, and ambitious, does not yet provide an *explanation* of its disruptive capacity, and Hobbes takes care *not* to suggest that it does, although he *is* concerned to call attention to the unsavory *motives* of those who disseminate these false doctrines inimical to the maintenance of social order. For Hobbes, it is the *ideas* and not the actors that are important. I would thus disagree with Deborah Baumgold's thesis that Hobbes took the struggle for power among ambitious elites to be the cause of disorder, not just because it oversimplifies Hobbes's view as to the sources of disorder (which I discuss at length in Chapters 3, 5, and 7), but also because it seems to suggest a more personal account of this source of disorder than Hobbes himself was prepared to give (see Baumgold, *Hobbes's Political Theory*).

8 Hobbes writes that "to increase [the people's] disaffection to his Majesty, [the Parliament] accused him of a purpose to introduce and authorize the Roman religion in this kingdom: than which nothing was more hateful to the people. . . . And this was indeed the most effectual calumny, to alienate the people's affections from him, that could possibly be invented" (77).

9 "And because opinions which are gotten by education, and in length of time are made habitual, cannot be taken away by force, and upon the sudden: they must therefore be taken away also, by time and education" (*EL* 2.9.8).

10 "The right of judging what doctrines are . . . to be taught the subjects, is . . . inseparably annexed . . . to the soveraign power

civill. . . . For it is evident to the meanest capacity, that mens actions are derived from the opinions they have of the good, or evill, which from those actions redound unto themselves; and consequently, men that are once possessed of an opinion that their obedience to the soveraign power will bee more hurtfull to them, than their disobedience, will disobey the laws, and thereby overthrow the commonwealth, and introduce confusion, and civill war" (*L* 295).

11 The view that hope of success is a necessary condition of rebellion is discussed at some length in the *Elements:* "To dispose men to sedition three things concur. The first is discontent. . . . The second is pretence of right; for though a man be discontented, yet if in his own opinion there be no just cause of stirring against, or resisting the government established . . . he will never show it. The third is hope of success; for it were madness to attempt without hope, when to fail is to die the death of a traitor. Without these three: discontent, pretence, and hope, there can be no rebellion; and when the same are all together, there wanteth nothing thereto, but a man of credit to set up the standard, and to blow the trumpet" (2.8.1). Hobbes continues, "there is required, in the third place, hope of success, which consisteth in four points: 1. That the discontented have mutual intelligence; 2. that they have sufficient number; 3. that they have arms; 4. that they agree upon a head. For these four must concur to the making of one body of rebellion, in which intelligence is the life, number the limbs, arms the strength, and a head the unity, by which they are directed to one and the same action" (2.8.11).

12 Baumgold discusses Hobbes's view that depriving the ambitious of their bases of support is necessary in her account of the role Hobbes's remarks on the art of government play in his theory (see Baumgold, *Hobbes's Political Theory*).

13 This formulation was suggested to me by Perry Anderson.

14 It is true that *Behemoth* was written in the light of the unstable religious settlement of 1662 and the religious struggles of the 1660s, whereas *Leviathan* was not. But more than half of *Leviathan* is devoted to a detailed discussion of religion, and this obviously indicates some substantial concern with religion at the time of its composition.

15 God's power is a different case. God does not have to have supporters in order to have power, nor does he need to be

given authority (be authorized) in order to have a right to rule. "Whether men will or not," writes Hobbes, "they must be subject alwayes to the divine power. By denying the existence, or providence of God, men may shake off their ease, but not their yoke. . . . The right of nature, whereby God reigneth over men, and punisheth those that break his lawes, is to be derived, not from his creating them, as if he required obedience, as of gratitude for his benefits; but from his irresistible power. . . . To those therefore whose power is irresistible, the dominion of all men adhaereth naturally by their excellence of power; and consequently, it is from that power, that the kingdom over men, and the right of afflicting men at his pleasure, belongeth naturally to God Almighty; not as creator, and gracious; but as Omnipotent" (L 186–7). But the power of human rulers consists in the support of the people.

16   And authority draws further power to itself. Also, perceived power may draw further power to itself, for, in Hobbes's view, "reputation of power is power" (L 41).

17   The intimate connection between authority and that support in which power consists is made clear by Hobbes's *equating* the notions of having authority and being authorized. Harrington criticizes Hobbes for what he sees as a conflation of the ideas of authority and power: "A learned writer may have authority, though he have no power; and a foolish magistrate may have power, though he have otherwise no esteem or authority" (*Oceana*, ed. F. B. Liljegren [Westport, Conn.: Hyperion Press, 1979], p. 14). But for Hobbes, this way of talking is wrongheaded. To have authority (being authorized by others to use their strength and their means as one thinks fit) is to have supporters, which is, in turn, to have power. Hobbes's deliberate discussion of authorization in Chapter 16 of *Leviathan* suggests that Hobbes was not simply mistaken in his use of what he was taking to be our ordinary understandings of these notions, but was rather attempting to work out a new and more politically useful understanding of the relationship between the notions. Their connection, and the primacy of the concept of authority in Hobbes's system, are obscured by the standard philosophical interpretation's insistence that might alone makes order.

18   At least not *qua* governing concepts. The pride–iniquity version of the prudence–duty distinction does appear, for example, in

Chapter 33: "If every man should be obliged to take for God's law, what particular men, on pretence of private inspiration or revelation, should obtrude upon him, (in such a number of men, that out of pride, and ignorance, take their own dreams and extravagant fancies and madnesse for testimonies of Gods spirit; or out of ambition, pretend to such divine testimonies falsely, and contrary to their own consciences,) it were impossible that any divine law should be acknowledged" (205).

19 In fact, this sort of pride is closely related to madness. Hobbes holds that to assume oneself divinely inspired bespeaks that excessive pride which, in Hobbes's view, is a form of madness. Hobbes writes: "And if there were nothing else that bewrayed their madnesse; yet that very arrogating such inspiration to themselves, is argument enough. If some man in Bedlam should entertaine you with sober discourse; and you desire in taking leave, to know what he were, that you might another time requite his civility; and he should tell you, he were God the Father; I think you need expect no extravagant action for argument of his Madnesse" (L 36). Likewise, the divinity disputation of schoolmen, is a form of madness resulting from excessive pride: "There is yet another fault in the discourses of some men; which may also be numbred amongst the sorts of madnesse; namely, that abuse of words . . . by the name of absurdity. . . . And this is incident to none but those, that converse in questions of matters incomprehensible, as the Schoolemen; or in questions of abstruse philosophy. . . . What is the meaning of these words: 'The first cause does not necessarily inflow any thing into the second, by force of the essentiall subordination of the second causes, by which it may help it to worke'? They are the translation of the title of the sixth chapter of Suarez first booke, *Of the Concourse, Motion, and Help of God*. When men write whole volumes of such stuffe, are they not mad, or intend to make others so? . . . So that this kind of absurdity, may rightly be numbred amongst the many sorts of madnesse; and all the time that guided by clear thoughts of their worldly lust, they forbear disputing, or writing thus, but lucide intervals" (L 39–40).

20 Hobbes writes, "And Job, how earnestly does he expostulate with God, for the many afflictions he suffered, notwithstanding his righteousness? This question in the case of Job, is decided by God himselfe, not by arguments derived from Job's

sinne, but his own power. For whereas the friends of Job drew their arguments from his affliction to his sinne, and he defended himselfe by the conscience of his innocence, God himself taketh up the matter, and having justified the affliction by arguments drawn from his power, such as this, 'Where wast thou when I layd the foundations of the earth,' and the like, both approved Job's innocence, and reproved the erroneous doctrine of his friends" (L 188).

21 Leo Strauss, *The Political Philosophy of Hobbes; Its Basis and Its Genesis* (Chicago: University of Chicago Press, 1963), p. 13, emphasis added.

22 Ibid., pp. 27–8.

23 Ibid., p. 21.

24 Ibid., p. 22.

25 J. W. N. Watkins, *Hobbes's System of Ideas*, pp. 14–16.

26 Ibid., pp. 166–7. Ironically, Watkins presents as evidence for the falsity of Hobbes's "overriding fear of death principle" Frazer's discussion of the willingness of the members of certain tribes to become kings, even though they knew they would be ceremonially killed at or before the time of their first signs of aging, and their subsequent willingness to submit to their execution when the time came. This example is hauntingly reminiscent of Hobbes's own discussion of the Ethiopian kings who killed themselves when the priest so commanded them (B 119), which Hobbes gave precisely as an example of how one's religious beliefs can override one's fear of death.

CHAPTER 7. HOBBES'S RESOLUTIVE ANALYSIS, PHASE ONE

1 The closest thing to an exception here is Hobbes's enumeration of the laws of nature. These laws are subsequently used as premises in Hobbes's argument that we have a moral reason to adhere to his principle of political obligation.

2 If we need an account of our natures in order to build a rational science of politics, and if natural science cannot provide us with one, it would seem we will need a social scientific account of ourselves. This may be why experience, rather than mere postulates and observations of physics, is such a crucial concept in the argument of *Leviathan*. Hobbes is not deriving necessary political institutions from a scientific analysis of

fundamental human nature. He is relying on our social experience, and on our knowledge of our natures as socially formed beings, arguing that given these our tendencies, this is what we need for a stable state. "I have derived the rights of soveraigne power, and the duty of subjects hitherto," Hobbes writes, "from the principles of nature onely, such as experience has found true . . . that is to say, from the nature of men known to us by experience" (195). But our experience is social, and we know ourselves as creatures with particular interests, allegiances, ends, and affections, concerning religion, moral duty, our self-conceptions and our ties to others, formed by culture and education.

3   It is worth noticing that this passage appears in the *Leviathan expansion* of Hobbes's earlier *Elements of Law* discussion of dreams. When Hobbes revised his "scientific" chapters, he *systematically* expanded his discussions of the *religious* implications and applications of his scientific remarks; *not* the science itself. This strongly suggests that the science is there for religious purposes.

4   David Johnston, in contrast, holds that Hobbes fundamentally aimed to destroy Christian belief by discrediting the Scriptures and undermining belief in the central Christian tenet of salvation, in order to do away with the transcendent religious interests that upset social order. I do not find any textual evidence to support the claim that Hobbes sought to discredit, rather than rationalize, religious belief (and of course Hobbes denies it); nor does it seem, given Hobbes's intended audience, a very plausible project to have undertaken. I discuss this matter in greater detail in the following chapter. See Johnston, *The Rhetoric of Leviathan*.

5   These chapters have more in common with Chapters 7 through 11 than they do with Chapters 1 through 3 and Chapter 6, relying, as they do, more on social abuses of speech than on an account of individual physical operations. If we count these as chapters on linguistic errors, then there are a mere four chapters of physical scientific discussion in *Leviathan*, a very slim grounding for a science of politics, and surprisingly little if this were the function Hobbes intended physical science to serve.

6   Hobbes returns to this point in Chapter 11: "Ignorance of the signification of words, which is want of understanding, dis-

poseth men to take on trust, not onely the truth they know
not, but also the errors, and which is more, the non-sense of
them they trust: For neither error, nor non-sense, can without
a perfect understanding of words be detected" (50).

7   Hobbes writes that "they that have no science are in better,
and nobler condition with their naturall prudence than men,
that by mis-reasoning, or by trusting them that reason wrong,
fall upon false and absurd generall rules [and] that trusting
onely to the authority of books, follow the blind blindly. . . .
[And so] in any businesse whereof a man has not infallible
science to proceed by, to forsake his own natural judgement,
and be guided by generall sentences read in authors, and subject to many exceptions, is a signe of folly. . . . And even of
those men themselves, that in councells of the commonwealth,
love to shew their reading of politiques and history, very few
do it in their domestique affaires, where their particular interest
is concerned . . . but in publique they study more the reputation of their owne wit, than the successe of anothers businesse" (21–2).

8   Every single topic introduced in Part 1 either lays a premise
for a later crucial argument, or serves as an abbreviated preliminary discussion of a later crucial point. That is, each topic
in Part 1 is introduced for a purpose that only becomes fully
clear farther on in *Leviathan* where it is put in context and
elaborated. It would be extremely tedious to compile a complete catalog of all the connections between the points in Part
1 and the passages throughout the rest of the text that use
them, but perhaps some further examples are in order: The
Chapter 6 discussion of the passions comes into the Chapter
29 discussion of how thinking qualities infused leads to disorder; the distinctions of Chapter 7 are employed in the Chapter 43 argument that our relation to Christian doctrine is one
of belief rather than knowledge; Chapter 10 lays the foundation
for the discussion in Chapter 18 of distinctions in honor among
subjects, and in Chapter 30 of how wrong notions about honor
disturb order; the Chapter 12 discussion of the bogus distinction between temporal and spiritual power reappears in the
crucial arguments of Chapters 39, 40, and 42; the Chapter 13
description of a state of nature is employed in the Chapter 19
discussion of the need for settled rules of succession; the Chapter 16 discussion of persons is used in Chapter 22 on systems,

in Chapter 33 on the authority of the Scriptures, and in Chapter 42 on the topic of liberty of conscience versus liberty of action. Many more such examples could be produced, and would serve as further evidence that Part 1 ought not to be taken to stand on its own, or to contain the bulk of Hobbes's most important arguments, or to provide a deductive ground for Hobbes's political theory.

9 Hobbes presents this view more starkly in *EW* 2.5 than at *L* 10: "But though the benefits of this life may be much furthered by mutual help; since yet those may be better attained to by dominion than by the society of others, I hope no body will doubt, but that men would much more greedily be carried by nature, if all fear were removed, to obtain dominion, than to gain society."

10 Hobbes's *theory* is not atheistic – that is, it cannot be captured in a way that omits all references to belief in God and religion – even though parts of it could be used to understand and to order an atheistic society if one existed. Atheism is certainly no assumption, nor any part, of Hobbes's own theory. Still, one might assert that Hobbes himself was an atheist whose theory assumes theism only because, as a matter of sociological fact, the people whom he was intending to persuade were theists (and theists of a very particular sort). The problem of knowing the real content of other minds prevents us from evaluating this assertion in a completely definitive way; nonetheless, the evidence is against it. Not only did Hobbes deny he was an atheist, implying of himself, as he said of Thucydides, that he was religious but not superstitious, but he proclaimed that one could (indeed, that it is impossible not to) arrive at knowledge of "one God, eternall, infinite, and omnipotent" through a persistent inquiry into the causes of things, using an analogy that indicates Hobbes believed God to be real, and really to exist, "for as a man that is born blind, hearing men talk of warming themselves by the fire, and being brought to warm himself by the same, may easily conceive, and assure himselfe, there is somewhat there, which men call fire, and is the cause of the heat he feeles; but cannot imagine what it is like, nor have an idea of it in his mind, such as they have that see it: so also, by the visible things of this world, and their admirable order, a man may conceive there is a cause of them, which men call God; and yet not have an idea, or

image of him in his mind" (51). More tellingly still, if Aubrey is to be believed, Hobbes actually took confession when he thought he was dying (and hence when he thought he had no need to fear the wrath of ecclesiastics). Aubrey writes, "That he was a Christian 'tis cleare, for he received the sacrament of Dr. Pierson, and in his confession to Dr. John Cosins, on his (as he thought) death-bed, declared that he liked the religion of the church of England best of all other" (Oliver Lawson Dick, ed., *Aubrey's Brief Lives* [Ann Arbor: University of Michigan Press, 1957], p. 156). Interestingly, Hobbes also believed in the existence of spirits, and criticized the Sadducees, who, in rejecting demonology, "erred so farre on the other hand, as not to believe there were at all any spirits, which is very neere to direct atheisme" (38).

11 Notice also that the kind of fear Hobbes refers to in the passage quoted is fear of God; thus the passage cannot be used to support the standard philosophical interpretation. Hobbes writes: "The force of words being (as I have formerly noted) too weak to hold men to the performance of their covenants, there are in mans nature but two imaginable helps to strengthen it. And those are either a feare of the consequence of breaking their word, or a glory, or pride in appearing not to need to breake it. This later is a generosity too rarely found to be presumed on. . . . The passion to be reckoned upon is feare, whereof there be two very generall objects: one the power of spirits invisible; the other, the power of those men they shall therein offend. . . . The feare of the former is in every man his own religion, which hath place in the nature of man before civill society. The later hath not so, at least not place enough to keep men to their promises. . . . So that before the time of civill society, or in the interruption thereof by warre, there is nothing can strengthen a covenant of peace agreed on . . . but the feare of that invisible power which they every one worship as God; and feare as a revenger of their perfidy" (70).

12 Commentators frequently express the view that fear of death *ought* to be the overriding motivational force for Hobbes's people because that is, they think, an implication of what they take to be his mechanistic physical science. But once we see that Hobbes's scattered physical scientific remarks are not intended as a deductive ground for a theory of human nature, but are rather aimed at very particular erroneous religious

370

views, and note further that even if they were, the outcome of any conflict between a fear of death "repelling" one from a contemplated action and a desire for such a thing as honor or God's approval propelling one toward it is a matter left undetermined by what physical scientific account there is in *Leviathan*, then we can see that there is no warrant for the view that Hobbes ought to take fear of death to be overriding. He needn't, and he doesn't. For the view that Hobbes thought fear of death ought to be made to be overriding, see Johnston, *The Rhetoric of Leviathan*.

13 Keith Thomas, "The Social Origins of Hobbes's Political Thought," in Brown, ed., *Hobbes Studies*, pp. 185–236.

14 One could argue that a duty to obey an existing sovereign comes out of the first law of nature (to seek peace); the second (to be willing to lay down one's right to all things when others are willing also); the third (to keep one's covenants); the fourth (gratitude); the tenth (against arrogance); or the sum of the laws of nature (not doing to others as one wouldn't have done to oneself).

15 I think it likely this is the argument Hobbes had in mind, because in Chapter 42 he offers an argument of a similar form (although he presents it as a "separation of cases" argument): "This we may say, that whatsoever a subject . . . is compelled to in obedience to his soveraign . . . that action is not his, but his soveraigns. . . . If any man shall accuse this doctrine, as repugnant to true, and unfeigned Christianity; I ask him, in case there should be a subject in any Christian common-wealth, that should be inwardly in his heart of the Mahometan religion, whether if his soveraign command him to bee present at the divine service of the Christian church, and that on pain of death, he think that Mahometan obliged in conscience to suffer death for that cause, rather than to obey that command of his lawful prince. If he say, he ought rather to suffer death, then he authorizeth all private men to disobey their princes, in maintenance of their religion, true, or false: if he say he ought to bee obedient, then he alloweth to himself, that which hee denyeth to another . . . contrary to the law of nature (which is the indubitable everlasting law of God), 'Do not to another, which thou wouldest not he should doe unto thee'" (271–2). (Hobbes is assuming here that his readers would be quite unwilling to have people disobey their sovereigns in the name

of false religion.) This argument is very like the one I've re-constructed, although mine has a more straightforward form: (1) You must not reserve to yourself any right you would not be willing to have others retain as well. (2) You are not willing to have others retain right *x*. (3) Therefore, you must not retain right *x* yourself. See also Hobbes's similar argument at *L* 152.

16 Of the promise to obey one's political authority Hobbes writes, "this promise may be either expresse, or tacite: Expresse, by promise: Tacite, by other signes. As for example, a man that hath not been called to make such an expresse promise (be-cause he is one whose power perhaps is not considerable;) yet if he live under their protection openly, hee is understood to submit himselfe to the government" (391). If this is enough for consent, then virtually all of Hobbes's readers had consented.

17 Officeholders and other important people, as well as suspected troublemakers, like recusants, did take oaths of allegiance in Hobbes's day. Two of the most famous of these oaths, the Oath of Supremacy and the Oath of Allegiance, were required by acts of Parliament. The 1606 "Act for the better discovering and re-pressing of Popish recusants" required that suspected recusants take the following oath: "I, A.B., do truly and sincerely acknowl-edge, profess, testify and declare in my conscience before God and the world, that our Sovereign Lord King James is lawful and rightful king of this realm and of all other his Majesty's domin-ions and countries. . . . Also I do swear from my heart that not-withstanding any declaration or sentence of excommunication or deprivation made or granted or to be made or granted by the Pope or his successors . . . I will bear faith and true alle-giance to his Majesty, his heirs and successors, and him or them will defend to the uttermost of my power against all conspiracies and attempts whatsoever which shall be made against his or their persons, their crown and dignity. . . . And I do make this recognition and acknowledgement heartily, willingly and truly, upon the true faith of a Christian. So help me God" (J. P. Kenyon, *The Stuart Constitution* [Cambridge: Cambridge University Press, 1966], pp. 458–9). In 1673 "an Act for preventing dangers which may happen from Popish recusants" extended the scope of the oaths of supremacy and allegiance, requiring that they be taken by "all and every per-

son or persons, as well peers as commoners, that shall bear
any office or offices, civil or military, or shall receive any pay,
salary, fee or wages by reason of any patent or trust from or
under his Majesty, or any of his Majesty's predecessors, or by
his or their authority derived from him or them within the
realm . . . , or shall be of the household or in the service or
employment of his Majesty or of his royal highness the duke
of York, who shall inhabit, or reside or be within the city of
London or Westminster or within thirty miles distant from the
same on the first day of the Easter Term . . . 1673" (ibid. p. 461).
The Act of Supremacy of 1534 acknowledged the king's supremacy in religion: "Albeit the King's majesty justly and
rightfully is and oweth to be the supreme head of the Church
of England, and so is recognized by the clergy of the realm in
their convocations [yet it was thought right] for corroboration
and confirmation thereof [to enact that he and his successors
should be] taken, accepted and reputed the only supreme head
in earth of the Church of England called Anglicana Ecclesia"
(G. R. Elton, *The Tudor Constitution: Documents and Commentary*,
2nd ed. [Cambridge: Cambridge University Press, 1960],
p. 364).

18 Again: Doubtless Hobbes had independent scientific interests
and wished to develop a defensible science of nature as part
of his broader philosophical project. But he does not conceive
his science as grounding his political theory. The science that
appears in his political works is partial, and a mere corrective
to particular pieces of bad science that have underwritten socially disruptive doctrines. If we look at the evolution of his
political writings, from the *Elements* to *De Cive* to his crowning
achievement *Leviathan*, we see that in each case the development of Hobbes's theory involves expanded discussion of religion and of the religious applications of his sketchy scientific
arguments. He *never* in these works develops the science itself,
as he surely would have done had he viewed it as foundational
to his argument. This conclusion is in no way mitigated by the
fact he was in a hurry to publish his political theory: He did
vastly revise his theory, and the point is in *how* he chose to
revise it. Indeed, in *De Cive*, he simply omits the section on
human nature altogether; telling evidence that he did not regard his political theory as based on it.

CHAPTER 8. THE TREATMENT OF TRANSCENDENT
INTERESTS

1 Contrast my view here to that of David Johnston, *The Rhetoric of Leviathan*.

2 "And therefore the first founders and legislators of common-wealths among the gentiles, whose ends were only to keep the people in obedience and peace, have in all places taken care; First, to imprint in their minds a beliefe that those pre-cepts which they gave concerning religion, might not be thought to proceed from their own device, but from the dic-tates of some God, or other spirit; or else that they themselves were of a higher nature than mere mortalls, that their laws might the more easily be received.... Secondly, they have had a care, to make it believed, that the same things were dis-pleasing to the gods, which were forbidden by the laws. Thirdly, to prescribe ceremonies, supplications, sacrifices, and festivalls, by which they were to believe, the anger of the gods might be appeased... their anger [being] from the neglect of their worship, or the forgetting, or mistaking, some point of the ceremonies required.... And by these, and such other institutions, they obtayned in order to their end (which was the peace of the commonwealth,) that the common people in their misfortunes, laying the fault on neglect, or errour in their ceremonies, or on their own disobedience to the lawes, were the lesse apt to mutiny against their governors. And being entertained with the pomp, and pastime of festivalls, and pub-like games, made in honour of the gods, needed nothing else but bread, to keep them from discontent, murmuring, and commotion against the state.... And thus you see how the religion of the gentiles was a part of their policy" (57). More-over, Hobbes thought that *all* religion was nurtured to the end that people should render civil obedience: "these [naturall seeds of religion] have received culture from two sorts of men. One sort have been they, that have nourished, and ordered them, according to their own invention. The other have done it, by Gods commandment and direction: but both sorts have done it, with a purpose to make those men that relyed on them the more apt to obedience, lawes, peace, charity, and civill society" (54).

3 I think that David Johnston, in his otherwise illuminating book

The Rhetoric of Leviathan, makes this mistake, and it leads him to conceive Hobbes's project as one of transforming irrational superstitious human beings into the rational egoists they would need to be if the standard philosophical interpretation's solution to the problem of social disorder were possibly to be effective. Although it is important that Hobbes purge the superstitious elements from Christianity, so that transcendent religious interests can work for, rather than against, order, it is an error to *identify* religion with superstition, for this leads one to misunderstand not only Hobbes's project, but also his solution to the problem of disorder.

4   Even during the Interregnum, toleration didn't extend to Catholics. For example, in the 1657 "Humble Petition and Advice," Parliament urged Cromwell to tolerate differences in profession and practice among adherents to "the true protestant Christian religion" but urged that "this liberty be not extended to Popery or Prelacy, or to the countenancing such who publish horrid blasphemies, or practice to hold forth licentiousness or profaneness under the profession of Christ" (Kenyon, *The Stuart Constitution,* p. 355). And toleration of Protestant differences was firmly rolled back with the Restoration. The Uniformity Act of 1662 reads in part as follows:

> Now in regard that nothing conduceth more to the settling of the peace of this nation . . . nor to the honour of our religion and the propagation thereof than a universal agreement in the public worship of Almighty God . . . be it enacted . . . that all and singular ministers in any cathedral, collegiate or parish church or chapel or other place of public worship within this realm . . . shall be bound to say and use the Morning Prayer, Evening Prayer, celebration and administration of both the Sacraments, and all other the public and common prayer in such order and form as is mentioned in the said Book annexed and joined to this present Act and entitled "The Book of Common Prayer and Administration of the Sacraments and other Rites and Ceremonies of the Church according to the use of the Church of England, together with the Psalter or Psalms of David appointed as they are to be sung or said in churches, and the form and manner of making, ordaining and consecrating of Bishops, Priests and Deacons" . . . And to the end that uniformity in the public worship of God . . . may be speedily effected, be it further enacted . . . that every parson, vicar or other minister whatsoever who now hath and enjoyeth any ecclesiastical benefice or pro-

motion within this realm of England shall in the church, chapel
or place of public worship belonging to his said benefice or
promotion . . . openly and publicly before the congregation there
assembled declare his unfeigned assent and consent to the use
of all things in the said Book contained and prescribed . . . and
that all and every such person who shall . . . neglect or refuse to
do the same . . . shall *ipso facto* be deprived of all his spiritual
promotions, and that from henceforth it shall be lawfull to and
for all patrons and donors of all and singular the said spiritual
promotions . . . to present or collate to the same as though the
person or persons so offending or neglecting were dead. . . . And
be it further enacted . . . that every dean, canon and prebendary
of every cathedral or collegiate church, and all masters and other
heads, fellows, chaplains and tutors of or in any college, hall,
house of learning or hospital, and every public professor and
reader in either of the universities and in every college elsewhere, and every parson, vicar, curate, lecturer and every other
person in holy orders, and every schoolmaster keeping any public or private schools, and every person instructing or teaching
any youth in any house or private family as a tutor or schoolmaster . . . shall before the Feast Day of St Bartholomew [24 Au-
gust], 1662 . . . subscribe the Declaration or Acknowledgement
following:

I, A.B., do declare that it is not lawful upon any pretence
whatsoever to take arms against the King, and that I do abhor
that traitorous position of taking arms by his authority against
his person or against those that are commissioned by him, and
that I will conform to the liturgy of the Church of England as it
is now by law established. (Kenyon, *The Stuart Constitution*,
pp. 379–81)

Other examples of the Restoration push to reaffirm a uniform
state religion can be found in the Corporation Act of 1661 and
the Conventicles Act of 1670.

5 This is a supposition that our intention to honor God dictates
that we make. We can, of course, have no natural knowledge
of God's particular characteristics.

6 According to Hobbes's view, not only is there a unity of practical reason, but there is a unity of speculative reason, and a
coherence between the two. Every truth about the world finds
its place in a coherent unified system. Not only normative
truths but also non-normative truths must be compatible with
peace: If heliocentric theories threaten peace, it is because
either heliocentric theories are false or our religious interpre-

tations are (partially) false: "Every day it appeareth more and more that years and dayes are determined by the motions of the earth. Nevethelesse, men that have in their writings but supposed such doctrine, as an occasion to lay open the reasons for and against it, have been punished for it by authority ecclesiasticall. But what reason is there for it? Is it because such opinions are contrary to true religion? *that cannot be, if they be true*" (380).

7 Clarendon, for example, wrote: "If Mr. Hobbes would take a view of the Insurrections and Civil Wars which have at any time been stirred up in Western parts, he will not find that they have been contrived or formented by men who had spent much time in the reading of Greek and Latin authors, or that they have been carried upon the Maxims and Principles which they found there. Jack Straw and Wat Tyler, whose insurrection in respect of the numbers and progress it made, was as dangerous as hath happened in any age or climate, had never read Aristotle or Cicero" (*A Brief View And Survey Of The Dangerous and Pernicious Errors To Church and State In Mr. Hobbes's Book Entitled Leviathan*, p. 85).

8 This is part of the explanation of why Hobbes doesn't conceive of damnation as eternal torment. He writes that "it seemeth hard to say that God who is the father of mercies, that doth in heaven and earth all that hee will; that hath the hearts of all men in his disposing; that worketh in men both to doe and to will; and without whose free gift a man hath neither inclination to good, nor repentance of evill, should punish mens transgressions without any end of time, and with all the extremity of torture, that men can imagine, and more" (345).

9 Perhaps a loose analogy will help us to see Hobbes's point here. Suppose one is sitting on a park bench tossing beernuts to a single hungry bird. Here the bird has practical freedom. Now suppose that four more hungry birds discover the gravy train: Each time the feeder tosses out a beernut, each of the birds attempts to get it, the actions of the others decreasing the practical freedom of each. Even if the feeder humanely tosses out a handful of beernuts, five at a time, the birds will still reduce one another's practical freedom because their activity is not coordinated, and their private judgments overlap with the effect that they all aim at some subset of the beernuts, interfering with one another. When each acts on its private

judgment, the practical freedom of all is decreased, and the more birds there are, the less (other things equal) the practical freedom of each.

10   Cf. Kavka's similar conclusion concerning Locke's discussion of a like case, in *Hobbesian Moral and Political Theory*, ch. 5.5, p. 227.

11   Hobbes presents this rather peculiar view in Chapter 21.

12   Kavka, impressed by the peculiarity of this view, reconstructs for Hobbes an argument to the effect that we trade off some practical liberty for more, and thereby obtain a net gain in liberty via law (Kavka, *Hobbesian Moral and Political Theory*). But this is a reconstruction and not, I think, Hobbes's actual view.

Now, what about this peculiar view? Of course, one can imagine certain sorts of invasive laws that regulated activities, which if left to people's private judgment, would not have diminished the practical freedom of others (for example, a law regulating people's hair-styles), and these *would* result in a net decrease in practical freedom. But Hobbes does not think the sovereign will make such laws. First of all, Hobbes views such totalitarian regulation as being quite impossible: "For seeing there is no common-wealth in the world, wherein there be rules enough set down, for the regulating of all the actions, and words of men, (as being a thing impossible;) it followeth necessarily, that in all kinds of actions, by the laws praeter-mitted, men have the liberty of doing what their own reasons shall suggest, for the most profitable to themselves" (109). But more importantly, Hobbes holds that "to the care of the sov-eraign belongeth the making of good lawes. . . . A good law is that, which is needfull for the good of the people, and withall perspicuous. For the use of lawes, (which are but rules au-thorised) is not to bind the people from all voluntary actions, but to direct and keep them in such a motion, as not to hurt themselves by their own impetuous desires, rashnesse, or in-discretion. . . . Unnecessary lawes are not good lawes" (181–2).

13   Closer to absurd is Hobbes's claim that with respect to liberty, all states are very much alike: "There is written on the Turrets of the city of Lucca in great characters at this day, the word LIBERTAS; yet no man can thence inferre, that a particular man has more libertie or immunitie from the service of the com-monwealth there, than in Constantinople" (110). Harrington

criticized this view, writing: "The mountain hath brought forth, and we have a little equivocation! For to say that a Lucchese hath no more liberty or immunity from the laws of Lucca than a Turk hath from those of Constantinople, and to say that a Lucchese hath no more immunity or liberty by the laws of Lucca than a Turk hath by those of Constantinople, are pretty different speeches. The first may be said of all governments alike, the second scarce of any two; much less of these, seeing it is known that whereas the greatest bashaw is a tenant, as well of his head as of his estate, at the will of his lord, the meanest Lucchese that hath land is a freeholder of both" (*Oceana*, p. 170).

CHAPTER 9. HOBBES'S ABSOLUTISM

1   I discussed these points in Chapter 1. For the clearest presentation of these arguments, see Kavka, *Hobbesian Moral and Political Theory*, ch. 5.5, pp. 224–6. See also Gauthier, *The Logic of Leviathan*, ch. 4.4, pp. 161–70.

2   Watkins holds the view that absolutism and anarchy are not the only alternatives, and that of these two, anarchy may not be the less desirable: "We know that a middle possibility does exist, that a sovereign body may be limited by something which is not a superior body: an elected body of men may enjoy unlimited legislative powers, yet face the possibility of dismissal at the next election" (*Hobbes's System of Ideas*, p. 174). And Hobbes "knew of only one political calamity (external wars excepted) besides which others pale into insignificance. We know of two: civil war *and totalitarianism*. And the question is whether his drastic remedy for civil war – an all-powerful sovereign upon whom there is no constitutional check – is not likely to lead to a situation as grim as the one it replaces" (p. 172).

3   David Gauthier endorses this position in *The Logic of Leviathan*, p. 170.

4   Watkins, *Hobbes's System of Ideas*, p. 179.

5   We should not be alarmed by this conclusion because, as we shall see, acknowledging its truth does not commit us to endorse absolutism ourselves.

6   Kavka, *Hobbesian Moral and Political Theory*, p. 168.

7   H.L.A. Hart, *The Concept of Law* (Oxford: Clarendon Press,

1961, pp. 77–96). I am indebted to Larry Solum for bringing this useful distinction to my attention.

8 Ibid., p. 92.

9 We ignore here the complication that there will in any system have to be some criterion for determining what counts as sovereign speech that can distinguish between, for example, the king's edicts and what he mumbles in his sleep, or says in his capacity as a private person.

10 Hart provides a very simple example of this sort: "Of course if there is a social structure so simple that the only 'source of law' is legislation, the rule of recognition will simply specify enactment as the unique identifying mark or criterion of validity of the rules. This will be the case for example in the imaginary kingdom of Rex I depicted in Chapter IV: there the rule of recognition would simply be that whatever Rex I enacts is law" (Hart, *The Concept of Law*, p. 93). I am assuming here that there are no significant constraints on what is to count as enactment.

11 Recall the condition on obedience, discussed in Chapter 2, that obedience is due only to an *effective* sovereign, and only insofar as the sovereign is effective in protecting subjects. This condition came from Hobbes's concept of a commonwealth and his conception of membership, and in no way represented an exemption from obedience. Because, on Hobbes's view, membership is suspended or terminated *whenever* protection is absent, (i.e., when a sovereign is ineffective in protecting a subject), it remains *strictly true* that all *members* of a commonwealth are under an absolute obligation of obedience to its sovereign. Thus, although persons need not obey a sovereign who is not effective in protecting them – at least in those things that he cannot protect them – this effectiveness condition on obligation does not weaken the absolutist character of Hobbes's theory. See Chapter 2 above.

12 Obviously, this is to say more than just that there are no *legal* grounds for disobeying the government. If what it meant to say that a government was absolute were that subjects held no legal rights against the government, it would seem to be true by definition that all governments were equally absolute, supposing that for something to count as a legal right it must be given by the government, and so that any governmentally given right could not be properly thought of as a right against the govern-

ment. On this trivial account subjects have all and only those legal rights that the government (understood as the sum total of all political processes and institutions) gives them, and there can be no independent source of legal rights against the government. The conclusion, then, is that every government is an absolute sovereign because it is subject to no legal limits (as it would be if subjects held any legal rights against it).

If this argument held, then its conclusion would be only trivially true, and would not bear on the obvious differences among forms of government that concern us in political theory, and over which historic struggles have been waged. But, in fact, the argument does not hold good. See, for example, Hart's classic discussion of the errors involved, in *The Concept of Law*, ch. 4, and ch. 6, pp. 102–3. I am indebted to Shelly Kagan for calling the trivial sense of absolutism to my attention.

13 Deborah Baumgold describes Hobbes's views on this point in her discussion of how governmental forms may institutionalize avenues for rebellion. See Baumgold, *Hobbes's Political Theory*.

14 Baumgold's treatment lays less emphasis on this latter equally important aspect (ibid.).

15 *EL* 2.8.1. Notice that the "hope of success" condition cannot be addressed in theory, but only in practice – it cannot be removed until a system of reeducation is firmly in place, depriving would-be insurgents of the necessary confederates and making effective law enforcement possible.

16 The Prometheus story illustrates this point. Although Zeus was understood to have supreme authority, and the severity of Prometheus's punishment indicated how thoroughly he had defied Zeus, Prometheus is presented in all accounts of the tale as a hero who was morally justified in his disobedience. I owe this example to Nick Pappas.

17 This might be because one trusts that God will not command anything (say, morally) impermissible even if it seems so, or alternatively, that faith involves a teleological suspension of the ethical. For this latter view, see Kierkegaard's *Fear and Trembling*, especially "Problem I."

18 Hobbes would not, I think, have had to hold that an unbeliever could have no transcendent interests. Hobbes thought that atheists were *rationally* defective but was not committed to the view that they were morally defective. Hobbes's position is most plausible when we consider Christians who wholeheart-

edly believed in God but were unable to bring themselves to give fulfillment of their duties to God priority over their narrow self-interest; *these* people would be unlikely to have any transcendent interests at all. Hobbes's claim is most plausible when its scope is restricted to believers, but this restriction, given how few unbelievers there appear to have been in the seventeenth century, hardly weakens Hobbes's position.

19 Obviously, the fact that Hobbes's views on religion were widely rejected suggests that Hobbes's redescription argument did not actually work in practice, but we are here concerned primarily with the logic of the argument for absolutism.

20 To say that absolutism follows is to say that the argument is valid. Whether it is also sound depends, of course, on the truth of Hobbes's premises.

21 Indeed, we might conclude from the fact that Hobbes's argument was rejected that these conditions did not hold, even in Hobbes's day. Here, I think, the problem was with P2 about the content of religious duty rather than P1 concerning the status of religious interests. Many people didn't buy Hobbes's argument on the basis of his interpretation of Scripture for what our duty to God actually involves. (Note that this raises the question of plausibility – convincingness – rather than of soundness, that is, the truth of the premises since they may be true even if people are unconvinced of their truth.) Can we conclude from people's rejection of it that Hobbes's view on what our duty to God is was implausible? To assess fully the *plausibility* of Hobbes's premise *to his contemporaries*, we would need to enlist the aid of an intellectual historian who could, among other things, determine the actual content of the contending theories opposed to Hobbes's, and how they were received, in order to assess the strength of Hobbes's arguments against these rival positions as judged by enlightened or popular opinion, and to analyze the strength of their objections to Hobbes's theory as judged by his contemporaries. We can make our own judgment about the validity and soundness of Hobbes's argument, and about its plausibility for us, but we must defer to Hobbes's contemporaries on the question of its plausibility to them. What we *can* say is that Hobbes thought his premises true; and that if he was right about this, then his argument for absolutism is sound as well as valid.

22 Although he did not see its significance, Clarendon noted and

objected to the fact that Hobbes's theory put the Scriptures "in the same scale with Al-Coran, which hath as much authority by the stamp which the Grand Signior puts upon it in all his Dominions; and all the differences and controversies, which are no fewer in number, nor prosecuted with less animosity between them, than the disputes of Christians in matters of religion, have all proceeded from the several glosses upon, and reading the Al-Coran, which are proscribed or tolerated by the several princes in their respective Dominions, they all paying the same submission and reverence to Mahomet, but differing much in what he hath said and directed." Clarendon continues, "This is a degree of impiety Mr. Hobbes was not arrived at when he first published his book *De Cive*, where tho he allowed his sovereign power to give what religion it thought fit to its subjects, he thought it necessary to provide it should be Christian, which was a caution too modest for his *Leviathan*" (Clarendon, *A Brief View and Survey* . . . , p. 198).

23   This notion is elaborated in, for example, Rawls's idea of an overlapping consensus.

Index

Abraham, 304
absolute property, doctrine of, 212
absolutism, 190, 277–8, 379n2, 379n5;
 historical contingency/general
 application of Hobbes's arguments
 for, 309–16; of Hobbes, 287–8, 289–
 321; Hobbes's arguments for, 299–
 308; necessity and desirability of, 5,
 22, 289–90, 308, 314–16, 327n22;
 status of Hobbes's arguments for,
 309–16; two senses of, 290–9
absolutist form of government, 9, 50,
 291, 293–5, 296–9
acceptability criterion for truth of
 interpretations, 346n12
action, 331n3; and belief, 353–4n32,
 369n8
Adam, 137, 153
adiaphora, 347n13
agreement, 8–9, 319–20
ambition, 201–3, 204, 205, 206–7, 210,
 214–15
anarchy, 27, 289, 379n2
Anglicans, 194, 198
antisocial behavior, 10, 14, 34;
 rationality of, 26, 27, 33
Aristotle, 170, 180–3, 187, 197, 199;
 doctrinal error from, 181–3
arrogance, law of nature against,
 267
Ashcraft, Richard, 323n2
assembly, 62, 293, 296
atheism, 253, 369n10; attributed to
 Hobbes, 13, 14, 17, 241, 268, 273
atheists, 20, 55, 103, 357n41
attachments, 3, 235, 310
attitude(s) toward government, 67–8,
 295
Aubrey, John, 272, 370n10

authoritarianism: in religion, 272,
 274–5
authority: appropriate, 130; and
 being authorized, 364n17; in/of
 clergy, 185–8, 198, 199; counterposed
 to sovereign, 184; distribution of,
 40; divided, 86–7, 223, 224–6,
 340n19; multiple, overlapping, 81,
 82–3, 85, 86–7, 341n20; power and,
 222–4; in religion, 109, 110, 111;
 temporal/spiritual, 137–8, 222; unity
 of secular and religious, 129–30, 138–
 42; *see also* civil authority; spiritual
 authority
authorization (concept), 223
Aylmer, G. E., 343n4

bad faith, 147, 148, 153
baptism, 133, 286, 287
Barry, Brian, 7
Baumgold, Deborah, 323n2, 362n7,
 363n12
Behemoth (Hobbes), 3, 190–1, 192–212;
 implications of, for interpretation,
 212–33
belief(s), 1, 3, 39, 235, 310, 319; and
 action, 353–4n32; competing, 42–3;
 differing, and duty to God, 106–7,
 108, 109, 114; disruptive, 211;
 experience and reason in, 121, 123–
 4; false, 43–4; as function of whom
 we believe, 108–9, 110, 125, 216–17,
 223; in/and passions, 163, 249;
 passionately held, 45, 46;
 rationalizing, 3, 310–11
Bellarmine, Cardinal, 144, 361n1
Beza, Théodore de, 361n1
Bible, *see* Scripture(s)
Bramhall, Bishop, 37

384

Index

Index

consent, 9; as source of sovereignty, 144–5; *see also* tacit consent
contextualist approach to writing, 323n2
Conventicles Act of 1670, 376n4
cooperation, 10, 31, 32; with political authority, 101
cooperation problem, 25–6, 33, 35, 327n22
Corporation Act of 1661, 376n4
covenants, 66, 72, 79, 94; and justice, 286; obligation to keep, 356–7n40
crime, 160
Cromwell, Oliver, 192, 213, 375n4
Cromwell, Richard, 192

damnation, 173–4, 287, 377n8
De Cive (Hobbes), 281, 361n3
De Summo Pontifice (Bellarmine), 144
deductive method, 237, 239, 242, 269
defense, 64, 65, 66, 154–5, 157
democracy, 85, 292, 293, 295
demonology, 169–70, 174–6, 184, 186, 242, 244, 249
description(s): of interest in fulfilling duties to God, 113–14, 115, 119, 123, 125, 128, 129, 149–51; generality/ formality of, 110, 316
desire to rule, 251–2
determinism, 214
diffidence: as source of disorder, 264
Diodorus, 42
disagreement, 275–6, 294, 315; causes of, 263–4; in religious interests, 306–7
discontent: as condition for social disorder, 298–9
disobedience, 8, 18, 19, 34, 155–6, 219; to God, 74–5; grounds for, 53, 54, 69, 75–6, 87–8, 297, 340n19; as injustice, 286; justification for, 150–1, 184, 209, 303–4; to laws of God, 153; as means to reforms, 155; narrowly prudential reasons for avoiding, 98; in principle of political obligation, 95, 98; religious grounds for, 118, 301–2; right to, 60–1; and salvation, 128; sanctions for, 11; in self-defense, 331n2; threat of punishment and, 32–3
disorder, 10–11, 157, 329n37; causes of, 39, 40, 263–5, 313; competing religious interests as primary cause of, 308; conditions necessary for, 298; different account of causes of,

36–47; Hobbes's analysis of, 190–1, 212–16, 264–8, 269, 271, 275–8, 289, 297–8, 309–16; method in Hobbes's analysis of, 235–41, 268, 309–10, 311, 314, 315; mistaken beliefs as cause of, 208–9; opinions as cause of, 41–2; private judgment in, 63–4; recurrent, 27, 29–36; religion as source of, 66, 118, 330n40; religious interests in, 170–1, 176–7; as result of bad education, 160; sources of, 35, 53, 59, 167–8, 312; sources of, in Hobbes, 24–36; as substantive problem, 45; transcendent interests as cause of, 57; *see also* problem of social disorder
dispute resolution, 9, mechanisms of, 83, 87, 101, 183
dissenters, 307–8
divided sovereignty, 30–1, 214, 327n22; Hobbes's argument against, 22; principle of, 81–8, 297; private judgment in, 294; rule of recognition, 291
divine law, 183; *see also* laws of God
divine right, 148
diversity, 276–7, 306–7
doctrine(s), 39, 40–1, 145, 310; attempts to suppress pernicious, 207–12; competing, 215–16, 217; erroneous, 182–8; right of determining, 222
doctrines disruptive to social order, 212, 213, 215, 217, 244–5, 249, 362n7; in English Civil War, 193–7, 201–4, 215–16; universities in dissemination of, 196–9, 201–2, 204, 205–9, 211
dominion, 251–2
dreams, 121–2, 128, 243–4
dueling, 37
Dunne, John, 323n2
duty: argument from, 227–8, 270; of obedience, 68–9; and self-interest, 326n15; teaching men about, 46
duty(ies) to God, 38, 43, 44–5, 51, 52, 151, 152–3, 195, 214; and civil obedience, 286; claim of divergence from religious authority, 131–5, 141– 2; conflict with duty to man, 222; knowledge of, 113; knowledge of, through natural reason, 113–20; known through personal revelation, 120, 121–8; known through prophecy, 120, 121–8; and obedience

386

Index

moral errors, 241, 256, 269, 271
moral ideals, 1–2
moral interests, 103, 151, 157, 234,
  305–6; argument from, 102–3;
  education in, 163; in principle of
  political obligation, 51, 52, 54, 55–6,
  68, 89, 98, 102; proper conception of,
  159, 166
moral obligations, 51; of obedience,
  48–9; and principle of political
  obligation, 93–4, 98
moral philosophy: ancient, 181–2
moral reasons: for adhering to
  principle of political obligation, 299,
  302; not to disobey, 156
moral relativism, 320
moral subjectivism, 7, 233, 234, 241,
  254–60, 266, 269
moral terms: use of, 258–61, 269
moral theory in Hobbes, 13–14, 248,
  255–60, 265–70
moral virtue, 254–5; teaching of,
  164–6
morality, 12, 311, 343n4; argument
  from, 99, 100; basic rule of, 343n3;
  secular, 89, 94
Moses, 136, 140
motivating forces, 7, 14, 18–19
motivation(s), 35, 191, 235; egoistic,
  12–13, 46; in national defense,
  357n42; for obedience, 11–12, 101–2;
  opinions, doctrines as, 40–1; in
  rebellion, 32
multiple sovereignty, see divided
  sovereignty

Nagel, Thomas, 6, 26, 325n9
naming, 246–7
narrow prudence, 279; argument from,
  89–93, 94–8, 99, 308
narrow self-interest, 75, 311;
  overridden by religious interests, 19–
  20; political obedience and, 159; and
  principle of political obligation, 91–3,
  94, 95, 96, 100; transcendent
  interests and, 102, 271
narrowly prudential interests: in
  principle of political obligation, 51,
  52, 54, 55, 88, 89, 93, 98, 105
narrowly prudential reason, 344n7; in
  principle of political obligation, 100
national civil sovereign: as authority
  on both secular and religious
  matters, 129, 130, 135, 138–42, 143,

144, 146–51; divine right in, 148; see
  also civil sovereign; sovereign(s)
natural duty(ies), 266–7, 268, 279, 299,
  302, 311; arguments from, 90, 93–4,
  98; as reason to obey government,
  293, 298
natural kingdom, 114
natural knowledge, 89
natural philosophy, 239
natural reason, 102, 105, 107, 108, 120,
  162, 265, 312; and absolutism, 302;
  duties to God from, 124, 128, 129,
  132, 134, 149–50; God's positive laws
  compatible with, 279; in obligation
  to obey, 356–7n40; prudence and
  morality accessible to, 311; as source
  of religious knowledge, 113–20, 239;
  and sovereignty, 147
natural religion, 279, 305, 350n24, 359n1
natural science (Hobbes), 214

Oakeshott, Michael, 7
Oath of Allegiance, 372n17
Oath of Supremacy, 372n17
obedience, 8, 15, 18, 67, 68, 101–2,
  130, 218–19; absolute obligation of,
  290, 291–3, 301; condition on, 70–3,
  74, 78, 295; in divided sovereignty,
  81–8; duty of, 68–9, 103–5;
  effectiveness condition on, 300,
  334n16, 380n11; exemptions from,
  54, 69–78, 79–80, 82, 83–4, 87–8, 89,
  93, 103–5, 110, 129, 149, 292, 299,
  300–2, 313, 339n17; fear of death as
  foundation for, 19–20; to God, 38; to
  law, 183–4; to laws of God, 102, 154;
  to laws of nature, 154; in limited
  sovereignty, 78–80; moral obligation
  in, 48–9; motivation for, 11–12, 39,
  231; and narrow self-interest, 159;
  oaths of, 267; obligation of, 94, 286,
  356n40; passive, 157; perfect, 115;
  power requires, 144–5; as primary
  moral duty, 266–8; in principle of
  political obligation, 50–1, 53–4, 69–
  73; private judgment in, 265;
  protection and, 31–2, 60, 70, 74, 75–
  6, 94, 159–60; rationality of, 11;
  reasons for, 279, 293; religious
  reasons for, 302; restrictions on,
  300–1; and salvation argument,
  151–2; social order depends on,
  100–1; unconditional, 157, 280, 289,
  296, 299, 300, 306, 308

390

Index

prophecy: as source of religious
  knowledge, 113, 119–20, 121–8
prophets, true, 123–4, 125, 127,
  351n26
protection, 90; and obedience, 31–2,
  60, 70, 74, 75–6, 94, 159–60
Protestants, 19, 148–9, 274
prudence, 12, 14, 49, 151–7, 245;
  accessible to natural reason, 311;
  argument from, 227–8, 270; as
  reason to obey government, 293;
  rule of, 279; see also narrow
  prudence; special prudence
prudential duties, 279, 280
prudential interests, 52; in principle of
  political obligation, 51–2, 56, 57
prudential reasons, 7–8; to accept
  principle of political obligation, 151,
  302; not to disobey, 156
psychological egoism (in Hobbes), 12,
  13, 14, 21, 214, 215, 234, 241, 250,
  329n39, 346n12; assumption of, 30,
  231–2, 327n22
public authority: as religious authority,
  143
public judgment, 261, 262, 264, 265
punishment, 10, 15, 64, 86, 95, 155–6;
  by God, 96, 114; natural, 152; see also
  threat of punishment
purgatory, 175–6, 180, 184, 186

rational self-interest: passions
  overriding, 34–5, 36–7, 41; and
  rebellion, 32–3; in state of war, 24–6;
  in submission to political authority,
  7–9, 11
rationality, 10–11; individual/collective,
  10, 26, 32; short-term/long-term, 32;
  in standard philosophical
  interpretation, 31, 32, 33
reason, 347n15; faulty, 246, 247–8;
  passions overriding, 36–7;
  perturbation of, as source of
  disorder, 32, 34–5
rebellion, 46, 95, 155, 197; conditions
  for, 159, 298, 300; faulty education
  in, 160; hope of success necessary
  condition for, 363n11; justification
  of, 317; law enforcement and,
  329n36; liberty and, 281; moral
  considerations in, 266; narrow self-
  interest and, 98; passions in, 249;
  pride in, 228; religious interests in,
  253–4; and self-preservation, 38;

theory of, 32–3; threat of force and,
  218
recognition, rule of, 291
redescription, 44–5, 276, 278, 316;
  argument, 159, 301, 306–8; of
  Christianity, 269; of interests, 3, 310–
  11; of transcendent interests, 3, 99–
  157, 189, 216–17
reeducation, 43–5, 251, 269, 276; in
  eradication of disruptive opinions,
  219–21; religious, moral, and civic
  duty, 207–10, 211; and social order,
  159, 168
Reformation, 153, 199–200
relativism, personal, 7, 13, 14, 320
religion: corruption of, 166; doctrinal
  differences in, 124–5, 127; Hobbes's
  treatment of, 272–5, 287; private
  judgment in, 179, 199–201, 202, 209,
  216, 217, 228, 230, 265; as private
  matter, 344–5n8, 353n32; and
  redescription of transcendent
  interests, 99–157; revealed, 89, 313;
  right understanding of, 168; and
  social order, 272–3; as source of
  disorder, 118; teaching about, 46;
  true, 188; see also natural religion
religious authority, 109, 110, 111, 127,
  167; appropriate, 129, 134–6, 142,
  149; claims of divergence from, 131–
  5; competing claims in, 120; in
  determination of miracles, 126–7;
  distinct from civil, 209, 222; included
  in civil sovereign, 167–8; in matters
  of revelation, 128; sovereignty in,
  142–51; state as locus of, 194
religious beliefs, 244, 251, 252–3;
  differing, 109–10, 112–13; and
  disorder, 330n40; disruptive, 248; of
  Hobbes, 112; overriding fear of
  death, 366n26
religious differences: reconciling, 277
religious duty, 18, 75, 112, 113, 269,
  279, 280; argument from, 102;
  competing characterizations of, 215–
  16; obedience in, 159; opinions of,
  42–3; proper conception of, 168;
  reeducation in, 209–10; stability-
  supporting conception of, 166; see
  also duty(ies) to God
religious errors, 240, 241, 269, 271
religious factions, 41, 106–7, 111,
  112, 168, 179, 191, 193, 194, 209,
  215–16, 277, 344n6; competing

393

Index